Pentecostal Christology

Christian Heritage Rediscovered

The Series, as the name suggests, is meant to focus on Christian Faith & Living vis-à-vis topics like Literature & Poetry, Indigenous Philosophizing, Ethical response towards Agriculture, Health & Healing, Science & Technology, Ecofeminist Theology, Sociological approach towards Human Rights, Law & Politics, Arts, History of Ideas, Ancient Civilizations, Cultural Contiguity, Religious Cosmologies & Mysticism, Footsteps of famous Theologians, World Peace & Harmony, Global Capitalism, Network Marketing, Cybertheology, Population & Demographics, Epigraphic Studies, Contextualized Education, and many others. We welcome a Mss. on any topic/s mentioned, whether they are original works, scholarly monographs, collections of conference papers, revised dissertations, or translations of historical documents. Through the Series we, the Publishers, are striving to put forward published works that may help Institutions, Academic Bodies, Researchers, Scholars and the World at large in furthering their respective knowledge and understanding on the concerned subject. We welcome your comments on our efforts and further suggestions on how we can foster the upcoming thoughtful theologically grounded books.

Christian Heritage Rediscovered - 82

Pentecostal Christology

Empirical Approach in Indian Context

Shaibu Abraham

CWI

Christian World Imprints

First Published in 2019 by

Christian World Imprints
Christian Publishing & Books from India
C-3, Shop No. 14, Ground Floor
Wazirpur Industrial Area, **Delhi-110052**
cwidelhi2017@gmail.com
www.ChristianWorldImprints.com
Phone: +91 11 41526079

ISBN: 978-93-5148-379-3

Printed in India.

To

Sheena
with love

Contents

Preface

The Pentecostal movement is one of the major Christian denominations in India today. In the Indian sub-continent, the Pentecostal movement is growing fast. The *World Christian Encyclopedia,* the reputed source book of World Christianity terms India as one of the major hubs of Pentecostal and Charismatic Christianity. As we stand at the verge of the third decade of the twenty first century, religious observers, sociologists and Christian theologians acknowledge the remarkable growth of Pentecostalism all over India, especially in north India among the Tribals, Dalits, and lower castes in rural areas as well as among middle class in urban centres. Nevertheless, until recently, the growth and expansion of the movement in India has not been noticed or documented. Even now it is hard to ascertain the extent and pace of its growth and consolidation, however, the recent testimonies and researches have shown that the movement is growing fast.

Even though the movement has been growing at a fast pace, it faces adverse external challenges such as religious pluralism, cultural diversity, poverty, caste-oppression, communalism and especially a recent spate of violence against Christians. These elements have affected the growth and consolidation of the movement negatively. On the other, there are various issues within the movement like schism, caste-consciousness, leadership conflicts and cross-cultural differences. Within this context, the movement faces a fundamental problem, namely the lack of an articulated theology, especially with regard to Christology which can affect the movement in the long run.

The task of retrieving the theology of the Indian Pentecostal movement is painstaking. The pioneers of the movement were so engrossed in their mission that they were wary of developing a carefully articulated theology of their vibrant faith. Nevertheless, a close observation reveals that Indian Pentecostals have a rich tradition of oral theology informed by their experiences. Given the above-mentioned community struggles, the time has come to systematise those rich experiential elements into popular theological categories.

Any growing Christian movement needs a well articulated Christology relevant to its context. Such a contextual Christology should be sensitive to the socio-political, religio-cultural, and economic milieu if it is to be relevant. Since the interface of culture and the Gospel has created a new form of Pentecostal culture in India combining positive aspects of Indian culture with Gospel values by which Pentecostals live and carry out their evangelistic and mission activities. This poses the challenge of religious pluralism, which sometimes escalates into violence and persecution. Here, a contextual Christology can help the faithful to face such challenges.

Moreover, a strong contextually-oriented Christology is vital for an active involvement in the society. Ordinary Pentecostals enthusiastically participate in evangelistic activities which result in many being liberated from the dismal situation they are in. This has led to a rapid proliferation of Pentecostalism among the poor. A contextual Christology can add further momentum to such activity. Besides, it can also provide theological validity for involvement in society and addressing social concerns around them. Such a pattern can be seen in the New Testament. The gospels and epistles give us sufficient evidence to demonstrate that the early church used various facets of the person and work of Christ to face particular situations.

Therefore, a well articulated Christology is vital for the growth and consolidation of Pentecostal movement in India. To achieve this end, a research has been conducted to unearth the intricate threads of Christological formulations of Pentecostal believers, informed by their Spirit-experience; socio-political, religio-cultural and economic situations. As a result, the unique Indian Pentecostal traits are being identified and analysed. Taking these elements into consideration, this study suggests a Biblical Christological model faithful to believers' Spirit-experience, socio-political, religio-cultural and economic situations and particularly the intense persecution they face. It is anticipated that the model of Christology suggested here is faithful to their situation and biblical tradition as well as a model that will do justice to the larger Pentecostal tradition.

This book is a modified form of my PhD research, carried out in the University of Birmingham, England. I owe to many people for the successful completion of the research and the publication of the project. I am particularly grateful to Dr. Mark J. Cartledge who guided me meticulously throughout this project, by patiently correcting and encouraging me and also by understanding all of my concerns. I also want to thank Dr. Andrew Davis for reading the draft and giving helpful comments, which enabled me to turn it into a better piece of work.

I would like to thank my wife, Sheena, who stood with me throughout this project, supporting me to finance my studies and our life in Birmingham, as well as for her enduring prayers. I also extend my love to my parents, P. M. Mathew and Saramma Mathew, who taught me to love the Bible and the people of God, as well as for their love and prayers.

I am greatly indebted to The Birmingham Pentecostal Fellowship Church members and Pastor, Dr Wesley Lukose, for the prayers, financial support, love and respect showered upon me. Needless to say, their support was of great help in the completion of the project. Here I also acknowledge the encouragement and help of Dr Finny Philip, the Principal of Filadelfia Bible College, Udaipur, Rajasthan, in this project. I would also like to extend my thanks to the publisher, Christian World Imprints for speedy publication of the work. I also wish to extend my love and thanks towards many 'ordinary' Indian Pentecostals who shared their testimonies, views and ideas with me, a fact that helped enrich this research.

Abbreviations

ABD	The Anchor Bible Dictionary
AJPS	Asian Journal of Pentecostal Studies
BJP	Bharatiya Janata Party
BSP	Bahujan Samaj Party
CLS	Christian Literature Society
CMS	The Church Missionary Society
CNI	Church of North India
Dharma Deepika	A Journal of South Indian Missiological Research
DJG	Dictionary of Jesus and the Gospels
DPL	Dictionary of Paul and His Letters
EPW	Economic and Political Weekly
GDP	Gross Domestic Product
IBMR	International Bulletin of Missionary Research
IJST	International Journal of Systematic Theology
IMR	Infant Mortality Rate
JEPTA	Journal of the European Pentecostal Theological Association
JPT	Journal of Pentecostal Theology
MLA	Member of Legislative Assembly
MP	Member of Parliament
NCRB	National Crime Records Bureau
NDBT	New Dictionary of Biblical Theology
NDT	New Dictionary of Theology
NFHS	National Family Health Survey
NIB	The New Interpreters Bible

NICNT	The New International Commentary on the New Testament
NIDPCM	The New International Dictionary of Pentecostal and Charismatic Movements
NIGTCe	New International Greek Testament Commentary
PHC	Public Health Centre
Pneuma	The Journal of the Society for Pentecostal Studies
RSS	Rashtriya Swayamsevak Sangh
S.C.	Scheduled Castes
S.T.	Scheduled Tribes
TS	Theological Studies
UNDP	United Nations Development Programme
UP	Uttar Pradesh
VHP	Vishwa Hindu Parishad
VKA	Vanvasi Kalyan Ashram
WBC	Word Biblical Commentary
WHO	World Health Organisation
WMUS	Women's Union Missionary Society

Glossary of Indian Terms

adivasis	Tribal people
advaita	non-dualism (Hindu philosophy)
Anganwadi	government run nursery school in villages
antaryamin	in-dweller
avatara, avatar	Incarnation
Babri-Masjid	a Muslim Mosque at the site of Ram's birth in Ayodhya
Bhaktas	Devotees
bhakti	devotion
bhakti marga	way of devotion
Bhoots	ghosts, evil spirits
bhopa, bhua, bhuva-bhagat	traditional healers
Brahman	the ultimate (absolute) reality
brahma Sutra	precepts of Brahman (Hindu Philosophy)
Bramanic	related to *brahmin* caste
Crore	10 million
Crorepati	billionaire
Dakan	evil spirit
Dalit	'untouchable'
Deeksha	initiation ceremony
devara	Shrine
ekal vidyalayas	one teacher school
Guru	religious teacher, advisor
Hindu Dharma	Hindu moral order
Hindutva	political Hinduism, Hinduness
Isvara	god
jadhu tona	black magic
jadi-booti	roots and leaves

jnana marga	way of knowledge
jungali	uncivilised with bad customs and manners
karma	Deeds
karma marga	way of deeds
Lok Sabha	lower house of the Indian Parliament
malik, ooparwala	master, God
mantras	Chants
mata, mataji	female deity of Tribal people
Mimamsa	interpretation of Hindu scripture
mukti	Salvation
nirguna Brahman	the ultimate reality without attributes
padre, padri	pastor, priest (Christian)
panchayat	village council
pooja, puja	rituals, Hindu worship
puranas	Hindu scripture
purna avatara	complete and final incarnation
Rajya Sabha	upper house of the Indian Parliament
Ram-Janmabhoomi	movement the movement to build a temple of Ram to replace the Babri Masjid at the site of Ram's birth in Ayodhya
rath-yatra	chariot procession
sadhus	saints, monks
saguna Brahman	God with attributes
Saiva Siddhanta	precepts related to *shiva* sect
sakshi	Testimony
samsara	the world
Sangh-Parivar	the RSS family of organisations
Sarpanchs	elected head of a village council
sati	immolation of widows
Satyagrahi	one who pursues the truth
Shaivism	related *shiva* sect
shakti	Power
Shifa	healing
Shuddhikaran	purification ceremony, reconversion to Hinduism
tantric, tantric	black magician
Trishuls	Tridents
Upanishadic	related to *upanishads* (Hindu Scriptures)
vaisnava tradition	tradition related to god *Vishnu*
vedantic	related to *vedas*
Vrata	religious vows
Yishu	Jesus

Chapter 1

Pentecostalism in India

The southward shift of Christianity has facilitated pioneering inquiries into the phenomenon of Pentecostal growth in Asia, a movement thought to be marginal, if not nonexistent.[1] It was estimated that in 2000, Asian countries had 135 million Pentecostals/Charismatics, second only to Latin America.[2] Such a phenomenal growth has compelled many researchers and observers to investigate Asian Pentecostalism with new vigour and sympathy.[3] This change in approach has resulted in considering Pentecostalism as a significant social and religious movement in the Asian scene. Theologians and religious observers have begun to consider the beliefs and practices of the movement and critically appreciate its social and theological relevance.[4] However, researchers face two inherent obstacles. First, Pentecostalism exists in a diverse socio-cultural milieu within Asia.

---

[1] To have a glimpse at the impact of Christianity in the Southern hemisphere see, Philip Jenkins, *The New Faces of Christianity: Believing the Bible in the Global South* (Oxford: Oxford University Press, 2006); Philip Jenkins, *The Next Christendom: The Coming of Global Christianity* (Oxford: Oxford University Press, 2002).

[2] David B. Barrett, George T. Kurian, & Todd M. Johnson, *World Christian Encyclopedia,* 2nd ed. (New York: Oxford University Press, 2001), 13-15.

[3] Allan Anderson, *Spreading Fires: The Missionary Nature of Early Pentecostalism* (London: SCM Press, 2007), 75-108; Michael Bergunder, *The South Indian Pentecostal Movement in the Twentieth Century* (Cambridge: Eerdmans, 2008); Allan Anderson and Edmond Tang (eds.), *Asian and Pentecostal: The Charismatic Face of Christianity in Asia* (Carlisle: Regnum Books International, 2005).

[4] Donald E. Miller and Tetsunao Yamamori, *Global Pentecostalism: The New Face of Christian Social Engagement* (Berkeley, California: University of California Press, 2007); Allan Anderson, 'Revising Pentecostal History in Global Perspective,' *Asian and Pentecostal*, 147-173, especially, 166.

Therefore, there is a danger of over-generalisation from very specific expressions of its doctrines and practices. Second, the lack of historical and theological documentation of Pentecostalism in Asian countries has made the study of the movement a difficult task.[5] These days efforts are being made to gather oral traditions, and local research projects have been carried out in order to salvage the mission stories and local theologies from the margins. These endeavours resulting from self-awareness among Pentecostals keen to understand and articulate local expressions which are peculiar and unique, however, have met with limited success.[6]

1.1 Pentecostalism in India

What is said about Asian Pentecostalism is also true concerning Indian Pentecostalism. On the Indian sub-continent the Pentecostal movement is growing rapidly. According to the *World Christian Encyclopedia,* by 2000, over half of India's 62 million Christians were Pentecostals/Charismatics.[7] Almost two decades after, there is exponential growth, especially in North India among the Tribal people, Dalits, and lower castes in rural areas, as well as among the middle class in urban centres. However, until recently, the expansion of the Pentecostal movement in India had not been documented. Even now it is hard to ascertain the extent and pace of its growth and consolidation. Anyone who travels in cities and villages of India can see ample evidence of the increased growth of Pentecostalism among the common masses. Today, some of the largest Christian congregations in India are Pentecostal churches in such cities as Chennai, Kolkata, Mumbai and New Delhi.[8] My own research over the past 25 years has shown that many are joining the movement.

---

[5] Wonsuk Ma, 'Asian (Classical) Pentecostalism: Theology in Context,' *Dharma Deepika* 6/2 (July-December 2002): 13-33, 14.

[6] Anderson, *Spreading Fires;* Bergunder, *The South Indian Pentecostal Movement;* In Kerala Pentecostal History Saju Mathew has done a fairly good job of bringing up many forgotten pioneers of Pentecostalism; see Saju Mathew, *Kerala Penthecosthu Charithram,* 2nd ed. (Kottayam, India: Good News Publications, 2007); A. C. George, 'Pentecostal Beginnings in Travancore, South India,' *AJPS* 4/2 (2001): 215-37; A. C. George, *Trailblazers for God: A History of the Assemblies of God of India* (Kothanur, Bangalore: SABC Publications, 2004); Paulson Pulikottil, 'Emergence of Indian Pentecostalism,' *Dharma Deepika* 6/2 (July-December 2002): 47-58; Paulson Pulikottil, 'As East and West Met in God's Own Country: Encounter of Western Pentecostalism with Native Pentecostalism in Kerala,' http://www.pctii.org/cyberj/cyberj10/paulson.html (accessed 10 January 2010); Ivan M. Satyavrata, 'Contextual Perspectives on Pentecostalism as a Global Culture: A South Asian View,' in *The Globalization of Pentecostalism*, edited by M. W. Dempster, B. D. Klaus & D. Petersen (Carlisle: Regnum, 1999), 203-221.

[7] See, Barrett, et. all, *World Christian Encyclopedia*, 360.

[8] Chief Editor, 'Editorial – Pentecostalism,' *Dharma Deepika* 6/2 (July-December 2002): 2.

From its inception at the beginning of the last century with the revival movements,[9] Pentecostalism has grown into a stream of important religious and liberating forces in Indian society. In South India, the movement has considerable influence among the middle class and the urban population. For example, in Chennai city itself, two Pentecostal churches claim a membership of 25,000 to 30,000 each, who meet in multiple services, and include people from all walks of life.[10] Similarly, another church in Bangalore boasts of more than 10,000 members.[11] Even North Indian cities like Mumbai and the states of Punjab and Delhi have seen the springing up of many indigenous Pentecostal and Charismatic churches.[12] For instance, the New Life Fellowship (NLF) in Mumbai itself has more than one thousand house churches while extending its activities into other states.[13] Recently, the NLF has been targeted by some fundamentalists in the state of Karnataka for allegedly converting Hindus to Christianity.[14] Similarly, another indigenous Pentecostal movement known as *Yeshu Darbar* in Allahabad, Uttar Pradesh claims a gathering of thousands of people of every caste and religion who were healed and delivered from evil possession.[15] South Indian states like Kerala, Tamil Nadu and Andhra Pradesh have also seen major growth of indigenous Pentecostal movements.[16] Furthermore, India is the largest missionary sending

---

[9] See G. B. McGee, 'Pentecostal and Pentecostal-like Movements (1860-1910),' in *NIDPCM,* edited by Stanley M. Burgess (Michigan: Zondervan, 2002), 118-119. Also see G. B. McGee, 'Pentecostal Phenomena and Revivals in India: Implication for Indigenous Church Leadership,' *IBMR* 20/3 (July, 1996): 112-114.

[10] New Life Assembly of God (AoG) Anna Salai Little Mount, Chennai; for more details see website: http://www.nlag.org.in/about_us.htm (accessed 22 December 2009). Another church Apostolic Christian Assembly (ACA), Purasavakkam, Chennai, claims 30,000 members and it also claims to have 250 branches in Chennai city.

[11] Full Gospel Assembly of God Church (FGAG), see website: http://salvationband. wordpress. com/2009/01/30/revpaul-thangiah-%E2%80%93-fgag/ (accessed 22 December 2009).

[12] Roger E. Hedlund, 'Indigenous Pentecostalism in India,' *Asian and Pentecostal,* 218. Also see Roger E. Hedlund, *Quest for Identity: India's Churches of Indigenous Origin, The 'Little Tradition' in Indian Christianity* (Delhi: ISPCK, 2000), 193.

[13] Hedlund, 'Indigenous Pentecostalism,' 230-232; Satyavrata, 'Contextual Perspectives,' 218.

[14] Vikhar Ahmed Sayeed, 'Now, Karnataka,' *Frontline* 25/20 (27 September - 10 October 2008), http://www.frontlineonnet.com/fl2520/stories/20081010252002500.htm (accessed 23 December 2009). *Also see* Interview with *Karnataka Home Minister* Dr. V. S. Acharya; Sanjana, 'There is a Limit to Religious Freedom,' *Tehelka 5/38* (27 September 2008), http://www.tehelka. com/story _main40.asp?filename=Ne270908incoldblood.asp (accessed 23 December 2009).

[15] See website: http://www.aaidu.org/yeshuDarbar.htm (accessed 23 December 2009).

[16] See Bergunder, *The South Indian Pentecostal Movement*; Hedlund, 'Indigenous Pentecostalism'; Roger E. Hedlund, *Christianity is Indian: The Emergence of an Indigenous Community,* rev. ed. (Delhi: ISPCK, 2004).

nation in Asia;[17] and most of these missionaries are Pentecostals. It is claimed that the Indian Pentecostal Church of God (IPC) has about 6000 churches all over India, while the Assemblies of God has 5,000 churches all over India.[18] In addition, there are many Pentecostal denominations working in the south as well as in the north who have established hundreds of churches.[19] According to Hedlund, in 1999 there were 60 Pentecostal Bible colleges in Kerala alone.[20] In Kerala many adherents of the mainline denominations have moved from their respective churches and joined Pentecostal churches, a fact noticed by the secular press. Shaji reports, 'The Pentecostal movement's growing clout has alarmed the Syrian Christian church, which commands the largest following. Several of its denominations – like the Jacobites and Marthomites – have witnessed a sharp erosion in their ranks'. Heavenly Feast, a neo-Pentecostal church that opened in Kottayam, Kerala, just five years ago, has grown to a congregation of 8,000 in this town alone and is popular among new converts, not least because it permits members to wear jewellery, unlike the more austere Pentecostals.[21]

In North India and certain parts of South India the situation is rather different. Pentecostal growth has taken place primarily in rural areas – among the poor, Tribal people, Dalits and lower castes. The Tribal-belt of North India, states like Rajasthan, Gujarat, Maharashtra, Madhya Pradesh, Jharkhand, Chhattisgarh and Orissa, have experienced remarkable growth. The recent spate of communal violence against Christians by *Hindutva* forces in these states provides us with evidence of the perceived threat of the growing number of Pentecostal churches.[22] Unfortunately, exact facts and figures are not yet available. Most of these Pentecostals are poor, illiterate and live in small hamlets in remote villages, where facilities like transportation, medical help and schooling are limited. Arun Jones, who has undertaken some research in North India says that middle-class mainline

---

[17] See Todd M. Johnson, David B. Barrett, and Peter F. Crossing, 'Christianity 2010: A View from the New Atlas of Global Christianity,' *IBMR* 34/1 (January 2010): 30; http://www.internationalbulletin.org/system/files/2010-01-029-johnson.pdf (accessed 9 January 2010).

[18] Y. Jeyaraj, 'Comments,' in George, *Trailblazers for God*; Y. Jeyaraj is the General Superintendent of All India Assemblies of God. K. A. Shaji, 'Holy Ghost on Malabar Coast,' *Tehelka* 4/42 (27 October 2007), http://www.tehelka.com/story_main34.asp?filename=Ne271007 holyghost.asp (accessed 22 December 2009).

[19] See Hedlund, 'Indigenous Pentecostalism,' 215-244.

[20] Roger E. Hedlund, 'Critique of Pentecostal Mission by a Friendly Evangelical,' *AJPS* 8/1 (2005): 83.

[21] Shaji, 'Holy Ghost on Malabar Coast.'

[22] For example, commenting on the violence against Christians which took place in August 2008 in Kandhamal, Orissa, Vijay Simha says, 'The rise in the number of Christians in Kandhamal is offering radical Hindu outfits like the Vishwa Hindu Parishad (VHP) the perfect alibi to launch an aggressive anti-Christian movement.' See Vijay Simha, 'In the Name of God,' *Tehelka 5/36* (13 September 2008), http://www.tehelka.com/story_main40.asp?filename=Ne130908CoverStory.asp (accessed 23 December 2009).

Protestants are generally not anxious to welcome low caste, poor people into their churches. However, Pentecostals welcome whoever they can get. Thus, Pentecostal fellowships tend to have more appeal to lower class and lower caste populations.[23]

The Pentecostal movement in India has acquired diverse forms which have been expressed differently, depending on geographical locations, culture, people-group. There can even be a distinction between Pentecostal denominations existing in the same geographical area, in terms of tenets and practices. Some Pentecostal groups consist of only a single ethnic group. Nevertheless, there are certain features that bind them together as a movement. The most significant of these is the emphasis on the work of the Holy Spirit. Most of the people who joined the movement in the beginning were either underprivileged members of the society or people with physical or spiritual troubles (often diagnosed as demonic). The majority who join Indian Pentecostal churches belong to the younger generation. There are several possible reasons: the lively worship style of Pentecostalism which turns to songs and dance, life-changing messages and prayer meetings, all attract the younger generation.[24] Older people appear to be more bound by their religious or denominational traditions finding it difficult to integrate into the movement. Furthermore, Pentecostalism is attracting people from Dalits, Tribal-groups and lower castes because it provides them with a sense of dignity and hope that is non-existent in other sections of Indian society.

The Indian Pentecostal movement is highly contextual and indigenous in nature; the worship, practices and life-style of its members reflect the culture and practices of the locality. Roger Hedlund underlines this fact:

> Indigenous Indian Christianity is found in the Little Tradition of the so-called fringe sections largely (not exclusively) of Pentecostal, Charismatic or Evangelical origin. Questions of contextualisation, adaptation, accommodation, and the cultural transformation of the Christian faith are topics of hot debate in the traditional Catholic, Orthodox and Protestant denominations – all churches of 'Great Tradition' in religious studies – whereas cultural incarnation of the faith is a normal expression in churches of Little Tradition.[25]

This is especially true in North India where Pentecostal churches are being targeted for dogmatism and rigidity in their outlook in relation to doctrine, especially when it concerns the uniqueness of Christ; albeit they are able to attract many people from other religious traditions. Arun Jones contrasts mainline protestant churches and the Pentecostals:

---

[23] Arun W. Jones, 'Faces of Pentecostalism in North India Today' sent by the author through e-mail on December 22, 2009. It is also published in *Society* 46/6 (November 2009): 504-509.

[24] Reuben Louis Gabriel, 'Reflections on the Indian Pentecostalism: Trends and Issues,' *Dharma Deepika* 6/2 (July-December 2002): 67-76, 69.

[25] Hedlund, *Quest for Identity*, 3.

> Thus in North India at least, we are left with a rather paradoxical situation. Mainline Protestantism, whose rhetoric and theology tend towards liberalism, is currently experienced sociologically and ideologically as a somewhat closed and calcifying Christian tradition, with little room for new people and fresh religious perspectives. Pentecostalism on the other hand, whose rhetoric tends towards the conservative and dogmatic, is in reality a highly adaptable social and religious movement, twisting and turning and transforming itself to adjust to the realities of a civilization whose ancient roots continue to sprout new branches and leaves.[26]

In addition, Pentecostals are strict in outlook on holiness and fervent in mission activities. These elements have enabled them to develop a form of Pentecostalism true to its neighbourhood, to proclaim Christ as Lord.

1.2 Need for a Contextual Pentecostal Christology

Even though the movement has been growing at a fast pace, it faces adverse external challenges such as religious pluralism, cultural diversity, poverty, caste-oppression, communalism and especially a recent spate of violence against Christians. These elements have affected the growth and consolidation of the movement negatively. On the other, there are various issues within the movement like schism, caste-consciousness, leadership conflicts and cross-cultural differences. Within this context, the movement faces a fundamental problem, namely the lack of an articulated theology, especially with regard to Christology.

The task of retrieving the theology of the Indian Pentecostal movement is painstaking. The pioneers of the movement were so engrossed in their mission that they were wary of developing a carefully articulated theology of their vibrant faith. Even when we find some description of their doctrines, they are compilations of biblical references apologetic in nature, seeking to prove the distinctive Pentecostal doctrinal positions such as Spirit baptism, water baptism, holiness, and the prohibition of the wearing of ornaments. Nevertheless, as a whole, it is clear that Indian Pentecostals have a rich tradition of oral theology informed by their experiences. Given the above-mentioned community struggles, the time has come to systematise those rich experiential popular theological categories.

Closely related to the aforesaid handicaps is the lack of adequate theological training for the movement's leaders, especially in North India. Although, missions were developing at a rapid pace, and many churches were established, there were no facilities to provide theological education until recently. Pastors were not able to give believers in-depth biblical teachings or lead them to a higher level of Christian understanding. This had a negative effect-on the spiritual growth of the community. Although, recent effort have place more emphasis on educating pastors and lay leaders, the courses offered are insensitive to the socio-cultural and

[26] Jones, 'Faces of Pentecostalism.'

religious context of India and are, therefore, less relevant to the pressing needs of the congregations. This lack of contextual expressions of faith formulation is detrimental to the ministry and the mission of the Church. Therefore, it is important to retrieve contextual theological expressions to educate the pastors and lay leaders for both ministry and mission.

It could be argued that any growing Christian movement needs a well articulated Christology relevant to its context. Such a contextual Christology should be sensitive to the socio-political, religio-cultural, and economic milieu if it is to be relevant. Among other things this involves the incorporation of values and worldviews by bringing them to interface with the gospel. In the process it is essential to draw clear lines wherever alienating and oppressive elements are found in the culture. Since the interface of culture and the Gospel has created a new form of Pentecostal culture combining positive aspects of Indian culture with Gospel values by which Pentecostals live and carry out their evangelistic and mission activities, this poses the challenge of religious pluralism, which sometimes escalates into violence and persecution. A contextual Christology therefore needs to consider the cultural and religious plurality of the context at face value.

Such a pattern can be seen in the New Testament. The gospels and epistles give us sufficient evidence to demonstrate that the early church used various facets of the person and work of Christ to face particular situations.[27] In India various theological traditions such as Dalit theology, Tribal theology, and the Indian version of liberation theology have developed their own contextual Christologies. There are other indigenous expression of Christologies which co-exist with traditions and culture of the Indian context.[28] To date, such efforts have not been made in the Pentecostal movement.

The Indian situation has many parallels with first century Palestine. These include such things as the purity laws, caste system, poverty, armed struggle (such as Maoism), linguistic-cultural rivalries, and communalism. The mixing of politics and religion with the resultant cultural-nationalism has turned out to be detrimental to the unity of the country. It has also affected the safe existence of minority populations, including Christians. The Indian Pentecostal movement needs a well articulated Christology akin to the New Testament pattern to sustain its momentum, as it seeks to impact its immediate surroundings.

The aim of this research is not to impose any Christological models upon the people. Instead, it seeks first to discover what Christological ideas believers

---

[27] Dean Flemming, *Contextualization in the New Testament: Pattern for Theology and Mission* (Illinois: IVP, 2005); Mesa and Wostyn, *Doing Christology*, 215-298; Ben Witherington III, *The Christology of Jesus* (Minneapolis: Fortress, 1990).

[28] We shall explore some of them in Chapter 5. Robin H. S. Boyd, *Kristadvaita: A Theology for India* (Madras: CLS, 1977); Hubert Manohar Watson, *Towards a Relevant Christology in India Today: An Appraisal of the Christologies of John Hick, Jürgen Moltmann and Jon Sobrino* (Frankfurt am Main: Peter lang, 2002).

have developed in their complicated situation and how they use them in their personal, family and community life, ministry and mission of the church. We will then seek to develop these ideas in clear concise systematic way.

A strong contextually-oriented Christology is vital for an active involvement in the society.[29] Ordinary Pentecostals enthusiastically participate in evangelistic activities which result in many being liberated from the dismal situation they are in. This has led to a rapid proliferation of Pentecostalism among the poor. Even political parties have begun to acknowledge Pentecostal's by attending Pentecostal conventions. This progressive momentum happened because of the positive changes and the testimonies of ordinary members; their new-found faith, the spiritual urge and the better condition of life they enjoy rather than as a result of a conscious effort or social program Pentecostals developed.

However, a contextual Christology can add further momentum to such activity. Moreover, it can also provide theological validity for involvement in society and addressing social concerns around them. It is natural that after becoming Pentecostals, members shrink from society due to their holiness understanding and avoid any overt religious and cultural practices. Moreover, members find themselves powerless and ineffective in the larger society, due to their poor condition and the opposition they face. However, a realisation of the worth of their own Christological articulation as well as of a portrayal of Christ which is relevant may change the inhibitions, and the psychosis they inherit. Once ordinary believers are convinced about something, they are ready to forfeit their life for a cause. Thus a picture of Christ, anchored in biblical tradition, a Christ consciously involved in his society, would certainly impel ordinary members to move outward with a clear agenda of 'liberation'. This liberation motivation should not be equated to Marxian economic categories or formal Liberation theology models. It needs to spring from spiritual and individual aspects of Pentecostal experience, and then move toward social, economic and political realms.

To achieve this end, the author conducted qualitative research to unearth the intricate threads of Christological formulations of Pentecostal believers, informed by their Spirit-experience; socio-political, religio-cultural and economic situations; and particularly the intense persecution they face. Once those traits were identified, it was possible to analyse them and suggest a Biblical Christological model faithful to their Spirit-experience, socio-political, religio-cultural and economic situations and particularly the intense persecution they face. Once we identify those traits, it is possible to analyse and even suggest a model of Christology which is faithful to their situation and biblical tradition as well as a model that will do justice to the larger Pentecostal tradition.

---

[29] Stephen B. Bevans, *Models of Contextual Theology*, rev. ed. (Maryknoll: Orbis Books, 2002), 3-15; A. Alangaram, *Christ of the Asian People: Towards an Asian Contextual Theology* (Bangalore: Asia Trading Corporation, 2001), 144.

1.3 Overview

Chapter two focuses on the methodology of the study discussing the importance of ordinary theology, especially an ordinary Christology for an Indian context. Further, it also explains various methodological tools used in the research to collect the relevant information from the people.

Chapters three and four form the background of the study and deal with contextual aspects. To understand and articulate the Christology of a people it is vital to know their context and the issues they face and Christological traditions around them. Therefore, chapter three deals with major issues encountered by ordinary Pentecostals and the way in which they are affected by them. These issues add colour and content to their Christological articulation. We shall concentrate on issues like lack of health-care facilities, economic disparity, poverty, illiteracy, the caste system and communalism, which are the most pressing issues people face. These aspects decisively impact and shape ordinary Indian Pentecostal Christology.

Within the formulation of a Christology, existing Christologies in the context can make valuable contributions. They may also help a Christology to identify its salient features as well as its limitations. Therefore, chapter four will elaborate on the Christological articulations existing in the theological scenario in India. It is not possible to discuss all these strands but we shall choose the more representative of them to find out what they can contribute to a Pentecostal Christology. We shall divide them into various categories such as religious, cultural, political and so on.

Chapters five, six and seven form the core aspects of the study; the articulation of ordinary Indian Pentecostal Christology, its evaluation and development and the constructive proposal, respectively. Chapter five deals with our main findings from the research among the ordinary Pentecostals. This chapter portrays their Christological insights as articulated through their testimonies, songs, conversations, both formal and informal, and messages preached in the churches. These themes have been coloured by their context and the spiritual fervour they cherish. Their Christological articulations have been elaborated in various themes such as Jesus as healer, exorcist and provider and so on.

Chapter six endeavours to critically evaluate Indian Pentecostal Christology closely, by looking into its various aspects. We shall also analyse and elaborate its nature and characteristics, to see what it looks like. This chapter also will try to tally this Christology with the Christology of the larger Pentecostal tradition, as well as the New Testament testimony of the person and work of Christ.

Chapter seven ventures to construct an appropriate model of Christology for the Indian context. Here we shall rescript ordinary Christology in the light of Pentecostal scholarship to present it to the wider scholarship. In the light of evaluation, rescription and contextual factors, we shall also propose certain Trinitarian, dialogical and liberative elements to ordinary Christology. These elements may enrich Christology and help ordinary people to engage in their context.

Chapter eight will conclude the discussion. It will also highlight this Christology's contribution in the wider context and point out certain vital areas for further research in Pentecostal scholarship. In short, this research seeks to construct a Pentecostal Christology from the perspective of ordinary people, which may help to consolidate the movement and its mission, theological enterprise and Christological articulation in global Pentecostalism and Christianity.

Chapter 2

Indian Pentecostal Christology: Methodology

Theology has been often referred to as *fides quaerens intellectum,* 'faith seeking understanding' (Anselm) in classical definitions. It is 'faith' venturing to inquire and find out possible solutions for puzzling questions about God and the world. Theology thus grows out of 'faith' that incites reflection, inquiry, and pursuit of the truth not yet possessed, or only partially possessed. There are at least two fundamental roots of this quest. First, this 'faith' is the faith in God, and God is, and remains a mystery beyond human comprehension. However, the incomprehensible God has been revealed in Jesus Christ, as sovereign love, and experienced through the work of the Holy Spirit. Second, this 'faith' presupposes a 'situation of faith'. Believers do not live in a vacuum. Like all people, they live in particular historical situations that have their own distinctive problems and possibilities. These two aspects, the 'faith in God' and the 'situation of faith', bring up new questions, insights and disclosures.[1] However, this 'understanding' which 'faith' seeks is deeply coloured by the cultural context and the experience of the people.[2]

Human beings are open when they ask questions and keep seeking; when they are, as Augustine says, 'ravished with love for truth'.[3] There are certain questions that arise from the context: Do the faith and proclamation of the community

---

[1] Daniel L. Migliore, *Faith Seeking Understanding: An Introduction to Christian Theology*, 2nd ed. (Michigan: Eerdmans, 1991), 3-4.

[2] Robert J. Schreiter, *Constructing Local Theologies* (New York: Orbis Books, 1985), 75-78.

[3] Migliore, *Faith Seeking Understanding*, 4.

lead to the transforming praxis in the personal and social life of its members as well as in the larger society? Are the proclamation and practice of the community true to the revelation of God in Jesus Christ, as attested in the scripture? Similar questions lead us into the larger issue of the nature of theology.[4]

Although, modern thought tends to regard theology as a theoretical science of God, there is a strain originating in the earliest Church and developed in the Middle Ages that identifies theology as 'a cognitive disposition and orientation of the soul, a knowledge of God and what God reveals.'[5] According to Edward Farley, theology in its original and most authentic sense is a fundamental dimension of every Christian's piety and vocation. It is the insight, understanding or wisdom proper to the life of the believer and concerned with the believer's ways of existing in the world before God.[6] Further, Gustavo Gutiérrez, the liberation theologian argues that theology is reflection on *praxis* in the light of faith and is a dialectical movement between action and reflection. He understands theology as a tool to alleviate the injustices of humanity. Thus the role of theology is to speak to those inequities, thus becoming a critical reflection on 'praxis.'[7] These definitions of theology presuppose that what we call 'theology' is not a defined system of metaphysics put forth by professionals. Rather, it emerges out of people's experience, while looking for possible solutions. Therefore theology is always contextual, practical and 'ordinary'.

2.1 Theology as 'Contextual' Faith

This description leads us to understand theology as 'contextual' rather than 'theoretical'. Theology should be determined by the context, i.e. by the insights and resources from the life of the people to whom it is being directed. Otherwise theology will become a tool of ideological manipulation to justify the status quo rather than to give hope and liberation to the people. Therefore, 'the contextualisation of theology is really a theological imperative,' asserts Bevans.[8] Even though various reasons are cited by the scholars for contextualisation, the rapid growth of Christianity in the southern hemisphere and the widespread oppression in those contexts make the contextualisation of theology an urgent task.[9]

[4] Migliore, *Faith Seeking Understanding*, 10-15.

[5] Edward Farley, *Theologia: The Fragmentation and Unity of Theological Education* (Philadelphia: Fortress Press, 1983), 35.

[6] Farley, *Theologia*, 156-159; also see Jeff Astley and Ann Christie, *Taking Ordinary Theology Seriously, The Grove Pastoral Series* (Cambridge: Grove Books Limited, 2007), 5.

[7] Gustavo Gutiérrez, *A Theology of Liberation: History, Politics, and Salvation*, rev. ed. (London: SCM, 2001).

[8] Stephen B. Bevans, *Models of Contextual Theology*, rev. ed. (Maryknoll: Orbis Books, 2002), 3.

[9] Sigurd Bergmann, *God in Context: A Survey of Contextual Theology* (Hants: Ashgate, 2003), 5-20.

According to Bevans, doing theology contextually means taking into account two things: first, the faith experience of the *past* that was recorded in the scripture and kept alive in tradition; and second, the experience of the present – the *context.*[10] The context includes the experiences of a person's or group's personal life which allow a person to, or prevent a person from, experiencing God in their lives. There are also experiences of life – personal or communal – in our contemporary world: the moments of tragedy such as genocide, revolutions and so on. Moreover, personal or communal experience is possible only within the context of the culture whether it is secular or religious. We can also speak of context in terms of a person's or a community's 'social location'. Finally, the notion of present experience in our context involves the reality of social change; a change for better or worse.[11] However, here we need to be cautious to interpret Christian faith authentically by considering the specific traits of Christian Scripture. Balancing both these aspects is vital for theology; Moltmann calls these 'identity and relevance.'[12]

2.2 Theology as 'Practical' Faith

When we take the people's experience as a valid source on which to ground theology, theology becomes 'practical'. 'Practical theology focuses on human experience in the specific context and endeavours to reflect theologically on that experience,' contend Swinton and Mowat.[13] It seeks to explore the complex dynamics of particular situations in order to enable the development of a transformative and illuminating understanding of what is going on in the context. The authors define Practical theology as '*critical, theological reflection on the practices of the church as they interact with the practices of the world with a view to ensuring faithful participation in the continuing mission of the triune God*'.[14] The fundamental aim of practical theology is to participate in the mission of God and to reflect critically and theologically on situations in order to provide insights and strategies enabling faithful change in the context.[15] It also recognises and respects the diversity of

[10] Bevans, *Models of Contextual Theology*, 5.

[11] Schreiter, *Constructing Local Theologies*, 24; According to Bevans, in the globalised world, two factors are influencing social change. First, the cultural impact of modernity, with the revolution brought about by electronic media and the contemporary expansion of global connectedness (with its materialistic outlook). Second, the idealist side of modernity has encouraged oppressed people to struggle for their rights and privileges; see Bevans, *Models of Contextual Theology,* 5-7

[12] Bergmann, *God in Context*, 7.

[13] John Swinton & Harriet Mowat, *Practical Theology and Qualitative Research* (London: SCM, 2006), iii; Paul Ballard & John Pritchard, *Practical Theology in Action: Christian Thinking in the Service of the Church and Society* (London: SPCK, 1996).

[14] Swinton & Mowat, *Practical Theology,* 25 (italics original).

[15] Swinton & Mowat, *Practical Theology,* 25; Duncan B. Forrester, *Truthful Action: Explorations in Practical Theology* (Edinburgh: Clark, 2000), 7.

interpretation within the various expositions of the Gospel and seeks to ensure and encourage the Christian community to remain faithful to the narrative of the original God-given plot of the Gospel and to practise faithfully in the context as that narrative unfolds.

Moreover, practical theology locates itself with a creative tension between revelation formulated historically within scripture, doctrine, tradition, and the continuing innovative performance of the Gospel as embodied and enacted in the life and practices of the Church as the latter interact with the life and practices of the world.[16] Similarly, Bevans also endorses that theology needs to consider culture, history and contemporary thought forms along with scripture and tradition, as valid sources for theological expression.[17] Thus, theology becomes a venture, which reflects critically on the shared dialogue of a particular community.[18] Consequently, practical theology is essentially contextual.

2.3 Theology as 'Ordinary' Faith

A contextualised theology, which is essentially practical, presupposes that theological endeavours must listen to the voice of the ordinary people to understand how they appropriate the Gospel message in their particular context. According to Groome, theological enterprise should not be in the exclusive domain of the specialist, but instead,

> Theology should arise from the faith of a community reflected on in the light of the Story/Vision and not from a group of scholars isolated from the community to reflect on the community's behalf. This later kind of 'theology' (and we have it in abundance) contributes little to the ongoing faith life of the Christian community.[19]

Taking the cue from this understanding, Jeff Astley has developed a form of practical theology which listens to the heartbeats of the ordinary people; he calls it 'ordinary theology' or 'popular theology'. He defines it as *'the theology and theologising of Christians who have received little or no theological education*

---

[16] Swinton & Mowat, *Practical Theology,* 5.

[17] Bevans, *Models of Contextual Theology,* 4.

[18] Mark J. Cartledge, *Practical Theology: Charismatic and Empirical Perspectives* (Waynesboro, GA: Paternoster Press, 2003); Bevans, *Models of Contextual Theology*; Schreiter, *Constructing Local Theologies.*

[19] Thomas H. Groome, *Christian Religious Education: Sharing our story and Vision* (San Francisco: Harper & Row, 1980), 229; According to Schreiter, in the development of local theologies, the professional theologians can help the community to clarify its own experience and to relate them to the experience of other communities past and present. Thus, the professional theologian has an indispensible but limited role. The theologian cannot create a theology in isolation from the community's experience; see Schreiter, *Constructing Local Theologies*, 18.

of a scholarly, academic or systematic kind.'[20] Therefore, it is a theology emerging from the experience of ordinary believers. According to Astley and Christie, 'ordinary theology' is often both fundamentally secular but also deeply religious and spiritual. It is secular in the sense that it is grounded in our experience of the everyday roles of ordinary life. It is also religious as a form of theology that keeps close to the religious impulses and especially to the spirituality that drives people and heals them. It is, therefore, significant and intimate to the person who cherishes it and, hence intensely personal.[21]

According to Astley, justification for an ordinary theology lies in the fact that those who are involved in religious education and pastoral care need to be familiar with the religious beliefs and thoughts of their learners, and the process of their religious believing and thinking. He further adds that the church needs to study ordinary theology, the language and logic of the believers so that it may properly exercise its ministry of pastoral care, worship, Christian education, apologetics, preaching and evangelism, and all other concerns.[22]

Moreover, ordinary theology may unravel the hidden dimensions of the believers' intimate faith and understanding of God and the wider implications this faith brings to their lives. This understanding can be useful for professional theologians engaged in the systematisation of theologising.[23] However, the role of the community in forming theology is vital since the members articulate their own faith experiences in their own dialects. The larger community often raises questions of faith, provides experience of their struggle and recognizes the response and solutions at hand. According to Schreiter, gifted individuals within the community such as poets, prophets, and teachers working on its behalf, actually shape the theology, which is then in turn accepted or rejected by the community. Recent research into oral traditions indicates that it is individuals capturing the spirit of those communities who do the actual shaping of folk songs and epics.[24]

2.4 Empirical Theology

The ultimate aim of practical theology is to explore the experience, beliefs and practices of individuals and communities and for this it uses a few tools and

---

[20] Jeff Astley, *Ordinary Theology: Looking, Listening and Learning in Theology* (Hants: Ashgate, 2002), 56, (Italics Original); Ann Christie & Jeff Astley, 'Ordinary Soteriology: A Qualitative Study,' *Empirical Theology in Texts and Tables: Qualitative, Quantitative and Comparative Perspectives,* edited by Leslie J. Francis, Mandy Robbins & Jeff Astley (Leiden: Brill, 2009), 177-196; Also see, Jeff Astley, 'In Defense of "Ordinary Theology,"' *British Journal of Theological Education* 13/1 (August, 2002): 21-35.

[21] Christie and Astley, 'Ordinary Soteriology,' 179-180; also see Stephen Pattison, *The Challenge of Practical Theology* (London: Jessica Kingsley Publishers, 2007), 18-19.

[22] Astley, *Ordinary Theology*, 146-147.

[23] Swinton & Mowat, *Practical Theology*, viii-ix.

[24] Schreiter, *Constructing Local Theologies*, 17.

methods of the social sciences. However, this does not mean that theology is relegated to a subset of social sciences.[25] Moreover, every nuance of 'faith' and experience very often cannot be adequately grasped by the methodological tools of social science. It is in this context some people like Johannes van der Ven from the Roman Catholic University at Nijmegen and the British group around Leslie Francis began to propose what is known as 'empirical theology' which enables 'the direct use of empirical tools and methods in theology.'[26]

Van der Ven has understood theology as an empirical discipline to explore the theological ideas of the people in a particular context. He has extensively incorporated social-scientific research to provide an intra-disciplinary enquiry, in which theology provides an overall framework that incorporates the appropriate techniques and methods of the social sciences to further its own work. The term intra-disciplinary refers to the idea of borrowing concepts, methods and techniques from other disciplines with a view to integrating them into another science.

Empirical methodology enables ordinary theology to study the religious convictions, beliefs, images and feelings of people. In this endeavour, the theological problem and its goal are first posed and a theological question formulated. Then it is translated into publically verifiable measurements. Using social scientific research methods, empirical testing is carried out and the results are then subjected to theological interpretation, so as to answer the original theological question and in so doing, explain the meaning and relevance of the study.[27]

Given the unique Indian context, this empirical approach will be helpful in taking ordinary Pentecostal believers' experiences seriously and the articulation of their faith at its face value. In the Pentecostal movement, the believers cherish their Spirit-experience and consider it as the primary source of their Christological understanding. Moreover, the hostile situation in which they are deeply involved evokes challenging 'experiences'. However, human experience is not a flawless source for theology. It has its own limitations, not least due to the imperfection of human experience itself, and complications related to cultural and social backgrounds. Nevertheless, when the Spirit works in human experiences, the Bible is seen in a new light and creates an interpretative context. This raises new

---

[25] Mark. J. Cartledge, 'Empirical Theology: Inter-or Intra-disciplinary?,' *Journal of Beliefs & Values* 20/1 (1999): 98-104.

[26] Johannes A. van der Ven, *Practical Theology: An Empirical Approach* (Kampen: Kok Pharos, 1993), 27; Johannes A. van der Ven, 'An Empirical or a Normative Approach to Practical Theological Research?,' *Journal of Empirical Theology* 15/2 (2002): 5-33; Ottmar Fuchs, 'Relationship between Practical Theology and Empirical Research,' *Journal of Empirical Theology* 14/2 (2001): 5-19.

[27] Astley, *Ordinary Theology*, 106-107; Gerben Heitink, *Practical Theology: History, Theory, Action Domain* (Michigan: Eerdmans, 1999), 220-230.

questions and challenges and brings answers from the Gospel, which are not always obvious when the Bible is reflected on in abstraction.[28]

2.5 Pentecostal Theology and Empirical Research

Now it is important to see the possibility of using empirical research methods in Pentecostal theology to draw out the ordinary theology of Pentecostal believers. Pentecostalism, from its inception, has been a people's movement, and was originally a movement of the poor and the rejected of the society.[29] Even today this is true almost everywhere the movement takes root. A systematic analysis of the contributions of this movement worldwide shows that the liberational role (spiritual as well as social) it plays even today is commendable. For example, after undertaking a full year of empirical, sociological and theological analysis of the Pentecostal movement in Latin America, Shaull and Cesar conclude that the movement became a major liberative force among the poor of the Majority World. Shaull explains the radical changes taking place in the lives of the disadvantaged and the way they respond to their surroundings:

> The Pentecostal message and experience had radically transformed their understanding and experience of their world and enabled them to restore their broken lives and thus find new life and energy. Poor marginalised women and men had found the power they needed for the physical, mental and often material renewal and for a successful struggle to overcome the most destructive forces around them.[30]

Therefore, it is not a surprise that *The Oxford Dictionary of the Christian Church* terms Pentecostalism as 'originally "a religion of the poor."'[31]

This character of Pentecostal spirituality and for that matter Pentecostal theology is essentially practical and touches the lives of ordinary people in every aspect.[32] For instance, J. D. Johns suggests that Pentecostals are inclined towards an epistemology and corresponding approach to social reform, which is generally compatible with Freire's model of *praxis*.[33] However, he sees it as a

[28] Swinton & Mowat, *Practical Theology*, 6.

[29] Jeffrey T. Snell, 'Beyond the Individual and into the World: A Call to Participation in the Larger Purpose of the Spirit on the Basis of Pentecostal Theology,' *Pneuma* 14/1 (Spring 1992), 54.

[30] Richard Shaull & Waldo Cesar, *Pentecostalism and the Future of the Christian Churches* (Michigan: Eerdmans, 2000), 119.

[31] F.L. Cross & E.A. Livingston (eds.), 'Pentecostalism,' *The Oxford Dictionary of the Christian Church*, 3rd ed. (Oxford: Oxford University Press, 1997), 1254.

[32] Browning conducted a study on the practical theology of a Pentecostal church and underlines that its spirituality is practical and contextual; see Don S. Browning, *A Fundamental Practical Theology* (Minneapolis: Fortress Press, 1991), 243-277.

[33] For a detailed exposition and analysis of this nature of the Pentecostal movement see, Cheryl Bridges Johns, *Pentecostal Formation: A Pedagogy among the Oppressed* (Sheffield: Sheffield Academic Press, 1993).

contemporary expression of the epistemology found in the Scriptures. The Pentecostal epistemology is formed by the knowledge that is grounded in God and God is known through encounter.[34] Moreover, for Pentecostals truth is not just propositional truth, but truth leads them to experience God and transformation in life. According to Land, the Pentecostal paradigm of truth is known and expressed through *orthodoxy* (right praise-confession), *orthopathy* (right affections) and *orthopraxy* (right praxis).[35]

Now if *Praxis* is a type of knowledge in which a learner engages and transforms the social realities of his existence and empowers the oppressed so they can read their own plights, and gives them a voice to speak to those situations, as Freire understands, then Pentecostal theology even transcends this definition. The reason is, as Pentecostals understand, *praxis* is not mere human endeavour instead of divine action through the agency of the Spirit. The Spirit-filled person engages with his/her environment with the power of the Spirit.[36] When a person is filled with the Spirit, God infuses the human spirit with *dunamis*, opening the way for transforming vertical discipleship into horizontal responsibility. Lovett explains:

> For 'Where the Spirit of the Lord is, there is liberty' is a claim long attested to and affirmed by Pentecostal-charismatic believers…The Spirit is God and God is expressed in community, shattering and renewing, rending and healing, revealing and transforming, lifting and liberating a people unto God. When the human spirit is grasped and energised by the Holy Spirit, it is given the necessary power to go beyond itself enabling it to perform tasks beyond our normally anticipated human ability and comprehension.[37]

Hence, it is right to call Pentecostal theology 'ordinary theology' on the basis of the definitions we have explored in this section, since it brings radical

---

[34] Jackie David Johns, 'Yielding to the Spirit: The Dynamic of a Pentecostal Model of Praxis,' in *The Globalization of Pentecostalism: A Religion Made to Travel,* edited by M.W. Dempster, B.D. Klaus & D. Petersen (Carlisle: Regnum, 1999), 70-84, 75; Jackie David Johns & Cheryl Bridges Johns, 'Yielding to the Spirit: A Pentecostal Approach to Group Bible Study,' *JPT* 1/1 (1992): 109-134.

[35] Stephen J. Land, *Pentecostal Spirituality: A Passion for the Kingdom* (Sheffield: Sheffield Academic Press, 1993), 41.

[36] Johns, 'Yielding to the Spirit,' 73-80.

[37] Leonard Lovett, 'Liberation: A Dual-Edged Sword,' *Pneuma* 9/2 (Fall, 1987): 166; Bridges Johns also says, 'The role of the Holy Spirit is that of one who activates conversion in which a person enters into a new realm, and new level of consciousness. The Holy Spirit is the agent of sanctification and also gives power for service with a concept of mission being grounded in historical experience but with consequences which go beyond present history. The Holy Spirit enables a person to experience the paradox of suffering and the power of renunciation. One is enabled to side with the oppressed and to become a servant of the poor by becoming poor in the spirit (humility)', Johns, *Pentecostal Formation*, 100.

transformation among the disadvantaged to bring about change in themselves and to change others.

These features of Pentecostal theology justify the use of empirical methodological tools for the exploration of the ordinary theology of Pentecostal believers. Pentecostalism has its base among the ordinary folks in India and this entails the need to use interviews, focus groups, and the collection of oral stories for the formation of Pentecostal theology, especially a Pentecostal Christology.

2.6 Ordinary Christology

In every period of history, Christology has been shaped by the needs and concerns of the context. A close reading of the New Testament and the history of Christian theology will show that Christology always is normed by soteriological requirements.[38] In the post-modern world, however, the threats of human suffering and injustice are at the forefront of our needs. Therefore, human suffering and injustice must set boundaries for an adequate Christology today. This dire need presumes that Christology should be translated into the realm of 'ordinary people'.

This understanding has a valid theological justification, since the incarnation itself is seen as 'translation into ordinariness' or contextualisation *per se*. Nicholls presents the case:

> Contextualization is not a passing fad or a debatable option. It is essential to our understanding of God's self-revelation. The incarnation is the ultimate paradigm of the translation of text into context. Jesus Christ, the Word of God incarnate as a Jew, identified with a particular culture at a limited moment in history though transcending it. In his life and teaching he is the supreme model of contextualization.[39]

The implication of this process of translation is seen in the apostolic witness and the life of the New Testament Church.[40] That the individual Christologies found in the four Gospels and the Epistles vary according to the life situations

---

[38] Religion confronts a wide range of fundamental human needs. Paul Tillich sees the predominant need in the ancient world to be anxiety about death, in the medieval world to be anxiety about guilt, and in the modern world to be anxiety about meaninglessness. Paul Tillich, *Courage to Be* (New Haven: Yale University Press, 1952); also see Tyron L. Inbody, *The Many Faces of Christology* (Nashville: Abingdon Press, 2002), 19-59; Jose M. De Mesa & Lode L. Wostyn, *Doing Christology: The Re-Appropriation of a Tradition* (Quezon City, Philippines: Claretian Publications, 1989), 30-40.

[39] Bruce. J. Nicholls, 'Contextualisation,' *NDT,* edited by Sinclair B. Ferguson & David F. Wright (Illinois: IVP, 2000), 164; Bruce. J. Nicholls, *Contextualization: A Theology of Gospel and Culture* (Exeter: Paternoster, 1979).

[40] The difference in theological emphasis and preaching method between Paul's address to the synagogue in Pisidian Antioch (Acts. 13:16-41) and his address to the Areopagus in Athens (Acts. 17:22-31) is but one notable illustration of the sociological and theological inevitability of this translation; Nicholls, 'Contextualisation.'

of the communities in which they evolved proves the essential nature of contextualisation and the plurality of Christologies.[41] In the history of dogma the affirmations of the truths of God's revelation in the Scriptures have always involved a selection of themes and contextualized language in response to the particular theological and ethical issues confronting the Church in a particular moment of history. The creeds, confessions and statements of faith reflect this process.[42]

Christ is at the heart of Christian belief, thought and practice; therefore Christ is at the heart of Christian theology. What Christians claim to know as distinctive and authentic about God is because of Christ. According to Marsh, given the Gospel history and the narrative about Jesus Christ, which truly portray a genuine effort of contextualisation, the task of interpreting God's presence and action will draw interpreters to the margins of their own social worlds.[43] Küster also endorses a similar view:

> *The biblical stories about Jesus Christ, the narratives of believers, men and women, on the one hand, and the themes which determine them on the other, are the two complementary forms shaping the text. They came to interact with the stories of men and women the generative themes of the con-text which govern them. As a result a dense fabric of stories and themes takes shape.*[44]

What will result is a practical theology with Christology at its heart; an ordinary Christology born of deep exploration of the experience of Christ in 'in-between' worlds – that is, in the biblical narrative world and in the believers' experiences today – a Christology that is done from the perspective of the people, from a particular location.[45]

According to Küster, Christological discourse is a hermeneutical event. The story of Jesus can be told from different viewpoints: his birth and public activities, suffering and death on the cross, and resurrection. People interpret their own stories through these Christological stories and *vice versa*. Here the stories evoke a whole web of *generative themes*. The generative words and themes of local community, when linked together, enable the full disclosure-linguistic or

---

[41] Veli-Matti Kärkkäinen, *Christology: A Global Introduction* (Michigan: Baker Academic, 2003), 19-58; Dean Flemming, *Contextualization in the New Testament: Pattern for Theology and Mission* (Illinois: IVP, 2005).

[42] De Mesa & Wostyn, *Doing Christology*, 223-298; Flemming, *Contextualization in the New Testament*; Anton Wessels, *Images of Jesus* (London: SCM, 1990).

[43] Clive Marsh, *Christ in Focus: Radical Christocentrism in Christian Theology* (London: SCM, 2005), 18.

[44] Volker Küster, *The Many Faces of Jesus Christ* (London: SCM, 2001), 32 (Italics original).

[45] Marsh, *Christ in Focus*, 3-17; Ann Christie, 'Who Do You Say I Am?: Answers from the Pews,' *The Journal of Adult Theological Education* 4/2 (2007): 181-194.

thematic universe-of a community.[46] Christological interpretations emerge from a creative dialogue between the biblical text and the contemporary context in which an interpreter or a community engage with an ancient text as a dialogue partner with specific questions that arise from a contemporary context.[47]

In recent times, theologians have tended to bring two sets of priorities from their own contexts to the process of contextual interpretation. Liberation theologians bring socioeconomic, political and gender concerns to brush up the portrait of Jesus, while theologians of inculturation integrate religio-cultural issues. In the Indian context both of these issues are relevant while shaping a Christology. However, as Nicholls cautions us, valid contextualization takes place only where there is unreserved commitment to the path of discipleship; loyalty and commitment to Jesus Christ as Saviour and Lord of all of life, personal and social, and to his Gospel.[48]

2.7 Ordinary Indian Pentecostal Christology

When the story of Jesus passes through the hermeneutical grid of the Pentecostal community in the power of the Spirit, it produces *generative themes* that liberate people from the tyranny of evil leading them to freedom and joy. Consequently, the Pentecostal community becomes the harbinger of a truly context-oriented Christology which is in every sense an 'ordinary Christology,' since it stems directly from the experience of ordinary people in their context. It is a 'Christology from below', originating from the pain and suffering of the people in which they experience Jesus as in the Synoptic Gospels. It is a Christology that sprouts from the struggles of the community; hence it is 'practical,' 'contextual' and 'ordinary'. Further, it is not a Christology that is systematically articulated or created by professional theologians, but instinctively articulated by the people. In other words, it emerges from the context of the community without the conscious effort of the people who are theologising. Moreover, it is a corporate affair; every single member of the community unknowingly partakes in this process. This Christology or rather 'Christological themes' take shape and texture in the worship context of the community; the Spirit experience and the miraculous elements of the Gospel act as essential ingredients.[49] It can be named elemental spirituality and it is very close to the Christology of the early church. This Christology acts as a beacon of

[46] Küster, *The Many Faces of Jesus Christ*, 30, 33; These options are typically represented by incarnational theology in Roman Catholic confession; the theology of cross in the Protestant confession; and resurrection theology in the Eastern Orthodox confession.

[47] J. Levison & P. Pope-Levison, 'Christology,' *Global Dictionary of Theology*, edited by William A. Dyrness & Veli-Matti Kärkkäinen (Nottingham: IVP, 2008), 176.

[48] Nicholls, 'Contextualisation.'

[49] For instance, Schreiter affirms that one cannot speak of a community developing a local theology without it being filled with the Spirit and working under the power of the Gospel. Theology is the work of God through a human, graced community; Schreiter, *Constructing Local Theologies*, 24.

liberation and becomes a pedagogical process awakening consciousness, inciting members to action just as Schreiter maintains, 'the role of the community in the development of the theology shows how the poor become the subject of their own history.'[50] Therefore, it is vital to retrieve these Christological themes to fully comprehend the overall Christological understanding of Pentecostal believers.

However, no scholarly literature has been produced on Indian Pentecostal Christology and this work is an initial attempt to articulate the ordinary Christology. Therefore, it is methodologically necessary to select few churches as representatives to investigate and map 'ordinary Christology.'[51] But India, as we know, is a huge and diverse country with a population of more than one billion people. It is a country of contrasts with an incredible diversity of religions, languages, customs, and landscape. Moreover, Pentecostals in India come from various cultural contexts, religious backgrounds, languages and geographical locations. Therefore, to form a standard and uniform Christology is a difficult task. Nevertheless, the majority of Pentecostals all over India are first generation believers and go through similar situations, which we shall explore in the Indian context. The only exception is the Pentecostals from the South-Indian states of Kerala and Chennai city who are third or fourth generation Pentecostals having a different set of problems.[52] They are socially and economically better off and may hold a slightly different understanding of Christ owing to their improved status. Nevertheless, even in Kerala most of the people joining the Pentecostal movement face similar issues as those in the rest of India, even if it is perhaps to a lesser degree. These shared features of Pentecostals allow us to envision a Christology with certain characteristics in common.

2.7.1 Sources of Ordinary Indian Pentecostal Christology

It is well known that Pentecostalism is rooted in oral culture, rather than literary culture.[53] One of the forms *par excellence* of communication of the Pentecostal religious experience is the personal testimony. It is directed both inward toward the community of believers and outward toward the world.[54] Pentecostals make their theological-world with their personal testimonies, what God has wrought in their lives. Telling of one's personal story of God's activity is central to the

[50] Schreiter, *Constructing Local Theologies*, 17.

[51] Richard J. Mouw, *Consulting the Faithful: What Christian Intellectuals can Learn from Popular Religion* (Michigan: Eerdmans, 1994).

[52] Even in Chennai city the condition of the majority of the Pentecostals are similar to the North Indian Pentecostals; see Bergunder, *The South Indian Pentecostal Movement,* 121-180.

[53] Walter J. Hollenweger, *Pentecostalism: Origins and Developments Worldwide* (Peabody: Hendrickson Publishers, 1997), 18.

[54] No Author, 'Pentecostal Conversion in the Popular Perception of the Sacred: Some Methodological Elements for its Analysis,' *Voices from the Third World* XIV/2 (December 1991): 55.

ordinary expression of faith.[55] It attempts to represent in verbal form the shape of a life.[56] Moreover, testimony not only has the capacity to generate the knowledge, but also gives proper weight to our dual nature as both socially indebted and individually rational creatures.[57] In Pentecostal churches, ordinary members articulate their theological world with their testimonies. There is a popular saying among Indian Pentecostals that 'a testimony begets another testimony'. In the testimonial narrative, one communicates his experience to another or to others.[58]

According to Cartledge, Pentecostal testimony could be said to function by means of three interrelated modes: personal story, congregational story and denominational story.[59] Along with the testimonies of believers, the sermons, missionary stories, auto/biographies, and worship as well as related activities in the local church contribute to the larger testimony of the community. They include stories of healing, exorcism, miraculous provision and protection. These testimonies form the bedrock of ordinary Indian Pentecostal Christology, since Christologies of the gospels are similarly formed by testimony.[60] Christology emerges when the Gospel is interpreted by 'a congregation of men and women who believe it and live by it.'[61] Therefore, these testimonies reflect a combination of personal values, corporate beliefs and particular circumstances of ordinary people. Moreover, they also point to the wider Pentecostal traditions, as well as to the larger Christian faith. Cartledge argues that testimony is a means of social knowledge construction which integrates other forms of knowledge such as perception, memory, consciousness and reason. In Pentecostal spirituality it acts as a mechanism of reinforcement and commitment and also as a means of integrating social knowledge enabling us to enter into the world of Pentecostal theology.[62]

Cartledge calls this narrative world a 'script' and, along with David Martin, he argues that scholarly engagement with this ordinary expression of faith can be said to be a 'rescription'. This 'rescripting' process, however, is not for 'a damaging

---

[55] Mark J. Cartledge, *Testimony in the Spirit* (Farnham: Ashgate, 2010), 17; Alan Jacobs, *Looking Before and After: Testimony and the Christian Life* (Michigan: Eerdmans, 2008).

[56] Jacobs, *Looking Before and After*, 24.

[57] Jennifer Lackey, *Learning from Words: Testimony as a Source of Knowledge* (Oxford: Oxford University Press, 2010), 3; Jan Vansina, *Oral Tradition: A Study in Historical Methodology*, translated by H.M. Wright (New Jersey: Transaction Publishers, 2006), 47-113.

[58] No Author, 'Pentecostal Conversion in the Popular Perception,' 55.

[59] Cartledge, *Testimony in the Spirit*, 17.

[60] The Gospels themselves are the testimony of the eye witness; see Richard J. Bauckham, *Jesus and the Eyewitnesses: The Gospels as Eyewitness Testimony* (Michigan: Eerdmans, 2006), 5; also see Richard J. Bauckham, *The Gospels as Eyewitness Testimony* (Cambridge: Grove Books, 2008).

[61] Lesslie Newbigin, *The Gospel in a Pluralist Society* (Michigan: Eerdmans, 1989), 227.

[62] Cartledge, *Practical Theology*, 52-57.

revisionist account, which seeks to surplant Pentecostal presupposition with alien categories'; rather,

> It seeks to maintain a tension between a revised script that is *both* in continuity with *and* in discontinuity with the existing script. It seeks to move ordinary theology forward through a deeper analysis of its testimony mode and a broader dialogue with the Christian theological tradition, illuminated by the insights of the social sciences.[63]

In our study, this 'rescription' is carried out taking into account (a) the New Testament scholarship regarding the person and work of Christ, (b) Pentecostal tradition as well as contemporary Pentecostal scholarship, (c) the context of the believers and (d) the Christological formulation of other Christian traditions in India.

There are different levels of conversation in the methodological process of ordinary Pentecostal Christology. The first level consists of the ordinary discourse of the believers and this is the main focus of the study. However, the second level, namely denominational or confessional theology as Cartledge puts it,[64] has not been distinctively developed by the denominations of the congregations of the present study. Therefore, sermons preached in the congregations and articles in the popular magazines can be taken as confessional theology. They can give a clue to the particular denomination's concept about Christ and their practices. Even this level can be understood as a reproduction of the primary level. The third level is the academic discourse on Pentecostalism and wider contextual theological enterprise of India and the Majority World.

2.8 The Researcher

It is important to give an exact picture of the researcher in relation to his/her denominational and theological position since, as Swinton and Mowat affirm, qualitative research as a mode of knowledge-formation cannot be understood apart from the person of the researcher who carries it out. A researcher should enter into the context of the study with the right questions and methods. While doing the research, s/he needs to understand the impossibility of standing outside of the research field and, therefore, it is vital to carry out critical self-reflection (*reflexivity*) which may help to monitor and respond to the contribution to the proceedings.[65]

Taking the cue from the above understanding, here I confess that I am a Pentecostal in my faith and an insider to the community I have studied. Having had two decades of involvement with the movement in North India and knowledge and experience of the Pentecostal spirituality, I have seen my research

[63] Cartledge, *Testimony in the Spirit,* 16-18.

[64] Ibid., 19-20.

[65] Swinton & Mowat, *Practical Theology,* 59.

greatly enriched.[66] Many years of exposure and participation in the context, culture, language and struggles of the common believers, and my experience as a Pastor and a Bible College teacher has helped me comprehend the ordinary theology of the members with more insight. Interaction with the Bible College students from various parts of India, several visits to various churches, ministerial responsibilities and close contact with members of the Pentecostal community in different states of India showing language and cultural diversities enabled me to appreciate their Christology in their own particular situations which has been of great help. Familiarity with the people and pastoral experience acted as added advantages, by enabling believers to express their Christological understanding as well as the issues they face without hesitance. Due to my affinity with people and inside knowledge of the situation, I may 'act as a catalyst' and can 'enable people to develop their own analysis.'[67] Simultaneously, my South-Indian background within a different cultural context, life-style and many years of theological education in ecumenical settings has enabled me to view the movement and its theology with critical distance. Thus, both the insider (*emic*) and outsider (*etic*) orientations allowed me to be sensitively critical and yet constructive.

2.9 Research Methods

The primary aim of this project is to find out what the common Pentecostal believers' ideas on the person and work of Christ are in their particular situations. To achieve this end, the research was carried out using qualitative research methods such as personal interviews, focus groups, participant observation and informal interaction with Pentecostals. This is exploratory research into the ordinary *beliefs, practices and consequences* of the Christology of Pentecostal believers.[68]

The data was collected using various qualitative research methods such as participant observation of worship services, personal interviews, focus group interviews, and documentary analysis. The data was also triangulated, so as to essentially crosscheck the veracity of the materials, both oral and written. This

[66] John W. Creswell, *Research Design: Qualitative, Quantitative, and Mixed Methods Approach* (London: Sage Publications, 2003), 184-185, 200.

[67] Ernest T. Stringer, *Action Research*, 2nd ed. (London: Sage Publications, 1999), 25.

[68] Three Pentecostal churches were selected which are located in North India. They were selected owing to the fact that they represent the character of the membership pattern of Indian Pentecostalism. The names of particular churches and their locations are withheld, owing to the hostility shown against Christians. One is from an inner village with almost 200 members; another one is in a city and has more than 600 members while the third one is in a town and has 100 members. Moreover, the three churches also represent the participation of various people groups: Tribal-groups, Dalits, various caste-groups from Hindu background, and also Christians from South India and the locality. Other churches of Kerala, Tamil Nadu, Rajasthan, Gujarat, Maharashtra were also visited while members from states of Andhra Pradesh, Orissa, Chhattisgarh, Madhya Pradesh and Punjab were also interviewed so as to accommodate the diverse nature of Pentecostalism in India.

is done to eradicate any possible distortion in the data and avoid any extreme positions or ideological views.

2.9.1 Participant Observation

Participant-observation is one of the best ethnographic methods because it allows the researcher to immerse in a group for a period thus observing the life-styles, listening to people's experiences and asking questions directly.[69] This is done overtly, after the people concerned have agreed.

2.9.1.1 Sunday Services

I attended Sunday services of each church for three weeks simultaneously and took notes. I also participated in their worship (singing, Psalm-reading and Holy Communion) and also explained the aims of the project to the believers. The songs, sermons from the pastors and the testimonies of believers in the services were recorded using the audio recorder and also noted down. Furthermore, as mentioned, I also visited other churches in the states of Rajasthan, Gujarat, Maharashtra, Tamil Nadu and Kerala. In general the essential content of the worship in these churches is similar. However, there were perceived differences also. For instance, in the village church, the songs were sung in local dialect or in Hindi, while in the city church both Hindi as well as English songs were sung. In the town church the majority of the songs were sung in Hindi. Worship in the village church lasted four hours, while in the city church it lasted only two hours. The songs, sermons and particularly testimonies proved to be rich sources of the people's understanding of Christ. Testimonies (which were often rather lengthy) by members explained their struggles and the way God had answered their prayers. Immediately after the service, people gathered for special prayer for healing and other matters. Bottles of oil and water were prayed over to be used later in the case of any sickness.

2.9.1.2 Prayer Meetings

I also attended the Friday fasting prayer of both the village and town church and participated in prayer meetings of the above mentioned states as well. In these meetings people prayed for healing; exorcisms were carried out and special prayers for blessing and protection were offered. Moreover, a sermon was preached by the Pastor and special prayers were offered for church growth and evangelistic activities. In the village church, I got the opportunity to attend the baptism service of new converts and also listened to their conversion stories as they were told before baptism took place.

All these churches have regular 'area prayer' in different locations, in the evenings; these prayers are conducted in believers' homes. I attended many of

[69] Colin Robson, *Real World Research: A Resource for Social Scientists and Practitioner-Researchers* (Oxford: Blackwell, 2002), 320-322; Bryman, *Social Research Methods*, 292.

these prayer meetings during the research period. Personal testimonies were often given in these meeting and a short exhortation or message was given by the leader. This is a time of fellowship, prayer and of sharing a meal.

2.9.2 Personal Interviews

Interviewing the Pastors, lay leaders and members is another important method to draw out the contextual experiences and the Christological framework of Indian Pentecostalism. Both formal and informal interviews were conducted to accommodate wider views. Semi-structured interviewing was used as most of the people are illiterate or semi-literate in a village context. Since many of the interviewees were not formally educated, Pastors selected the people for me, as they knew those who could speak and articulate the Christological notions. I asked the Pastors to select members from a wide range of categories such as women, men, youths, the newly converted as well as members with long experience and those who were involved in church activities and so on to get more inclusive views. Here more participation was given to women as a few of them only participated in focus groups (due to the nature of much of Indian society). When women were being interviewed, one more person accompanied them for the duration of interview, because of cultural sensitivities.

2.9.2.1 Interviews

Interviewers were asked to narrate their life-stories specifically, their life before conversion (including their religious lives, suffering, sickness etc); the circumstances in which their conversion had taken place; the opposition they faced, and the transformation that had happened in their lives.[70] After hearing the stories, they were asked a few questions such as, how they understand Christ in their personal, family and community lives; what changes (spiritual, financial) their lives have experienced; how they testify about Christ to others, and so on.

To accommodate the wide variety of voices of Pentecostalism in India, informal interviews were conducted among people from the different states mentioned above. These include ordinary members, area leaders, evangelists and pastors, male and female, young and old. Seventy five people were interviewed in thirteen different places. Besides, I interacted informally with a large number of people on several occasions and noted down their views regarding Christ. Data was recorded using an audio-recorder.

2.9.3 Documentary Analysis

The village and the town churches that were studied do not have, as yet, any documents regarding their faith affirmation or doctrinal statements. These churches were established recently and the members are generally poor and

[70] Uwe Flick, *An Introduction to Qualitative Research* (London: Sage Publications, 1998), 98-101; Creswell, *Research Design*, 185-188.

uneducated. Therefore, there is a complete lack of documents. The city church, however, does have its own formal faith affirmation though not documents of any significance. The denomination of the city church and the village church (both of them belong to same denomination) has significant amounts of information regarding mission, charity and spiritual activities. There are two magazines that published periodically in English and Hindi. I acquired several copies of them and also copied electronically some of the old issues where copies were unavailable. These magazines give us valuable information on various mission activities, stories of church growth, healing miracles, their conception of Christ and other doctrinal statements. I have obtained some biographies, compact discs containing testimonies and programmes, and song books published by the respective denominational headquarters of the various churches.

2.9.4 Focus Groups

To understand the deeply-rooted Christological perception of the Pentecostal community in the Indian setting, it is central to gather their collective views on the person and work of Christ. This is possible through the practice of testimony by members participating in conversations. In the Pentecostal setting, the usual practice of narrating the personal and corporate testimony in a worship context, as well as in informal gatherings, was found to be an excellent method to obtain the communitarian understanding on Christ.[71] Therefore, I decided to conduct informal 'focus groups' where people speak about their testimonies and views freely in a non-threatening environment; while keeping the subject focus in view.[72] It was a suitable method to go deeply into the theme we intended to explore and also a means to 'develop an understanding on *why* people feel the way they do.'[73] It was the best way to appreciate the testimony in context, as participants were completely at ease about sharing their personal stories with one another. Moreover, the believers were able to bring forth the issues that they deemed to be significant and came out with a general consensus, or difference. It was also helpful to listen to conversations among the participants: their reactions and facial expressions enabled me to have a better grasp on the subject in question.

The participants were selected from diverse age groups, new and experienced believers, and those who were involved in the Christian ministry. The village church consisted of people of the same ethnicity, language and culture. In the city and town churches, the participants were selected in part by looking into the ethnicity, language, education and financial condition of the members. The Pastors were careful to select the believers who were competent enough to speak about the subject. The number of women was kept lowest in the village and town

---

[71] Cartledge, *Practical Theology*, 52-60.

[72] Helen Finch & Jane Lewis, 'Focus Group,' in *Qualitative Research Practice*, 170-198; Robson, *Real World Research*, 284-286.

[73] Bryman, *Social Research Methods*, 348.

church owing to the cultural setting of these contexts. I was also informed by one pastor that some people might be unable to speak about the subject and that the language barrier can create a communication gap.

Over the discussion sessions, some of the participants were asked to narrate their testimony – the conversion experience, the way they experienced Christ on a daily basis and the changes triggered in their lives. Taking the clues from the testimonies, a number of questions related to the person and work of Christ were asked to the believers and a lively discussion followed.

Each focus group recording was subsequently transcribed using content analysis which highlights the major Christological themes emphasised by the participants. These themes were compared with other sources appearing in published documents and songs as well as the data collected from participant observation and personal interviews.[74]

2.9.5 Data Analysis

The data created from participant observations, personal interviews and focus groups was transcribed, typed and read carefully. Then the data was broken down into discrete parts, closely examined, compared for similarities and differences, and questions were asked about the phenomena as reflected in the data.[75] The sections of them which seemed to be distinct incidents and stated opinions about important topics were then highlighted. Then prominent ideas and topics were *coded* and these codes gave rise to seven themes. These themes are closely interconnected and form a *grounded theory* which will be explained later.[76]

The data collected has a wide range of implications in personal, family, community and the social lives of the people. They point to intimate experiences and life situations of the respondents and larger sections of the society and can be useful in drawing out various levels of conceptualisation in the spiritual, social, political and economic realms.

Summing up, it is obvious that Indian Pentecostals cherish an 'ordinary' Christology emerging from their experiences in their contexts. To unearth and comprehend this Christological heritage, it is essential to carry out our research using empirical methodological tools. Therefore, we turned to interviews, focus groups, participant observation and so on for data collection. In the following chapter we shall explore the general Indian context to find out what the contextual experiences of the people are. The study will focus on various issues arising in Indian society, which affect the Pentecostals and act as catalysts to their Christological articulations.

---

[74] Bryman, *Social Research Methods*, 275; Creswell, *Research Design*, 195-196.

[75] Juliet Corbin & Anselm Strauss, *Basics of Qualitative Research: Grounded Theory Procedures and Techniques* (Newbury Park, CA: Sage Publications, 1990), 62.

[76] A. Strauss & J. M. Corbin, *Basics of Qualitative Research: Techniques and Procedures for Developing Grounded Theory* (Thousand Oaks, CA: Sage Publications, 1998), 12.

Chapter 3

Indian Pentecostal Christology: Contextual Factors

This chapter will address the contemporary Indian society in which Pentecostal churches are emerging and growing in order to understand the contextual experiences of Pentecostals, by placing their Christology firmly within the context. To achieve this aim we need to consider the general socio-political, religio-cultural and economic conditions which affect the Pentecostals, so as to understand how theology, especially Christology, is being shaped by these factors. It has already been mentioned that the Pentecostal movement is growing fast among Tribal people, Dalits and other lower castes in Indian society, who are mostly poor and illiterate or semi-literate. Therefore, the Christological perception among these people is intricately conjoined to their immediate context, as well as their struggles. Besides, the former factors essentially offer multilayered interpretations to their Christological understanding. Hence, it is important to consider the context in which the various Christological features are continuously being added and explained. There are many issues to consider; however, here we will limit our focus on some of the most pressing issues directly affecting common Pentecostal believers; these are discussed in the pages that follow.

The structure of the Indian society has undergone considerable change in the last decade; currently, India is undergoing one of the most dramatic and transformational events in its history. Its tremendous growth in the industrial and commercial sectors, showing massive economic growth potential for the coming years, makes India a genuine world power candidate.[1] However, in the

[1] Sunil Bharati Mittal, 'Market Unbound,' *India Today* XXXIV/34 (18-24 August 2009): 60.

midst of incredible economic advances, a major chunk of the population has been left behind to fend for themselves in utter poverty and impoverishment due to corruption, nepotism and faulty policies of successive governments, as we shall see. Paradoxically, the Indian Constitution claims India to be a sovereign, democratic republic, assuring its citizens justice, equality and liberty and promoting fraternity among them all. By constitutional amendment in 1976, the concepts of socialist and secular ideals were added to promote and keep the real spirit of democracy and freedom of religions among all citizens. However, a cursory glance into the grass-root strata of Indian society would definitely persuade most people that India is a nation of teeming paradoxes.

3.1 India: An Emerging Power

India is the world's fifth largest economy and an expanding market; it now stands amongst the leading powers of the world.[2] India's GDP rate has been one of the highest in the world for the past several years. 'Within five years, India's growth rate will overtake China,' claims Kaushik Basu.[3] Experts have projected that, 30 to 40 years from now India will be a developed country.[4] Various reasons can be argued in favour of this perception. India is blessed with enormous and unique resources; it has huge tracts of fertile land with significant climate and coastal diversity, which help the country grow anything and everything.[5] Besides, more than half of India's population today is under 25 years of age and, more importantly, about 40% is under the age of 18. India has a stable democracy and, most significantly, its youth have a very strong entrepreneurial spirit.[6] 'A longstanding productive working population and a huge domestic consumer market, India is predicted to become the fifth largest consumer market in the world by 2025,' predicts Sunil Mittal, the Chairman of Bharti Enterprises.[7]

India has achieved significant growth in information and communication technology, as in both the medical and educational fields. India has some of the

---

[2] Dilip Bobb, 'Year of Revival,' *India Today* (11 January 2010); http://indiatoday.intoday.in/site/ Story/77320/Cover%20Story/Year+of+revival.html (accessed 14 January 2010).

[3] Kaushick Basu is the prime minister's chief economic advisor, Kaushick Basu, Interview given to NDTV News Channel on 6 January 2010, http://www.ndtv.com/news/videos/video_player.php? id=1190535 (accessed 6 January 2010).

[4] For instance, Hans Rosling, 'Asia's Rise - How and When,' *TED India 2009*, (Filmed November 2009, Posted November 2009), http://www.ted.com/talks/hans_rosling_asia_s_rise_how_and_ when.html (accessed 4 January 2010); Hans Rosling is a professor of global health at Sweden's Karolinska Institute and he gives an excellent and scholarly projection of the economic growth of India.

[5] Jagdish N. Sheth, 'Great Ideas, Great Minds,' *India Today* (6 October 2008), http://indiatoday. intoday.in/site/story?sId=16109&secid=30 (accessed 16 December 2009).

[6] Samit Basu, 'Brave New Demography: Youth Power,' *India Today* (14 December 2009), http://indiatoday.intoday.in/site/story?sId=73519&secid=30 (accessed 16 December 2009).

[7] Mittal, 'Market Unbound,' 60.

finest colleges in the world, specialising in various disciplines.[8] Indian scientists are not lagging behind in key areas of cutting edge research and are rubbing shoulders with the developed world. Even in the latest stem cell research, India has proved its mettle. 'India now has a global presence in both basic and clinical research in stem cells. We are in the big league now,' says D. Balasubramanian.[9]

The introduction of free market economy and its neo-liberal policies, as well as the resultant rapid economic growth of the past few years, have created a new brand of urban upper and middle class who have purchasing power. A recent survey conducted by market researcher Nielsen across 35 cities shows that, for affluent individuals, gyms, spas and beauty parlours are the new hangout zones, while fine dining and shopping are high priorities. The survey estimates a total of 2.5 million affluent households in India.[10]

A recent book by Australian author Geoff Hiscock, an expert on Asian economies, concludes that, as the Indian consumer seeks new experiences from food and wine, installs luxuries such as in-home spas and holidays in exotic destinations, modern retail is on its way to becoming the key driver of the country's economy. India's consumer demand, like China's, is simply unstoppable. Younger Indians are more confident and are willing to borrow to finance their consumption.[11] A MasterCard study estimates that, by 2015, the growing affluent class will spend $36 billion on shopping, dining and leisure; $15.3 billion on automobiles, personal computers, mobile phones, health and medicine and, consequently, in so doing they will stimulate the cycle of consumption, investment and job creation.[12] Of course, these facts and figures present a euphoric impression for those who see from the peripheries.

---

[8] Raj Chengappa, 'India's Best Colleges,' *India Today* (2 June 2008), http://indiatoday.intoday.in/site/story?sId=8688&secid=30 (accessed 16 December 2009).

[9] Quoted by Raj Chengappa, 'How Stem Cells can Save your Life,' *India Today* (25 January 2010), http://indiatoday.intoday.in/site/Story/79189/Cover%20Story/How+stem+cells+can+save+your+life.html (accessed 29 January 2010); D. Balasubramanian is the L.V. Prasad's director of research and recently chairman of the apex government committee overseeing stem cells work in India.

[10] No Author, 'What's Hot,' *India Today* (9 November 2009), http://indiatoday.intoday.in/site/ Story/68638/Lifestyle/What (accessed 16 December 2009); Eight in 10 Upper Middle and Rich (UMAR) eat out regularly and shopping is a craze: nine in 10 shop at modern retail stores, mainly for footwear, jewellery, handbags, sunglasses, cosmetics, fragrances, pens and watches. Nine in 10 affluent individuals own a house and two in five have a home theatre and/or modular kitchen.

[11] Geoff Hiscock, *India's Store Wars: Retail Revolution and the Battle for the Next 500 million Shoppers* (Singapore: John Wiley & Sons (Asia) Pte. Ltd, 2008). According to the latest research in the India Retail Report 2009, retail spending by Indian consumers is expected to rise from $300 billion now to $400 billion by 2010; See No Author, 'What's Hot.'

[12] Malini Bhupta, 'The Job Bonanza,' *India Today* (7 May 2007), http://www.indiatoday.com/itoday/20070507/cover1.html (accessed 9 November 2009). Also see V. Sridhar, 'Retail Invasion,' *Frontline* 24/13 (30 June – 13 July, 2007), http://www.frontlineonnet.com/fl2413/stories/20070713005300400.htm (accessed 18 December 2009).

3.2 India: A Nation of Inequalities

Ironically, all these achievements have been enjoyed by a section of Indian society only. A close scrutiny gives us a picture which is entirely different from the above-mentioned facts and figures. It is important not to lose sight of the fact that the recent economic growth has been more lopsided than ever before. Furthermore, large sections of the country's population continue to suffer, very acutely, with reference to a whole range of development deficits. Rather than alleviating the wretched condition of the poor and the downtrodden, the so-called liberalisation of the economy and globalisation have only helped the politically powerful and the rich few.[13] The glaring inequality that exists in the country is vividly portrayed by Aiyer:

> In a country where over 77% of the populace, or an estimated 836 million people, earn an income of Rs. 20 per day and over 300 million are living below the poverty line, nearly half the Rajya Sabha members and nearly a third of those from the Lok Sabha are worth a crore (10 million) and more.[14]

The stark contradiction between the condition of the state and the wealth of the legislators is baffling. The disparity between the rich and the poor is increasing day by day. The income of the minority indeed has been rising fast but, at the same time, the income of the majority has been stagnating or falling.[15] Among wage and salary earners, the top 20% of the population in urban India earns 56% of the income while the bottom 20% earns barely 3.4% of the income.[16]

The social and economic conditions of indigenous peoples like Dalits and Tribal groups have been adversely affected by their integration into the global economy through market-driven processes. Simultaneously, India is also home to at least 36 dollar-billionaires. At the height of the stock market boom, the wealth of just five individuals in the country exceeded $100 billion, or 10% of the GDP. One could argue that much of this is anecdotal evidence and that poverty has come down in the post-liberalisation era. Indeed, there is some evidence of a trickle-down effect.[17]

---

[13] See Praveen Jha & Mario Negre, 'Indian Economy in the Era of Contemporary Globalisation: Some Core Elements of the Balance Sheet,' *Macroscan* (17 May 2007), http://www.macroscan.org/anl/may07/anl170507Indian%20Economy.htm (accessed 10 November 2009).

[14] See Shankkar Aiyer, 'Richest Politicians,' *India Today* (23 February 2009), http://indiatoday.intoday.in/site/story?sId=28888&secid=30 (accessed 10 November 2009).

[15] Utsa Patnaik, 'A World of Distress,' *Frontline* 26/07 (28 March - 10 April 2009), http://www. frontlineonnet.com/fl2607/stories/20090410260701100.htm (accessed 11 November 2009).

[16] Shankkar Aiyar, 'Inclusive Inequality,' *India Today* (24 September 2007), http://indiatoday.intoday.in/site/story/Inclusive+inequality/1/1235.html (accessed 12 November 2009).

[17] Aiyar, 'Inclusive Inequality.'

The poverty level has dropped by 8.38%, from 35% to 27%, in the two 10-year periods; between 1993-94 and between 2004-05. 'Perhaps, the high tide of the last two years of 9-plus per cent growth may have lifted many more boats to the shore. But has the theory of percolation worked?' 'Not quite,' says Aiyar.[18] Yes, there is marginal growth and a few poor are earning more, but the distance between the poor and the rich, whether in villages or in metros, is widening. An *India Today* study based on data from the National Sample Survey Organisation for the periods 1993-94 and 2004-05 reports that expenditure and income show that inequality, as measured by the Gini coefficient,[19] has gone up across the country. 'Inequality, indeed, is the only constant across states, castes, religions and segments,' laments Aiyar.[20]

3.2.1 Poverty

India is fast earning the dubious distinction of being 'the hunger capital of the world'. The nutritional status of children has not improved over the past five years.[21] India has 40% of the malnourished children of the world. Roughly one-third of all children in India are under-weight.

Paradoxically, a survey in a private school in Delhi has found that roughly one-third of the children there are obese.[22] 'The rise in per capita total grain demand of the minority, which is getting richer and demanding more animal products, is being more than cancelled out by an enforced fall in per capita grain demand of the majority which is stagnating or getting absolutely poorer,' observes Patnaick.[23] The result is an overall decline of food intake of the poor and increase in mass hunger. The National Sample Survey data on consumption shows that, between 1993-94 and 2004-05, over 60% of India's rural population has seen a substantial absolute decline in the intake of both cereals and animal products such as milk, eggs and meat, while the top 10% registered a sharp rise in animal product intake, though not in cereal intake.[24] 'Rapid aggregate income growth over the

[18] Aiyar, 'Inclusive Inequality.'

[19] The Gini coefficient is a measure of statistical dispersion developed by the Italian statistician Corrado Gini and published in his 1912 paper 'Variability and Mutability'. It is commonly used as a measure of inequality of income or wealth. It has, however, also found application in the study of inequalities in disciplines as diverse as Health Science, Ecology, and Chemistry.

[20] Aiyar, 'Inclusive Inequality.' The reason behind this is, the Integrated Child Development Services (ICDS) aimed at promoting child health and nutrition is not working properly.

[21] R. Ramachandran & T. K. Rajalakshmi, 'Unhealthy Trend,' *Frontline* 26/07 (28 March - 10 April 2009), http://www.frontlineonnet.com/fl2607/stories/20090410260702100.htm (accessed 14 November 2009).

[22] Bibek Debroy, 'A Case for India Whining,' *India Today* (24 September 2007), http://indiatoday.intoday.in/site/story?sId=1230&secid=30 (accessed 14 November 2009).

[23] Patnaik, 'A World of Distress.'

[24] Patnaik, 'A World of Distress.' Also see, G.C. Manna, 'On Calibrating the Poverty Line for Poverty Estimation in India,' *EPW* (28 July 2007): 3108-3115.

past two decades has not addressed the basic issue of ensuring the food security of the population. Instead, nutrition indicators have stagnated and per capita calorie consumption has actually declined, suggesting that the problem of hunger may have got worse rather than better,' observes Ghosh.[25] At the same time thousands of tonnes of food grains are rotting away in the states like Punjab.[26] Such a state of affair negatively affects the Pentecostals who are mostly poor.

Rural unemployment is rampant and this leads to poverty and affects the poor badly. Even after 61 years of Independence, 318 million Indians do not have access to safe drinking water.[27] Even when they have, as the UNDP report reports, poor people 'still have to pay for their water, sometimes 10 to 20 times more than their richer neighbours.'[28]

The struggles of the common people, especially farmers, are increasing day by day. Agrarian depression continues, as do farmer suicides. Every year, over 20,000 farmers commit suicide out of despair over failing crops and impossibly high debt.[29] Mujumdar sarcastically comments the evil effect of the liberalisation of the economy on the poor masses:

> In the euphoria of liberalisation and globalisation of the Indian economy, agriculture became the Cinderella of Indian policy-makers. Blessed were they who debunked the whole philosophy of planned economic development: those who exulted in the alleged miraculous powers of the market-led economy believed that they have begun to live in heaven. Economic reforms created an adversarial environment for agricultural growth and rural development.[30]

'The situation is deteriorating rapidly and the entire farming sector is heading for a total collapse, if no rapid remedial measures are taken,' warns eminent agriculture scientist M.S. Swaminathan.[31] Similarly, Professor K. Nagaraj's

---

[25] Jayati Ghosh, 'Securing Food for the People,' *Macroscan* (18 August 2009), http://www.Macroscan.org/cur/aug09/cur180809Food.htm (accessed 16 November 2009).

[26] NDTV News, 'Pawar Promises Action after NDTV Report on Wasted Wheat,' *NDTV News* (18 March 2010), http://www.ndtv.com/news/videos/video_player.php?id=1209941 (accessed 19 March 2010).

[27] N. R. Narayana Murthy, *A Better India, A Better World* (New Delhi: Penguin Books India Pvt. Ltd, 2009), xiii.

[28] Quoted by Jayanta Bandyopadhyay, 'Endless Thirst,' *India Today* (6 October 2008), http://indiatoday.intoday.in/site/story?sId=16141&secid=3 (accessed 17 November 2009).

[29] N. A. Mujumdar, 'Rural Development: New Perceptions,' *EPW* (28 September 2002): 3983, http://epw.in.ezproxyd.bham.ac.uk/epw/uploads/articles/4601.pdf (accessed 16 November 2009).

[30] Mujumdar, 'Rural Development,' 3983; Also see Utsa Patnaik, 'Neoliberalism and Rural Poverty in India,' *EPW* (28 July 2007): 3132-3150.

[31] Quoted by Raj Chengappa & Ramesh Vinayak, 'Grain Drain,' *India Today* (11 June 2007), http://www.indiatoday.com/itoday/20070611/cover1.html (accessed 17 November 2009); M.S. Swaminathan is currently chairman of National Commission on Farmers.

recent study of farmer suicides shows a higher incidence in states that produce export crops, as well as in certain Tribal population-predominant states.[32] Such a predicament badly affects the common populace, especially Dalits and *Adivasis* (Tribal people) who form most of the Pentecostal believers in North India.

3.2.2 Incapacitated Education

Today, India has the largest number of illiterate people in the world, over 390 million. Twenty five million Indian children are out of school, accounting for 20% of the world's total.[33] The reason is Primary Education is in shambles. Going by enrolment statistics in India's schools, one may think that the country is doing well; however, as per recent count, around one-fifth of all primary rural schools in the country do not have a building to house students and another one-fourth have only one room and one teacher for all five classes. This number rises to 40% in states like Assam and Arunachal Pradesh.[34] According to Murthy, a survey by Harvard University's Michael Kremer found that one out of four teachers in government owned elementary schools was absent at any given time. A recent national survey revealed that close to 35% of children in the 7-14 age group surveyed could not read a simple paragraph and almost 60% could not read a simple story. The average drop-out rate in state schools is 53%. According to an assessment undertaken at a national level, there is an estimated shortage of about one million classrooms and 2.5 million school teachers.[35] However, in cities there are schools of international standard which are affordable only to the rich.

Indian higher education also faces difficulty.[36] Just one out of nine children finishing school joins a college. A study by the National Assessment and Accreditation Council showed that 90% of the colleges and 70% of the universities that the Council graded were of average or poor quality. Indian students now spend $7 billion to go abroad and study in foreign universities, because of the poor quality of education at home.[37] Such a condition of the educational system badly affects the Pentecostals who are poor and live in inner villages.

[32] K. Nagaraj, 'Farmer Suicides in India: Magnitudes, Trends and Spatial Patterns,' *Macroscan* (March 2008), http://www.macroscan.org/anl/mar08/pdf/Farmers_Suicides.pdf (accessed 18 November 2009).

[33] Narayana Murthy, *A Better India*, 138.

[34] Jha & Negre, 'Indian Economy.'

[35] Narayana Murthy, *A Better India*, 139.

[36] See Narayana Murthy, *A Better India*, 135-138.

[37] Raj Chengappa, 'Higher Education: How to Clean the Mess,' *India Today* (13 July 2009), http://indiatoday.intoday.in/site/Story/49794/Higher+Education:+How+to+clean+the+mess.html?page=0 (accessed 18 November 2009).

3.2.3 Incapacitated Health Care

The state of the nation's health is in disarray. It is a well-known scandal that India is practically at the bottom of a list of more than 170 countries, in terms of the proportion of total health expenditure that is financed by the government.[38] Even today, 250 million do not have access to basic medical care.[39] The findings of NFHS-3 shows that the infant mortality rate (IMR) before one year of age, is 57, which means more than one in 18 infants dies before they are one year old. 'The country may be witnessing an 8-9% economic growth and the government may think that India is a world power in the making,' cautions Ramachandran, 'but these findings tell the real story of where all that growth is headed.'[40] More tellingly, this is equal to the average of all the Least Developed Countries, 2.5 times that of China and eight to 10 times higher than that of developed countries.

The outreach and delivery of integrated child development services is extremely poor. As per NFHS-3 data, the services of an *anganwadi* are available only to a third of the children and the supplementary food scheme reaches only 26%. As a result, nearly half the children under the age of five are stunted, which reflects their childhood nutritional status. Under-nutrition extends to adults as well. Over half the women and nearly one-fourth of the men are anaemic. This is a direct consequence of the continued lack of balanced nutrition from childhood into adulthood, especially among women.[41]

Women are the worst hit in terms of access to health services. According to the NFHS-3 data, only 17.3% of women have ever received any service from a health care worker. Only 17.9% of the public health centres have a woman doctor. As a direct consequence, 56.2% of women (aged 15-49) are anaemic, which actually represents an increase from the NFHS-2 data of 51.8%. The percentage of pregnant women who are anaemic has also increased from 49.7 to 57.9%.[42] This condition has greatly affected the health of the poor and was clearly testified to in the interviews.

3.2.3.1 Commercialisation of Health-Care

In addition, health-care has slipped into the hands of the private sector, to the peril of the poor. In an environment of private-sector-dominated health care, unnecessary treatments abound. It is estimated that in India two-thirds of the money spent on medical treatment goes towards buying unnecessary drugs because

---

[38] Venkatesh Athreya, 'Far from Healthy,' *Frontline* 27/01 (2-15 January 2010); http://www.Frontlineonnet.com/stories/20100115270108400.htm (accessed 4 January 2010).

[39] Murthy, *A Better India,* xiii.

[40] Ramachandran & Rajalakshmi, 'Unhealthy Trend.'

[41] Ibid.

[42] There is a proliferation of brand names in India, with as many as 80,000 brands in the market. Even so, only 20-40% of the people have access to all the essential drugs they need. See Ramachandran & Rajalakshmi, 'Unhealthy Trend.'

of unnecessary prescriptions by private practitioners. Such an environment has enabled the pharmaceutical industry to thrive. Many drugs are sold at huge profit margins of 200-400%, thus putting essential drugs beyond the reach of the common masses. Ramachandran & Rajalakshmi remark:

> The prices of drugs have grown at a disproportionately high rate when compared with the Wholesale Price Index (WPI). Yet, policymakers are reluctant to impose any price control because of the industry lobby prevailing over politics. The existing price control regime is far from effective as most essential medicines are outside its purview.[43]

Besides, the government subsidy for health does not reach the poorer sections of the population either. According to a WHO report, only 10% of the total subsidy goes towards the benefit of the poorest 20% of the population, whereas the richest 20% avails itself of 33% of the subsidy.[44] A study conducted by the Economic Research Foundation, New Delhi, remarks, 'The greater reliance on private delivery of health infrastructure and health services, therefore, means that overall these will be socially underprovided by private agents, and also denies adequate access to the poor.'[45] According to the Report of the National Commission on Macroeconomics and Health, 2005, households undertook nearly three-fourths of all the health spending in the country. Public spending was only 22%, and all other sources accounted for less than 5%. There are many states where households undertake more than 80% of all health spending, indicating an exceptionally high burden upon them.[46] Naturally, the poor fall into debt burden or look for alternative healing methods. This explains the popularity of Pentecostal healing and the significance of the Christological perception of Jesus as divine healer.

3.2.3.2 Ill-Health and Poverty

Ill-health and poor access to health services are increasingly seen as major dimensions of poverty.[47] Poor people are caught in a vicious circle: poverty breeds ill-health; ill-health results in impoverishment and indebtedness.[48] Health-care

---

[43] Ramachandran & Rajalakshmi, 'Unhealthy Trend.'

[44] Ibid.

[45] Economic Research Foundation, (New Delhi), 'Government Health Expenditure in India: A Benchmark Study,' *Macroscan* (30 October 2006), http://www.macroscan.com/anl/oct06/anl301006Health_Expenditure.htm (accessed 4 January 2010).

[46] Economic Research Foundation, 'Government Health Expenditure.'

[47] Adam Wagstaff, 'Poverty and Health Sector Inequalities,' *Bulletin of the World Health Organisation* 80/2 (2002); http://www.scielosp.org/scielo.php?pid=S0042-96862002000200004&script=sci_arttext&tlng=en (accessed 3 January 2010).

[48] World Bank, 'India: Raising the Sites-Better Health Systems for India's Poor: Findings, Analysis, and Options,' *Health, Nutrition, and Population Series* (Washington DC, 2002).

expenditure cuts poor households' budgets in two ways. They have to spend a large amount of money and resources on medical care. They are also unable to earn when ill. Moreover, rural people have a relatively higher burden of indirect costs (such as: expenses on transport; food/stay; tips given to secure access to any person or facility, opportunity; cost of lost wages of the sick, as well as the accompanying person, etc).[49] Very often the poor have to borrow funds at a high interest rate to meet both medical expenditure and other household consumption needs, which takes them into indebtedness.[50]

Some sources, such as the Commission on Macroeconomics and Health of the World Health Organisation (2001), have argued that better health care is the key to improving not only health but economic growth also. However, it seems difficult to improve the quality of health care delivery in developing countries. A recent survey conducted in 100 hamlets of a poor rural area of Udaipur district, Rajasthan, which is one of the poorest districts in India, with a large Tribal population and an unusually high level of female illiteracy has shed some light on this issue.[51] Villagers' health is poor despite the fact that they use health care facilities and spend a lot on health-care. The quality of the public service is abysmal and unregulated and private providers, who are often unqualified, provide the bulk of health care in the area. 'The current health scenario in India is often described as dismal or disturbing,' comments Bose.[52] Except for a few states like Kerala, Goa and Tamil Nadu which have done relatively well, the situation in most parts of the country is a cause for worry.[53] Such neglect of people's welfare, by both state governments and central government, have played a major role in the emergence

---

[49] P. R. Sodani, 'Determinants of Demand for Healthcare in Surveyed Tribal Households of Selected Three Districts of Rajasthan,' *Demography India* 28/2 (1999): 257-271; also see K. V. Narayana, 'Changing Health Care System,' *EPW* (22-29 March 2003): 1230-1241; Sonia Andrews & Sailesh Mohan, 'User Charges in Health Care: Some Issues,' *EPW* (14 September 2002): 373-375.

[50] Akash Acharya & M. Kent Ranson, 'Health Care Financing for the Poor: Community-based Health Insurance Schemes in Gujarat,' *EPW* (17 September 2005): 4141, http://epw.in.ezproxye.bham.ac.uk/epw/uploads/articles/1133.pdf (accessed 25 November 2009); Also see No Author, 'Expansion for Profit: Health Care,' *EPW* (24 August 2002): 3476, http://epw.in.ezproxye.bham. ac.uk/epw/uploads/articles/9714.pdf (accessed 25 November 2009).

[51] Abhijit Banerjee, Angus Deaton & Esther Duflo, 'Health Care Delivery in Rural Rajasthan,' *EPW* (28 February 2004): 944, http://epw.in.ezproxye.bham.ac.uk/epw/uploads/articles/7389.pdf (accessed 25 November 2009). The data collection took place between January 2002 and August 2003 and at the time of the 1991 census, only 5% of women were literate in rural Udaipur. One of the churches selected for our research belongs to one of these Tribal villages of the Udaipur district.

[52] Ashish Bose, 'India's Disturbing Health Card,' *EPW* (15 December 2007): 10-13. http://epw.in.ezproxye.bham.ac.uk/epw/uploads/articles/11314.pdf (accessed 25 November 2009).

[53] Anit N Mukherjee & Krishanu Karmakar 'Untreated Morbidity and Demand for Healthcare in India: An Analysis of National Sample Survey Data,' *EPW* (15 November 2008): 71-77; also see Deepa Sankar & Vinish Kathuria, 'Health System Performance in Rural India: Efficiency Estimates across States,' *EPW* (27 March 2004): 1427-1433.

of Maoist armed insurgencies (naxalism) in the states of Jharkhand, Orissa, West Bengal and Bihar. Now they are a major security threat for the governments of these states.[54] This poor condition of the health care system gives credence to healing ministries of the Pentecostal churches.

3.2.4 Lack of Roads and Transportation

Another perennial problem people of interior villages are facing is the lack of good roads and transportation facilities. The villagers have to walk miles to get their provision, medical help and employment. This has adversely affected the overall development and the standard of living.[55] Out of 600,000 villages existing in India only about 50% have road access.[56] India's road quality is well below global standards and results in inefficiencies. The road construction has been hamstrung by bureaucratic red-tape, funding difficulties and land acquisition problems, and these factors have slowed economic development of the rural populace. The existing network of 2.7 million kms of rural roads is neglected, under-funded, and under-maintained.[57] States like Madhya Pradesh and Chhattisgarh have barely 15% road connectivity. This leads to income disparity between those living in urban areas and those in rural areas.[58] This situation affects the poor, economically, and so Pentecostals who live in remote areas.

3.2.5 Superstitious Practices

Poverty, lack of education and health care, coupled with strong religious and cultural bindings, has led to the prevalence of superstitious cultural and religious practices mostly among villagers and the lower strata of the society. Even though these practices have existed historically, it is believed that occurrences are declining as time moves on. However, it is obvious that some of the practices like witchcraft

---

[54] Amarnath K. Menon, 'Tackling the Red Terror,' *India Today* (26 October 2009), http://indiatoday.intoday.in/site/Story/66450/Cover%20Story/Tackling+the+Red+Terror.html (accessed 5 January 2010). Also see Bernard D'mello, 'What is Maoism?,' *EPW* 44/47 (21 November 2009): 39-48, http://epw.in/epw/uploads/ articles/14167.pdf (accessed 5 January 2010); Tilak D. Gupta, 'Maoism in India: Ideology, Programme and Armed Struggle,' *EPW* (22 July 2006): 3172-3176, http://epw.in/epw/uploads/articles/791.pdf (accessed 5 January 2010).

[55] Jagdish Khattar, 'The Paths to Prosperity: Low Cost Transport,' *India Today* (14 December 2009); http://indiatoday.intoday.in/site/Story/73518/Cover%20Story/The+paths+to+prosperity.html (accessed 20 December 2009).

[56] I. Prasada Rao, B. Kangadurai, P. K. Jain, & Neelam Jain, 'Information System for Rural Road Network Planning - A Case Study,' *GIS Development* (8 October 2009), http://www.gis development.net/application/Utility/transport/mi03218.htm (accessed 18 November 2009).

[57] Vineeta Pandey, 'The Road to Development in Rural India is Literally a Road,' *DNA* (10 December 2009), http://www.dnaindia.com/india/report_the-road-to-development-in-rural-india-is-literally-a-road_1322070 (accessed 18 December 2009); she says, 'In 2000, about 40% of India's villages lacked all-weather roads and nearly 74% of the rural population was not fully integrated into the national economy.'

[58] Aiyar, 'Inclusive Inequality.'

for curing diseases, female infanticide, child marriage and traditional healing methods are widely practised in rural areas.[59] Even the old practice of burning a wife on the funeral pyre of the husband (*sati*) also reappears now and then.

Traditional healers have found a strong foothold due to the lack of sufficient medical facilities to villagers. The uneducated villagers are more susceptible in falling prey to baseless superstitions. The evil of human sacrifice still continues with many women sacrificing lives to get a baby themselves.[60] Infanticide in India occurs mostly among poor, rural populations. Daughters are considered economic burdens because of the high cost of weddings and dowries, while sons provide income, and are seen as insurance policies by their parents. New prenatal sex-determination techniques, such as ultrasound, have led to an increase in the abortion of female foetuses rather than female infanticide, in urban centres.[61]
Even though child marriage is now prohibited by law, the fact remains that, in 2005-06, nearly half of adult women aged 20 to 24 years were married before the legal age of 18. That the rural poor, less educated girls and those from the central and eastern regions of the country are most vulnerable to this practice points to a huge failure in public policy when dealing with the determinants of its prevalence. Some are as young as six or seven years old when they are married. The girls themselves rarely have any say in the matter.[62]
The prevalence of *Sati* in UP and Rajasthan has been reported; witchcraft and other dangerous customs still persist in rural India. The prohibition of widow re-marriage among upper caste Hindus is rampant.[63] In such situations the Pentecostal message of Spirit-empowerment and spiritual liberation sound encouraging to many while strengthening the credibility of the missionary activities of Pentecostals.

3.2.6 Communal Violence

Another significant issue that is detrimental to the Christian minority, especially to the groups such as the Pentecostals who are mission minded, is the violent communal activities of certain 'fundamentalist organisations'. Communalism is

---

[59] Dipesh Chakrabarty, 'The Power of Superstition in Public Life in India,' *EPW* (17 May 2008): 16-19.

[60] In a gruesome incident, a *tantrik* advised a couple to sacrifice 11 boys to get a child for themselves while 5 boys were sacrificed in Hingoli, Maharashtra. Five Children "Sacrificed" by Childless couple,' *NDTV News* (18 March 2010), http://www. ndtv.com/news/videos/video_player.php?id=1209886 (accessed 18 March 2010).

[61] L. S. Vishwanath, 'Female Foeticide and Infanticide,' *EPW* (1 September 2001): 3411-3412 and Yogesh Snehi, 'Female Infanticide and Gender in Punjab,' *EPW* (11 October 2003): 4302-4305; Also see Rashmi Dube Bhatnagar, et. al., *Female Infanticide in India: A Feminist History* (New York: State University of New York Press, 2005).

[62] See B.S. Negi, *Child Marriage in India* (New Delhi: Mittal Publication, 1993).

[63] L.S. Vishwanath, 'Female Infanticide: The Colonial Experience,' *EPW* (29 May 2004): 2318.

politics based on religious identity. It could be argued that no other phenomenon has affected life in the subcontinent so adversely as communalism.[64] In India today, the main communal offensive comes from *Hindutva* ideology as played out by *Rashtriya Swayamsevak Sangh* (RSS) and its related organisations like *Vishwa Hindu Parishad* (VHP), *Bajrang-Dal* (BD) and the political wing *Bharatiya Janata Party* (BJP). The Hindutva movement concerns itself with building a strong Hindu Nation based on the tenets of '*Hindu Dharma.*'[65]

3.2.6.1 Communalisation of Political Discourse

Even though communal tensions and riots prevailed in the Indian society even before Independence (1947), the post-1989 phase of political instability and electoral stalemate helped the BJP and *Sangh-Parivar* members to create divisions in communal lines by exploiting Hindu sentiments. They raised and orchestrated a nationwide debate on cultural nationalism, and sustained it politically by launching the *Ram Janmabhoomi* movement.[66] According to Sheth, the objective of this political agenda was to convert the demographic majority of Hindus into a political majority, ensuring a durable electoral majority – a step in the direction of making India a Hindu nation. To achieve this end, the BJP along with the *Sangh-Parivar* worked continuously on various fronts, in a longer time frame. Further, he explains how the BJP achieved their communal goal:

> First, the BJP transited smoothly from the discourse which it had itself created, of genuine versus pseudo-secularism (as if the party really was committed to secularism), to the new one of Hindu unity. This was initially articulated defensively in terms of cultural nationalism, but later, brazenly as Hindutva – a political doctrine holding that India belongs to Hindus and asserting that all people living in India must identify themselves historically and culturally as Hindus, even as they follow their different religions. Second, the BJP devised a new electoral strategy, forging alliance with regional parties. Its objective was to create communal polarisation nationally and in the process secure and durably consolidate the Hindu majority support in its favour.[67]

---

[64] Saumya, 'Communalism: Narratives in Chhattisgarh,' *EPW* 43/2 (12 January 2008): 39, http://epw.in.ezproxye.bham.ac.uk/epw/uploads/articles/11428.pdf (accessed 2 December 2009).

[65] Ram Puniyani, 'Communalism and Minorities,' *Religion and Society* 49/1 (March 2004): 1; Rizwan Qaiser, 'Communalism and the Conceptualisation of "Hindu Rashtra,"' *Social Action* 44 (January-March 1994): 81-96.

[66] K. Gopalakrishnan, 'Ideals of Secularism on Test in India,' *Indian Currents* (15-21 February 1999): 22-23; V. Karthikeyan, 'Religion in Politics,' *Indian Currents* (15-21 February 1999): 13.

[67] D. L. Sheth, 'Political Communalisation of Religions and the Crisis of Secularism,' *EPW* XLIV/39 (26 September 2009): 74, http://epw.in.ezproxye.bham.ac.uk/epw/uploads/articles/ 13967.pdf (accessed 2 December 2009); Ashok Nehru, 'Selling the Fascist Ideology: RSS Strategy,' *Indian Currents* (25-31 October, 1999): 15-18.

To this end, according to Sheth, the BJP engaged in a series of campaigns beginning with the *rath-yatra* (chariot procession) and then mobilising grass root support of Hindus by involving them in the supposedly pious act of carrying bricks to Ayodhya from different parts of the country for building a Ram temple at the site of the *Babri-Masjid*. 'It may not build the temple on the site of the mosque' comments Sheth, 'but it literally built, brick-by-brick, the political edifice of Hindutva in wider society.'[68]

However, the extent to which it has succeeded in this endeavour is difficult to ascertain, but it is fairly apparent that a conscious policy to induct the *Sangh-Parivar* cadre into the nation's administrative machinery was followed.[69] A good example is the Police Force.[70] It is widely reported that the Police Force in states ruled by the BJP, such as Rajasthan, Madhya Pradesh and Gujarat, has been 'saffronised'[71] by inducting recruits from the *Sangh-Parivar*. The consequences are by now well known. In the communal conflagrations, the police not only refused to intervene to save the victims but actually abetted members of organisations such as the VHP and the *Bajrang-Dal* in their crimes.[72] This explains the frequent attacks upon Pentecostals and inaction of police while some are still languishing in prisons.[73]

3.2.6.2 Hindutva and Violence

In fact, in many cases, a communal division is created by riots in an area where no communal tension existed before, where even a communal consciousness did not exist.[74] Today communal riots are being manipulated for reinforcing the communal divide and instilling communal ideology to the Tribals and Dalits who were not the target groups of the *Sangh-Parivar* earlier. Riots, in return, reinforce

---

[68] Sheth, 'Political Communalisation,' 74.

[69] See Richard Bonney, *Harvest of Hatred: The Concerned Citizen's Tribunal Report of Gujarat, 2002* (Delhi: Media House, 2004).

[70] For example, see Asghar Ali Engineer & Amarjit S. Narang (eds.), *Minorities and Police in India* (New Delhi: Manohar Publishers, 2006).

[71] Saffronisation is used to denote the pushing in of the extremist Hindutva ideology in social, educational and governmental institutions.

[72] K. N. Panikkar, 'Ways of Hindutva,' *Frontline* 26/07 (28 March-10 April 2009), http://www. frontlineonnet.com/fl2607/stories/20090410260702600.htm (accessed 2 December 2009).

[73] Editor, 'Arrested on False Charges,' *Cross & Crown* 37/3 (January-February 2008): 21; See another incident of false charges slapped on believers for proclaiming Christ; Editor, 'A Plan for me...even in Prison,' *Cross & Crown* 36/2 (July-August 2007): 12.

[74] See Lancy Lobo, 'Adivasis, Hindutva and Post-Godhra Riots in Gujarat,' *EPW* (30 November 2002): 4844-4849, http://epw.in.ezproxye.bham.ac.uk/epw/uploads/articles/9761.pdf (accessed 2 December 2009).

the communal identity.[75] Generally, it is relatively the poor and the deprived who are the victims of riots.

The work of Christian missionaries among Tribals in remote areas has come as rough and ready fuel for the RSS ideology to identify a new 'communal issue'. 'RSS propaganda tactics has always resorted to demonising Christian missionary activities using the bogey of conversion,' comments Sarkar.[76] For the last decade, the *Sangh* and its front organisations like the *Vanvasi Kalyan Ashram* and the VHP have been targeting the Tribal belt of India, which includes Madhya Pradesh, Chhattisgarh, Bihar, Jharkhand, Rajasthan, Orissa and Gujarat.[77] For example, while surveying the riots that took place in 2003-2004, Asghar Ali Engineer describes a riot fomented by the BJP among Tribals. In Madhya Pradesh, state elections took place in December 2003 and the BJP won. The BJP was trying to Hinduise Tribals in Jhabua and created enmity between Christian Tribals and other Tribals, in order to win their political support. Thus, Jhabua became communally sensitive and clashes took place there between the *Bhil* tribe and Tribal Christians.[78] As a result many Pentecostals suffered.

Similarly in Karnataka, the Hindutva forces have unleashed violence against the Christian community, especially against Pentecostals, in the name of forcible conversion, and destroyed many churches while attacking innocent people.[79]

3.2.6.3 Atrocities against Tribal Christians

Similarly, the *Sangh-Parivar* persistently perpetrated atrocities on Tribal Christians in various states.[80] A list of these atrocities, such as the burning of churches and prayer halls, beating up *adivasi* Christians, performing forcible purification ('*shuddhikaran*') ceremonies on them and other forms of harassments, are well

---

[75] Angana Chatterji, 'Hindutva's Violent History,' *Tehelka* 5/36 (13 September 2008), http://www.tehelka.com/story_main40.asp?filename=Ne130908HindutvasViolentHistory.asp (accessed 10 December 2009); Saumya, 'Communalism: Narratives in Chhattisgarh,' 39.

[76] Sumit Sarkar, 'Conversion and Politics of Hindu Right,' *EPW* (26 June 1999): 1691-1700; Benjamin Lakra, 'Conversion and Tribals of India,' *Indian Currents* (8-14 February, 1999): 39-41.

[77] Editorial, 'Communal Violence in Orissa,' *EPW* (5 January 2008): 6; Also see Saumya, 'Communalism,' 39; Panikkar, 'Ways of Hindutva.'

[78] Asghar Ali Engineer, 'Communal Riots, 2004,' *EPW* (5 February 2005): 518, http://epw.in.ezproxye.bham.ac.uk/epw/uploads/articles/142.pdf (accessed 2 December 2009); Jhabua has many Pentecostal churches and many are joining the movement recently.

[79] Sanjana, 'An Unholy Crusade,' *Tehelka* 5/39 (4 October 2008); http://www.tehelka.com/story_main40.asp?filename=Ne041008coverstory.asp (accessed 22 December 2009).

[80] Francis Gonsalves, '"Destroy Christians, Kill them, Jai Sriram!": The Traumatic Experience on a Black Christmas Day,' *Indian Currents* (4-10 January, 1999): 20-22.

documented.[81] Lobo speaks about the then BJP Prime Minister A.B. Vajpayee's response, 'When *adivasi* Christians were in intense anguish there came the Prime Minister of India to Dangs, not to console the victims of atrocities but to score a point for the *Sangh-Parivar* saying a national debate on conversions was the need of the hour.'[82] In a relatively peaceful south Gujarat Tribal area these atrocities shook the confidence of the people; many of the victims were Pentecostals.

Lobo explains the strategy of the *Sangh-Parivar*. Attempts were made to establish branches of the *Bajrang-Dal* and VHP in each village and make non-Christian Tribals members. *Deeksha* (initiation ceremony) was given to persons joining the *Bajrang-Dal* in which '*trishuls*' (tridents) and saffron headbands were distributed. Non-Christian *sarpanchs* and economically better-off persons and unemployed youth of villages were made members. *Sangh-Parivar* widely distributed calendars depicting the Hindu god Hanuman and idols of gods and goddesses during the Navaratri and Ganapati festivals. Financial help was also given. Moreover, *Sangh-Parivar* published anti-Christian pamphlets and orchestrated an anti-Christian campaign through newspapers. *Sangh-Parivar* showed open hostility against Christians after the instalment of the BJP government; anti-Christian meetings were organised. Personal conflicts in the villages were converted into Hindu-Christian communal conflicts.[83] In one documented case, the *Sangh-Parivar* recruited four educated unemployed youth from each village. They were given training and an honorarium of 250 rupees per month to collect information about their own village and pass it to the *Sangh-Parivar* centres. Generally 20 villages constituted a centre. Information collected included the names of opinion makers in the village, leaders, Christians and non-Christian Tribals, movements of the missionaries, factions and quarrels in the village, and so on.[84]

---

[81] Lancy Lobo, *Globalisation, Hindu Nationalism and Christians in India* (Jaipur: Rawat, 2002), 182ff. Of the 51 instances of atrocities, 41 took place in the Dangs, nine in Surat and one in Valsad districts of south Gujarat. Of 41 atrocities in Dangs, 24 were to do with burning of churches and prayer halls, eight with beatings, and four with various kinds of harassment. Of nine instances in the Surat district four had to do with burning churches, two with beatings and three with other forms of harassment.

[82] Lobo, 'Adivasis, Hindutva,' 4846; Tisy Jose, 'Conversion: A Convenient Mask,' *Indian Currents* (18-24 January 1999): 10-13; Valson Thampu, 'National Debate on Conversions,' *Indian Currents* (18-24 January 1999): 16-17.

[83] Lobo, 'Adivasis, Hindutva,' 4845-6. People of these areas testified, '*Baharthi loko aveene dhamal kare chhe, ame to shantithi raheta hata*' (outsiders have come and created disturbances when we were living in peace). It must be noted that these atrocities were preceded by certain activities of *Sangh-Parivar* in the adivasi areas.

[84] Lobo, 'Adivasis, Hindutva,' 4845-6. For instance, the Dang district being small was divided into four centres: Subir in the north, Ahwa in the south, Waghai in the east and Narkadi in the west. Each centre was headed by leaders known for their notoriety in the area.

3.2.6.4 Ideology of Hindutva

According to M.S. Golwalkar, the ideologue and second head of the RSS, minorities may stay in the country, but should be wholly subordinated to the Hindu nation, claiming nothing and deserving no privileges at all, far less any preferential treatment, not even citizen's rights.[85] Golwalkar developed the 'ethnic-racist and national content' of the concept of 'Hinduness' and Hindutva was thus marked with high discipline, puritan, ritualistic and rigid hierarchies. According to Saumya, this agenda is achieved through the systematic penetration of Hindutva ideas into the young hearts of Tribal children by running schools on the pretext of eradicating illiteracy in remote areas while in fact spreading Hindutva education with an aim to stopping conversions to Christianity and encouraging reconversions to Hinduism. A crucial role is played by *Vidya Bharti*, an educational unit of RSS which educates young children through primary and secondary schools (*Saraswati Shishu Mandirs*) when following the RSS Hindutva ideology. In addition to this, there are '*ekal' vidyalayas* (one teacher school) with the aim of 'saving the Tribals from undesirable foreign influence.'[86] However, the proponents of this ideology send their children to Christian mission schools for 'convent education' and do not fear the conversion of their children, but do not want Tribals to go to Christian schools for they fear 'forcible conversion.'[87]

Recently the common masses, especially Tribals, Dalits and even the urban middle class began to realise the insidious agenda of Hindutva cadres. Faced with the prospect of losing political power, Hindu communalism has been resorting to violence and even terrorism to consolidate its position. Violence, both spontaneous and premeditated, has always been an integral part of communalism.[88] For instance, in Kandhamal, Orissa State, houses belonging to Christians were set on fire and pastors and members of the community were attacked and burnt alive. Scores of churches and prayer houses were burnt down. Informed sources said that the policemen on duty at various police stations made no attempt to prevent the protesters from attacking Christians and their property. According to Prafulladas, the evidence suggests that they were acting on the instructions of their political bosses.[89]

---

[85] M.S. Golwalker, *We or Our Nationhood Defined* (Nagpur, India: Bharath Publications, 1939), 48.

[86] Saumya, 'Communalism,' 39.

[87] Francis Gonsalves, 'Debating Conversions,' *Indian Currents* (8-14 February, 1999): 35.

[88] Panikkar, 'Ways of Hindutva.'

[89] Prafulladas, 'Project Orissa,' *Frontline* 25/19 (13-26 September 2008), http://www.frontline onnet.com/fl2519/ stories/20080926251900400.htm (accessed 10 December 2009).

Large-scale displacement of the population has been a common consequence in almost all communal incidents in recent times.[90] In Orissa, thousands of Christians have taken shelter in the forest, to escape from the attacks of the members of Hindu communal organisations. A condition of their return to their homes is reconversion to Hinduism. The state was controlled by the BJP has not discharged even the basic duty of protecting the lives and property of citizens.[91]

3.2.6.5 The BJP and Communalist Politics

According to Sheth, the strategy of the BJP was shrewd: to convert and co-opt the caste politics of Indian society into the Hindutva communalist movement. As a result, regionally powerful castes began to be subfused gradually with the culture of religious communities, thereby transforming faith communities into ethno-religious communities. This was marked by the growing participation and power of Other Backward Castes (OBC), Dalits and Tribals in organisational activities and events of popular Hinduism often sponsored and promoted by the *Sangh-Parivar* – religious congregations and festivals as well as management of religious establishments.[92]

Even though the Hindus and the Muslims had a strained relationship even before the independence, the conflict has been aggravated after the demolition of the *Babri-Masjid*, a Muslim shrine which was supposedly built on Lord Ram's birth place, Ayodhya in Uttar Pradesh and the subsequent communal conflagration in 1992 by members of various Hindu nationalist organizations. Ten years later, Gujarat riots of 2002, perhaps the most intense Hindu-Muslim conflict in India since the bloodshed that accompanied the partition of India created a wide chasm between the communities which resulted in enhanced terrorist activities and communal disturbances and caused lasting wounds in Hindu-Muslim relations that may take decades to heal.

There are various theories and arguments forwarded by scholars who have expertise in this field of study.[93] For instance, Ashutosh Varshney in his work on ethnic violence, in which he almost absolves politicians and the *Sangh-Parivar,* that has been associated with most post-independence Hindu-Muslim conflict, by stressing that the absence of civic ties between members of communities as the

[90] In Gujarat, more than 100,000 people belonging to the Muslim community fled their homes and lived for months in camps. It is estimated that about 80% of them have not been able to return to their homes.

[91] Vijay Simha, 'In the Name of God,' *Tehelka* 5/36 (13 September 2008), http://www.tehelka. com/story_main40.asp?filename=Ne130908CoverStory.asp (accessed 22 December 2009); also see Panikkar, 'Ways of Hindutva.'

[92] Sheth, 'Political Communalisation,' 78.

[93] See Roshni Sengupta, 'Communal Violence in India: Perspectives on Causative Factors,' *EPW* (14 May 2005): 2046-2050.

major factor that leads to violence.[94] However, Wilkinson convincingly argues that ethnic riots are far from being spontaneous eruptions of anger. Instead, they are often planned by politicians for a clear electoral purpose. These violent conflagrations are, according to Wilkinson, caused by political elites who play on existing communal tensions to advance a political agenda.[95] Similarly, Paul Brass in his book demonstrates that communal tensions are maintained with lethal rioting, and how this is essential for the development of militant Hindu nationalism and for other organisations and individuals.[96] This issue has adversely affected the Pentecostals all over India.

3.2.7 The Caste System

Another issue that badly affects the Pentecostals is the caste system. Even after 60 years of Independence, the biggest disadvantage in Indian society is the caste-system and its evil practice of untouchability.[97] Indian society is divided into different castes and sub-castes. Lower castes, Dalits and Tribals are being denied their right to live in mainstream society. The Dalits are not only discriminated against, but their women are raped, their men are physically assaulted and their children are made to work as bonded labourers. They have no access to the land, are forced to work in degrading conditions and are often beaten up by the police and the dominant caste groups.

The state, instead of coming to their rescue, has always acted against their interests in close nexus with the upper class. The Dalits are being pushed into peripheries of the society and are often considered to be worse than animals.[98] Although, Tribals are not part of the Hindu caste-system, they are also considered to be 'untouchables'.

However, it should be noted that the Indian Constitution abolished caste and untouchability, and states that discrimination on the grounds of caste stands prohibited. In addition, there is a 'directive' emerging from the state to promote

---

[94] Ashutosh Varshney, *Ethnic Conflict and Civic Life: Hindus and Muslims in India* (New Haven: Yale University Press, 2002).

[95] Steven I. Wilkinson, 'Communal Riots in India,' *EPW* (29 October 2005): 4768, http://epw.in.ezproxyd.bham.ac.uk/epw/uploads/articles/1313.pdf (accessed 10 December 2009); Also see his *Votes and Violence: Electoral Competition and Communal Riots in India* (New Delhi: Cambridge University Press, 2005), 1-10.

[96] Paul R. Brass, *The Production of Hindu-Muslim Violence in Contemporary India* (Washington, DC: University of Washington Press, 2003), 5-7. Also see his 'Development of an Institutionalised Riot System in Meerut City, 1961 to 1982,' *EPW* (30 October 2004), http://epw.in.ezproxyd.bham.ac.uk/epw/uploads/articles/8354.pdf (accessed 10 December 2009).

[97] M.P. Raju, 'Thou art Untouchable, Thou shalt Remain so,' *Indian Currents* (9-15 August, 1999): 24-28; Ambrose Pinto, 'Dalits: Victims of an Oppressive Caste System,' *Indian Currents* (9-15 August, 1999): 29-31, 34.

[98] Kancha Ilaiah, *Why I am not a Hindu: A Sudra Critique of Hindutva Philosophy, Culture and Political Economy*, 2nd ed. (Calcutta: Samya, 2005).

socio-economic development of Dalits and other weaker sections. Yet the caste system not only continues to exist, but has strengthened its grip as well. The powerful vested interest groups have found it convenient to continue with the system because practically all the labour force who work as scavengers, sweepers and other menial jobs are Dalits.[99] Although, there have been some movements which have come up in mainstream politics, they become established political parties and run after political power. For example, even in the state of Uttar Pradesh where a Dalit party is ruling (BSP), the condition of the Dalits is not only deteriorating but considered to be worse than that of many other states.[100]

3.2.7.1 The Caste System and Economic Deprivation

The caste system not only exerts its influence on the social arena, but also becomes a mechanism to oppress the Dalits, Tribals and the lower castes economically.[101] Caste has long been used to regulate economic life in India.[102] A community-based system of enforcement regulates caste privileges by means of social ostracism, violence, and economic penalties that find their justification in elements of the Hindu religion.[103] Amartya Sen has shown that there is social exclusion which results in economic disparity.[104] Without intervention, the untouchables, who lie at the very bottom of the social order, find themselves restricted to the most despised occupations and the lowest wages. At this point, it is central to look into the market behaviour.

While elaborating on economic discrimination on the basis of caste, Thorat and Newman argue that caste-based discrimination is prevalent in the Indian market and that this causes a series of adverse consequences not only on income

---

[99] Pinto, 'Dalits: Victims,' 29-30.

[100] Venkitesh Ramakrishnan & Ajoy Ashirwad Mahaprashasta, 'Victims Always,' *Frontline* 26/24 (21 November - 4 December 2009), http://www.frontlineonnet.com/fl2624/stories/200912042624 00400.htm (accessed December 15, 2009); Also see Ilaiah, *Why I am not a Hindu*, 47-49.

[101] K. Srinivasan & S. K. Mohanty, 'Deprivation of Basic Amenities by Caste and Religion,' *EPW* (14 February 2004): 728-735, http://epw.in.ezproxyd.bham.ac.uk/epw/uploads/articles/9484.pdf (accessed 15 December 2009).

[102] Nicholas Dirks, *Castes of Mind: Colonialism and the Making of Modern India* (New Jersey: Princeton University Press, 2001).

[103] B. R. Ambedkar, 'Philosophy of Hinduism' in *Dr. Babasaheb Ambedkar: Writings and Speeches,* Vol. 3, edited by Vasant Moon (Bombay: Department of Education, Government of Maharashtra, 1987) (first published 1936), 194. Also see Deepak Lal, *The Hindu Equilibrium: Cultural Stability and Economic Stagnation – India 1500BC-AD1980*, vol. I (Oxford: Clarendon Press, 1989).

[104] Amartya Sen, 'Social Exclusion: Concept, Application, and Scrutiny,' *Working Paper, Social Development Paper No 1,* (Manila: Asian Development Bank, June, 2000). http://scholar.google. co.uk.ezproxyd.bham.ac.uk/scholar?hl=en&rlz=1R2RNTN_enGB348&q=author:%22Sen%22+intitle:%22Social+exclusion:+Concept,+application,+and+scrutiny%22+&um=1&ie=UTF-8&oi=scholarr (accessed 10 December 2009).

distribution but also on the economic growth of the Dalits and Tribals,[105] though some would deny it.[106] In fact these workers are discriminated against both in the public and private sectors, but the discrimination effect is much larger in the private sector and results in low wages to Dalits and Tribals.[107]

3.2.7.2 The Caste System and Discrimination

Discrimination is rampant in higher educational institutions as in Engineering and Medical colleges where in the name of merit the percentage of Dalits and Tribals allowed to enrol is a meagre 2%.[108] This is because, as Marc Galanter has pointed out, three broad kinds of resources are necessary to produce the results in competitive exams in terms of merit, such as economic resources (for prior education, training, materials, freedom from work, etc); social and cultural resources (networks of contacts, confidence, guidance and advice, information, etc); and intrinsic ability and hard-work. The above-mentioned are lacking among the untouchables.[109] Having conducted field work in three important universities of India, Deshpande and Newman portray that Dalit students are being discriminated against in the universities as well as in the job market and lack many advantages that turn out to be crucial when shaping their employment outcomes in comparison to higher castes.[110]

The acts of discrimination which show their ugly head in these areas include the refusal by public health personnel to vaccinate Dalit children, denial of access to water sources, and refusal to serve Dalits tea at teashops and to cut their hair at barber shops. They are not allowed to join the queue with caste

---

[105] Sukhadeo Thorat & Katherine S. Newman, 'Caste and Economic Discrimination: Causes, Consequences and Remedies,' *EPW* (13 October 2007): 4122, http://epw.in.ezproxyd.bham.ac.uk/epw/uploads/articles/11132.pdf (accessed 12 December 2009).

[106] For example, Thorat and Newman *quotes the Economist* magazine, 'There is no evidence that [Indian] companies discriminate against [the lower castes], and argued that the relegation of low caste Indians to the bottom of the social structure is a function not of discrimination in the private sector but of the actions of a different culprit altogether: 'government, and the rotten educational system it has created.'

[107] S. Madheswaran & Paul Attewell, 'Caste Discrimination in the Indian Urban Labour Market: Evidence from the National Sample Survey,' *EPW* (13 October 2007): 4146-53, http://epw.in. ezproxyd. bham.ac.uk/epw/uploads/articles/11136.pdf (accessed 12 December 2009).

[108] Satish Deshpande, 'Exclusive Inequalities: Merit, Caste and Discrimination in Indian Higher Education Today,' *EPW* (17 June 2006): 2438-2444, http://epw.in.ezproxyd.bham.ac.uk/epw/ uploads/articles/2212.pdf (accessed 15 December 2009). Also see S. Srinivasa Rao, 'Dalits in Education and Workforce,' *EPW* (20 July 2002): 2998-3000, http://epw.in.ezproxyd.bham.ac.uk/epw/uploads/articles/4367.pdf (accessed 15 December 2009).

[109] Marc Galanter, *Competing Equalities: Law and the Backward Classes in India* (Oxford, New Delhi, 1984).

[110] Ashwini Deshpande & Katherine Newman, 'Where the Path Leads: The Role of Caste in Post-University Employment Expectations,' *EPW* (13 October 2007), http://epw.in.ezproxyd.bham. ac.uk/epw/uploads/articles/11134.pdf (accessed 15 December 2009).

Hindus at government-run fair-price shops. Access to burial grounds and temples are also barred to them in many places.[111] Even educational institutions are not free from the practice. Higher caste parents ask their children to skip the noon meal provided in schools, if the food is cooked by Dalits.[112] Behind these trends of dominant caste behaviour is the classic Hindu understanding of purity and pollution, according to which food prepared by a Dalit – an 'untouchable' – is considered 'polluted', by virtue of its contact with the intrinsically-polluted Dalit. 'On another level,' comments Thorat, 'dominant caste opposition to Dalit cooks also represents a power struggle over livelihood rights and functions to break Dalit economic aspirations.'[113] This issue badly affects the Dalit Pentecostals who form a sizeable number in North-Indian context socially and economically.

3.2.7.3 The Caste System and Hindutva

The State of Gujarat which is known as the 'Hindutva laboratory' abounds in atrocities against Dalits and Tribals. Ironically, the same Dalits and Tribals who suffer such discrimination willingly became foot soldiers of Hindutva in the Muslim carnage of 2002 and Christian persecutions of their own kith and kin later. According to Puniyani, this was accomplished through the successful co-option of Dalits and Tribals in their fold by offering deceptive discourses and practices to achieve its larger political objective: to expand the BJP's electoral base.[114] The vulnerability of Dalits to Hindutva politics has a variety of explanations as Panikkar rightly suggests: Dalits and Tribals, who traditionally lived with a sense of deprivation in the margins of Hindu cultural life, find 'Hinduisation' attractive; when Hindutva invites them to be part of a larger and 'superior' tradition, many of them accept it with a sense of pride.[115]

Moreover, to prevent the Dalits and Tribals from joining egalitarian religions like Christianity and Islam, Hindutva forces have exerted pressure on state governments and enacted anti-conversion laws[116] in the name of a 'Freedom of

---

[111] S. Viswanathan, 'Cracks in the Wall,' *Frontline* 26/08 (11-24 April 2009), http://www.frontline onnet.com/fl2608/stories/20090424260804200.htm (accessed 16 December 2009).

[112] Sukhdeo Thorat & Joel Lee, 'Caste Discrimination and Food Security Programmes,' *EPW* (24 September 2005): 4199-4200, http://epw.in.ezproxyd.bham.ac.uk/epw/uploads/articles/1149.pdf (accessed 16 December 2009).

[113] Thorat & Lee, 'Caste Discrimination,' 4199-4200.

[114] Ram Puniyani, *Contours of Hindu Rashtra: Hindutva, Sangh Parivaar and Contemporary Politics* (Delhi: Kalpaz Publications, 2006), 233-243. Also see Pralay Kanungo, 'Co-opting Dalits into the Hindutva Fold,' *EPW* (19 May 2007), 1852, http://epw.in.ezproxyd.bham.ac.uk/epw/uploads/articles/10631.pdf (accessed 16 December 2009).

[115] K.N. Panikkar, 'Foreword,' *Hindutva and Dalits: Perspectives for Understanding Communal Praxis* (Kolkata: Samya, 2005), xi-xi.

[116] South Asia Human Rights Documentation Centre, 'Anti-Conversion Laws: Challenges to Secularism and Fundamental Rights,' *EPW* (12 January 2008): 63-73; Cyriac Thomas, 'Anti-Conversion Laws in India.' *Indian Church History Review* 41/2 (2007): 126-41.

Religion Bill', so as to harass them and keep them under their control. However, Omvedt aptly reasons against such propaganda:

> It is a matter of fact that India saw the birth of the first great missionary religion of the world – Buddhism. It is also true that the major 'inducements' offered by Christianity to the rural low castes were those of self-respect – and, while the established churches today, which do show reflections of caste, have mostly given up conversion efforts, the evangelical Christians who are carrying these on show hardly any sign of caste distinctions. In any case, to argue that a person should stay in his or her 'ancestral religion' is a denial of human freedom; to put legal obstacles to this is an infringement of the Constitution – which was presided over and presented to the nation by an ex-untouchable who himself felt the necessity of saying, 'I was born a Hindu but will not die a Hindu.'[117]

3.2.7.4 The Caste System and the State

The apathy of successive central and state governments and their mindless policies has further deteriorated the conditions of the Dalits and the Tribals. State Governments across the country have shown a remarkable reluctance to use the Schedule Caste/Schedule Tribe Atrocities Act which was meant for their protection.[118] Quoting figures from the 2007 Annual Report of the National Crime Records Bureau (NCRB), the Asian Centre for Human Rights' the publication 'Torture in India 2009' states that the NCRB reported a total of 30,031 cases – including 206 cases under the Protection of Civil Rights Act and 9,819 cases under the S.C./S.T. Act – against the S.C.s in 2007. Although, the average charge-sheeting rate for the crimes against the S.C.s was 90.6%, the average conviction rate was only 30.9%.[119]

In September 2001, the most contentious issue for Indians was the demand for the inclusion of caste discrimination as a specific form of racism. The government, led by the BJP, blocked any reference to caste in the documents of the Durban Conference by using a combination of legal as well as academic

[117] Gail Omvedt, 'Caste System and Hinduism,' *EPW* (13 March 2004), 1180, http://epw.in.ezproxyd.bham.ac.uk/epw/uploads/articles/8133.pdf (accessed 10 December 2009).

[118] Debashis Chakraborty, D. Shyam Babu & Manashi Chakravorty, 'Atrocities on Dalits: What the District Level Data Say on Society-State Complicity,' *EPW* (17 June 2006): 2478-2481, http://epw.in.ezproxyd.bham.ac.uk/epw/uploads/articles/2221.pdf (accessed 16 December 2009). Also see Somen Chakraborty, 'Blood Bath in Bihar: Caste Unabated,' *Indian Currents* (15-21 February, 1999): 16-20.

[119] Lyla Bavadam, 'Growing Unease,' *Frontline* 26/24 (21 November - 4 December 2009), http://www.Frontlineonnet.com/fl2624/stories/20091204262400900.htm (accessed 16 December 2009).

arguments and the diplomatic power of the emerging superpower.[120] According to Visvanathan, it was obvious that a government led by the Hindu nationalist BJP would thwart any international scrutiny of Hindu social practices.[121] However, eight years later, the Congress-led government has showed a similar inflexibility in allowing any discussion of caste discrimination at the Durban Review Conference. The charge that the obstinate blocking by the Indian government of all discussions on caste in international fora is merely a symptom of the proclivity of upper caste India[122] to deny the very existence of caste discrimination may, therefore, have a fair element of accuracy to it.[123]

3.2.8 Tribal and Dalit Situation

A sizeable number of Pentecostals are from Tribal and Dalit background. Therefore, it is important to comprehend their context and outlook. Centuries of social conditioning and deprivation have seriously wounded the Tribal and Dalit psyche; they deeply long for recognition and respect. Very often they are reluctant to change, perhaps because of the terrible bitterness and indifference they developed through many years of suffering. As we have seen the caste system and untouchability have pushed them into the peripheries of villages, deep into the jungles and mountainous locations.[124]

They have a three-tier worldview, based on a close relationship between nature, human beings and various spirits; their priority is in the order of material things, spirits and a high God. Proximity to the jungle, a primitive worldview and strong faith in supernatural elements made them fearful of spirits and ghosts.[125] A sick person is usually not taken to hospital, instead treated with *jadi-booti* (roots

---

[120] The Durban Conference is the World Conference against racism, racial discrimination, xenophobia and related intolerance.

[121] Shiv Visvanathan, 'The Race for Caste: Prolegomena to the Durban Conference,' *EPW* (7 July 2001): 2512-2516, http://epw.in.ezproxyd.bham.ac.uk/epw/uploads/articles/5628.pdf (accessed 17 December 2009) and also see, Shiv Visvanathan, 'Durban and Dalit Discourse,' *EPW* (18 August 2001), 3123-3127, http://epw.in.ezproxyd.bham.ac.uk/epw/uploads/articles/5776.pdf (accessed 17 December 2009).

[122] Sam Paul, 'Christian Council Disappointed with Treatment of Dalit Issues at Un Anti-Racism Conference,' *All India Christian Council* (30 April 2009), http://indianchristians.in/news/content/ view/2986/42/ (accessed 15 December 2009).

[123] Editorial, 'Caste Out, Yet Again,' *EPW* XLIV/20, (16 May 2009): 5, http://epw.in.ezproxyd. bham.ac.uk/epw/uploads/articles/13508.pdf (accessed 15 December 2009).

[124] James Massey, *Down Trodden: The Struggle of India's Dalits for Identity, Solidarity and Liberation* (Geneva: WCC Publications, 1997), 23-40; James Massey, *Bharat ke Masihi Dalit* (Dalit Christians of India) (Delhi: ISPCK, 2003).

[125] Sathianathan Clarke, *Dalits and Christianity: Subaltern Religion and Liberation Theology in India* (New Delhi: Oxford University Press, 1999), 71; Chad M. Bauman, *Christian Identity and Dalit Religion in Hindu India, 1868-1947* (Michigan: Eerdmans, 2008), 40; Stephen Neill, *Out of Bondage: Christ and the Indian Villager* (London: Church of England Zenana Missionary Society, 1930), 21-34.

and leaves); they turn to traditional religious practices to ward off malevolent spirits, which are believed to be the cause of illness. They often consider *jadi-bootis* and traditional religious practices to be more powerful than allopathic medicines.[126] According to Saxena, their priority is for 'magico-medical and indigenous treatment' and therefore, it seems that they often seem to disregard sanitation and hygiene.[127] However, we should not forget the fact that it is their downtrodden condition and lack of resources which contributes such an outlook to a large extent.

Tribals and Dalits believe in a number of spirits, both benevolent and malevolent. Their whole social and religious life is intricately related to the spirit world.[128] The people consider these spirits as powerful enough to keep their children from sickness, make them fertile, provide rain, and the welfare of domestic animals. Various categories of spirits such as village spirits, clan spirits, and spirits of the ancestors are identified.[129] The fear of these spirits motivates the people to worship and offer sacrifices to the spirits. Every village worships a female spirit which is considered to be the guardian spirit and generally known as *mata*. These spirits are thought to protect people in distress and if the village got polluted, it is thought they would withdraw protection. If these spirits are not placated or offered sacrifices, they are supposed to be angry and it is believed that they can cause harm to life and property.[130]

There are many malevolent spirits, which are to be dreaded and warded off by any means. Certain spirits create nuisance by playing tricks on people. There are dangerous spirits too; they cause illness, accidents and calamities. It is believed

---

[126] Abraham T. Cherian, 'Contribution of Churches and Missions to the Bhils of Rajasthan' (unpublished PhD Thesis, Asian Institute of Theology, Bangalore, India, 2005), 25-26; Interview by author, Rajasthan, 7 July 2009.

[127] L.L. Saxena, *The Bhils of Rajasthan – Their Habitat, Economy and Society* (Jodhpur, India: Books Treasure, 2000), 171-172.

[128] For a comprehensive understanding of the names of spirits worshipped by various Tribal groups in different states of India see, H. H. Risley and E. A. Gait, *Census of India 1921, Religion* (Calcutta: Superintendent Government Printing, India, 1923); also see http://www.archive.org/stream/cu31924014522746#page/n179/mode/2up (accessed 11 July 2010). Paul G. Hiebert, 'Spiritual Warfare and World View,' in *Missiology for the 21st Century: South Asian Perspective*, edited by Roger E. Hedlund & Paul Joshua Bhakiaraj (Delhi: ISPCK, 2004), 472.

[129] Ghanshyam Shah, 'Conversion, Reconversion and the State: Recent Events in the Dangs,' *EPW* (6 February 1999): 315, http://epw.in/epw/uploads/articles/8620.pdf (accessed 2 May 2010); Cherian, 'Contribution of Churches and Missions,' 33; Abraham M. Ayrookhuziel, 'Distinctive Characteristics of Folk Traditions,' in *Religions of the Marginalised: Towards a Phenomenology and Methodology of Study*, edited by Gnana Robinson (Delhi: ISPCK, 1998), 2-4.

[130] Daniel Katapali, 'Indigenous Missions and the Savara Tribal Church of Srikakulam,' *Christianity is Indian: The Emergence of an Indigenous Community*, rev. ed, edited by Roger E. Hedlund (Delhi: ISPCK, 2004), 270; Clarke, *Dalits and Christianity*, 71-75; Bauman, *Christian Identity and Dalit Religion*, 40-41; Ayrookhuziel, 'Distinctive Characteristics of Folk Traditions,' 2-3; Ilaiah, *Why I am not a Hindu*, 91-96.

that the dead are a part of the community and have dealings with those who are still alive.[131] Images of dead men and women, riding on horseback with bows and arrows are found engraved on stone tablets in villages, to give protection to the people from malevolent spirits. Some spirits are thought to help those who engage in robbery, beating, killing and snatching others' property.[132]

If any benevolent spirit possesses anybody, it may show itself through various actions and signs and is not considered to be harmful. A message spoken by such a person is counted as prophetic, as coming from the spirit. Even though Tribals and Dalits believe in a benevolent high God, no offering or sacrifice is made for such a God, as he does not harm them. That God is known as *malik* or *ooparwala*, which means master or one who is transcendent. The belief in malevolent spirits has made them increasingly preoccupied with fear. Their material needs or physical problems are immediately attached to spirits, the benevolent high God is sought only as a last resort.[133]

It is also important to discuss the idea of sin among these people. For them, sin is essentially related to the community and inter-relationships between its members. To break a taboo is sin because breaking taboos results in provocation of the spirits, which a fact which carries adverse aftermath and penalty by the village council.[134]

Every village has a *devara* (shrine) and a *bhopa* or *bhua* who acts as the village priest.[135] People rush to village shrines whenever they face any natural calamity or epidemic to seek the protection of the guardian spirits of their village.[136] It is believed that the spirit to whom they offer sacrifices and food has become angry and is, therefore, tormenting them. The *bhopa* wields great power and authority over the villagers and his words are obeyed with awe, as it is believed that the spirits possess him regularly. The priests usually ask for money, alcohol, cockerel, or goats for the ceremonies; some demand bigger amounts, unaffordable to the poor villagers, and even threaten the victims with consequences of spirit affliction, if they fail to give what they demand.[137] In the act of exorcism, the *bhopa* is either possessed by the spirit or acts as if controlled by it. The terrified family would bring the demanded items somehow, spending hard-earned money. S/He would declare that the spirit has descended on the sacrificed animal and left the house. Then gleefully, s/he would collect the money and other items and

---

[131] Clarke, *Dalits and Christianity,* 73.

[132] Cherian, 'Contribution of Churches and Missions,' 33.

[133] Cherian, 'A Study of the Religion of the Bhils,' 43; Clarke, *Dalits and Christianity,* 76-77, 87-89; Cherian, 'Contribution of Churches and Missions,' 42.

[134] M.C. Raj, *Dalitology* (Tumkur, India: Ambedkar Resource Centre, 2001), 245-246.

[135] Ebenezer, Focus Group Interview, Tabor Church, Gujarat, 23 August 2009; Clarke, *Dalits and Christianity,* 76-77, 85; A female who has the power to heal is known as *bopi.*

[136] Focus Group Interview, Tabor Church, Gujarat, 23 August 2009.

[137] Interview, Rajasthan, 5 July 2009.

walk away.[138] However, in most cases, after a few days, the patient would develop symptoms of possession or sickness. Then s/he would demand more money and materials to appease greater spirits. Having found no recovery, the family would look for a *bhopa* with greater powers, who would in turn demand more money and items; ultimately, the family becomes penniless and falls into irrevocable debt and poverty.[139]

In addition, according to the respondents, magical practices are widespread among these people.[140] Several of the interviewees acknowledge that many people are oppressed by the infestation of demonic spirits, as they claim. Some people even claim that using evil spirits (*dakan*) through magic and chants one can dry a plant or tree within a few hours. It is also believed that with the help of these spirits, witches can steal away the harvest produce or spoil the financial security of a person. Some claim that women are being sexually exploited using wicked spirits. More surprisingly, some people afflict their enemies with illness with the help of witches or even kill others. Evil spirits are also seen as causing illnesses such as paralysis, swelling all over the body, urinary problems and so on.[141] While exploring the religion of Dalits in Chhattisgarh, Bauman also portrays a similar picture:

> The religion of rural Chhattisgarh in the nineteenth and early twentieth centuries was (and in many ways still is) about power and control, about survival, protection and order. It was about the concerns of everyday, about diagnosing illness, interpreting omens and signs and about performing rituals intended to smooth one's path in this life and the next.[142]

There are many other beliefs concerning the spirit world. The people believe that the 'evil eye' causes diseases and ill-luck.[143] It can destroy family members, ruin the fortune of a person, and bring harm to domestic animals, crops and houses. To avert the evil eye, the villagers place skulls and monkey tails on poles outside their homes. Chickenpox is considered to be the blessing of *mata* and

[138] Focus Group Interview, Hebron Church, Rajasthan, 9 August 2009; Cherian, 'Contribution of Churches and Missions,' 27-28.

[139] Cherian, 'Contribution of Churches and Missions,' 28.

[140] Focus Group Interview, Hebron Church, Rajasthan, 9 August 2009.

[141] If a person needs protection from these witches, s/he has to get the help of the master witch, who gives some bangles to be worn over the shoulder, uttering certain *mantras*, which are believed to be powerful over all witchcraft. He is considered to be more powerful than a *bhopa*. Interview by author, Maharashtra, 2 September 2009. Focus Group Interview, Tabor Church, Gujarat, 23 August 2009.

[142] Bauman, *Christian Identity and Dalit Religion*, 40.

[143] The evil eye is a look that is believed by many cultures to be able to cause injury or bad luck to the person at whom it is directed for reasons of envy or dislike. It also refers to the power of certain persons of inflicting injury or bad luck by such an envious or ill-wishing look.

no treatment is undergone for it.[144] Moreover, they ascribe diseases like measles, typhoid and others to a spirit's attack. This attitude becomes a major reason for their ill-health and untimely deaths of many, along with overconsumption of alcohol.[145] They believe that gods drink alcohol and taught them to brew it and, hence, there are no ceremonies, whether it is worship, traditional hospitality, death or marriage, without serving alcohol. Some even say that 'my god is my alcohol.'[146]

Besides, by chasing the Tribals and Dalits into the jungles and the peripheries of villages, others have deprived them of their livelihood and 'caste Hindus look down upon them as backward and "jungali", i.e., uncivilised with bad customs and manners.'[147] Governmental developmental plans like industrialisation as well as onslaught of greedy contractors and middlemen have destroyed the natural resources and cures Tribals used, affected their life and health profiles. The forest dwellings, lack of education and natural resources, have made them very poor.[148] The complex worldview and lack of health care have a severe impact upon their psyche and health.[149] A large number of Tribal and Dalit Pentecostals come from such a context.

To summarise our discussion, we have outlined the most pressing issues which affect the Pentecostals. In the formulation of an Indian Pentecostal Christology, these issues are to be considered to get a true portrayal of their understanding of Christ. Obviously, the life struggles of Pentecostals colour the Christological articulation while the hostile situations they confront enrich their outlook of Christ as we shall see later.

---

[144] Focus Group Interview, Hebron Church, Rajasthan, 2 August 2009.

[145] The drinking habit of the Tribals, even by borrowing money from unscrupulous money lenders, pushes them into debt and poverty. Mohender Singh Bedi, *Drinking Behaviour and Development in Tribal Areas* (Udaipur, India: Himanshu Publications, 1998).

[146] David Hardiman, 'Healing, Medical Power and the Poor: Contests in Tribal India,' *EPW* (21 April 2007): 1406.

[147] Shah, 'Conversion, Reconversion and the State,' 315-316.

[148] Manna, 'On Calibrating the Poverty.'

[149] Wagstaff, 'Poverty and Health Sector Inequalities'; Sodani, 'Determinants of Demand for Healthcare.'

Chapter 4

Indian Christology

Christology of any given context cannot stand apart from other Christologies in the context or similar contexts, lest it may fall into the trap of self-sufficiency, short-sightedness and exaggeration of its own worth. It should engage in conversation with other Christologies to understand its limitations and rectify those flaws by taking cues from these dialogue partners. Moreover, by engaging in dialogue these Christologies may eventually enrich one another to serve people better. Therefore, we shall look into some dominant theological strands of Indian Christianity to find out how they portray Christ and whether they may become potential dialogue partners of ordinary Pentecostal Christology. Owing to the constraints of this research, we shall only provide a brief and cursory analysis of the major theological strands, grouping lines of thought which appear to be similar and dividing them into broad categories. Our aim is to find out whether the Christological concepts developed by the dominant theological traditions contribute to ordinary Pentecostal Christology, not so much to explore and evaluate them in detail.

First one might expect to have a glance into Indian Christologies' relation to wider Asian Christologies. However, the discussion of Asian theologies or Christologies begins in Indian soil itself, as Christianity reached India 2,000 years ago, even though it was dormant for centuries in the southern tip of India. The Christians of Kerala did not develop any Christology; however, they held to a tradition known as the 'Syrian tradition' and hence became known as Syrian Christians.[1] The message of Christ was accessible to them only through prayers,

[1] See E.M. Philip, *The Indian Christians of St. Thomas* (1950); Mundadan, *History of Christianity in India*; Varghese & Philip, *Glimpses of the History of the Christian Churches in India.*

songs, folk stories and liturgy in Syriac, since the Bible was not available in their local languages.[2] The establishment of the Roman Catholic Church in 1498, by Portuguese, and later the arrival of Protestant missions in 1706 did not give rise to any significant Christology. The only exception to this, perhaps, was the effort of Robert De Nobili at the beginning of the 15th century.[3] Thus, whatever meagre Christological formulation had taken place in and around Asia happened in India. Asian nations were under colonialism and whatever existing Christologies were prevalent were imported from the West. It was only in the 19th century that some sort of Christological formulations began to appear as a result of Hindu-Christian encounter.[4] The rest of the Asian countries lagged behind India in Christological formation. However, later many theologians have come up with their own theologies in various locations of Asia.

Indian Christology can be termed as the conceptualisation and interaction of the person and message of Christ into the socio-economic and religio-cultural realities of Indian people. However, what was widespread in Indian churches and seminaries was an imported western Christology with its philosophical categories and underpinnings, which were alien to Indian Christians. By the end of the 19th century, the theological scenario began to change and Indian theologians began to realise that Christologies articulated in the West were irrelevant to Indian people. This was partially due to the socio-political and religio-cultural change which occurred in that period which detonated the freedom struggle and gave rise to patriotic feelings among Christians.[5] This realisation facilitated the proliferation of Christological articulations in the 20th century. We should not misunderstand them as voluminous systematic works, rather they were small and arose within the context.

Various people have classified Indian theologies into different headings, according to their own personal perspective.[6] We shall divide Indian Christologies

---

[2] The complete Bible was translated into Malayalam only in 1841. However, some writers argue that the theological contributions of St. Thomas Christians are unique and significant; see A.M. Mundadan, *The Path of Indian Theology* (Bangalore: Dharmaram Publications, 1998), 31-62.

[3] Robert De Nobili was a Portuguese Jesuit missionary; he came to India 1605 and attempted to appropriate the philosophy and language of India for the communication of the message of Christ. However, he was not so successful; for more details see, Boyd, *An Introduction to Indian Christian Theology*, 11-14 and David Jenks, *Six Great Missionaries of the Sixteenth and Seventeenth Centuries* (London: A. R. Mowbray, 1930).

[4] Boyd, *An Introduction to Indian Christian Theology*, 17-18; it is through the writing of Raja Ram Mohan Roy we see some Christological articulation in India, even though he was not a Christian in the conventional sense.

[5] Here we shall not deal with the socio-political and religio-cultural context of India; we have already explored them briefly in the History of Pentecostalism and also in general Indian context in Chapter 3.

[6] For example see Boyd, *An Introduction;* Sumithra, *Christian Theologies;* Hubert Manohar Watson, *Towards a Relevant Christology*, 52-94; Mundadan, *The Path of Indian Theology.*

into four broad categories, considering their field of study and the way they portray Christ; Christologies from: 1) secular perspective 2) religious perspective 3) cultural perspective and 4) socio-political perspective. Chronologically speaking, 1 and 2 emerged earlier while 3 and 4 were developed recently and are numerous. From each group we shall consider some to be representative in their depiction of Christ.

4.1 Christologies from Secular Perspective

The people who endeavoured to present Christ in the secular perspective were mainly social and political leaders who attempted to reform Indian society and leaders of the Indian Freedom Movement. The Christologies from secular perspective primarily emerged as a reaction to the western mode of Christianity. It was also equally due to the captivating power of the person and the message of Christ, which became an inspiration for their reform movement.[7] This group belonged to Hinduism but had a secular outlook. After hearing the Gospel, they grappled with the person and teachings of Jesus and tried to appropriate what was feasible for them but rejected the western interpretation of Christ as well as what was incompatible with their own traditions.[8] They portrayed Jesus as a great moral teacher. Prominent among them are Raja Ram Mohan Roy (1772-1833), Mahatma Gandhi (1869-1948) and S. Radhakrishnan (1888-1975) amongst others.[9] We shall take Mohan Roy as a representative, to see how these people understood Christ.

4.1.1 The Christology of Raja Ram Mohan Roy (1772-1833)

Roy was one of the greatest social reformers, scholars and rationalists attracted by the teachings of Jesus and often called 'the father of modern India'. He was instrumental in abolishing harmful practices like *sati*, child-marriage and enacting legislation for widow-remarriage.[10] He was influenced by the Islamic teachings of monotheism and his contact with 'Unitarians' resulted in his rejection of the polytheism of popular Hinduism. Roy was attracted to Christian ethics rather than

[7] Jacob Parappally, *Emerging Trends in Indian Christology* (Bangalore: IIS Publications, 1995), 6.

[8] Anantanand Rambachan, 'A Hindu Look at Jesus,' *Vidhyajyoti Journal of Theological Reflection* 58/12 (December 1994): 773.

[9] Balwant A.M. Paradkar, 'Hindu Interpretation of Christ from Vivekananda to Radhakrishnan,' *Indian Journal of Theology* 18/1 (January-March 1969): 70-73 and 77-80; P. Fallon, 'A Critical Evaluation of the Hindu Interpretation of Christ,' *Indian Journal of Theology* 18/1 (January-March 1969): 81-87; Ronald Neufeldt, *Hindu-Christian Dialogue: Perspectives and Encounter,* edited by Harold Coward (Maryknoll: Orbis Books, 1989), 162-175; Parappally, *Emerging Trends,* 6-9; Watson, *Towards a Relevant Christology,* 53-57; Boyd, *An Introduction,* 19-26; Sumithra, *Christian Theologies,* 209-230.

[10] In Hinduism widow remarriage was not allowed and not only he brought legislation for it but also proved it by marrying a widow.

dogma.[11] We may summarise his fundamental ideas into the following points: first, monotheistic faith in the unity of God; second, morality is the essence of true religion, and moral degradation is the accompaniment of polytheism and idolatrous worship; third, rationalism demands that religious beliefs should be reasonable and reason should purify religion of superstition and unnecessary mysteries and miracles.

Roy was inspired by the *Upanishadic* teachings on *Brahman* as Supreme-being and Jesus' ethics, especially the Sermon on the Mount which shaped his Christology. He published a book called '*The Precepts of Jesus*' based on the teaching of Jesus which was inspired by the four Gospels; his intention was to provoke Hindu intellectuals in the cause of the moral reform of Hindu society.[12]

Roy ultimately denied the full divinity of Christ. For him, Jesus was a great teacher and 'messenger of God'. According to him, the 'Son of God' title was just the expression of the created nature of Christ, although the most highly exalted of all creatures.[13] Roy proved what he called 'the natural inferiority of the Son to the Father' by quoting many passages from Bible.[14] He held that Jesus is merely authorized with power from God, but did not possess this power, intrinsically. Roy explained the Johannine text which speaks about the unity of the Father and the Son, as 'a subsisting concord of will and design, such as existed among his apostles and not identity of being.'[15] For him, the claim that Jesus was God-man cannot be accepted, as it is incompatible with the *vedantic* understanding of the supreme-being.[16]

Although, Roy affirms the virgin birth, miracles, and even the bodily resurrection of Christ, he does not give much emphasis to these aspects. He believes that the saving work of Christ is accomplished only through his teachings. For this reason, he does not see any significance in the vicarious suffering, death and resurrection of Jesus.[17] For him, Christ's death is merely the supreme illustration

---

[11] Boyd, *An Introduction,* 19.

[12] Ram Mohan Roy, *The Precepts of Jesus* (Calcutta: The Baptist Mission Press, 1820).

[13] Boyd, *An Introduction,* 22; He elaborates: Jesus is the Son of God, a term synonymous with that of Messiah, the highest of all the prophet; and his life declares him to have been, as represented in the scripture, pure as light, innocent as a lamb, necessary for the eternal life as bread for a temporal one, and great as the angels of God or rather greater than they; see Raja Ram Mohan Roy, *Second Appeal* (Calcutta: Printed by the Baptist Mission Press, 1821), 69, cited by Boyd, *An Introduction,* 23.

[14] Mohan Roy, *Second Appeal,* 12.

[15] Roy, *Second Appeal.*

[16] Parappally, *Emerging Trends,* 8; Ironically, he believed in the Virgin birth and the miracles of Christ, however, rejected the personality of Holy Spirit as the agent of Christ's birth saying that it would mean the Godhead having had intercourse with a human female. The miracles of Jesus did not carry any weight in India where so many other miracles are believed.

[17] Parappally, *Emerging Trends,* 8.

of those precepts, whose communication invited the sole object of his mission.[18] In Roy's thinking, 'the blessing of pardon' is available 'from the merciful Father through repentance, which declared the only means of procuring forgiveness of our failures.'[19] Thus, Roy negates the need for an atoning death. He finds divine injustice, if God inflicts suffering on an innocent person on behalf of others.[20]

Similarly, others in this group appreciated the person and message of Jesus, but were wary of acknowledging the divinity of Jesus and accepting him as God, which was impossible for them. Parapally rightly comments, 'Commitment to the person of Jesus Christ must remain a pre-requisite for understanding the person and message of Christ.'[21] Hence, their interpretations of Christ remained that of 'outsiders'.

4.2 Christologies from Religious Perspective

This strand of Christologies emerged in response to Hinduism and we can mainly divide them into two areas: the Christologies which emerged in response to the Hindu philosophical system[22] and popular Hindu religious piety. The former mainly utilises the *vedantic* tradition of Upanishad, expounded by Sankara but the latter uses popular devotional (*bhakti*) tradition (especially Ramanuja's *Vishishta-advaita* - modified non-dualism). We shall look into both in due turn.

Advaita Philosophy

The Hindu sacred scriptures can be divided into sections dealing with action (*karmakanda*) and knowledge (*jnanakanda*). The *mimamsa* maintains that ritual actions are of primary importance because performing dharma is the central purpose of the *Vedas*. Sankara, on the other hand, maintains that the knowledge is of greater importance, for liberation is the central message of the Vedas and only knowledge leads to liberation.[23] This liberating knowledge is referred to in the 'great sayings' (*mahavakya*) of the Upanishads, namely: 'I am the absolute' (*aham brahmasmi*); 'this self is the absolute' (*ayam atma brahma*); 'everything is

[18] Sumitra, *Christian Theologies,* 44.

[19] M.M. Thomas, *The Acknowledged Christ of Indian Renaissance* (Madras: Christian Literature Society, 1970), 27; According to him, repentance is the only means for salvation. He affirms that there is not 'a single passage pronounced by Jesus enjoining such a doctrine of the Cross, as all sufficient and indispensable for salvation.'

[20] Boyd, *An Introduction*, 24.

[21] Parappally, *Emerging Trends,* 9.

[22] For a brief description of Indian philosophical systems, especially *advaita* philosophy, see Ramakrishna Puligandla, *Fundamentals of Indian Philosophy* (New Delhi: D.K. Printworld, 1997) and Aravind Sharma, *The Philosophy of Religion and Advaita Vedanta* (Delhi: Sri Satguru Publications, 1997).

[23] Raimundo Panikkar, *The Unknown Christ of Hinduism: Towards an Ecumenical Christophany* (London: Darton, Longman & Todd, 1981), 110-116. K.P. Aleaz, *The Relevance of Relation in Sankara's Advaita Vedanta* (Delhi: Kant Publications, 1996), 25-30.

indeed absolute' (*sarvam khalu idam brahma*); and 'you are that' (*tattvamasi*). To realise the existential force of these claims is to be liberated and to distinguish pure being and worldly phenomena. The ultimate or *Brahman*, in its timeless essence as identical with the self, is beyond all predicates and qualities (*nirguna*).[24]

However here we face a problem when explaining the existence of the world. If Brahman is without even existence how did the reality come to be one? There will be dualism. To sort out this difficulty the Upanishads explain Brahman as the efficient and, at the same time, the material cause of the world. *Brahma Sutra* 1.1.2 says, '*that* by which the world originates, etc.,' 'Brahman is the omniscient and omnipotent cause of the origin, persistence and passing away of the world'. It is from *that* which all beings spring into existence, in which they live, and into which they return at the end.[25] This is *saguna Brahman, Brahman* endowed with attributes; also called *Isvara*. Thus, in its temporal mode, Sankara presents a personal Lord (*Isvara*), with attributes (*saguna*), so that people with a lower level of knowledge can approach him through devotion.[26]

It is the *saguna Brahman* that people worship in different names and forms. It is God as *saguna Brahman* that was endowed with such qualities as love, kindness, mercy who stands in relation to humans and the world. In short, *saguna Brahman* is a personal God. *Brahman* is also designated as *sat-cit-ananda* (being-consciousness-bliss), and in Sankara's theology we can see him using these three words to explain *Brahman*.[27]

Some of the Indian theologians like Keshab Chandra Sen, Brahmabandhav Upadhyaya, Raimundo Panikkar and others employed Vedanta philosophy to re-interpret Christian spirituality so that it would make sense to the Hindus. In this endeavour they explained Christ in these philosophical categories. Here we shall explore the idea of Upadhyaya briefly to see how Vedanta philosophy is used to explain the person and message of Christ.

4.2.1 The Christology of Brahmabandhav Upadhyaya (1861-1907)

According to Upadhyaya, Christianity came to India in western garb, with its purity and originality hidden under a series of unfamiliar terms and structures. Therefore, it was essential to adapt the message of Christ to the Indian thought system and for this he found Sankara's philosophy as the best medium. He

---

[24] P. Nagaraja Rao, *Introduction to Vedanta,* 3rd ed. (Bombay: Bharatiya Vidya Bhavan, 1966), 113-133 and Eric Lott, *Vedantic Approaches to God* (London: The MacMillan Press, 1980), 20-26. Brahman is the inexpressible, invisible, inaudible and unthinkable ground of all existence. Brahman is neither a he nor a she but is the It. Brahman is neither to be identified with any God or gods men worship. Brahman can never be captured by the senses or intellect, but can only be examined in a flash of the highest mystical intuition. This is *nirguna Brahman*; see Puligandla, *Fundamentals of Indian Philosophy.*

[25] Panikkar, *The Unknown Christ,* 106-107.

[26] Aleaz, *The Relevance of Relation,* 49-60.

[27] Panikkar, *The Unknown Christ,* 148-155; Also see Aleaz, *The Relevance of Relation,* 49-50.

writes, 'The Hindu mind is extremely subtle and penetrative, but is opposed to the Greco-Scholastic method of thinking. We must fall back on the *vedantic* method, in formulating the Catholic religion to our countrymen.'[28] He had also advocated that it was possible for a Christian to be culturally Hindu but religiously Christian.[29] His argument was that if Greek philosophy and culture could be the vehicle of Christian theology in the West, similarly, Indian philosophy and culture could be the best means to establish the Gospel in India.

4.2.1.1 Christ the God-Man

Using the *saccidananda* concept, Upadhyaya explained the Christian understanding of Trinity to conceptualise his Christology.[30] For him God the Father is *sat* (Being), Christ as *cit* (consciousness) or revelation of God's inner being and Spirit as *ananda* (bliss).[31] The uniqueness of Christ lies in 'his unfolding the mystery of God's inner life'. This is also Christ's claim to his divinity.[32]

In one of his Sanskrit hymns – the *Hymn of the Incarnation* – he expounds his Christology.[33] Christ is the image of God, *Brahman* and in him the eternal Word (intelligence, *cit*), the fullness of the Godhead dwells. Here he calls Christ *Nara-Hari* (Man-God). He held the conviction that Christ was fully God and fully man. Christ is infinite, the upholder of the universe, and yet was born of a virgin; though he is 'infinite in being' (*nirguna*), yet he is also 'with relations' (*saguna*) and so personal and knowable. His use of *Hari*, in fact a proper name used for god Vishnu, and, for this reason, many Christians opposed this.[34] However, he rejected the idea of Christ as *avatara* such as Rama or Krishna of Hindu *Vaisnava* tradition to denote the incarnation of Christ. For him, there was only one incarnation, that of Christ, in whom God himself became incarnate. There was a qualitative difference between Hindu *avatars* and the incarnation of Christ.[35] According to Upadhyaya, humans are composed of five sheaths: animate, vital, mental, intellectual and spiritual. In human beings these five sheaths are controlled by personality (*aham*), however, in Christ they are activated by *logos* or *cit* of Trinity. Hence, Christ is different from *avatars* of the Hindu *puranas*.[36]

---

[28] B. Animananda, *The Blade: Life and Work of Brahmabandhab Upadhyaya* (Calcutta), 68.

[29] Sumitra, *Christian Theologies,* 62.

[30] Julius Lipner & George Gispert-Sauch (eds.), *The Writings of Brahmabandhab Upadhyaya,* vol.1 (Bangalore: The United Theological College, 1991), 126.

[31] Earlier Keshab Chander Sen also explained the Trinity in terms of *Saccidananda.*

[32] Sumitra, *Christian Theologies,* 66.

[33] Brahmabandhab Upadhyaya, 'The Hymn of the Incarnation,' *The Twentieth Century* 1/1 (1901): 7-8.

[34] Boyd, *An Introduction*, 78-79; It is, however, commonly used in Hindu circle as a synonym for God.

[35] Boyd, *An Introduction*, 80-81.

[36] Lipner & Gispert-Sauch (eds.), *The Writings of Brahmabandhab,* 190.

Upadhyaya also describes the work of Christ. Christ's deeds are holy and this shows the essential connection between God and morality. Christ pours out his life for others, giving himself as a sacrifice, acting as both priest and victim. He destroyed the poison of sin, won victory over sin and death. He is the 'soother of the human heart' and 'vanquisher of fierce death.'[37]

This theological position of explaining Christ in the *advaita* philosophical system accentuates the dominant trend of Hindu intellectualism in the national scene. Upadhyaya and others attempted to present a Christ relevant to that context. It seems that they could make an impact among highly educated Hindus; however, this philosophy was beyond the reach of the common masses.

Bhakti Tradition

The second strand from religious perspective is the Christologies which use the *bhakti* tradition. The main tenet of the *bhakti* tradition is the existence of a personal god, *Isvara,* however, unlike *advaita* it never blurs the differences between God and humans. For Ramanuja, the impersonal *Nirguna Brahman* of Sankara was a useless God. God is related to the world as a human soul is related to the body, and since this is not a relation of identity; a personal relationship is possible between God and a devotee. In this relationship there is warmth and love and personal devotion, there is experience of God's grace, there is utter self-abandonment to the love and the power of God.[38] *Bhakti* tradition also rejected the caste system. These qualities attracted many Indian Christians. Theologians belonging to this strand are Appasamy, Narayan Vaman Tilak, H. A. Krishna Pillai, Vengal Chakkarai and so on. Here we shall focus on Appasamy.

4.2.2 The Christology of Appasamy (1891-1975)

Appasamy regards Jesus as the *avatara* of God; however, not like *avataras* in Hinduism. In Hinduism *avatara* is of a recurring nature, incomplete and comes to the destruction of the wicked. However, for Appasamy Christ is the only *purna avatara,* in whom the fullness of Godhead dwells bodily (Col. 2:9). The incarnation of Christ is once and for all and is unique.[39] Christ came to seek and save the lost and sinful. He regards the Hindu *avatara* as theophanies, rather than incarnations; consequently not historical. Appasamy emphasizes the reality of humanity and historicity of Jesus.[40]

---

[37] Boyd, *An Introduction*, 79.

[38] Ibid, 112.

[39] V. P. Thomas, 'Indian Christian Approaches to the Knowledge of Christ,' *Indian Journal of Theology* 18/1 (January-March 1969): 90.

[40] Thomas, 'Indian Christian Approaches,' 90.

4.2.2.1 Christ and God

Appasamy rejected the Chalcedonian formula that Christ is metaphysically one with the Father. Instead, he expressed the union between Christ and Father as one of deep communion.[41] How is Christ related to the Father? Is the relation one of identity of substance? The Chalcedonian solution says that the Christ is the same substance (*homoousios*) as the Father. Accordingly, there is a metaphysical unity between the Father and the Son. Appasamy challenges this view and holds that the union of the Father and the Son is a moral unity. The Son from all eternity is so conformed to the Father's will, that the two persons are one, but in a moral rather than a metaphysical way.[42] He brings this view to refute the *advaita* philosophy's monist tendency which claims that Christ and the believers are one in a metaphysical way. The relation between the Father and Christ is not one of identity but rather of a completeness of harmony in thought and purpose.[43] In Gethsemane, Christ surrenders his will entirely to the Father. The doing of the Father's will was the essence of his oneness with the Father. Appasamy's explanation was intended to show that Christ and the Father are not 'one' in the *advaita* sense.[44]

For Appasamy, similar to Christ's union with his Father, the union of believers with Christ is a moral union based on love and obedience (Jn.14:28; 10:30). In Jn. 17:20 Jesus prays, "… that they may be one, as thou Father, art in me, and I in thee, that they also may be one in us". This 'as,' according to Appasamy, implies that the two relationships are of the same kind. That is, Christ and the Father are not one in the *advaita* sense. There is a difference of function and a difference of person too.

Appasamy also connects the Johannine idea of *logos* and the Hindu idea of immanent God-the *antaryamin*, in-dweller. He exegetes Jn.1:10; 'He was in the world' and interprets this as the immanence of Christ, the presence of the *logos* in the world even before his incarnation.[45] He supports this idea with Ramanuja's commentary on the *Taittiriya Upanishad*, 'Having created that, He then entered the same'. Appasamy holds that because men have not understood Him, even though He is immanent in them, He has become flesh.[46]

---

[41] Sumitra, *Christian Theologies,* 101; Appasamy takes John 10:3, 'I and my Father are one' as moral union not as a metaphysical unity.

[42] Boyd, *An Introduction*, 120.

[43] A.J. Appasamy, *What is Moksa?* (1931), 59.

[44] Boyd, *An Introduction*, 121.

[45] Sumitra, *Christian Theologies,* 102-103.

[46] Boyd, *An Introduction*, 124-125.

4.2.2.2 The Work of Christ

Christ's life of selfless love, which leads to suffering and death, is the supreme illustration of God's love. As a result, humanity is morally influenced by it to a life of faith-union with Christ and to a life of *bhakti*.[47] According to Appasamy, the cross indicates the universal need of suffering. Human sin brought suffering and the death of Christ on the cross. However, he interprets the suffering of Christ in terms of moral influence, rather than vicarious suffering or sin bearing. The central fact of the cross is not a negative fact of sin-bearing, but a positive fact of faith-union with Christ. This union is strengthened and given added depth by the revelation of suffering love on the cross.[48]

It is obvious that the Christologies of the *bhakti* strand attempted to present Christ in the light of the religiosity and devotion of the common people, like Christ as the *avatara* God. They also rejected highly philosophical categories which might sound inaccessible to the ordinary people. In this effort, however, they seem to have diluted the person of Christ, by connecting him too closely to the stature of a mere human being.

4.3 Christologies from Cultural Perspective

The third category of Christologies emerged in the Indian theology in response to the cultural situation of Indian society attempted to present Christ in the categories of the common masses. These Christologies were indigenous in nature and reflected a mystical and popular religiosity. The people who were behind them were evangelists in the true sense of the word, who ministered among the common people. Their mystical experiences acted as the fountainhead of their theology while the cultural elements added shape and colour. Moreover, they were pioneers in contextualising the Gospel to make it understandable to the culture, language and concepts of the ordinary people. Their spiritual experiences led them to develop Christologies which were highly mystical but at same time down to earth. Notable among them are Sandu Sundar Singh, Sadhu Kochu Kunju and Subha Rao. Here we shall explore the ideals of Sundar Singh and recent developments in this field.

4.3.1 The Christology of Sadhu Sundar Singh (1889-1929)

Sadhu Sundar Singh can be considered to be the most famous Indian Christian who has yet lived; his influence has extended to most of the western world as an evangelist and mystic.[49] He used stories and parables in local languages to convey the message of the Gospel. His famous adage, 'Indians greatly need the Water

---

[47] Thomas, 'Indian Christian Approaches,' 91.

[48] Watson, *Towards a Relevant Christology*, 60-61.

[49] A. J. Appasamy, *Sundar Singh: A Biography* (Madras: Christian Literature Service, 1966) and C.F. Andrews, *Sadhu Sundar Singh: A Personal Memoir* (London: Hodder and Stoughton, 1937).

of Life, but they do not want it in European vessels,' shows his commitment to develop a spirituality in Indian cultural setting.[50] Here it is important to have a glimpse at his mystical theology, before we turn to his Christology.

4.3.1.1 Mystical Theology

His theology was mystical as well as practical. Moreover, he emphasised the supernatural elements in his theology. The basis of Sadhu's mystical theology was his direct experience of Jesus Christ. His own conversion experience and visions of Jesus contributed to the formation of his theology, especially Christology. He says:

> It was not imagination. If Buddha or Krishna had shown himself it would have been imagination, for I worshipped them. But for Christ to show himself, he whom I hated, is a miracle and clear proof that he is a living Christ.[51]

Most of his theological writings developed as parts of trances or visions and he often spoke about having visited heaven.[52] He gave prominence to the visions and ecstatic experiences he had. He explains this way:

> There are pearls in the sea but to get them you have to dive to the bottom of spiritual things; it is not a trance but it is like a dive because as a diver has to stop breathing so in the ecstasy the outward senses must be stopped.[53]

Moreover, his spiritual life was founded on constant communion with Christ, through prayer. Unlike many Hindu *bhaktas* his prayer was not just a self immersion in the Absolute but, rather a continuous practice of the presence of Christ. For Sadhu, the aim of prayer was the union with God, however, this was the union of two free personalities rather than absorption in the divine.[54] He explains:

> If we want to rejoice in God we must be different from Him; the tongue could state no sweetness if there were no difference between it and that which it tastes.[55]

---

[50] Friedrich Heiler, *The Gospel of Sadhu Sundar Singh* (London: George Allen & Unwin Ltd., 1927), 232.

[51] Quoted in Sumitra, *Christian Theologies,* 93.

[52] His main writings are, *At the Master's Feet, Religion – Meditations on God, Man and Nature, The Search After, With and Without Christ, Visions of Spiritual World, The Real Pearl* and many other articles.

[53] Burnett Hillman Streeter & A. J. Appasamy, *The Sadhu: A Study in Mysticism and Practical Religion* (London: Macmillan and Company, 1922), 132.

[54] Boyd, *An Introduction*, 95.

[55] Heiler, *The Gospel of Sadhu,* 242.

The ecstatic experiences were part of his life and these took place in a walking, not a dream state. Moreover, suffering held a significant place in Sadhu's experience and theology. He underwent severe hardship; however, his asceticism was not rigid. His aim was to bear witness to Christ's love and grace and he often spoke of the joy of suffering.[56] He says,

> Through suffering God strikes us in love. The Cross is the key of heaven. The Cross will bear those who bear the Cross, until it bears them up to heaven, into the actual presence of glorious Redeemer.[57]

4.3.1.2 Christology

'Sundar Singh was always Christocentric in his thought and his theology stems from his own experience of Christ, rather than from theistic consideration,' comments Boyd.[58] Sadhu considered Christ to be fully God. Christ was the content of his visionary experiences. He says, 'I do not believe in Jesus Christ because I have read about him in the Bible. I saw him and know him in my daily experience.'[59]

Sadhu contends that our immediate experience is of Christ and it is only through him, in the power of the Spirit, that we can know the Father. Sadhu expounds the idea through one of his visions:

> The time I entered heaven I looked round about and asked, 'But where is God?' And they told me, 'God is not seen here anymore than on earth, for God is infinite. But there is Christ, He is God, He is the image of the invisible God, and it is only in him that we can see God...[60]

In another vision he speaks about Christ in relation to the Trinity, especially to the Spirit. He had thought of three separate persons sitting as it were on three separate thrones; but through a vision it was made plain for him. He illustrates it:

> I entered in an ecstasy into the third heaven...And there I saw Christ in a glorious spiritual body sitting on a throne...Christ is always in the centre, a figure ineffable and indescribable...And streaming out from Christ I saw, as it were waves shining and peace-giving, and going through and among the saints and angels, and everywhere bringing refreshment, just

[56] Boyd, *An Introduction*, 95.

[57] Heiler, *The Gospel of Sadhu*, 117.

[58] Boyd, *An Introduction*, 98.

[59] Sadhu Sundar Singh, 'The Living Christ,' in *Readings in Indian Christian Theology*, edited by R.S. Sugirtharaja & Cecil Hargreaves (London: SPCK, 1993), 73.

[60] Streeter & Appasamy, *The Sadhu: A Study in Mysticism*, 54.

> as in hot weather water refreshes trees. And this I understood to be the Holy Spirit.[61]

Sundar Singh fully accepts the idea of incarnation. Christ is like a king going about *incognito* among his people to help them; men saw him and still see him, but do not recognise his divinity. Men without faith and direct experience cannot accept the divinity of Christ. 'Faith in the divinity of Christ grows out of the immediate experience of the heart.'[62]

To appreciate Sadhu's idea of the work of Christ fully, it is essential to explore his idea of sin. According to Sadhu, human beings are sinners and the smallest sin, even an evil thought, is sufficient to keep us outside the kingdom. He connects it with the popular Hindu doctrine of *karma* but rejects the related doctrine of *samsara*. Moreover, he considers sin as the negation of goodness, rather than an active principle. Human beings are unable to do good by their own power. The sinful nature brings its own retribution, as well as the degradation of the whole personality, which can be termed *karma*. This *karma*, can cast us into hell, unless we avail ourselves of the salvation offered in Christ.[63] Christ, through his suffering and death, brings salvation to humanity.

He frequently spoke of Christ's death and the revelation of the love of God through Christ's suffering. He describes it:

> Christ knew that neither silver nor gold, nor diamonds nor any other jewels would suffice to produce life to the soul, but that what was needed was the surrender of life for life, the surrender of soul in order to save the souls of men. That is why He gave His life for the redemption of the world.[64]

According to Boyd, here we come to the idea of the substitutionary theory of atonement.[65] There can be no *karma marga*, no possibility of obtaining salvation by our own works. While other religions say, 'Do good and you will become good,' Christianity says, 'Be in Christ and you will do good.'[66] For Sadhu, the work of Christ is not finished with the forgiveness of sin, rather it involves bringing of freedom from sin; 'sanctification'. He explains:

> Jesus Christ came not only to forgive sin, but to make us free from sin. We receive from Christ a new vital power which releases us from sin...

[61] Sundar Singh, 'The Living Christ,' 76.

[62] Boyd, *An Introduction*, 98.

[63] Ibid., 101.

[64] Heiler, *The Gospel of Sadhu*, 150.

[65] Boyd, *An Introduction*, 102.

[66] Ibid., 101.

> To be saved by Christ is to receive new life from Him, to become a new creature.[67]

The attempt of this strand to present Christ in terms of the people's thought form by using stories and metaphors had wider impact. This strand attempted to serve 'the water of life in Indian cup'. The miraculous and mystical aspects of spirituality have a greater audience among the religiously-minded Indian village population.

4.3.2 Recent Cultural Christologies

Recently, theologians from various theological traditions and affiliations have come up with Christological articulations to address various cultural and social issues in Indian society. One of the most significant approaches is the presentation of Jesus in Indian cultural images and metaphors familiar to the common people. Here Michael Amaladoss and his practical presentation of Jesus in various images, is worth mentioning. According to Amaladoss, Jesus was born and lived in Asia, however, due to historical circumstances he comes back to India as a European.[68] Therefore, it is vital to present Christ in Indian cultural images to make sense to Indians. He is cautious to avoid the images with significance in other religious traditions; instead, he chooses metaphors with a cultural tone which is common to all.[69] Following the New Testament pattern of titles of Jesus, he proposes various titles such as *sage, guru, avatar, satyagrahi, servant, pilgrim* and so on. He advises us that these images should not be compared. 'Each one has its special appeal in particular situations to particular people at particular times.' He contends that these metaphors would help 'to discover the Asian Jesus, to follow him in an Asian way and to witness him before other Asians in a meaningful manner.'[70] He advocates Jesus as the only saviour; through him, God's saving love reaches out to all people.[71]

Similarly, Thomas Thangaraj depicts Jesus as the 'crucified *guru*.'[72] He seeks to establish a 'dialogue between the Christian understanding of Jesus the Christ and the Saiva Siddhanta concept of *guru*.'[73] Alangaram also portrays Jesus in a

---

[67] Quoted in Heiler, *The Gospel of Sadhu*, 62.

[68] Michael Amaladoss, *The Asian Jesus* (Delhi: ISPCK, 2005), 1.

[69] Amaladoss, *The Asian Jesus*, 7-9.

[70] Ibid., 200.

[71] P. R. John, 'Towards Indian Christology,' in *Seeking New Horizons*, edited by Leonard Fernando (Delhi: ISPCK, 2002), 63.

[72] Unfortunately, the constraint of this work does not allow us to deal them in detail. M. Thomas Thangaraj, *The Crucified Guru: An Experiment in Cross-Cultural Christology* (Nashville: Abingdon Press, 1994).

[73] Thangaraj, *The Crucified Guru*, 89.

similar way within the wider context of India and Asia, with titles like Jesus as *evangelist, liberator, servant* and so on.[74]

In another approach, Felix Wilfred suggests a *kenotic* Christology in the context of communal frenzy and marginalisation of the poor.[75] In Jesus, the divine mystery has limited itself in a particular culture to be a Jew. This particularity is an inextricable part of the mystery of Christ. Therefore, he advocates:

> ...*kenosis* is the permanent horizon for the understanding both of his divine as well as human nature in their inter-relatedness. This opens up development of contextual Christologies based on the particular cultural and historical experience of peoples and nations. Self-emptying was at the origin of the message of the Kingdom of God which Jesus preached and represented in his person.[76]

Moreover, the experience of Jesus suffering for others, which is truly an experience of kenosis, is something that relevant to the poor of India, irrespective of their religions.[77]

4.4 Christologies from Socio-Political Perspective

The fourth category of Indian Christologies emerged in response to the socio-political changes and advocates dialogue with secular and religious movements; it emphasises liberation from the socio-economic evils existing in Indian society. Religious conflicts, antagonism between communities and socio-political ideologies have threatened the integrity and safety of Indian society. Moreover, caste discrimination, religious oppression, and rampant economic exploitation also became sources for the development of Christologies. Therefore, dialogue and liberation are considered to be indispensable acts in the Indian context because they both reinforce and contribute efforts to address the struggles which exist in socio-economic and religious realms. Thus, some Indian Christians have felt the need of dialogues between different religions for peace and harmony among communities, while others have emphasised dialogue with socio-political and economic forces to bring liberation to the oppressed and the poor. Prominent among the first group are P. D. Devanandan, Swami Abhishiktananda, and Stanley Samartha. The second group consists of persons as well as of theological movements; M. M. Thomas, Sebastian Kappen and K. C. Abraham are well-known among the people; Dalit theology, Tribal theology, and an Indian version of liberation theology are important among the movements. Here we shall explore

[74] A. Alangaram, *Christ of the Asian Peoples: Towards an Asian Contextual Christology* (Bangalore: Asian Trading Corporation, 1999).

[75] Felix Wilfred, *On the Bank of Ganges: Doing Contextual Christology*, rev. ed. (Delhi: ISPCK, 2005), 175-181.

[76] Wilfred, *On the Bank of Ganges*, 176.

[77] Ibid., 176.

the idea of M.M. Thomas, who advocates dialogue, for nation-building and for liberation. We shall also look at Dalit theology to see its explanation of Christ in the context of caste-system and economic oppression. Lastly we shall turn to the recent development of Spirit Christologies taking one example, which also focuses on liberation.

4.4.1 The Christology of M. M. Thomas (1916 –1996)

The socio-political changes in the sub-continent and the renascent Hinduism with its powerful ideology for social change led Thomas to search for a theology relevant to the postmodern India. He calls his theological framework 'theological anthropology'. Humanisation is in the core concept of his thinking.[78] He begins his theology from the world, it is a contextual or situational approach, and, therefore, it is action-oriented. He insisted that four essential factors should be maintained in dialogue, 'first, Scripture; then, Christian tradition; next, *Koinonia* of the Church, and finally its mission in the contemporary world.'[79] Here his understanding of Christ bears a unique status.

The human quest and struggle for liberation has its answer in Jesus Christ. To Thomas, the historicity of Jesus Christ is the essential part of Christology. Jesus Christ is 'the meeting point in history where God fully reveals Himself and where humanity realises itself fully.'[80] He is the 'redemptive centre' of world history.

4.4.1.1 Lordship Christology

Thomas advocates that the ultimate framework of reference for Christian thought is neither God nor humanity but Jesus Christ who is God-Man.[81] Thomas developed his Lordship Christology in the context of contemporary revolutionary changes, its meanings and the implications of the Christian faith to such a context.[82] In his book *The Acknowledged Christ of the Indian Renaissance,* he sought to expound the presence of Christ in renascent Hinduism,[83] and advocated the need for Christians to engage in dialogues with other religious traditions and secular ideologies to accomplish the mission of Christ.

He interprets lordship in terms of the kingly rule of Christ over all realms of life, from a starting point, that Jesus Christ is the agent of creation and redemption (Col.1:16-20). This kingly rule should be understood in terms of 'overcoming

[78] M. M. Thomas, *Salvation and Humanisation* (Bangalore: Christian Institute for the Study of Religion and Society, 1971), 6-9.

[79] Boyd, *An Introduction*, 314.

[80] T. M. Philip, *The Encounter Between Theology and Ideology: An Explanation into the Communicative Theology of M.M. Thomas* (Chennai: CLS, 1986), 57-58.

[81] Thomas, *Salvation and Humanisation*, 6.

[82] M. M. Thomas, *The Secular Ideologies of India and the Secular Meaning of Christ* (Madras: CLS, 1976) and *The Christian Response to the Asian Revolution* (London: SCM, 1966).

[83] M. M. Thomas, *The Acknowledged Christ of the Indian Renaissance* (Madras: CLS, 1991).

sin and all the structures of evil, and finally death itself and of the end-event, namely the conversion of the kingdoms of this world into the Kingdom of God through Christ.'[84] Thomas was criticized for his identification of revolutions with the revelation of God in Christ;[85] nevertheless, Thomas clarifies that his notion of Lordship was developed so as to emphasize the historical person of Jesus Christ.

The lordship Christology of Thomas tries to provide a theological interpretation of history. For him, Christ is the meeting point of history where God fully reveals God-self and where humanity realises itself fully. He criticised Christian *advaitic* tradition, which interpreted Christ in mystical terms, dissociating the historic person of Jesus from his Hebraic background. He also rejects the Christian theological interpretation of history in a sense of pietistic evangelical spirituality which emphasises individualism, for they are *ahistorical*.[86]

4.4.1.2 Christ as the Dynamic of Revolutionary Humanism

Thomas sees Jesus Christ as the revelation of God in solidarity with the poor and the oppressed.[87] The crucifixion of Jesus provides a potent vision in uplifting the downtrodden as well as in working for the transformation of society. The crucifixion also points to the question of the ultimate destiny of suffering humanity. Thomas is of the opinion that the Crucified Christ liberates humanity from Satan; and Satan is the spiritual consolidation of the forces of dehumanization, poverty, oppression, disease, sin and death.[88] He interprets Jesus' crucifixion, resurrection and glorification as the dynamics of a revolutionary humanism to which Jesus' person is central and is the way to the kingdom of God.

Thomas' Christology is thoroughly based on his interpretation of the Cross. God's love is manifested on the Cross.[89] Thomas believes the message of the Cross of Christ offering divine forgiveness is relevant to present humanistic ideologies like Marxism from degenerating into instruments of totalitarian schemes of dehumanization. The crucified and risen Christ justifies every human ideology and releases them for works of love to the redemption of humanity; and hence, makes the ideology of Marxism-Leninism a truly secular humanism.[90]

---

[84] Philip, *The Encounter Between*, 56.

[85] Sunand Sumithra, *Revolution as Revelation: A Study of M. M. Thomas's Theology* (New Delhi: Theological Research and Communications Institute, 1984).

[86] Philip, *The Encounter Between*, 57. He asks not to reduce the Gospel of redemption of all things in heaven and earth, and the message of Christ's renewal of humans in their total relations into a cult of pietism or the more sophisticated existentialist self-understanding which may motivate humanity to be liberated from the burden of history through a mystic self realization. See Philip, *The Encounter Between*, 58.

[87] Philip, *The Encounter Between*, 59.

[88] Ibid., 61.

[89] M. M. Thomas, *The Realisation of the Cross* (Madras: CLS, 1972), 44.

[90] Philip, *The Encounter Between*, 66.

Thomas views the Cross as a power releaser, as he identifies it with the Kingdom and says that the Cross is the Kingdom of God moving with power into the history of humanity, by taking control of the powers of this world.[91] This interpretation of the Cross has to do with his view on corporate aspects of sin. He says, 'Corporate sin has a momentum unknown to personal sins.'[92] To illustrate this he talks of the caste-system prevalent in India. He says that, when ideologies are absolutised, they tend to become 'principalities and powers'. Thomas interprets the Cross as power to redeem the principalities and powers and to release us from the power of our collective sins.

For Thomas, the resurrection of Jesus marks the inauguration of a new humanity. God's act of raising Jesus is viewed by Thomas as an act of 'New Creation'. All kinds of divisions created in society by nature, culture or history are broken down by the resurrection of Jesus Christ. Therefore, the life of Jesus, the crucified and risen serves as a model in the dialogue between the secular ideologies of India and the Indian renaissance. Christ is the revelation of God in secular solidarity with the poor and powerless.[93] Jesus identified Himself with the poor and oppressed in their struggle for human dignity and social justice. This will unite Christians and non-Christians in involving themselves with the political struggle for the transformation of Indian society.[94]

4.4.1.3 Salvation as Humanization

Thomas considers salvation to be humanisation. Sin prevented humans from freedom and creativity but God redeemed human beings in Christ. The God of the Bible is the God of history who liberates people from their bondage. Salvation involves social liberation. It includes community and unity among human beings.[95] True humanism is to be found in the humanity of Jesus. Therefore, the mission of the Church is humanization. He says, 'the Gospel of salvation must work itself out also in the realm of history and politics.'[96] The need of the hour is participation in the struggle of the people. 'The Churches cannot stand on the side-lines as spectators, but must involve themselves in contemporary Asian existence in solidarity with the human and spiritual struggle of the world of the Asian renaissance and revolution.'[97]

---

[91] Philip, *The Encounter Between*, 66.

[92] Thomas, *New Creation in Christ*, 20.

[93] Philip, *The Encounter Between*, 68-69.

[94] Ibid., 70.

[95] Thomas, *Salvation and Humanisation*, 8-9;Thomas, *The Secular Ideologies*, 194.

[96] Boyd, *An Introduction*, 319.

[97] Thomas, *The Acknowledged Christ*, 310; Also see M. M. Thomas, 'My Pilgrimage in Mission,' in *Frontiers in Asian Christian Theology: Emerging Trends*, edited by R.S. Sugirtharajah (Maryknoll: Orbis Books, 1994): 156-160.

The attempt to address the serious issues of emancipation of the poor and nation-building, which are inseparable aspects in theologising is an eye-opener to the traditional theological method employed in India. Their concept of the presence of Christ in authentic religions and in progressive secular ideologies may help to augment the process of dialogue. However, although dialogue is essential, the message of Christ can be blunted in the process of dialogue.

4.4.2 Dalit Christology

The emergence of liberation theology in Latin America has influenced Christians in India and they began to articulate theologies on similar lines, but also with certain differences.[98] The main concern of all of them is the articulation of the person and work of Christ for the liberation of the oppressed. We shall concentrate on the Christology of Aravind Nirmal, a prominent Dalit theologian.

4.4.2.1 Dalit Theology

Dalit theology is a theological movement developed on behalf of Dalits, irrespective of their religions, regions, background or languages. According to Nirmal, one of the pioneers of Dalit theology,

> It is a theology about the Dalits or the theological reflection upon the Christian responsibility to the depressed classes. Secondly, it is a theology for the depressed classes, or the theology of the message addressed to the depressed classes and to which they seem to be responding. Thirdly, it is a theology from the depressed classes, that is, the theology which they themselves would like to expound.[99]

Thus, Dalit theology is solely for the depressed people who are under pathos (suffering and pain) which speaks about their causes, emancipation in Indian churches and in larger society. It tries to create awareness among the Dalits about their rights and privileges and also among other people, especially among Christians. It also brings out the biblical and Christological understanding of the suffering of this people and looks for remedies from a biblical perspective.

4.4.2.2 Indian Church and Dalits

It is a fact that 70 to 85% of the membership of the Indian church comes from among Dalit communities; they became the backbone of the Indian church. The upper caste people consists of only 15 to 20%. However, upper caste converts had an edge over the Dalit converts because they were educated and naturally assumed leadership within the church. The caste system made way into the life of the

---

[98] Unlike liberation theology of Latin America, the Indian version of liberation theology is wary of uncritical use of Marxian ideology as well as of religious dialogue.

[99] A. P. Nirmal, 'Towards a Christian Dalit Theology,' in *A Reader in Dalit Theology,* edited by A. P. Nirmal (Madras: Gurukul, n.d.), 58.

Indian church. There were no inter-marriages among Dalits and non-Dalits. They would celebrate communion together but this did not result in social interaction over meals.[100]

4.4.2.3 Indian Christian Theology and Dalits

As mentioned, the leadership of the Indian church was in the hands of upper caste Christian coverts who were also the chief spokespersons of Indian Christian theology. These upper caste convert theologies basically witnessed continuity between the Christian faith and their former Hindu faith. Thus, Indian Christian theology concerned and obsessed itself with *bramanic* tradition. Therefore, the classical Indian Christian theology never noticed the social reality of the Indian church seriously. There existed a wide gap between the Indian church and Indian theology. It was only in the eighties that a new theological paradigm in the form of Dalit theology emerged. The pathos of Dalits now began to be articulated and found a theological expression of its own in this new paradigm. It was this pathos, this sense of suffering, which became the keynote of Dalit theology.[101]

4.4.2.4 The Dalitness of Jesus

For Nirmal, the Dalit who follow Christ are not just Dalit, but Christian Dalit. This means, 'First of all that we affirm that Jesus Christ whose followers we are, was himself a Dalit despite being a Jew. It further means that both his humanity and divinity are to be understood in terms of his Dalitness. His Dalitness is the key to the mystery of his divine humanity.'[102]

Nirmal reads the Gospels with a Dalit eye and from a Dalit perspective. He recapitulates some of the features of the Dalitness of Jesus. In the genealogy of Jesus, according to Matthew (1:1-17), the names of some of the women would startle and shock us; they were considered to be 'untouchable' and 'impure' in the eyes of the Jews. They were scandalised and reproached in their contemporary society.[103] They are the dalitness of Jesus. Jesus was also referred to as a 'carpenter's Son.' That sounds like looking down upon his father's profession.[104] In his birth he was in a Dalit condition, in a cattle shed, away from comfort, far from human activities.

---

[100] A. P. Nirmal, 'Dalit Theology,' *Transcending Boundaries* (Bombay: Vikas Adhyan Kendra, 1995), 74-75.

[101] Nirmal, 'Dalit Theology,' 74-75.

[102] Ibid.

[103] The first name is that of Tamar, the daughter-in-law of Judah. She outwitted her father-in-law by sleeping with him and conceiving from him (Gen. 38:1-30). Secondly there is Rahab, a gentile woman, a harlot who helped the Israelite spies (Josh. 2:1-21). Thirdly, Ruth, a Moabite woman, who was considered to be untouchable, became the great grandmother of King David and, fourthly, Bethsheeba, the illegitimate wife of King David.

[104] Nirmal, 'Towards a Christian Dalit Theology,' 66.

Another aspect of Jesus' dalitness is the fact that he preferred to use himself the title 'Son of Man'. Even though it is used in different ways, the use of the title to portray his suffering and death is used by Nirmal to develop his Christology. He quotes the 'Son of Man' saying of Jesus precisely to demonstrate the dalitness of Jesus.[105] Jesus encounters rejection, mockery and contempt, suffering and, finally, death. All this suffering originated from the dominant religious tradition of his time. He underwent these experiences as the prototype of all Dalits.[106] Another important aspect of Jesus' life is his total identification with the Dalits of his day. Again and again, Jesus was accused of eating and drinking with publicans, tax collectors and sinners of his day (Mk. 2:15-16). Moreover, his visit to Samaritan villages and cities is a good example of his attitude towards the rejected and Dalits of his day.[107]

The Dalit Jesus' 'Nazareth Manifesto'[108] in the Gospel according to Luke is very important for Dalit theologians. Balasundaram explains Nirmal's concept. The Dalit Jesus' Nazareth Manifesto speaks about who his liberation is meant for. The two illustrations Jesus uses (Luke 4:25-27) indicate that the liberation he is talking about is meant for the Dalits but not for non-Dalits. The gentiles were preferred to Israel; with reference to the widow of Zarephath and Namaan, the Syrian. While there were many widows in Israel, it was only to Zarephath that Elijah was sent. So, too was Namaan, the leper from Syria who Elisha cleansed. There were many lepers in Israel but they were not cleansed. Thus the Dalits were set over against Israel.[109]

The cleansing of the temple by Jesus is taken by Nirmal and used to illustrate Jesus' concern for the people and to restoring their right to worship. This act of Jesus is very important in the Indian context, as Dalits were not allowed to enter the Hindu temples and face segregation in the Indian churches. Nirmal contends that this episode is full of significance for a Christian Dalit theology. Owing to Lightfoot's interpretation of Mark 11:15-19, that Jesus, the messianic king, restores to the gentiles their religious right, Nirmal says,

> Jesus the messianic king thus restores to the gentiles their religious rights. Lightfoot's interpretation makes sense to the Indian Dalits who

---

[105] For example, 'And he began to teach them that the Son of man must suffer many things and be rejected by the elders and the chief priests and scribes and be killed, and after three days rise again' (Mk. 8:31); 'It is written of the Son of man that he should suffer many things and treated with contempt'(Mk. 9:12); 'For the Son of man also came not to be served but to serve and to give his life ransom for many' (Mk. 10:45).

[106] Nirmal, 'Towards a Christian Dalit Theology,' 66.

[107] Ibid., 67.

[108] "The Spirit of the Lord is upon me, because he has anointed me, to bring good news to the poor. He has send me to proclaim release to the captives. And recovery of sight to the blind, to let the oppressed go free, to proclaim the year of the Lord's favour" (Lk. 4:18-19).

[109] F. J. Balasundaram, *Contemporary Asian Christian Theology* (Delhi: ISPCK, 1995), 67.

> had to struggle for the temple entry rights…We the Indian Dalits know what it means to be denied the right to pray and worship…In his act of restoration of gentile right to worship, we see a pre-figuration of the vindication of the Dalit struggle for their prayer and worship rights.[110]

'There are many other examples of Jesus' sympathy for the Dalit of his day,' asserts Nirmal, 'but his dalitness is best symbolized by the cross.'[111] On the Cross, he was the broken, the crushed, the split, the torn, the driven-asunder man, the Dalit in the fullest possible meaning of the term. 'My God, my God, why hast thou forsaken me?' he cried aloud from the cross; the Son of God feels that he is forsaken. 'That feeling of being God-forsaken is at the heart of our Dalit experiences and Dalit consciousness in India. It is the dalitness of humanity and divinity that the Cross symbolises.'[112]

Thus, this strand shows the contextual needs and aspirations of the oppressed who suffer in the social, economic, religious and spiritual realms. By introducing Jesus as one who suffers with the victims and as a liberator does justice to the person and message of Christ. It also reminds the Church about its liberative mission.[113] Nevertheless, it seems that, in this liberative model, spiritual liberation which is a prerequisite for every other kind of liberation, is forgotten or pushed into the periphery

4.4.3 Spirit Christologies

Another recent development in Christological narrative within the Indian context is the emergence of Spirit Christologies. Earlier, the Spirit-dimension of Christology was either neglected or relegated in mainline denominations. Some Indian theologians endeavoured to explain Christology in terms of the Spirit's outworking. Prominent among them are Chenchiah, Swami Abhishiktananda and Chakkarai who consciously highlighted the relevance of the work of the Spirit in an Indian religious and cultural setting. Recently, Samuel Rayan has proposed a Spirit-Christology primarily to present Christ in his humanity so as to enhance the liberation. It also tries to replace 'the Christology from above' (*Logos* Christology) with 'the Christology from below'. Also, a number of published doctoral theses have been written which explain the Spirit-Christologies of Indian theologians.[114] We shall look into the Christology of Samuel Rayan, a Roman Catholic theologian and long-time campaigner for the rights of the Dalits of

---

[110] Balasundaram, *Contemporary Asian,* 169-170.

[111] Nirmal, 'Towards a Christian Dalit Theology,' 69.

[112] Ibid., 69.

[113] Wilfred, *On the Bank of Ganges*, 137.

[114] For instance, Kirsteen Kim, *Mission in Spirit: The Holy Spirit in Indian Christian Theologies* (Delhi: ISPCK, 2003) and Christina Manohar, *Spirit Christology: An Indian Christian Perspective* (Delhi: ISPCK, 2009).

India, who formulates a Spirit-Christology for the socio-political and economic liberation of the oppressed. He was critical of the Church's neglect of the poor and oppressed.[115]

In one of his books, *Breath of Fire,* he sees the Holy Spirit, the Spirit of God and of Jesus Christ, as the heart of the Christian gospel.[116] Drawing on the *shakti* tradition, he portrays the Spirit as a 'breath of fire,' who empowers us in committed historical action.[117] He advocates a spiritual struggle to overcome the forces of violence and oppression in society and to bring about justice. According to him, the Spirit is the 'breath' or yeast of new life that invigorates the 'bread,' which is the earth, and in so doing, brings about a redistribution of its resources to the benefit of all.[118]

Rayan outlines his Spirit-Christology and relates it to four key events in the Gospels, the annunciation, the baptism, the resurrection and Pentecost.[119] He considers the annunciation as a second act of creation by the Spirit and because the Spirit is at work in Jesus from annunciation, not just from baptism, he claims that his Christology avoids adoptionism. The baptism of Jesus was not the first but a fresh, more personal experience of the Spirit which guaranteed the coming of the Spirit upon us and on Earth.[120] The resurrection was Jesus' fullest and most decisive experience of the Spirit, an experience which wholly transformed him to provide humanity a decisive future. Moreover, the resurrection brought about by the Spirit is 'God's strongest act of dissent and most definitive rejection and subversion of the power and project of prince and priest,' who crucified Jesus. For him, Pentecost reveals the whole meaning of Jesus for human history and destiny, as the disciples are then empowered to participate in his mission.[121]

---

[115] He says, 'We go out of our way to secure enormous funds to run colleges, special schools, medical colleges and excellent hospitals, all of which we know only the richer classes can afford. Aid goes to the poor mainly in relief or in emergency cases...The churches seem to be saying something like this: "I am a rich Christian. So many (how many?) millions of rupees come into my hands every year from funding agencies abroad. With this I serve my class, the upper class, irrespective of religion. Now here are the poor Christians. Government, you, please, take care of them. You must if you are just."' See Samuel Rayan, 'The Justice of God,' in *Living Theology in Asia,* edited by John C. England (London: SCM, 1981), 217.

[116] Samuel Rayan, *Breath of Fire – The Holy Spirit: Heart of the Christian Gospel* (London: Geoffrey Chapman, n.d.).

[117] Rayan, *Breath of Fire*, vii.

[118] Kirsteen Kim, 'The Holy Spirit in Mission in India: Indian Contribution to Contemporary Mission Pneumatology,' *Oxford Centre for Mission Studies* (6 April 2004), http://www.ocms. ac.uk/docs/TUESDAY%20LECTURES_Kirsteen.pdf (accessed 10 November 2010).

[119] For a fuller analysis of Rayan's theology and Spirit Christology see Kim, *Mission in Spirit,* 138-194, especially 178-183; Also see Kirsteen Kim, 'Mission Pneumatology with Special Reference to the Indian Theologies of the Holy Spirit of Stanley Samartha, Vandana, and Samuel Rayan' (PhD Thesis, University of Birmingham, 2001).

[120] Kim, *Mission in Spirit,* 178.

[121] Kim, *Mission in Spirit,* 178-179.

However, in his Spirit-Christology, he does not consider Jesus as the exclusive source of salvation. For him, Jesus reveals salvation, realises it historically, and becomes its perfect exemplar. Jesus is unique as a normative manifestation of God; however, Jesus is decisive and absolute for Christians, though not exclusive, and we may expect other mediations of the same salvation.[122]

In the above pages we had a glance at the dominant strands of Christologies prevailing in the Indian scenario. They are diverse in form and disposition and have sprung up from divergent settings of theological thinking. Their efforts to depict Christ in a way that is intelligible has added shades and colours to Christological articulations worldwide. However, the mystery of the incarnation eludes the precise definitions and explanations and very often the use of philosophies or ideologies complicate their portrayal of Christ. Moreover, the most vexing question is how far these Christologies are appreciated and comprehended by common people. The situation is further complicated by the lack of participation in the theological process by believers of the churches these theologians belong to. Theologians seldom consult 'the faithful' and often forget to ensure the validity and utility of the Christologies they articulate for 'believers' and Christ-seekers. Many a time their notions and explanations stand above the grasp of ordinary folks.

Indian Christologies are attempts at presenting the mystery of Christ in a way that is intelligible to the unique and peculiar context of India. Unfortunately, Indian society is not a monolithic homogeneous structure but is made up of manifold elements put together. Hence, while presenting Christ, the communicators face various challenges such as religious pluralism, cultural diversities, the hierarchical structure of society and differences in languages. Additionally, each people group has its own set of beliefs and practices which is dissimilar to that of other groups. Even in a given locality or community there are sharp distinctions in beliefs, rituals and world-views. These differences pose challenges to the pioneers who venture out to present the person and message of Christ. Consequently, these circumstances presuppose a multiplicity of Christological articulations.

What we have seen in the pages above are the strenuous efforts undertaken by various pioneers to present Christ in a meaningful way to different sections of the society. However, due to the existence of diverse settings, very often a Christology directed towards a religious affinity does stand in contrast even to the people of the same religion.

For example, as we have seen, the *advaitic* strand of Christology is in opposition to the *bhakti* strand of Christology. Similarly, the ideals of liberation Christology stand in contrast to the philosophical branch. The liberation strand would condemn the latter as contributing to the superiority and caste feeling among the Christians. Likewise, the mystical strand seems to be incompatible with the dialogical strand, as the former speaks of Christ in exclusive terms while

[122] Ibid., 182-183.

the latter is open to comparison. The dialogical strand sounds good in the context of religious pluralism and social oppression; however, its worth and effectiveness are not communicated to Christians and they remain lofty ideals in text books. Cultural Christology though, attempts to contextualise the message in cultural and religious settings, but in doing so its use of the terms and metaphors often offend Christians and makes the message of Christ similar to dogmas of other religions.

Another concern is the neglect of a personal spiritual aspect in Christology. Many of these strands are not able to penetrate into the hearts and minds of the ordinary people. One of the reasons could be attributed to their inability to address the personal spiritual struggle of the people – a fact which may be counted as one of the root causes of many of the problems people face. Often these Christologies are general and broad and stand aloof from the experiences people undergo. Although, some of them claim to use the methodology of 'Christology from below,' often their articulations are exclusive and highly intellectual. Many of them are incapable of addressing the needs and aspirations of village folk who have been undergoing severe crises – sickness, harmful rituals, spiritual oppression, witchcrafts and so on.

Even though the Spirit Christologies emphasise the work of the Spirit, they have failed to apply the work of the Spirit in the lives of the suffering masses. The gifts of the Spirit such as healing, exorcism and other miraculous aspects, have been relegated or pushed aside due to the influence of western enlightenment ideology present in theological formulation. This proves detrimental to the personal liberation of the downtrodden, as the Spirit is the agent of liberation. If Christ carried out his ministry in the power of the Spirit, touching the lives of the ordinary people as the Gospels testify, the Indian Christologies need to use similar methods in the Indian context.

Furthermore, some Christologies do not take New Testament testimonies about the person and the message of Christ as their primary source; some of them are not even based on canonical writings.[123] These Christologies need to be critically evaluated and used with discretion for the articulation of Pentecostal Christology. Therefore, Pentecostal contextual Christology needs a critical and renewed approach, which takes the context, as well as biblical insights, in balance.

Now for Pentecostals these Christologies can give certain clues – how to articulate Christologies and what specific areas need addressing in an Indian setting. Christologies from religious perspective can be helpful in presenting Christ both to the intellectual, as well as to ordinary people. The emphasis on Christ's humanity and divinity by the philosophical approach can be useful in fortifying Pentecostal Christology.

---

[123] R. S. Sugirtharajah (ed.), 'Prologue and Perspective,' *Asian Faces of Jesus – Faith and Culture Series* (Maryknoll: Orbis Books, 1993), ix.

Besides, as the Pentecostals mostly come from the lower strata of the society, the elements of liberation and mystical Christologies are essential ingredients for an ordinary Pentecostal Christology. The emphasis on dialogue for nation building and religious amity is crucial for Pentecostals. They can also be helpful in identifying the pertinent issues of in the context and used as handy tools. The Spirit-Christologies come closer to the Pentecostal understanding of Christ, and therefore, can be useful concepts when applied to a Spirit-informed liberation Christology. We will highlight these positive ideals and draw on them in the construction of an ordinary Christology for Indian Pentecostals. However, for Pentecostals, given the situations in which they emerge, Christology cannot be a set of principles or system of doctrines; but Christology must be enacted in everyday lives. It should answer their questions and give them enough courage to face opposition and persecution.

So, far in the Indian Pentecostal setting, no Christological articulation has appeared, or no conscious effort has been made, to form a Christology. As Pentecostalism is growing fast among the poor, it is imperative to consider the Christological articulation of the common believers to find out what it looks like. Therefore, in the following pages we shall look into the ordinary Pentecostal Christology within the Indian context.

Chapter 5

Indian Pentecostal Christology

This chapter will explore ordinary Indian Pentecostal Christology as it emerges from the experiences of ordinary Pentecostals in India. Before we start, we need to address certain key questions: who are the people we will be examining and what contextual experiences have they gone through? How far do their experiences shape and give content to their Christology? Does the Christology they cherish make any differences to their lives? The majority of Pentecostals belong to the lowest strata of the Indian society and, therefore, this Christology is essentially an ordinary people's Christology. The Christology I will be describing here is certainly a 'Christology from below,' because it stems directly from the convictions of ordinary members who seek to follow Christ intimately, without any assistance from external agencies.

In North India, it is Tribal and Dalit members who form the majority of Pentecostals while a tiny minority are from Hindu religious backgrounds.[1] We also find a few South Indian Pentecostals and North Indian Christians who embraced Pentecostalism. Along with them, a sizeable number of Pentecostals belong to the South Indian states. Majority of the Pentecostals from the state of Kerala joined the Pentecostal movement from the Syrian Christian churches and

[1] According to Philip Jenkins the Dalits represent 90% of the membership of Protestant churches in India; Philip Jenkins, *The Next Christendom: The Coming of Global Christianity* (Oxford: Oxford University Press, 2002), 183-184. The actual condition of Tribals and Dalits has been discussed in Chapter 3. In the case of Pentecostalism in North India more than 90% of the Pentecostals are from Tribal and Dalit backdrop. The membership of all the major and smaller denominations in North India has similar constituents. They have a similar membership pattern, either in a single church or different churches for these three groups in the same locality.

many are second or third generation Pentecostals. Further, there are Pentecostals from Dalit background. Similarly, a large group of Pentecostals are found in the state of Tamil Nadu and Andhra Pradesh who has been embraced the Pentecostal spirituality from other Christian denominations, various religious and ethnic context and Dalit background. Some Pentecostals from these states also come from Hindu religious settings and their former beliefs and understandings are similar to the ideas expressed in 'Christologies from religious perspectives' in Chapter four.

With this background information we shall start the discussion of the Christological ideas held by the believers from such contexts and how they face the above-mentioned daily challenges. The ideas that emerged are very intimate and subjective in nature and often overlap; however, similar themes recur, again and again, in all the places where studies have been conducted whether it is in urban or rural settings; whether adherents are educated or illiterate.

The geographical locations, the difference in languages or the people-group members belong to, as it has surfaced in the research, rarely affected the Christological understanding people developed. Presumably the reason is in most of the Indian subcontinent, except south India (especially Kerala and Chennai in Tamil Nadu and in urban centres), Pentecostals live under similar circumstances. Therefore, it is not surprising that their ideas of Christ reveal identical thematic conclusions. The only difference we find is a slightly variant understanding held by second or third generation South Indian Pentecostals (even their views ultimately identical in most of the themes) which I shall attempt to include while discussing the Christological themes.

Besides, the Pentecostal movement's revival phenomena have contributed greatly to its Christology. It is obvious from the Pentecostal outlook on spirituality and of the world around them; these beliefs kept re-appearing in the interviews and focus groups. In the revivals, healings, exorcisms and miraculous feats were common and those experiences they cherish and bring to life even today.[2] The revival fervour is still alive and active in worship services, as well as in their private lives. This revival consciousness highly contributed to the theology they hold, especially as regards Christology and also Ethics. It is deeply ingrained in the Christological themes that have emerged during the study and active in their everyday spirituality. Several remarkable themes have emerged from the analysis of the data which overlap in their content and emphasis. We cannot draw rigid boundaries between these themes, however, they differ in their emphasis on various aspects of Christology. The following are some of the dominant themes.

[2] Shaibu Abraham, *The History of the Pentecostal Movement in North India: Unfolding its Social and Theological Contexts* (New Delhi: Christian World Imprints, 2017).

5.1 Jesus the Healer

One of the predominant themes of the Christology that emerged from research among the ordinary Pentecostals is the notion of Jesus as the healer. This is the primary level of Christological articulation and it forms the very basis of the Christological edifice of ordinary Pentecostals. As we already have explained, healthcare facilities are scant, as well as in disarray in remote villages and a large majority suffer from various illnesses while hundreds die every year. Besides, lack of financial resources, widespread poverty and inadequate transportation facilities have adversely affected the chances of healing even ordinary diseases. Obviously, it is not surprising that people understand Jesus as the divine healer. Many of the interviewees testified that they had experienced Christ and accepted him through the healing they had experienced. This is also a major reason why most of the people joined Pentecostal churches.[3] We need to remember that even when they seek medical help from physicians available in villages, in many cases, this results in the draining of their hard-earned resources. In practice, they may not even get the results they desire. In some cases even if a medical doctor is appointed to a Public Health Centre (PHC), either the doctor may not be available or the centre may not have any medicines to dispense to these poor people.[4] There are private practitioners, but several of them are either 'quacks' or extort money from the poor villagers.[5]

For instance, one of the persons interviewed, who also serves as a lay evangelist in inner villages says:

> My son was gravely ill in his childhood. As usual in the village, I consulted the *bhopa* and he said that the illness was due to the displeasure of an ancestor's spirit. I spent a good sum of money on sacrifices and rituals... yet the situation was getting worse day by day...Then I took my child to the city hospital which is 25 miles away...We spent a large sum of money on medicines and other things. Later I had to sell a portion of my land to pay off the debt incurred by the treatment...We had almost given up our hope of getting back our son. Then someone spoke about a Christian who would pray for the sick people. We were desperate and took the child to the church. The pastor said that Jesus could heal the child, if I could believe. Then the pastor put his hand upon the boy and prayed in the name of Jesus (*yishu ka naam me*). The boy showed some response and within a week he was totally healed.[6]

---

[3] Emma, Interview by author, Udaipur, India, 15 September 2009.

[4] Mathai, Focus Group Interview, Hebron Church, Rajasthan, 9 August 2009.

[5] Banerjee, Deaton & Duflo, 'Health Care Delivery'; Acharya & Ranson, 'Health Care Financing for the Poor.'

[6] Babu, Interview by author, Rajasthan, 5 July 2009.

According to him, having experienced this healing, he decided to become a member of the Pentecostal congregation where the healing took place. Later, with help of the pastor, he has started a church in his own village and also evangelises nearby villages.[7]

Another example of healing in which the recipient is more than convinced that healing comes in the name of Jesus and declares that Jesus is the healer and the only God. Shanti, who was miraculously healed of a blood issue (which is a widespread problem among Tribal women), testifies:

> I was suffering acutely from a blood condition...We approached the village *bhopa*, however, he was not able to heal me. Later we consulted a more powerful *bhopa*.[8] Even though for a week I got some relief, later the problem began to increase. Later I was taken to the Primary Health Centre and the doctor prescribed me medicines. Whenever I took medicines, it was eased, but later it would come back again. I was totally devastated. I was not able to work or do the household chores. My children began to go to school hungry. My husband had to toil day and night to make ends meet. Later I was bed-ridden and only with the help of someone could I get up. I was in a miserable condition (she cries). Then one of my distant relatives told me about the church and prayer for the sick people there. My husband took me to the church on a Sunday. The pastor shared with me the story of Jesus and the healing power of Jesus. I put my trust on Jesus for healing. The pastor and the believers together prayed for me and, suddenly, I felt something like lightening passing through my body. At that moment I realised that I had been healed; praise the Lord (she seems to be emotional and raises the voice)...Jesus is the real healer (*yishu such much me chanka denawala hai*) and he is our God.[9]

The incident is reminiscent of the Gospel story of the healing of the woman with 'issue of blood' by Jesus (Matt. 9:20-22; Mk.5:25-34). Such healings not only have an impact on the person who has been healed, but also the people around them. They themselves are also attracted to the healing power of Jesus and join the Pentecostal churches. According to an evangelist, the attitude of the people is 'first miracle, then worship' (*pahle chamatkar, phir namaskar*).[10]

Some people acknowledge that there are many such testimonies of healing taking place through the work of evangelists and even ordinary members, which

---

[7] Babu, interview, Rajasthan, 5 July 2009.

[8] She said that the *bhopa* had performed certain *pooja* and also sacrificed a cockerel. He considered the disease to be the displeasure of *bavazi mata* and also assured her that the problem would be over very soon as the anger of *mataji* had been placated.

[9] Shanti, Interview by author, Hebron Church, Rajasthan, Udaipur, Rajasthan, 28 July 2009.

[10] Biju, Focus Group Interview, Hebron Church, Rajasthan, 9 August 2009.

change the lives of the people. One pastor said: 'Church is like a hospital; many people come and get the healing and go back.'[11] See another example of the same nature from the mission field of the state of Orissa reported by *Cross & Crown* magazine:

> Evangelist Elias Digal from Lakoti church informed of the healing testimony of a lady who was suffering from a blood condition for a long time. She was fed up with medications and tried traditional religious practices, which in turn also proved futile. She spent lot of money and was totally disappointed. Three months back, one of her neighbours who is a believer guided her to church and there she came to know Jesus the healer. She requested prayer from the pastor and believers of the church for her healing. On that day the saints prayed earnestly for that expectant lady that she could receive her miraculous healing. Now she is the happiest one to attend the church with all her dear ones in her family as they all repented, believed and were baptised in the water to join the body of Christ.[12]

Some of the people who had received bodily healing not only joined Pentecostal churches, but began to involve themselves in the healing activities among the villagers. The story of Pastor Mathew, who had been bed-ridden due to paralysis for two years and tried both traditional healing methods and medical help in the city is the best example, he narrates:

> Not having any result, I was taken back to my village and just left in bed forever. For two years I was bed-ridden. I thought that my life had come to an end and I had given up any hope of recovery. However, someone told me that there was a pastor (*padri*) who would pray for the sick ... I never knew about Jesus Christ or healing in the name of Jesus. The pastor narrated the story of Jesus, how he healed paralysed man in the Gospel...The pastor prayed over me. Although, my body did not feel anything, my mind became calm and peaceful for the first time ... Day by day my condition began to change, within two weeks I was able to sit on my bed. When the recovery was fast enough, I could walk within one month. I was convinced that Jesus is true Lord and healer of all diseases. I had decided to serve this great Lord who is able to do great things. Now Jesus is doing many miracles of healing and exorcism through me.[13]

---

[11] Ponnachan, Focus Group Interview, Tabor Church, Gujarat, 6 September 2009.

[12] Editor, 'From our Mission Field: Report from Orissa,' *Cross & Crown* (September-October 2001):13.

[13] Mathew, Focus Group Interview, Tabor Church, Gujarat, 23 August 2009.

According to him, people are coming to the church through miraculous healings, even though there is intense opposition from extreme religious elements.[14] Such healing miracles are even noted by secular academicians. Ghanshyam Shah, professor of Social Science at Jawaharlal Nehru University, New Delhi, accounts for healing as the main reason for Tribals to accept Christianity. He writes:

> There are various reasons, as given by them, for accepting Christianity. The most common reasons are curing of diseases, relief from tension related to day-to-day problems, faith in prayer which helped them in their personal crises, particularly recovery from illness.[15]

Then he quotes a testimony:

> "I was sick and tried 'Bhuva-Bhagat' [traditional healers] but could not get relief. My neighbour, who is a Christian, suggested to me to meet the 'Padari' [priest] and ask him to offer a prayer for my recovery. I knew the Padari as he used to visit us. I told him about my illness. He asked me to join him for the prayer and I began to feel better. From that day I attended prayers regularly and later became 'Cristi' [Christian]."[16]

Similarly, David Hardiman of the University of Warwick, U.K. who conducted a study of healing among the Tribals of Gujarat claims that he too collected testimonies of Pentecostal 'faith healing'; he says, '...we managed to meet some of them [the Pentecostals] and attend their meetings for worship in the Dangs, in 2005, that incorporated healing testimonies ('sakshi').'[17] He further adds, 'Faith healing by bodies such as the Pentecostalists has come to the fore in recent years, as much in the rich countries of the West, as in the poor and underdeveloped tribal belts of India.'[18]

This is true in South India, even in Kerala state. Having conducted a field research among Syrian and Dalit Pentecostals in Kerala, P. G. Abraham shows that the participants testified that the majority of them had 'physical problems in their life' and joined Pentecostal churches because of 'deliverance of their troubles' and

---

[14] Mathew, Focus Group Interview, Tabor Church, Gujarat, 23 August 2009.

[15] Shah, 'Conversion, Reconversion and the State,' 315, http://epw.in/epw/uploads/articles/8620. pdf (accessed 2 May 2010).

[16] Shah, 'Conversion, Reconversion and the State,' 315.

[17] David Hardiman & Gauri Raje, 'Practices of Healing in Tribal Gujarat,' *EPW* (1 March 2008): 49; also see David Hardiman, 'Healing, Medical Power and the Poor: Contests in Tribal India,' *EPW* (21 April 2007): 1405-06.

[18] Hardiman, 'Healing, Medical Power and the Poor,' 1406.

'healing experience.'[19] Similarly, Siga Arles, a distinguished Indian missiologist, speaking about the Pentecostal churches in Karnataka (Kolar Gold Field), also highlights that the 'power of healing' attracts both Christians and non-Christians into Pentecostal churches.[20]

Interestingly, when anything happens in villages, people first approach traditional healers and when this fails they turn to medical help, and eventually approach pastors. However, in small towns, and sometimes in cities, a reverse trend is visible. First, people take medical help; when treatments do not yield the desired results, people consult mediums and resort to traditional religious practices and other means. When all these fail, they come to Christians because they believe that medicine is not working due to infestation of malevolent spirits. In towns and cities there are fake *sadhus* and god-men who take advantage of these innocent miserable people.[21]

Another interesting fact which is noteworthy is that not only does the healing occur before the conversion experience, but also even as believers, people come to depend on divine healing, in the name of Jesus. There are several testimonies in this regard. Listen to Jessy who has experienced the miraculous healing of a cyst in her ovary:

> Last year I had developed a cyst in my stomach [later it was known from her husband that it was an ovarian cyst]. It caused intense pain and I could not work or sleep. I was taken to hospital and doctors recommended surgery. However, I needed a big sum of money. It was difficult for us to raise such an amount. I was not able to work and the wages earned by my husband were only enough for daily expenses of the family. It was beyond our capacity. Therefore, we began to pray. The matter was put before the congregation and the pastor earnestly prayed for me. To our surprise within two weeks the cyst disappeared completely. I know that God loves me and heals his children.[22]

She swears that Jesus' healing power is available even today and he can heal any diseases.[23] It is a usual scene in village churches for people to come with bottles of oil and even water to be prayed over by pastors to be used for their

---

[19] He conducted the study to understand the caste discrimination among various Pentecostal denominations; P.G. Abraham, *Caste and Christianity: A Pentecostal Perspective* (Kumbhaza, Kerala: Crown Books, 2003), 116-118; He notes the response of the people: '1. I have experienced God's deliverance in my trouble. 2. I have experienced God's healing power in my sickness. 3. God had delivered me from devilish attack.'

[20] Siga Arles, 'Indigenous Pentecostal Church Growth at KGF (Kolar Gold Field), Karnataka,' in *Christianity is Indian*, 392-393, 395.

[21] Thomas, Interview by author, Udaipur, 8 July 2009.

[22] Jessy, Interview by Author, Tabor Church, Gujarat, 5 September 2009.

[23] Jessy, Interview, Tabor Church, Gujarat, 5 September 2009.

illness. The believers have strong faith in the efficacy of prayer. So, what they sing in a folksong tune within the worship context is true:

> In the name of Jesus, there is healing (*shifa*)
> See and read in the word of God
> In the name of Jesus, the power of illness is nullified
> Jesus has shed his blood, he saved us
> Jesus healed us of our entire sickness
> See and read in the word of God.[24]

Jesus as the healer is a prominent theme in worship songs; there are several songs in circulation.[25] It is also interesting to see that most of the pastors and evangelists in the village settings use Gospel stories for their preaching, which expound the themes which we discuss in this Chapter.

Some people have testified that they were not immediately healed, although they attended a Pentecostal church. However, they are convinced that Jesus is able to give enough grace to sustain their sickness. Above all, they feel the joy and presence of God.[26] Some respondents, who are third generation Pentecostals, do not consider Jesus to be a healer as the most important aspect of Christology, even though they believe in miraculous healing.[27] They usually seek medical help along with prayer when they are sick.[28] It is to be noted that there is no restriction in using medicines or consulting doctors in Pentecostal churches.

For ordinary believers the healing episode is not merely physical recovery or being healthy. Instead, the divine healing affects the totality of their life: physical, social, economic and spiritual. From the interviews, it is apparent that when a person is sick, it affects the net income of the family as one is not able to work.[29] Therefore being healthy or being delivered from sickness is all-round well-being and peace of mind. In the case of the illness of women, it means that children are not being adequately looked after and other household chores are not attended to. The cattle and the little cultivation they own are usually affected negatively.[30] Thus, healing of the body contributes the wholistic development of a person and his/her family.

---

[24] Participant Observation, Hebron Church, Rajasthan, 26 July 2009.

[25] Song of Fellowship (Udaipur, India: Filadelfia Bible College, 2005).

[26] Jerry, Interview by author, Kolenchery, Kerala, 26 June 2009; Adarsh, Interview by author, Chennai, 2 July 2009.

[27] Moncy, Focus Group Interview, Udaipur, 12 July 2009.

[28] Saji, Focus Group Interview, Udaipur, 12 July 2009; for these people Jesus as saviour and God are the most important aspects of Christology.

Shanti, Interview, Hebron Church, Rajasthan, 28 July 2009.

[29] Shanti, Interview, Hebron Church, Rajasthan, 28 July 2009.

[30] See Shanti, Interview, Hebron Church, Rajasthan, 28 July 2009; also Rosamma, Interview by author, Hebron Church, Rajasthan, 5 August 2009.

Furthermore, as Jessy said, healing is a definite proof that God loves them and takes care of them.[31] This understanding inculcates a new confidence in them: that they are someone special in the mind of God. This confidence, in turn, enables them to take 'a giant leap of faith' in the spiritual sphere and a renewed perception of themselves in society. When a person is convinced of the love and constant presence of God, he/she is able to overcome many of the nagging problems and obstacles which stand in the way of their progress whether it is financial, social, cultural, spiritual or personal. This new outlook situates a person in a higher pedestal and brings an attitudinal as well as a character change, which in turn results in a positive self-image and better perception of the realities surrounding the person.[32] Heredia, writing in *Economic and Political Weekly* agrees: 'For the convert, conversion at this level involves a change of worldview, of the root paradigm, the foundational myth of a people's religious tradition.'[33] Arles also comments, 'Karl Marx saw religion as the opium of the masses, but in Pentecostal churches there is an efficient use of religion for building a self-image for the poor.'[34]

Divine healing also enables a person to reject the old religious practices as well as fear of malevolent spirits and exploitation of traditional healers.[35] Now, they are no more under those intimidating and enslaving powers; some are even now empowered to heal others. Therefore, it is a spiritual liberation too. Moreover, this makes a difference to their social standing. Even today, being sick in a village society is considered as a misnomer and bad omen. When one is miraculously healed, the esteem and social standing in the community is enhanced. Breman, from the Amsterdam School for Social Science Research, when commenting on healing among Tribals, argued that such healings satisfy a continuing desire for community-based healing. He comments that the popularity of healing dramas performed by evangelical Christians should be understood in collective terms.[36] Thus, it has social implication too.

The healing is enacted by the power of the Holy Spirit and it is considered to be the direct intervention of the Spirit. It is through the work of the Spirit that healing takes place. It is considered to be the gift of the Spirit.[37] Thus, what

---

[31] Jessy, Interview, Tabor Church, Gujarat, 5 September 2009.

[32] Mani, Focus Group Interview, Hebron Church, Rajasthan, 2 August 2009.

[33] Rudolf C. Heredia, 'No Entry, No Exit: Savarna Aversion towards Dalit Conversion,' *EPW* (9 October 2004), 4546; also see his *Changing Gods: Rethinking Conversion in India* (New Delhi: Penguin Books, 2007).

[34] Arles, 'Indigenous Pentecostal Church Growth at KGF,' 395.

[35] Joel, Interview, Maharashtra, 2 September 2009.

[36] See Hardiman, 'Healing, Medical Power and the Poor.'

[37] Joel, Interview, Maharashtra, 2 September 2009; Mani, Focus Group Interview, Hebron Church, Rajasthan, 2 August 2009.

German Theologian Adolf von Harnack commented for Christianity is true for Indian Pentecostalism; it is 'a religion for the sick.'[38]

5.2 Jesus the Exorcist

Another dominant Christological theme appeared in the study is the understanding of Jesus as the exorcist. As with Jesus the healer, this theme is a primary level of Christological articulation. There are plenty of testimonies related to people being delivered from demonic possessions and the attack of malevolent spirits. According to villagers, many diseases are caused by spirit attack or perpetuated by evil practices.[39] An attack from wicked spirits can have severe repercussions and can be life-threatening.[40] Listen to the ordeal Yeshudas had gone through and how he was miraculously rescued from the attack of evil spirits:

> My father was the *bhopa* of my village ... Everything was fine until my father's death. After a month of my father's death, suddenly four of my sisters and mother fell ill in consecutive days. Their bodies were swollen and unable to pass urine. I realised that it was the attack of the spirits that were to be placated because no sacrifices had been offered after my father's death. In panic I began to run pillar to post, consulting other *bhopas* and *tantriks* but to no avail. After few days my wife, who was pregnant then, also fell ill. It was a shock to me. I brought a powerful *bhopa* from a different village but he could not do anything. We spent lot of money... After a week I became ill with the same symptoms. All of my body was swollen and aching and I was unable to eat anything or pass urine. I was also bed-ridden and unconscious for some time.
>
> One of my relatives, who was married off to a different village came to know about it; she was a believer. Knowing our condition, she came with her pastor. He prayed over me and in the name of Jesus rebuked the power of evil spirits. From that moment onward all of us began to feel better and within a few days we received complete release from the attack of the spirits. Now I know that Jesus is all powerful, greater than all other gods. He can do everything; he has power over every spirit. I will only worship him.[41]

Within the context of the focus group, some people also shared their experiences of spirit attack and the deliverance they have received in the name of Jesus. Moreover, the discussion mostly revolved around the power of Jesus to

---

[38] R.A.N. Kydd, 'Healing in the Christian Church,' *NIDPCM,* 698.

[39] See the beginning of this chapter.

[40] Mani, Focus Group Interview, Hebron Church, Rajasthan, 2 August 2009.

[41] Yeshu Das, Interview, Hebron Church, Rajasthan, 5 August 2009.

rescue from the evil influence of wicked spirits as well as witch-doctors.[42] These people experienced the delivering power of Jesus in their life and now they do not fear any demonic spirits or traditional religious practices. For example, a participant narrates his testimony of freedom from an evil spell:

> My first wife became ill and it turned out that she was infested with an evil spirit. I employed the services of the village *bhopa* and he had said that she was possessed by *hingotri mata*. I spent a large sum of money on sacrifices and other rituals; however, these could not save her. My wife and a four year old daughter died together. After a year I re-married. However, my wife was also attacked by evil spirits. Some people advised me that it was the work of some evil people, so I should go to the church and I would be delivered. Then I asked, 'what is church?' I did not know what church was. Then with my wife I came to the church. The pastor prayed for me and we got release from the torment of evil powers. Now it has been ten years and I have three children and we don't have any fear of spirits. Jesus is more powerful than all the spirits. I submit everything to God.[43]

In the focus group, participants claimed that many people in the inner villages are either affected by the attack of spirits or live fearfully.[44] People believe that these are the works of wicked spirits. Traditional healers first ask for a cockerel to sacrifice; if there is no relief, after seven days a goat is sacrificed. They also use alcohol, incense-sticks and other materials to either please the spirits or ward them off. A cockerel, even in the village will cost Rs. 250-300, and a goat more than Rs. 2000. Moreover, *bhopa* also may demand big amounts like Rs. 1,000-5,000. They claim that they can deliver the villagers from the spirits. When poor villagers fail to get any result through traditional religious practices, or dangerous events happen, as a last resort only they will approach pastors for their rescue. Many of the members who attend the churches share such incidents.[45] They also hand down their testimonies to the suffering people. This has resulted in a rapid growth of Pentecostalism among the poor villagers.[46] The *Economic and Political Weekly*, for instance, undergirds this fact. Commenting on the reasons why Oraons, a group in Orissa, accept Christianity, Pati says:

---

[42] Focus Group, Hebron Church, Rajasthan, 9 August 2009.

[43] Yohannan, Focus Group Interview, Hebron Church, Rajasthan, 9 August 2009.

[44] Focus Group Interview, Hebron Church, Rajasthan, 9 August 2009.

[45] Mathai, Focus Group Interview, Hebron Church, Rajasthan, 9 August 2009.

[46] Kuttappan, Focus Group Interview, Hebron Church, Rajasthan, 9 August 2009.

> In a context of uncertainties and insecurities the Oraons, for example, felt that Christianity protected them from the witches and 'bhoots', who were powerless against this system.[47]

In another incident, the children fell prey to curse and attack from wicked spirits. Parsing Baria, an evangelist of the Filadelfia Church in the Panchmahal district in Gujarat speaks about the miraculous recovery of a family:

> ...the Lord told me to go to a family that was being tormented with sickness and consistent deaths. Four children in that family had died following which even the cattle began to fall prey. The entire household moved to another locality to escape the curse, but the curse followed. Much prayer was done and the Lord through a miracle restored to them what they had lost over the years.[48]

Pastor Kuttappan narrated an incident of miraculous recovery of a young man who was insane for some years, as a result of his ministry. According to Kuttappan, the man used to wander in the forest and village with a sword. Due to his fear that his son would harm others, the father told the villagers that they might kill him if he harmed anybody. One evening people of the village came to kill him. However, his wife did not allow it.

The next day his sister, who was staying near Kuttappan's house, approached and requested whether he could heal him. This woman had seen that people prayed for deliverance. Then the man was brought to his home, hands tied. Kuttappan kept him in his home, providing food and everything for a month. Meanwhile he was constantly prayed by Kuttappan and the church there. Now he is completely healed and has been undergoing Bible training and is involved in evangelism. According to Kuttappan, due to this deliverance many people from the village joined the church.[49] It is remarkable that Pentecostal churches act as a refuge for tormented people. As Abraham has shown, even in Kerala (the state with 100% literacy rate), where we find third or fourth generation Pentecostals, a good number of new adherents were delivered from evil spirits and joined Pentecostal churches.[50]

Another interesting fact came out in the research is that very often the attack of malevolent spirits results in paralysis. Hear the story of a married woman narrated by her husband:

> My wife was troubled by evil spirits from her childhood. Even after the marriage they used to torment her, make her fall down and wound her

[47] Biswamoy, Pati, 'Identity, Hegemony, Resistance: Conversions in Orissa, 1800-2000,' *EPW* (3 November 2001), 4204.

[48] No Author, 'Field News,' *Cross & Crown* 26/6 (August-September 1996): 21.

[49] Kuttappan, Focus Group Interview, Hebron Church, Rajasthan, 9 August 2009.

[50] Abraham, *Caste and Christianity*, 116, 118.

> and sometimes make her unconscious. Later she was paralysed in one of her legs and became bed-ridden. We spent lot of money for traditional religious practices [He is a truck driver and earns good money]. All of my income would go towards traditional religious practices and treatment but without any results. However, somebody introduced me to the pastor and he prayed for her; she got some relief. Then she continued to attend the church and now she is totally healed.[51]

People not only suffer from the direct attack of evil spirits, but there are many instances of the use of wicked spirits by witch-doctors to extract money and torment gullible people. Merchand Masih, an evangelist narrates:

> A certain witch-doctor cast a spell on a simple villager and in the process, took nine hundred rupees from him. The man came seeking salvation in the church... When the people of God pray, something in the spirit realm happens. The villager got healed and the witch-doctor came and returned the money to him. This was an instant answer to prayer. This was enough to convince the man and several others to accept the Lord as their saviour.[52]

According to *Cross & Crown* magazine the influence of the person of Jesus is so powerful among the villagers that some powerful village-healers (*bhopa*) became pastors to deliver many from evil influences.[53] The story of Kesabhai, who was a highly placed *bhopa* around his locality, is an example. He was the chief sorcerer and villagers approached him, whenever ill fate and sickness fell upon them. But a day came when Kesabhai's own three year old son fell ill. He spared no magical devices he knew and practised for others, but in vain. When the villagers came to know about the death of his son, they said, 'the evil spirits whom he worshipped have snatched his child because they are displeased'. No sooner had he recovered from the trauma of the loss of his son than his only surviving child, his seven month old daughter was struck with jaundice.

It dawned on Kesabhai that, if traditional methods could not save his son, they couldn't work for his daughter. He took her to the Primary Health Centre where he met an old man named Vakta. Vakta explained the real healing power of Jesus to this 'healer'. Both of them met Pastor Tajendra Masih in Pai village, who shared the Gospel with him and prayed for the child. It is claimed in the magazine that within three days the child was healed. Moreover, it is also testified that he

---

[51] Reji, Focus Group Interview, Hebron Church, Rajasthan, 9 August 2009.

[52] No Author, 'Field News,' *Cross & Crown* 26/6 (August-September 1996): 20.

[53] C&C Reporter, 'Field News: How do we Plant a Church in Remote Villages?,' *Cross & Crown* 26/7 (January-February 1997): 2-5.

then became a Pentecostal and, through him, many were healed and delivered from evil spirits.[54]

For ordinary villagers being freed from the fear of malevolent spirits as well as liberation from spirit possession is more than a life regained. They live in constant fear of the supernatural and this fear affects all their activities. Just as we discussed when addressing divine healing, the deliverance in the spirit realm positively affects the people's social, economic and spiritual domains; the spirit infestation breaks their financial security, their physical as well as their mental well-being.[55]

In the testimonies of the participants, deliverance brings a new awareness of the spiritual world. Earlier, the worldview was infested with dread of spirits and enslavement to them; always trying to appease them. However, deliverance removes their fear of demonic activities and fear is turned into safety and joy. It is the peace of mind and body which rules in them after they receive deliverance in the name of Jesus.[56] Earlier, even if they may get respite, nothing guarantees the uninterrupted security and protection from these evil powers, who can return and trouble them. Bauman's description also tallies with this understanding. These people are obsessed with 'performance of daily rituals, the *ad hoc* utilization of amulets and charms, and the protective repetition of *mantras*.'[57] Thus, deliverance in the name of Jesus assures them a long-lasting safeguard from the demonic powers.[58]

Further, exorcism enacted in the name of Jesus is totally free of cost and it does not impinge their financial security. Pastors or members conduct exorcism without any rituals or chants. This raises a new consciousness: that satanic forces come to steal their financial resources (John 10:10). According to Dasan, the 'power encounter' with Christ, in which Tribals are healed, expelled the evil spirits that were blighting their lives, reformed their morals and ethics, broke the hold of the *bhagats*, and allowed them to stand up to the shopkeepers who exploited them.[59]

Later, believers are taught that they can also cast out demons in the name of Jesus. As one person explained, this understanding makes a huge shift in their worldview; they realise that they have control over evil spirits which have been torment-

---

[54] C&C Reporter, 'Field News,' 2-5.

[55] Focus group, Tabor Church, Gujarat, 23 August 2009; Focus group, Hebron Church, Rajasthan, 9 August 2009.

[56] Joel, Interview, Maharashtra, 2 September 2009.

[57] Bauman, *Christian Identity and Dalit Religion*, 40.

[58] See Yohannan, Focus Group Interview, Hebron Church, Rajasthan, 16 August 2009; Focus Group Interview, Hebron Church, Rajasthan, 9 August 2009.

[59] Ebenezer D. Dasan, 'Conversion and Persecution in South Gujarat,' in *Conversion in a Pluralistic Context: Perspectives and Context,* edited by Krickwin C. Marak & Plamthodathil S. Jacob (Delhi: ISPCK, 2000), 161-164.

ing them and proceed to rescue others from the clutches of tyranny. For example, Pastor Mathew claims that he has a special anointing to cast out demons.[60] The ordinary adherents come to know that through prayer and faith now they can counter the evil forces. Hardiman agrees with it, 'There is a strong emphasis on the healing of all maladies and sicknesses through the power of faith alone. They consider that malign forces cause ill health, and that these forces can be countered through prayer and faith.'[61] This brings spiritual empowerment and leads to what we call 'spiritual warfare' which is carried out as an everyday affair one where no specialists are needed. Additionally, as in the case of healing, the act of exorcism is also carried out in the power of the Spirit. Here the work of the Spirit is paramount to obtain the desired outcome.

This also results in a lofty understanding of the supremacy of Christ: he is more powerful than any other god. Besides, unlike their old deities which may get angry now and then, he is kind enough to deliver them from suffering and ready to keep them safe forever. He does not ask for any sacrifices. This perception leads them to the positive affirmation of the uniqueness of Christ over every other god they know. Eventually, they are not hesitant to proclaim that Jesus is the only God. Nevertheless, what we need to emphasise here is, that this does not happen by the rational articulation of arguments and counter arguments. Even this understanding does not come from a thoroughly Bible-based divinity and greatness of Christ. But it emerges out of their life experiences of Jesus' pervasive power over all gods. For they have knocked on every door they are aware of but with no results. Therefore, they do not debate to prove the uniqueness and supremacy of Christ; rather, they relate this idea to their experiences and persuade listeners to accept the lordship of Christ. This method is used in evangelism and mission. Evangelist Mathew said that he would approach people who were sick and troubled by demonic spirits and then narrate his own testimony and stories from the Bible. Then he would pray for the people in the name of Jesus.[62]

However, as in the case of healing, those respondents from city contexts and third-generation Pentecostals do not give much importance to exorcism. One has testified that she has seen exorcisms but believes that evil spirits affect those who worship satanic forces. For her Jesus is above every power and he protects his children.[63]

5.3 Jesus the Provider

Just as Jesus is the healer and the exorcist, another overarching theme that surfaced from the study is the notion that Jesus is the provider. This notion forms

---

[60] Mathew, Focus Group Interview, Tabor Church, Gujarat, 23 August 2009.

[61] David Hardiman & Gauri Raje, 'Practices of Healing in Tribal Gujarat,' *EPW* (1 March 2008): 49.

[62] Mathew, Focus Group Interview, Tabor Church, Gujarat, 23 August 2009.

[63] Jolly, Interview by author, Udaipur, 10 July 2009.

the second level of Christological affirmation which is drawn out of Jesus as the healer and exorcist. Concurrently, for some, Christological articulation begins with this theme. The curing of illness and miraculous rescue from demonic forces in the name of Jesus instils a new spiritual consciousness among the suffering people. Now they place their full confidence in the all-encompassing, all-powerful work of Jesus in all of their activities.[64] Their newfound experience widens the spiritual perception of the work of Jesus into other realms of their struggle, namely economic, social and household realms. 'He gives us blessings and prosperity freely,' asserts Yeshudas.[65] Jesus who has healed and freed them from the disintegrating powers is also able to provide them and liberate them from the rampant poverty they face. Reji says, 'After we became believers, we are better off people. God blessed us in every area of life: in cultivation, our animals and our works. Jesus gives us whatever we ask.'[66] That is, the notion that Jesus is a provider stems from the notions of Jesus as healer and exorcist. Nevertheless, for some people, the Christological perception starts with the notion of Jesus as provider for they were under debt and financial struggle, but after joining a Pentecostal church, their financial condition improved.[67]

This understanding of Jesus as provider in their mundane, hard and struggling life dawns a new epoch of hope and confidence.[68] Now they muster enough courage and strength to face the stark realties around them. Again, it is not a vain confidence or wishful thinking but an experience of miraculous provisions they are able to testify about in the worship context as well as in daily life.[69] Their condition explained in the chapter on the Indian context undergirds the significance of this Christological theme. Many of them were spending most of their meagre resources either for traditional religious practices or medical treatments and had come to a stage where they were burdened by debt and poverty. The options before them were either to borrow money from someone, or sell their property or to end their life. There are many men in villages who end their lives due to debt crisis and poverty, leaving behind women and children to mend their own lives.[70]

However, the healing and deliverance experience enables them to save their hard-earned resources to provide for life needs. The standard of living is enhanced: better food, clothing and new facilities at home bring a new sense of empowerment

[64] Wilson, Focus Group Interview, Hebron Church, Rajasthan, 16 August 2009; Raju, Focus Group Interview, Hebron Church, Rajasthan, 16 August 2009.

[65] Yeshudas, Interview, Hebron Church, Rajasthan, 9 August 2009.

[66] Reji, Focus Group Interview, Hebron Church, Rajasthan, 16 August 2009.

[67] Prince, Interview by author, Kolenchery, 28 June 2009.

[68] Papachan, Focus Group Interview, Hebron Church, Rajasthan, 16 August 2009.

[69] Testimony, Participant Observation, Udaipur; 19 July 2009; Pylee, Focus Group Interview, Udaipur, 26 July 2009.

[70] Blessen, Focus Group Interview, Tabor Church, Gujarat, 30 August 2009.

in them, as well as in the opinion of others.[71] There are several testimonies about the financial prosperity ordinary believers experience after conversion. At the end of the sessions on healing and exorcism testimonies, interviewees underlined this fact.

For instance, evangelist Babu testifies to the changes that occurred after conversion. He says, 'I had spent a huge amount of money on traditional religious practices and medical expenses for the treatment of my son. At the end, because of the debt, I had to sell my ancestral land.'[72] According to him, however, things began to change for the better after the healing of his son. The money they used to spend in traditional religious practices and treatment began to be used to supply them with better food and household needs. He continues:

> ...God blessed us greatly. Later I bought a buffalo and started cultivating the land remained with me. God helped our buffalo to produce good amount of milk. In the cultivation also there was a good yield. Then I brought one more buffalo. This is all by the grace of God (*sab prabhu ka anugrah hai*)...[73]

As he described in his story, it transpired that, after joining the church, his outlook began to change from a pessimism to enthusiasm. He worked hard and began to put all his problems before the Lord. He said that he experienced the providing hand of Jesus. 'Within four years I could buy back my land, although I had to pay more than what I received,' says Babu, 'it is only because of the grace of Jesus, not my ability'. Now he has a good house and his son is ready to join Bible training.[74]

Another person also testified in a similar vein. Thomas, who is an *ayurvedic* doctor with the state government hospital, gave a similar testimony:

> My wife was sick for a long time; she had stomach pain. We had taken her to best doctors available but there was no improvement. We had to spend minimum Rs. 3,000-4,000 every month on her treatment, doing sonography, X-ray and many other medical tests but the doctors could not find any problems in her. We were really fed up with her illness. It continued for three years. In 2004, someone introduced us to an evangelist and he prayed for her and she was healed. However, after one month the problem began to re-appear.[75] Again we started spending

[71] Thomas, Interview by author, Udaipur, 8 July 2009.

[72] Babu, Interview, Rajasthan, 5 July 2009.

[73] Ibid.

[74] Ibid.

[75] He says, 'We could not understand it and, moreover, we have never bothered to see how through prayer she was healed and there was no Christian fellowship. We lived in our old habits. We thought that the occurrence of the illness was natural.'

> money on her and it became routine in our life to spend minimum Rs. 2,000-4,000 every month. It continued for a time...With medicines and spending money there was no respite. Later I became also sick, always feeling tired and burdened.[76]

According to him, all this had started twenty years ago, because of evil religious practices which had led to his father's death. Since then they had been consulting a *tantrik* and every year a minimum Rs.10,000-20,000 were contributed towards traditional religious practices (*jadhu tona*) to avoid troubles in the family. The same person gave him some threads with some *mantras* to be worn, costing Rs. 3,000, and assured him of complete healing. However, there was no respite for their trouble. Then he was invited for a prayer meeting and got healing. The believers also prayed for his wife and she was freed from trouble. He says, 'Now we don't spend our resources on traditional religious practices and unnecessary treatment. Jesus has enabled us to save our financial resources.'[77]

Demonic torment is one of the main causes making people poor and destitute, taking away their resources and vitality. Among the interviewees, one of them sacrificed 20 goats for the deliverance from demonic attack of his wife.[78] At today's lowest market rate, a goat costs minimum Rs. 2,000-2,500 and thus he spend almost Rs.50000 on traditional religious practices! Spending such an amount by a poor villager places a huge constraint upon one's financial security and ultimately leads to destitution and irrecoverable poverty.

However, healing and deliverance save financial resources and enable them to either spend money on basic needs or save it. Abraham also underlines the financial aspect of traditional religious practices and comments, '...who were going after such practices and magicians spent a lot of money to get rid of satanic attacks, avoided such practices and used that sum of money for their livelihood.'[79] Moreover, their new experience in Christ gives them a sense of empowerment in the financial realm. Their faith in a God who loves them and cares for them empowers them and enables them to move forward in life.[80] The poor believers engage in hard work and many of them testify that Jesus provides for them in their crucial junctures of needs.[81] Besides, the conversion experience removes their old habits of consumption of alcohol, smoking, chewing pan, gambling and sexually immoral living.[82] This change of habits saves a good sum of money. A

[76] Thomas, Interview, Udaipur, 8 July 2009.

[77] Thomas, Interview, Udaipur, 8 July 2009.

[78] Testimony, Participant Observation, Hebron Church, Rajasthan, 16 August 2009.

[79] Abraham, *Caste and Christianity*, 123.

[80] Mariamma, Interview by author, Tabor Church, Gujarat, 2 September 2009.

[81] Peter, Focus Group Interview, Tabor Church, Gujarat, 6 September 2009; Reji, Focus Group Interview, Hebron Church, Rajasthan, 16 August 2009.

[82] Reji, Focus Group Interview, Hebron Church, Rajasthan, 16 August 2009.

believer has commented: 'Jesus in Cana turned water into wine, but for me Jesus has turned wine into chairs and tables.'[83] He was a drunkard and used to spend his earnings for alcohol. However, the conversion experience enabled him to spend money on household needs. Now children are sent to school and provided with better food and clothing. The believers spend more money on cultivation and in buying domestic animals which gives them financial stability and more money to spend on essential goods.[84]

This providential aspect of the work of Christ is not confined to money matters only; it is applied to the realm of childbearing also. A woman participant had no children eight years into her marriage. The family was desperate to have children and spent a lot of money on *pooja* and other rituals. They also spent money on medical treatment. However, through prayer they begot children. She exclaims, 'Jesus heard our prayer and provided us with children. He is our provider.'[85] In another incident, a woman was brought to the village church of evangelist Devadas Gamit in Gujarat. She was distraught because she had no child. Her two children had died at birth. She accepted Jesus and the whole congregation prayed for her; the lady gave birth to a baby boy.[86] Another woman whose thirteen children died immediately after birth conceived a son through prayer.[87] This is a reason for people to come to the church. Shah gives an account in *Economic and Political Weekly*:

> Another person who has proselytised recently told me, "I wanted a male child. I tried 'Bhuva' and also observed 'vrata' [religious vows] but it did not help. I talked to the priest and thanks to his prayer now I am a father of a male child. Hence, I developed faith in prayer and became Cristi [Christian]."[88]

The respondents claimed that they also experience the provision of the Lord in the education and growth of their children and testify to it in the worship services.[89]

The supernatural provision of Jesus is also extended to their livestock and agriculture. For instance, Joel tells the story of a poor believer whose land produces the best yield in that area:

> One of our brothers is an uneducated person. He does not know any of the latest method of cultivation. However, his land produces the highest

[83] Yohannan, Focus Group Interview, Hebron Church, Rajasthan, 16 August 2009.

[84] Johnykutty, Focus Group Interview, Tabor Church, Gujarat, 6 September 2009.

[85] Achamma, Focus Group Interview, Udaipur, 19 July 2009.

[86] No Author, 'From Harvest Field,' *Cross & Crown* 28/5 (September-October 1998): 23.

[87] No Author, 'From our Mission Field,' *Cross & Crown* (July-August 2001): 13.

[88] Shah, 'Conversion, Reconversion and the State,' 315.

[89] Testimony, Participant Observation, Hebron Church, Rajasthan, 2 August 2009.

yield in the village. Even people from nearby villages visit his land to see what sort of methods he uses to get such a harvest. God blesses the works of his people. He is the provider of all our needs.[90]

Pentecostal believers very often request prayers from fellow believers and pastors for their domestic animals and cultivation, as many of them depend on these for their livelihood.[91] In times of drought or disease they pray for them in earnest. Moreover, special prayers are offered for animals at the time of childbirth and sowing and harvesting seasons.[92] People attribute material prosperity to the providing work of Jesus and accordingly, bring part of their produce to the church.[93]

Another area of life in which the believers claim to experience the provision of Jesus Christ is in the realm of employment. As already mentioned, most of them are working as manual labourers and earn barely enough to garner two square meals a day. However, after turning believers, even in the midst of their deprived condition, many of them have improved their condition and earn better.[94] A better job, hike in wages or income from other activities are all attributed to the name of Jesus and his supernatural provision. The believers testify to such blessings via testimony in the worship services. For example, James, who is a self-employed small time contractor, testified that recently he had been offered a new job in a private firm which was bigger than any of the jobs he had been carrying out for the last few years. He attributes it to the miraculous provision of Jesus because there were bigger contractors tendering for that job. Eventually, he acknowledged the glory to Jesus for all of his material blessings.[95] Interestingly, even third-generation Pentecostals attribute the providing aspect to the work of Christ; they depend on Jesus for their material well-being and progress at work.[96]

In the churches, pastors preach messages attributing this source of all blessings to Jesus and exhort believers to enjoy these blessings with thanksgiving. For example, in the village church, the pastor begins a message with these words: 'How many of you have been blessed materially?' All of the people raise their hands and say *hallelujah* in unison. Then he asks, 'To receive all these blessings what have we done?' He himself answered the question, 'We have just said "yes" to Jesus; yes Jesus, we have just bowed down our head before you, that is why we

[90] Joel, Interview, Maharashtra, 2 September 2009.

[91] Testimony, Participant Observation, Hebron Church, Rajasthan, 9 August 2009.

[92] Pastor Nathan, Interview by author, Hebron Church, Rajasthan, 5 August 2009.

[93] This is a usual practice in the village churches.

[94] Saji, Focus Group Interview, Udaipur, 19 July 2009.

[95] James, Focus Group Interview, Hebron Church, Rajasthan, 16 August 2009.

[96] Praisey, Interview by author, Tabor Church, Gujarat, 29 August 2009; Jolly, Interview by author, Udaipur, 10 July 2009.

have all these blessings.'[97] He took Isaiah 43:1-6 and emphasised the phrase, 'you are mine' (v.1) and 'you are precious in my sight' (v.4) and exhorted believers on the provision and protection of believers by Jesus.[98]

This understanding of Jesus as provider and the increased income people make have contributed to an attitudinal change in their outlook. Earlier, they were mere earners or receivers but now have been transformed into generous givers. In North India, even today Christians are generally considered to be receivers of financial resources from missionaries and often called 'rice Christians'. Western missionaries provided converted Tribal and Dalit Christians with essential livelihood and education. This sort of help facilitated the emergence of a 'receiving mentality' among Tribal and Dalit Christians.[99]

However, the Pentecostal movement reversed this trend. Their change in spiritual perception empowers them to contribute generously to the cause of missionary activities and philanthropic work.[100] Even poor village believers bring their first fruits, the first produce from their animals and a portion of their income to the church. In village churches, every Sunday we can see believers placing these items prayerfully near the table of the pastor to be prayed for and blessed.[101] For example, in one of the churches under study, the pastor testified that poor believers contribute to the ministry generously. Four years before the church has started a five-day convention for evangelism and spiritual growth of the believers. Food is provided for all the participants three times a day. According to the pastor, a major portion of the expenses are borne by the poor believers. Even though they do not have much money to contribute, they contribute in terms of food grain, pulses, oil, milk, vegetables and other condiments. Besides, they are more than happy to provide for the sake of the ministry and the mission of the church.[102] The church in the city helps more than 40 evangelists and pastors who 'labour' in inner villages.[103] The believers find real joy and satisfaction in giving to the cause of ministry, and have strong faith: Jesus provides for them, although many of them are poor in relative terms.[104] Hardiman, countering the accusation of the Hindu right wing, that Gujarati Tribals are lured to Pentecostalism by foreign funds, says that now Pentecostal churches are 'largely run and financed by the Tribal peoples themselves.'[105] One respondent tried to explain the theology of

[97] Message, Participant Observation, Hebron Church, Rajasthan, 7 August 2009.

[98] Ibid.

[99] Bauman, *Christian Identity and Dalit Religion,* 71-100.

[100] Pastor Nathan, Interview, Hebron Church, Rajasthan, 5 August 2009.

[101] Participant Observation, Hebron Church, Rajasthan, 9 August 2009; Participant Observation, Tabor Church, Gujarat, 6 September 2009.

[102] Pastor Nathan, Interview, Hebron Church, Rajasthan, 5 August 2009.

[103] Participant Observation, Udaipur, 12 July 2009.

[104] Yohannan, Focus Group Interview, Hebron Church, Rajasthan, 16 August 2009.

[105] Hardiman & Raje, 'Practices of Healing in Tribal Gujarat,' 49.

blessing: 'God made human beings with all good things. In the Garden of Eden, nothing was lacking. For two people there were four rivers. There was abundance. However, because of sin poverty and illness entered into the world'. He continues, 'God's intention is to make us rich. For this purpose Jesus became poor. He took our poverty and pain to make us happy.'[106]

In the interviews, focus groups and informal conversations, members claimed that, in the villages, the Pentecostal believers prosper far better than other people in financial terms and in educating their children.[107] McGavran calls it 'redemption and lift.'[108] They wear better dress, improve cleanliness and are healthier. The obvious reason may be that they no longer spend their resources on alcohol, traditional religious practices or in activities regarded as sexually immoral.[109] Abraham also shows that the same is true in Kerala. He says, '...the majority responded that there has been a change in the economic life from their previous stage.'[110] This change has happened 'when they turned into Pentecostal churches, abolished all malpractices such as smoking, drinking and going for sorcery, etc. This resulted in the saving of huge amounts which could later be used for their family needs.'[111] Donald Miller and Tetsunao Yamamori observe it as one of the positive effects Pentecostalism:

> There is substantial evidence for the "social uplift" associated with Pentecostalism, in that Pentecostals have a competitive economic advantage over their neighbours because of their moral proscriptions against alcohol, drugs, gambling and womanising. Without these social evils, believers may produce surplus capital that can then be invested in business enterprises or in the education and welfare of their families.[112]

Further, financial improvements of the Pentecostals attract others. One person said:

> We have progressed in our works. Our children are sent to school. We don't spend our money on any useless things like alcohol or cigarettes. Seeing our blessings many villagers joined us.[113]

---

[106] Mani, Focus Group Interview, Hebron Church, Rajasthan, 2 August 2009.

[107] Reji, Focus Group Interview, Hebron Church, Rajasthan, 9 August 2009.

[108] Donald McGavran, *Understanding Church Growth* (Grand Rapids: Eerdmans, 1970), 260-277; also see C. Peter Wagner, *Look Out! The Pentecostals are Coming* (Illinois: Creation House, 1973), 93-94.

[109] Reji, Focus Group Interview, Hebron Church, Rajasthan, 9 August 2009.

[110] Abraham, *Caste and Christianity*, 122.

[111] Ibid., 112-123.

[112] Miller & Yamamori, *Global Pentecostalism*, 33.

[113] Reji, Focus Group Interview, Hebron Church, Rajasthan, 9 August 2009.

Moreover, in the Pentecostal churches, people are encouraged to spend their resources judiciously and to keep sanitation, as one of the evangelists said to me.[114] They are also encouraged to consult good doctors if they are sick, along with prayer.[115] The Pentecostal churches also conduct medical camps for their members as well as for others in villages. There are campaigns for health, safety and hygiene; specialists are invited to teach them and educated members are also trained to teach others.[116]

This study showed that Pentecostal believers fare better than believers of other denominations in finance, health and education. This fact is acknowledged by the believers of other Churches themselves.[117] According to a person who himself is from a Tribal background and a member of a denominational church, their believers still live like their counterparts in the larger society, consuming alcohol, indulging in smoking, gambling and other harmful practices, like traditional religious practices and so on.[118] Such activities affect their financial security and result in a reduced living standard. On the other hand, most of the Pentecostal churches are strict in their outlook on holiness and such practices are strictly prohibited. If people are found indulging in such activities, they are not allowed to be the members of the church. Such a stringent discipline helps keep people away from old habits. According Pastor Nathan, some people drop out from churches due to the strict holiness outlook and practice.[119] David Hardiman also comments, 'Conversion was seen as providing a means to transform their lives for the better, in which they abandoned the old wild ways of traditional tribal life, and became sober, hard-working and god-fearing.'[120] Thus, the concept of Jesus as the provider is a major Christological factor among the ordinary believers.

5.4 Jesus the Protector

Another prominent theme which resulted from the field research is the insight that Jesus is the protector. This perception regarding Jesus also springs from the intense personal struggle believers undergo. The above-explained notions of Jesus as the healer, exorcist and provider overlap with this perception of Jesus as the protector.

---

[114] Kuttappan, Focus Group Interview, Hebron Church, Rajasthan, 9 August 2009.

[115] There is a wrong assumption among others that Pentecostals prohibit the use of medicines. However, only a few Pentecostals follow such a rule.

[116] Pastor Nathan, Interview, Hebron Church, Rajasthan, 5 August 2009; The Organisation called Community Health Organisation (CHE) is instrumental in conducting medical camps for villagers in these areas. Coincidentally, my wife, Sheena was working as a community health educator and was also helping in medical camps.

[117] Informal conversations with believers of other denominations revealed that Pentecostals fare better in finance and education of their children.

[118] Informal conversation with Nathulal, Maharashtra, 7 September 2009.

[119] Pastor Nathan, Interview, Hebron Church, Rajasthan, 5 August 2009. It emerged in the research that a number of people have been turning to their earlier religions, due to various reasons.

[120] Hardiman & Raje, 'Practices of Healing in Tribal Gujarat,' 49.

This idea can be arrayed in different layers of the life situation of the ordinary Pentecostal believers. It can be explained as follows: Jesus not only has healed them but also continues to keep them from any possible sickness.[121] Similarly, Jesus has not only liberated them from demonic forces but keeps protecting them from all possible fears, attacks from evil spirits and persecutors. Again, Jesus not only provides them with help in coping with their existential struggles but also continues to protect their lives, their livestock, agriculture and finance from being manipulated or destroyed by demonic forces. Therefore, as in the case of Jesus as the provider, this theme is a second level Christological articulation of ordinary Pentecostals. Simultaneously, for some, Jesus is the rescuer from caste-ridden social ostracism and oppression. Members experienced liberation from the tyranny of the caste system and became part of a caring community. Therefore, for them, the notion of Jesus as the protector is the starting point of their Christological articulation.[122] Thus, the Pentecostals acknowledge and affirm with astute faith that Jesus is their protector in all of their everyday life situations.

For example, in the worship service a woman testified of her miraculous escape from a poisonous snake. Village houses are made of thatched roofs and mud walls and snakes and other poisonous reptiles may easily hide in them. While she was doing her household chores, a poisonous snake fell on her from the roof. According to her, the snake was so poisonous that had she been bitten by him, within an hour she would have died. But she attributed the protection to Jesus and said, '*prabhu yishu mujhe bacchaya*' (Lord Jesus has protected me).[123]

The believers also extend the protection of Jesus to their agriculture and livestock. Many of them are surviving on agriculture and the domestic animals they own. If rainfall fails or if there is excessive rain at the time of growth or harvest, this can ruin them. Therefore, at the time of sowing and harvest special prayers are conducted for agricultural prosperity. The believers have firm faith in the efficacy of prayer and in God's provision of rain and well-being to their harvest and animals.[124] There are testimonies by poor believers to the effect that their crops are protected from draught, pests and also from evil influence.[125] Some of them also testified that, after they began to attend the church, their agriculture started to show remarkable improvement and fared better than others.[126]

The protection of Jesus is acknowledged in relation to the prosperity of domestic animals too. Any disease spread to the animals may reduce believers' income. Therefore, they are not hesitant to bring their chickens or goats to churches to be prayed for in the name of Jesus by pastors, if they are sick. In the

---

[121] Jessy, Interview by Author, Tabor Church, Gujarat, 2 September 2009.

[122] Ginu, Interview by Author, Chennai, 3 July 2009.

[123] Testimony, Participant Observation, Hill-view Church, Rajasthan, 5 July 2009.

[124] Pastor Nathan, Interview, Hebron Church, Rajasthan, 5 August 2009.

[125] Testimony, Participant Observation, Hill-view Church, Rajasthan, 3 July 2009.

[126] Testimony, Participant Observation, Hill-view Church, Rajasthan, 5 July 2009.

worship services, it is not unusual to hear believers requesting prayers for their goats and cows or for their harvest.[127] For example, a woman testified that, in her village a severe disease affecting domestic birds spread and most of the villagers lost their cocks and hens. She had more than 15 of them and one died of the disease. Seeing this, she gathered them all and prayed over them in the name of Jesus. According to her, none of them perished after the prayer, while neighbours' birds all did.[128]

But above all the above mentioned, the notion of understanding Jesus as protector is predominantly related to the external struggles, namely the intense mental pressure and physical abuse and persecution they face as Christians. Many of the Pentecostals undergo severe mental and physical torture due to their new found faith in Jesus.[129] Such pressure and persecution emerges from various groups; from one's own family, village community and external agencies such as fundamentalist organisations which we explored in Chapter Four. Moreover, the believers who have experienced the touch of divine healing, or deliverance from demonic forces, place their complete trust in the overarching power of Jesus and are ready to forfeit all their old religious practices. They just refuse to worship their previous deities, or bow down their heads before any idols.[130] Besides, they even discard the cultural practices which are incompatible with their new understanding of Christ.[131] For example, it is usual and often customary in villages to greet another person with the common salutation, '*Ram Ram*'. However, when one becomes a believer, he or she stops greeting people in this way because this expression carries religious overtones. Instead, the Pentecostals usually greet people with '*Jai Yishu*' (victory to Jesus) or '*prabhu ka sthuthi ho*' (praise the Lord).[132] This sometimes creates a hostile environment for the Pentecostals.

In a society where religion and culture define the course of action of one's life and force people to fall in line with the system, such rebellious acts cannot be tolerated but are dealt with severity. The believers are both mentally and physically abused so that they fall in line with old practices.[133] If they resist, abuses and revengeful acts against them may increase. Besides, such rebellious behaviour can attract the scrutiny and judgment of the larger village community. The believers can be dragged into the village council and be dealt with severe punishment in the form of penalty or physical assault.[134] Even 'honour killing'

[127] Testimony, Participant Observation, Hebron Church, Rajasthan, 2 August 2009.

[128] Testimony, Participant Observation, Hebron Church, Rajasthan, 7 August 2009.

[129] Johnykutty, Focus Group Interview, Tabor Church, Gujarat, 6 September 2009.

[130] Chacko, Interview by author, Tabor Church, Gujarat, 2 September 2009.

[131] Shah, 'Conversion, Reconversion and the State,' 315.

[132] Message, Participant Observation, Hill-view Church, Rajasthan, 5 July 2009.

[133] Yeshudas, Interview, Hebron Church, Rajasthan, 16 August 2009; Yohannan, Focus Group Interview, Hebron Church, Rajasthan, 16 August 2009.

[134] Editor, 'Tortured for Christ,' *Cross & Crown* (July-August 1997): 12.

is also not uncommon. For example, in Madhya Pradesh, evangelist Benjamin was forced to pay a fine of Rs.1,500 and Suresh Alam was locked up for three days.[135] The total village community can turn against a single person for his/her faith. The administration or police only make the matters worse in this matter by supporting the opponents instead of extending help to believers.[136] Sometimes, even secular newspapers report against the believers and pastors accusing them of 'forcible conversion'.[137]

Moreover, the newfound faith and convictions of Pentecostals impel them to testify on their experience to the family members, village community and co-workers. This may further aggravate the situation and can get to a point where a person may be thrown out of home or village or his/her life be threatened.[138] In a village community, which is a closely-knit entity, people are averse to entertaining a new religion or faith or allow it to be established in their territory. Sometimes Pentecostals are not allowed to sit with other villagers.[139] It is usual for Pentecostals to be taken for 'untouchables' and to be disallowed from drawing water from village wells;[140] they may have to travel miles to fetch water.[141] At anyone's home, new believers may confront a hostile situation. A husband may assault his wife for the faith she professes or a father may throw out a son or a daughter from home. They may be forfeited of their rightful ancestral property or from any financial resources.[142]

There are many such incidents in which Pentecostals are abused in their homes, in the villages or in the groups they belong to. Some are being thrown out of their homes and villages. For instance, one woman testified that she has been suffering abuse from her husband and other family members, since she started attending the church. Sometimes her husband comes home drunk and physically abuses her and uses abusive language. Other members of the family also mentally torture her continuously by accusing her of accepting a new religion. However, she testified that she was very strong in her faith and whatever happens, even death would not separate her from the faith.[143] *Cross and Crown* narrates the story of Anita who had been thrown out of her house because she became a member

[135] Editor, 'From the Mission Field,' *Cross & Crown* 26/2 (December 1995-January 1996): 21.

[136] Editor, 'Arrested on False Charges,' *Cross & Crown* 37/3 (January-February 2008): 21.

[137] V. Sridhar, 'Numbers Game,' *Frontline* 16/25 (27 November 1999) and M.V. Kamath, 'Mission Impossible: Putting an End to Conversion Activity,' *Times of India* (13 October 1999).

[138] Anita Mathew, 'He Touched me: Testimony,' *Cross & Crown* 28/4 (July-August 1998): 13-14.

[139] Yeshudas, Interview, Hebron Church, Rajasthan, 16 August 2009.

[140] C&C Reporter, 'Field News: How do we Plant,' 2.

[141] Shiji, Interview by author, Tabor Church, Gujarat, 5 September 2009.

[142] Testimony, Participant Observation, Hill-view Church, Rajasthan, 31 July 2009; Raju, Focus Group Interview, Hebron Church, Rajasthan, 16 August 2009.

[143] Testimony, Participant Observation, Hebron Church, Rajasthan, 16 August 2009.

of a Pentecostal church. She was from another denominational background and announced that she accepted Jesus as her saviour and was going to be baptised. She says, 'Hearing this, they were furious and kicked me out of the house and threw away all my belongings.'[144] According to her, it was the protective hand of Jesus which enabled her to stand firm in the faith.[145]

Another person who had participated in the interview (Raju) was faced with a similar situation. An evangelist introduced Jesus to him and gave him a New Testament. He read it for some time and realised that what he used to worship are not true gods. He began to attend the church and was baptised. Then he was forced to leave his home and his father announced that he would be disowned from his father's inheritance. Moreover, other relatives gathered to beat him. However, somehow he escaped. He says, 'It was only because of the protection of Jesus I escaped their hands (*yishu ka anugrah se bacch gaya*). If Jesus had not protected me, then I would not have been speaking to you today!'[146] The pastor of the church kept him at his residence. However, after two years his whole family turned believers and now they go to church. At the same time, many of them suffer persecution but they claim that they take it as a privilege, for the glory of the Lord.[147] It is an interesting fact that the church acts as a 'refuge' for those who have been persecuted and rejected.

Another area of perpetual oppression emerges from the evil effect of the caste system. Some of the interviewees testified that they felt better and empowered after having joined a Pentecostal church. For instance, Tomy claims that he had been abused by his neighbours and even by his former employer due to his caste. He felt inferior before others and life was miserable for him. But, when he joined the church, the attitude of the believers was entirely different. He felt a sense of affection and love from the pastor and believers. He testified that one of the major reasons he joined the church was to escape the caste system and untouchability.[148] Similarly, Sam who became an evangelist testified that one of the results of his conversion was the escape from the inferior caste feeling he had been nursing all his life.[149] He says, 'Jesus pulled me up from the pit of caste-hierarchy and made me his beloved son and placed me with kings and priests.'[150] This positive effect of Pentecostalism is amply testified by non-Pentecostal scholars and considered to be one of the key reasons for its rapid growth among Dalits and lower castes.[151]

---

[144] Mathew, 'He Touched me,' 13-14

[145] Ibid., 14.

[146] Raju, Focus Group Interview, Hebron Church, Rajasthan, 9 August 2009.

[147] Pastor John, Interview by author, Tabor Church, Gujarat, 2 September 2009.

[148] Tomy, Interview by author, Chennai, 3 July 2009.

[149] Sam, Interview by author, Chennai, 3 July 2009.

[150] Ibid.

[151] Arles, 'Indigenous Pentecostal Church Growth at KGF,' 393; Jones, 'Faces of Pentecostalism in North India Today.'

Nevertheless, it is to be noted that this anomaly is not totally absent even in Pentecostal churches.[152]

More than this abuse, attacks of fundamentalist religious elements, however, create bigger trouble for the Pentecostal churches and believers. As already explained, these elements are consistently targeting the Pentecostal pastors and churches as well as many from other religious traditions, especially lower castes, Dalits and Tribals who join the Pentecostal churches.[153] According to Pastor John, they accuse pastors and believers of forced conversions and allege that people are being lured into churches by offering them money.[154] Then he acknowledged that it was only by the protective presence of Jesus the believers are safe.[155]

There have been many attacks carried out against pastors, believers and churches. In a gruesome incident narrated in a mission story, extremist religious fringe groups attacked a church in a village in Udaipur while worship was being conducted. They beat up evangelists Shantilal and Rajendra in front of the believers until they were left unconscious. These attackers bolted the single door of the church and cruelly attacked believers with rods and sticks, not even sparing women and children. It is described in the story that obviously, only the care and protection of God saved the lives of evangelists.[156] As a corollary of the story, the house and motor-bike of the leader of the group who attacked the church was destroyed in a fire. The villagers took it to be the result of the attack and consider it to be the vengeance of the God of Christians.[157]

The story of Jodharam, who is from Bikaner District of Rajasthan, is a classic example of the insidious scheme of extremist groups to persecute new believers. It also portrays how the Christological notion of Jesus as protector is fully realised in the ordinary believer's life. He was from an 'untouchable caste' and through a healing miracle of his wife he accepted Jesus. While having a meeting at his home, he was asked to appear before the village council, comprising of the leaders of Vshwa Hindu Parishad, Bajrang Dal, Arya Samaj and also the entire village. They forced him to recant his faith. However, he would not relent but boldly narrated his testimony. Meanwhile others took evangelist Pradeep and beat him badly. The next day most of the Hindi newspapers reported the event with headlines such as, 'Hunger and circumstances forced him to become a Christian,' 'Jodharam became Joseph,' and 'VHP expresses concern over the activities of missionaries to

[152] Abraham, *Caste and Christianity;* V. V. Thomas, 'Pentecostalism Among the Dalits in Kerala from 1909 to the Present: A Subaltern Reading,' *UBS Journal* 3/2 (September 2005): 89-94.

[153] See *India Persecution Update* which gives many incidents of attacks against Christians, especially Pentecostals; for instance, the issue of the month of May 2010 reports killing of two young evangelists; http://www.persecution.in/persecution_india_may2010 (accessed 25 June 2010).

[154] See Sridhar, 'Numbers Game'; Kamath, 'Mission Impossible.'

[155] Pastor John, Interview by author, Tabor Church, Gujarat, 2 September 2009.

[156] No Author, 'Tortured yet Triumphant!,' *Cross & Crown* 26/4 (April-May 1996): 19-20.

[157] No Author, 'Touching the Apple of God's Eye,' *Cross & Crown* 26/4 (April-May 1996): 20.

convert the natives of Bikaner,' and so on, for four consecutive days.[158] The fanatic elements attempted to harm him and continuously tried to force him to renounce his faith. As a result of the fact that he would not relent, the *sarpanch* (village headman) finally announced that Jodharam and his family would be thrown out of the village.[159]

According to Jodharam, he submitted his life, the family and their security in the hands of Jesus.[160] After much prayer he met the police commissioner and explained his newfound faith and sought protection from his oppressors. This gave him a respite, yet he was not safe. He exclaims, 'Jesus is our protector and he turns the hearts of officials like a stream, he is greater than all' (*Yishu hamara taranhara hai, woh subse badkar hai*).[161]

Thus, the notion of Jesus as protector is active and alive in the daily struggles of the Pentecostal believers as individuals and as a community. Even though they go through severe persecution, the idea that Jesus protects them, gives courage and a sense of safety helps them face dangerous situations fearlessly.

5.5 Jesus the Saviour

Another significant Christological theme that emerged from the study is the notion of Jesus as the Saviour. The firm faith of the believers identifies Jesus as the only one who saves them from their sins which has severe repercussions in their contexts as we have already seen. The saving act of Jesus, however, is not limited to the spiritual realm only; rather, it encompasses every aspect of their life: physical, material and social. Interestingly, this concept is derived from the perception of Jesus as the healer, exorcist, provider and protector. In other words, the saviour notion emerges from the reflections of their past life of fear and suffering juxtaposed to the safety and happiness they enjoy through the miraculous intervention and change Jesus accomplished in their lives. The believers were under the clutches of sickness, demonic powers, utter poverty and fear psychosis. Their social conditioning and cultural ethos burdened them with guilt. Some were under financial struggle and poverty and others were despised and denigrated by the caste system.

However, the encounter with Jesus transformed the old world to which they were tied down into a brave new world. We may summarise the reflective process in this way: initially, the believers experience healing and deliverance in the name of Jesus and come to the conclusion that Jesus is the healer and the exorcist *par excellence*; secondly, they realise that Jesus is far more powerful and merciful than their former deities; what their gods could not do and very often what their gods would not do, Jesus has accomplished. Therefore, Jesus is greatest of all. Thirdly,

[158] Quoted in Editor, 'Tortured for Christ,' *Cross & Crown* (July-August 1997): 12.

[159] Editor, 'Tortured for Christ,' 12.

[160] Ibid., 13.

[161] Ibid., 13.

after conversion they experience the providing and protective hand of Jesus in their daily lives of struggle. Fourthly, since what was impossible in the past has been accomplished by Jesus, that is, the peace, prosperity and safety now they enjoy fully, which leads them to elevate him to the role of *the* Saviour. In the case of second-or third-generation Pentecostals, or people who joined form other denominations, the Christological understanding starts from Jesus as Saviour and from this concept they reflect back to the former categories. Hence, the notion of Jesus as Saviour is experiential at the core and has nothing to do with *intellectual* articulations. They understand and envision Jesus as one who acts on their behalf and, therefore, this role can be considered to be a functional category. Simultaneously, they also understand Jesus to be divine and to be the only one who can deliver them from their sins.[162] Hence, this notion forms a bridge between the functional categories (such as healer, exorcist, provider, protector) and the ontological categories (such as Lord, God) which we shall discuss later. It is both functional as well as ontological. Thus, this notion forms the third level of Christological articulation of ordinary believers.

This idea has clearly emerged in the interviews and focus groups and is very much part of their testimonies in the worship services. The songs and hymns they sing, messages in the worship services and the published mission stories and testimonies also underline this notion of Jesus as Saviour *par excellence*. One of the songs often sung goes:

The name of Jesus gives peace, salvation and eternal life,

I will sing his greatness forever.
Mercy, goodness and life are with him,
He is eternal, loving, all-powerful Lord,
He loves us, gives us blessing and joy,
I will sing his greatness forever.[163]

Similarly, one of the testimonies given in the worship service points to the confession believers make in this regard:

> I was very sick and bed-ridden with paralysis and spent a lot of money for the treatment. I was from a Hindu family and consulted many god-men and also carried out *puja* and sacrifices for the healing. I have also visited many temples and called upon many gods. However, there was no relief for my suffering. When I put my trust in Jesus, without any rituals I got complete healing.[164]

[162] The idea of sin is explained in pages 239-241.

[163] Participant Observation, Hill-view Church, Rajasthan, 4 July 2009.

[164] Ponnachan, Focus Group Interview, Tabor Church, Gujarat, 6 September 2009.

When answering the question, 'how does he understand Christ,' he said without any hesitation that Jesus is the greatest of all gods. Moreover, he said that the gods and goddesses he had been serving were enslaving him to sinful activities.[165] However, Jesus gave freedom from sin as well as peace and therefore 'Jesus is the only saviour and is the greatest of all'; he continued,

> ...because Jesus has given me the healing I enjoy now; I have worshipped many gods and goddess but I could not get healing and the peace I was looking for. I got healing, peace of mind and joy through Jesus. *Yishu mera udharak hai, yishu mera pap mitha dhiya* (Jesus is my saviour and he has taken away my sins). He is greatest of all.[166]

The testimony of another respondent is worth considering, as he unambiguously affirms that Jesus is the Saviour. He is from a respected Hindu family and used to meditate on the contents of religious books. He has a good job in a company. While narrating the story of his conversion, he affirms that Jesus is the Saviour:

> My daughter who was 18 years old was infested with an evil spirit. Not only that, all my family was tormented by the influence of satanic powers. ...There was always quarrel and illness in the family. Even without any cause family members used to be sick. To get relief from this influence, we made special rituals in famous temples... However, in the name of Jesus Christ, my daughter got deliverance.[167]

He confesses that Jesus is the saviour (*Yishu hi udharak hai*) and only Jesus can save human beings from sins and suffering. He says:

> Jesus' name is greater than all names. His name is the true name. In his name all gods tremble. If we just utter his name or think his name, satanic powers will flee. His name has power over every power in the world. His power is eternal, never to be destroyed. Jesus' name is true from the beginning and that name gives me joy and happiness. Jesus is my saviour. He is the saviour of our family. Jesus has given us peace and deliverance from the torment of so-called gods we worshipped. Jesus is the saviour and only he can save us.[168]

In one of the churches during the worship service, the pastor was preaching from John 10:10, contrasting the work of Satan and Christ.[169] His words are

---

[165] Ponnachan, Focus Group Interview, Tabor Church, Gujarat, 6 September 2009.

[166] Ibid.

[167] Chacko, Interview by author, Tabor Church, Gujarat, 28 August 2009.

[168] Chacko, Interview, Tabor Church, Gujarat, 28 August 2009.

[169] Message, Participant Observation, Tabor Church, Gujarat, 6 September 2009.

a summary and typical representation of what the Pentecostal believers confess about Jesus.

> When we were away from Jesus, we were under the power of Satan. Satan comes and steals our money, health, prosperity of our animals and agriculture. He brings sorrows and illness, he kills our children and our animals. He leads us to sin, adultery, drinking habits and other sinful activities taking away our blessings. He makes us his slaves, gets us into trouble and makes us poor. However, Jesus gives us blessings and eternal life in abundance.[170]

Then he narrated some examples of healings and deliverance which took place in the name of Jesus, to persuade the believers. After he quoted Acts 4:12 and affirmed that no other gods can save human beings from Satan and sin, but only Jesus. He also quoted Rom 3:10-12 and said all have sinned and came under the power of Satan. He concluded this way, 'However, Jesus has saved us through his death and resurrection. He is the only saviour; he is the only true God.'[171]

Since the people's idea of sin is intricately related to the spirit world and to social relations, it is important to see how they understand Jesus as saviour. First of all, for them sin is the violation of the taboos which may provoke the spirits and lead to the destruction of life and property.[172] Therefore, the concept of Jesus as saviour and for that matter the idea of salvation does offer peace, safety and security. Jesus removes the burden of fear which looms large over their head and fills their mind and body with 'the peace which surpasses all the understanding.'[173] One of the respondents said:

> I was nervous in my mind and body because of the evil forces. I felt like I was carrying a heavy load on my head, something like 50 kgs, always. Now I feel very happy. My body became light. Jesus has taken away my burden and I feel it in practice. I was "carrying the heavy burden" just as we see in the Bible.[174]

Moreover, instead of the fear of the spirits, now the believers enjoy the close proximity of the presence of Jesus and of the Holy Spirit, which connect them to the spiritual world they once dreaded. This assurance of permanent safety and fearlessness permeate the spiritual realm and victory over demonic powers in the name of Jesus brings a new understanding of the person and of the work of

---

[170] Message, Participant Observation, Tabor Church, Gujarat, 6 September 2009.

[171] Ibid.

[172] Cherian, 'Contribution of Churches and Missions,' 41-43; Raj, *Dalitology*, 245-246; Pappachan, Focus Group Interview, 6 September 2009.

[173] Ponnachan, Focus Group Interview, Tabor Church, Gujarat, 6 September 2009.

[174] Thomas, Interview, Udaipur, 8 July 2009.

Christ. In other words, in their experience, Christology and Soteriology intersect with each other.

Secondly, the breaking of community rules which has an effect on oneself and on others in the community is also considered to be a sin. Every member of the community is so heavily interrelated that one's thoughtless actions can infringe the privileges of others which may cause rupture in the relationships. This in turn may affect the peace and tranquillity of the whole community.[175] Therefore, Jesus the saviour reconciles the relationship which was broken by sinful activities, such as enmity, and establishes peace and unity among the people.[176] In other words, Jesus is the mediator and reconciler. Such community relationships help a single person to bring many people to faith, which may also explain the rapid migration of Tribals and Dalits into Pentecostal churches.

All of the believers who participated in the study spontaneously affirmed their conviction of Jesus as the saviour while the second- or third-generation Pentecostals and people who joined from other denominations considered it as the most important Christological theme.[177] They hold a slightly different notion of sin, though. For them, sin is breaking God's law and results in guilt and judgment.[178] Moreover, believing in the suffering and death of Jesus brings salvation. The respondents who joined in from other denominations emphasised this strongly:

> Earlier I knew that Jesus was the saviour. However, I never experienced the meaning of salvation. My understanding was that because I was born to a Christian family, I was a saved person...When I joined the church, I fully experienced the meaning and significance of being saved. I understood the meaning of the suffering of Jesus for me. One has to experience the joy of salvation. I am happy and my guilt is removed. Now I know that salvation is an intimate relationship with Jesus. I am no more under the judgement of God. When I read the Bible I understand the saving power of Jesus.[179]

From their words it is obvious that they do not have any doubts or hesitation as to passing on this idea to others. The multi-religious context in which they live does not stop them from proclaiming Jesus as the only saviour. Their testimony of salvation experienced through Christ and the reflection of joy that this brings to their lives convince others of the notion that Jesus is a saviour beyond doubts. This

[175] Cherian, 'Contribution of Churches and Missions,' 41-43; Raj, *Dalitology*, 245-246.

[176] Kuttappan, Focus Group Interview, Hebron Church, Rajasthan, 9 August 2009.

[177] Moncy & Achamma, Focus Group Interview, Udaipur, 26 July 2009.

[178] Glory, Interview by author, Kolenchery, Kerala, 28 June 2009; Paul, Interview by author, Kolenchery, Kerala, 28 June 2009.

[179] Prince, Interview by author, Kolenchery, Kerala, 28 June 2009.

idea has evidently come out in a number of interviews. One of the interviewees said:

> After my healing experience, I accepted Jesus as my saviour. I know that he has removed all my sins. My relatives and villagers constantly discouraged me and forced me to renounce the faith. But, I cannot do that because I have experienced peace in my life. Now I feel joy. I tell about Jesus to others. I tell them that Jesus can save them from their problems. Jesus only can forgive their sins.[180]

In the focus groups this idea was aired very strongly.[181] All of them advocated Jesus as the only saviour. One said, 'Jesus is the only saviour, all other options are false. We should proclaim it to others.'[182] Another respondent said:

> We must tell everybody about Jesus. Those who have experienced this great salvation cannot stop telling it to others. It is our responsibility. When many people in the world are perishing without knowing Jesus, we are being saved to tell it to others. I have been called from my family to bring to its members real salvation. We cannot save others. But when the Holy Spirit works in the lives of the people, they will be transformed.[183]

Thus, for the Pentecostal believers evangelism is by default a life-style. It is not anything carried out by special agencies or highly trained experts. Rather, evangelism is deeply ingrained in the psyche and daily life of the believers and Jesus as the only saviour is proclaimed without any hesitation. This way of communicating and sharing of life-experiences explains the rapid proliferation of the Pentecostal churches in the Indian context.

5.6 Jesus the Lord

Another important Christological theme which is dominant among the Pentecostals is the notion that Jesus is the only true Lord. This forms the fourth level of Christological articulation and attributes divinity to Jesus. This idea is so widespread that in almost every worship service, personal testimony, even

[180] Ebenezer, Focus Group Interview, Tabor Church, Gujarat, 30 August 2009.

[181] One of the respondents said, 'Drinking habit is a big problem among the people around here. Many have ruined their lives because of this evil habit. However, when one believes in Jesus Christ, there is bodily healing, mental peace and also deliverance from the harmful habits of drinking and sorcery. Those who have experienced these changes testify to their fellow villagers. They encourage others to come and try what they have experienced and people quickly believe it. Moreover, many of the people come to Christ because of the fear of demonic powers. They accept Jesus as redeemer and saviour.' Joel, Interview, Maharashtra, 2 September 2009.

[182] Saji, Focus Group Interview, Udaipur, 26 July 2009.

[183] Mercy, Interview by author, Kolenchery, Kerala, 28 June 2009.

in informal conversion it emerges with clarity and alacrity. Even the common greetings between believers like *Prabhu ka Mahima ho* (Glory to the Lord), *Jai Yishu* (victory to Jesus) underscore this fact. The salutation '*Jai Yishu*' is a classical example of the affirmation of ordinary believers, attributing the glory and victory to their Lord who delivered them from their wretched conditions. A respondent made it clear, affirming victory to Jesus elevates him above all powers (*woh sub ka prabhu hai*).[184] Moreover, the word '*prabhu*' (Lord) is equated to Jesus Christ and connotes his glorious lordship over all other gods, the reason why he is to be worshipped.[185] Thus, this theme brings forth their strong conviction 'Jesus as victor' into the open.

Just as the notion of Jesus the saviour, the notion of Jesus the Lord emerged from a reflection upon the existential categories attributed to Jesus by the ordinary believers; namely, Jesus is the healer, exorcist, provider and protector. Along with these four notions, the believers also include the notion of Jesus the saviour in the reflective process. This inclusion, and subsequent reflective process and articulation, brings a new perception of Christ that lifts him above all. In other words, their present life situations as well as the exceptional status they enjoy in Christ, enable them to place Christ in an exalted position. If Jesus heals, delivers, provides, protects, and forgives their sins to grant them peace and joy, then he is greater than all and worthy of worship. Moreover, the worship atmosphere, the experience of the Spirit and biblical teachings in the church provide a strong base for this understanding; Jesus became the centre of their universe. They think of Jesus as Lord of their lives and, as a result, a very personal and intimate relationship is emphasised. One of the respondents unambiguously affirmed, 'He is the Lord of my life, worthy of worship and glory!' (*woh mera prabhu hai, aradhana aur mahima ka yogye hai!*).[186]

The idea of Jesus as Lord is a deep-rooted understanding among the believers. They attribute the lordship of Christ in every aspect of their life; whether it is personal, spiritual, social, economic or political. For them in applying this concept there is no differentiation between sacred and secular. It is obvious from their testimonies that, knowingly or unknowingly, they extrapolate this Christological theme to their family, community and larger society. In every worship service, the idea is echoed very clearly in the songs, testimonies as well as in the preaching. For example, one of the songs heard in the churches underlines the idea that Jesus is the victor and the Lord:

> Victory to the Lord
> Victory to the king

[184] Sabu, Focus Group Interview, Hebron Church, Rajasthan, 16 August 2009.

[185] Wilson, Focus Group Interview, Hebron Church, Rajasthan, 16 August 2009; Biju, Focus Group Interview, Hebron Church, Rajasthan, 9 August 2009.

[186] Jose, Focus Group Interview, Udaipur, 26 July 2009.

Victory to the Lord of lords
Victory to the Lord who listens to the prayers
Victory to the Lord who heals
Victory to the Lord who gives peace
Victory to the Lord who gives salvation.[187]

Even though they go through numerous untold miseries, their certainty and strong faith in the overarching power of Jesus helps them to confess Jesus as the Lord. A testimony which was heard in the worship service pointed to the conviction of ordinary Pentecostal believers in this regard. A woman who was severely abused by her husband testified her conviction. According to her, she accepted Jesus as her Lord, but her husband, an idol worshipper, opposed her becoming a Christian. Very often he abused her physically. (She cried during the testimony). In spite of all this, she has held on to her faith. She requested special prayers from the congregation to stand firm in the Lord.[188]

Listen to another testimony of a believer who was convinced of the greatness of Jesus, through a healing miracle:

> I was an idol worshipper and used to go to many temples. My wife was ill, suffering from constant stomach problems for many years. She could not eat anything. She was only a skeleton and about to die. I have sought the help of *bhopas* and carried out traditional religious practices, sacrificing 20 goats on various occasion for her healing but without any respite. Then a pastor came to my house at night for the first time. He has prayed for my wife and continuously visited me and encouraged me to put my trust in Jesus...I put my trust in Jesus... Slowly, my wife recovered from the illness...Then I began to attend the church and accepted Jesus as my saviour. Jesus is greater than all; all of my former deities. Jesus is my Lord (*yishu mera prabhu hai*).[189]

It is obvious from his testimony that his perception of Jesus as the Lord of his life, his family and all the aspects of life grew day by day.

The continuous reflective process of their newfound experience in Christ convinces the believers of the power and greatness of Jesus. This notion comes alive and emboldens the believers to face the thorny and gloomy junctures of life, disregarding the cost they have to pay. He portrays it:

> Then my daughter became gravely ill. People in my village accused me that it was because I have accepted a new religion. They have asked me to indulge in idol worship and get the help of *bhopa*. I said them, Jesus

[187] Song no. 716, *Songs of Fellowship*, (Udaipur, India: Filadelfia Bible College, 2005): 359.

[188] Testimony, Participant Observation, Hill-view Church, Rajasthan, 4 July 2009.

[189] Testimony, Participant Observation, Hill-top Church, Rajasthan, 2 July 2009.

is my Lord (*yishu mera prabhu hai*), he can heal my daughter; even if my child dies I do not worship idols. Even my parents accused me of killing my daughter. They asked me to leave Jesus and go for traditional religious practices. I felt very sad and cried. I said to them, Jesus can heal my daughter. Even if she dies, even if I die, even if all my family die, I do not worship idols; I won't leave Jesus because he alone is the true Lord (*kyonki woh hi succha prabhu hai*). Then I prayed and telephoned pastor. He prayed for her. Later she was taken to hospital and she got healed.[190]

From the testimony, it is clear that such life experiences, both painful and joyful, harden their commitment towards Christ and provide a deep-rooted experiential knowledge of Jesus as their Lord; their joys and sorrows, gains and losses, prosperity and poverty all come from him.[191] According to a respondent, they are ready to suffer and even forsake their lives for the sake of their Lord who is now the centre of all their activities. Furthermore, in their struggles, the believers experience the comforting presence of Jesus the Lord, who once delivered them from their predicament.[192] One of the women, who is totally uneducated, said that when she underwent any pain or trouble in her life, she used to see the vision of Jesus who came and comforted her.[193] Thus, in faith they anticipate the same miraculous intervention that materialises in their lives. This, of course, creates a victorious outlook in the midst of those spiritual, social and economic forces which would have otherwise overwhelmed them.

This victorious feeling is directed towards the liberation of fellow human beings from demonic oppression, caste hierarchy and other social evils prevalent in the society. One of the songs refers to this issue:

The 'good news' will be victorious
The demonic powers will be destroyed
In the name of Jesus heads of all humanity will be bowed down
That is the greatest joy
We will demolish the fortress of demonic forces
We will eradicate caste distinctions
We will raise the banner of love
We will unfurl the glorious banner of Jesus the king
The 'good news' will be victorious.[194]

Interestingly, one of the evangelists who performs exorcisms said that while evil spirits are cast out, the spirits make loud confession through the possessed

---

[190] Testimony, Participant Observation, Hill-top Church, Rajasthan, 2 July 2009.

[191] Achamma, Focus Group Interview, Udaipur, 26 July 2009.

[192] Yeshudas, Interview, Hebron Church, Rajasthan, 16 August 2009.

[193] Rosamma, Interview, Udaipur, 5 August 2009.

[194] Song no. 572, *Zion Geethavaly* (Tiruvalla, India: Immanuel Bible Depot, 2005), 346.

person to the effect that Jesus is the Lord. This happens when he rebukes the demonic spirits in the name of Jesus. Moreover, according to him, the possessed spirit often acknowledges that it is the deity of that particular area or the god or goddess which people usually worship. This sort of revelation opens the eyes of many people who realise that until now, they were being cheated and falsely worshipped evil deities, while others out-rightly forsake such god or goddess. When these deities are cast out in the name of Jesus, people are convinced of the lordship of Jesus over all spiritual powers and begin to acknowledge him as the Lord.[195] In the churches they are also taught that Jesus is the Lord of their entire life through biblical stories.[196]

The notion that Jesus is the Lord rings loudly in the evangelistic and mission activities. The ordinary Pentecostals are not hesitant of proclaiming Jesus as *the* Lord in their daily life; instead, they convey this message to anybody who they come across. 'We preach Jesus as Lord, King of kings and Saviour. People understand Jesus as Lord of their lives. They know that Jesus came as a human being but consider him as Lord of all,' asserts Biju.[197] An evangelistic song which is sung during worship also underlines this fact:

Let the name of Jesus be victorious
Let the strongholds of the Satan be broken down
Let the banner of 'good news' be raised
Let the Bible truths be echoed.[198]

Moreover, the life experiences of the ordinary believers play a vital role in the proclamation of Jesus as the Lord. Their experiences are shared with the neighbours and people who are in trouble. They also pray for others in the name of Jesus.[199] Through ordinary believers, many are being healed as well as delivered from evil spirits. One of the women explained that her family was the first one to become Christian in their village and through her testimony many have now joined the church.[200] Thus, through their testimonies and lives the notion of Jesus as Lord and victor comes alive and expands in the community.

5.7 Jesus the Supreme God

This notion is deeply engraved in the psyche and life-styles of the ordinary Pentecostal believers and becomes apparent in their daily life. The believers have no qualms or hesitations in affirming Jesus is unique or the incomparable God.

---

[195] Joel, Interview, Maharashtra, 2 September 2009.

[196] Pastor Nathan, Interview, Hebron Church, Rajasthan, 5 August 2009.

[197] Biju, Focus Group Interview, Hebron Church, Rajasthan, 16 August 2009.

[198] Participant Observation, Kolenchery, 28 June 2009.

[199] Mani, Focus Group Interview, Hebron Church, Rajasthan, 2 August 2009.

[200] Rosamma, Interview, Udaipur, 5 August 2009.

The uniqueness of Jesus, which they affirm and proclaim in their daily encounter with fellow human beings, is a category which emerged from their own life experiences and subsequent 'ordinary' theological reflection. They elevate Jesus above all gods and consider every other deity they know inferior to Jesus. For them Jesus is *God* Most-High. This notion clearly appears in their personal testimonies to outsiders, in worship services and in their evangelistic endeavours. For them Jesus' care and love, the peace and security he brings and his extraordinary power over other deities they followed earlier, enable them to elevate him to the status of 'High God'. This 'High God,' who earlier far removed from their life-struggles and pain is now very close to them in Jesus Christ. They experience his providing and protecting hand in every aspect of their lives. Along with such experiences, the conviction that Jesus is the saviour and the Lord impel them to proclaim Jesus as supreme and unique among all gods. Thus, they do not think twice to acknowledge the supremacy of Christ before anybody.[201] This notion, along with Jesus as the Lord, forms the fourth level of Christological articulation. However, at this point more emphasis is given to the supremacy and incomparability of his divine nature.

In the interviews and focus groups this conviction appeared specifically. One of the interviewees said:

> People who are worshipping the idols are actually worshipping Satan who is in disguise underlying idol worship. There are 330 million gods and goddesses. Even people do not know 330 of them. Jesus is the only God. Only through Jesus one can be saved. He is *the* God. It is my experience.[202]

This person was arrested and taken to the police station for his witnessing. According to him, there he narrated his testimony and reiterated that what he said resulted from his experience. His colleagues and superiors alleged that he was propagating Christianity and they wrote to the health secretary of the state as well as to the registrar, as he is a medical doctor. However, there was nothing they could do to harm him.[203] Even now he speaks boldly about Christ. He says, 'I testify to the people who are nervous and burdened like me, who spent lots of money on treatment, that Jesus can heal them. He is the only God who will save us. When one comes to Jesus a new perspective is established and old convictions are thrown away.'[204]

Even the uneducated women testify to the greatness of Jesus in their daily encounter with their neighbours and those who are in dire need. One of the women explained it:

[201] Thomas, Interview, Udaipur, 8 July 2009.

[202] Ibid.

[203] Ibid.

[204] Ibid.

> In my village I testify to the women who are suffering from various diseases and other problems. I pray for them in the name of Jesus. I tell them Jesus would heal them. Even though I am illiterate I tell them He is greater than all gods. People believe it.[205]

This conviction of Jesus' uniqueness and greatness is more fervent in the believers who have renounced their earlier religious faith. Most of the people interviewed came from similar backgrounds and they had been troubled by the consequences of the lives they led before turning to Christ. However, their encounter with Jesus brought a new vision of the spiritual reality. They realised and testified that what they were following was mere futility and now they have reached their destiny; the believers do not hesitate to call all those gods satanic and evil gods.[206] One of the persons who testified speaks: 'I was indulging in idol worship and all sorts of rituals (*puja patt*). I used to sacrifice for *bavazi.* Now I know that all those are satanic and futile. Jesus is God (*yishu hi parameshwar hai*).'[207]

The idea that Jesus is greatest of all and unique explicitly emerged in one of the testimonies:

> Earlier I was an idol worshipper...I thought that those gods would help me and bless me. However, instead of blessings I had many problems. My family suffered from illness and attacks by demonic spirits. But, when I accepted Jesus, things began to change. Now I feel peace and there is peace in my family. So, I proclaim the greatness of Jesus to everybody... Some people oppose me. There are 330 million gods. But Jesus is greater than all these gods. I firmly tell the people that Jesus is the only God. He is greater than all gods.[208]

Therefore, it is not surprising to hear this idea frequently echoing in the worship services through songs, personal testimonies and preaching as we have seen earlier. One of the songs portrays the theme in vivid language:

> The name of Jesus is wonderful
> The name that removes the sin of humanity
> The name that delivers demon possessed and various diseases
> The name that heals the blind, lame and lepers
> The name that is above every name
> The name that is powerful, before him every knee bows down

---

[205] Jainamma, Interview by author, Maharashtra, 8 September 2009.

[206] Joel, Interview by author, South Gujarat, 8 September 2009.

[207] Noble, Interview by author, Maharashtra, 2 September 2009.

[208] Pylee, Focus Group Interview, Udaipur, 19 July 2009.

The name that every power on heaven, earth, hell bows down
The name that defeats every authority on heaven and earth.[209]

The Sunday sermons as well as public testimonies are pregnant with the idea that Jesus is greater than all. However, it comes out very forcefully in evangelistic activities, where believers unashamedly proclaim that Jesus is God and only Jesus can save humans from their sins.[210] As one of the evangelists put it bluntly and humorously following Paul, 'If Jesus is not unique and not above all gods, our life and proclamation are in vain.'[211] This proclamation is not a neatly articulated theological argument or an academic presentation of the defence of the greatness of Jesus. Rather, it is the narration of their earlier life of misery and the miraculous intervention and rescue by Jesus, along with his power to do the same for others.[212] Thus, this notion is experiential and practical which is proved with signs and wonders.[213] Moreover, they do not engage in any debate or dialogue. The ordinary believers invite people who are in despair to 'come and taste what they have been experiencing.'[214] They pray for the needs of the people and miracles take place. Then they boldly proclaim that Jesus is greater than all.[215] As mentioned earlier, interestingly, village pastors use gospel stories prominently to proclaim Jesus as healer, exorcist and, ultimately, God.

This attitude has attracted the ire of fundamentalist elements of other religions. As we have seen, many of the pastors and believers have been abused and persecuted for this matter and even today opposition and attack continue. For instance, in a particular village in Madhya Pradesh, right after the worship service the local police came and took ten believers to the police station on charges that they were going from house to house forcing people to accept Jesus as their saviour. In reality, a believer testified to the greatness of Jesus to another person and, when that person realised that he was unable to counter the arguments of the believer, he sought the help of fundamentalists who then pressed a charge of 'forcible conversion.'[216] Even though such incidents are common, the ordinary Pentecostal believers seldom cease to proclaim the greatness of Jesus. Nevertheless,

---

[209] Participant Observation, Kolenchery, 26 July 2009.

[210] Focus Group, Interview, Udaipur, 19 July 2009.

[211] Joel, Interview, Maharashtra, 2 September 2009.

[212] Focus Group, Interview, Udaipur, 12 July 2009.

[213] Ibid.

[214] Mathew, Focus Group Interview, Tabor Church, Gujarat, 6 September 2009.

[215] Pastor Nathan, Interview, Hebron Church, Rajasthan, 5 August 2009.

[216] Editor, 'Arrested on False Charges,' *Cross & Crown* 37/3 (January-February 2008): 21; See another incident of false charges slapped on believers for proclaiming Christ; Editor, 'A Plan for me...even in Prison,' *Cross & Crown* 36/2 (July-August 2007): 12.

they are not wary of acknowledging the existence of other gods or spirits, who they formerly worshipped, and the evil consequences.[217]

Although, believers engage in the proclamation of the uniqueness of Jesus, it is not an exercise meant only for the physical world. It is in fact a war they are 'waging in the spiritual realm' as one of the respondents put it. He says, 'We are not against any other people. Our war is against evil forces that lead people to destruction. Therefore, our proclamation is a spiritual war against satanic forces.'[218] At this point the Spirit enables the believers to witness Christ with courage. It is firmly believed that only with help of the Spirit can one achieve it.[219] Besides, their newfound joy as well as the confidence in the efficacy of Jesus to change the predicament of their fellow humans, propel them to testify his uniqueness with urgency. According to Pastor Timothy, they have a burning desire in their heart to tell it to everybody. He narrated the story of an evangelist who used ingenious methods to proclaim Christ. An evangelist was sent to a hill-locked region of Gujarat for mission work and he could not make any foray there for more than one year. According to him, the evangelist began to pray and God put an idea in his mind. There were no barber shops around those places and people had to travel long distance for their hair cut. The evangelist asked for a set of scissors and other items from the pastor. With prayer he began helping people, freely giving his service, although he had never trained for this trade. While cutting hair, he would share the Gospel messages. Within a few months, more than forty people joined his church.[220] Thomas says, 'It is my desire that everybody should know about Christ. It is always in my heart as a burning desire to tell about Jesus to everybody. All should escape the futility of false worship and sinful life.'[221] Thus, the theme is intricately conjoined to mission and evangelism.

Some more interesting ideas emerged; even though believers understand Jesus is the incarnation of God, the humanity of Jesus has not been taken to be a crucial aspect. One of the respondents said:

> People here consider Jesus as Lord and God. He is greater than all. No power can stand before him. He is all powerful. Perhaps believers do not understand him as a human being like us. When we preach, we tell them that God became a man. I don't think that believers tell anybody that Jesus is a man like us. People always see Jesus as greater than all gods and goddesses.[222]

[217] Focus Group, Tabor Church, Gujarat, 23 August 2009.

[218] Joel, Interview, Maharashtra, 2 September 2009.

[219] Ibid.

[220] Timothy, Personal interview by author, Tabor Church, Gujarat, 26 August 2009.

[221] Thomas, Interview, Udaipur, 8 July 2009.

[222] Mani, Focus Group Interview, Hebron Church, Rajasthan, 2 August 2009.

Moreover, ordinary believers are not aware of the ontological identity of Jesus with the Father or the Trinitarian Christology.[223]

From the above discussion, it is obvious that the Christological concept underlying these themes holds that Jesus is able to accomplish anything in every aspect of a believers' life and that he is powerful and greater than all powers. We may summarise the interconnection between the themes and fundamental Christology underlying them below.[224] When people are healed of their illnesses or delivered from demonic attack or possession, they acknowledge Jesus as the healer and exorcist. This understanding gives them a new sense of empowerment. The healing and deliverance enable them to save their expenditure on medical treatment or traditional healing practices, which leads to financial security and all-round prosperity. They also experience providing grace in all aspects of their lives. Thus people understand Jesus as the provider. They also realise that Jesus not only heals and delivers from illness and evil spirits but also keeps them away from sickness and protects them from demonic attack. Moreover, he protects them from external forces (extreme elements). This results in acknowledging Jesus as the protector.

This new understanding – Jesus as the healer, exorcist, provider and protector – along with the peace of mind, joy and prosperity they enjoy as well as the experience of the Holy Spirit and the fervent worship atmosphere in the community enable them to elevate Jesus into an exalted position and confess him to be the saviour. The experience of the Holy Spirit acts as a catalyst in the confessions. Therefore, this notion stands between the functional and ontological categories. The process of reflection does not stop here. Their daily struggles, joy, sorrows and assurance of Jesus' presence in every aspect of their lives, coupled with preaching and teaching of biblical stories, especially Gospel stories enable them to proclaim Jesus as the Lord; now, the whole of their universe revolves around Jesus. This understanding, in turn, verbalised and communicated within the worship context and in evangelistic activities which proclaim that Jesus is *greater than all*. Consequently, they understand Jesus as *the* Supreme God. In certain cases, especially in the cases of those who come from denominational backgrounds or second and third generation Pentecostals, the reflective process may start from Jesus as the Saviour and read back to Jesus as healer, provider and so on.

223 Mercy, Interview by author, Kolenchery, Kerala, 28 June 2009.

224 Jesus as the healer and exorcist form the primary level of ordinary Christology, while Jesus as the provider and protector come out from previous themes, thus form the secondary level. Jesus as the saviour forms third level and this theme connects primary and secondary level to the fourth level Jesus as Lord and supreme God.

Chapter 6

Indian Pentecostal Christology: Discussion

Chapter five discussed the dominant Christological themes that ordinary Pentecostals appreciate in their broad religio-cultural, socio-economic and political contexts, as well as in their personal and immediate circumstances. It is significant to see that the Christology they embrace does make a marked difference to their spirituality, along with their socio-economic status. However, it is also important to discuss the feasibility of presenting this Christology systematically to a wider audience of Pentecostals as well as to Christians of other traditions. Several questions arise at this point: what are the limitations of this articulation? Does it show any special characteristics? Is it compatible with the Pentecostal tradition and the New Testament testimony of Jesus? Hence, in this chapter we shall attempt to offer a critical analysis of the scope and limitations of such a Christology. We shall also consider the nature and affinity of ordinary Christology with the larger Pentecostal tradition and with the New Testament testimony of the person and work of Christ.

6.1 Indian Pentecostal Christology: Evaluation

Ordinary Indian Pentecostal Christology is the product of the common believers' struggles, aspiration and remedies they draw out of utilizing biblical narratives, especially Gospel stories. It is in every sense a people's Christology; accordingly, far removed from the genre of scholarly and systematic theology. Hence, it is naive and even futile to attempt to seek every factor of a formal Christology in it. Given their context, it is natural for people to emphasise their immediate needs and concerns and to concentrate on those aspects of Christology that bring solace and immediate remedy. Consequently, the prominent components of this Christology are elementary in nature and can be used as the foundational building blocks of a Christological superstructure for the Indian context. Therefore, while we evaluate this Christology critically, it is vital to bear in mind the context, the experiences people go through and the solutions they seek.

On the other hand, a given Christology cannot be a stagnant entity; it needs to move from an elementary stage to more advanced categories to accommodate and answer changing situations. More seriously, the Christology of a people ought to develop into a more inclusive and balanced entity, more truthful and akin to biblical tradition. This pattern of progressive movement is apparent in the New Testament tradition. Various levels of Christological articulations have been proposed to supplement a more inclusive Christology. For example, while the Synoptic Gospels seem to propose a 'Christology from below' (functional), the Johannine Christology presents a 'Christology from above' (ontological). According to France, it is a progression from the former to the latter.[1] Therefore, it is significant to search for those essential factors that are lacking in this Christology, with a view to making it more constructive and meaningful; more inclusive and enduring.

6.1.1 An Ordinary Christology

Our starting point is a positive note. Close scrutiny will throw light on the salient features of this Christology which is a combination of a Christology from below and a Christology from above, with a qualification.[2] Justification of this observation is that, this Christology emphasises the works of Christ such as healing, exorcism and other miraculous events; it envisions a Jesus who is concerned about the poor and destitute and who comes to rescue them. Evidently its elementary components are based on Jesus' public activities and redemptive actions in relation to immediate situations which included the socio-political, the religio-cultural and the economic components. Jesus is the one who brings answers to their struggles in these spheres, as in the Gospels. Thus, it emphasises the work of Christ, as stated above.

Simultaneously, it also strongly asserts that Jesus is the Saviour, Lord and God. He is the only one who can save them from their predicament and sin. He is greater than all powers and he is God. Here we see a strong emphasis on the divinity of Jesus and in the assertion that he is unique and supreme. This sort of description of Jesus points towards highlighting his person. Consequently, we may term this a balanced Christology emphasising both the humanity and divinity of Jesus; a Christology with the right mix of functional and ontological elements.

---

[1] R.T. France, 'The Uniqueness of Christ,' *Evangelical Review of Theology* 17/1 (January-March 1993): 24.

[2] The following explanation expounds this statement.

However, this research showed that, although the work of Christ as a human being forms its basic ingredients, this Christology gives less importance to the humanity of Jesus.[3] The people understand and worship Jesus as God but they are unable to acknowledge Jesus as a human being.[4] Similarly, in asserting Jesus as Lord and God, this Christology seems to advocate the divinity of Jesus and a 'Christology from above'. However, it has emerged from this study that the Christology lacks an ontological conception of the person of Christ. People understand Jesus to be the Son of God but they do not give due importance to his pre-existence or to the Trinitarian relationship with the Father.[5] These are serious issues which need addressing and shall be discussed in the following pages.

6.1.2 Limitations in the Ontological Identity of Jesus

It is apparent from the discussion that this Christology is similar to the 'Christology of the Early Church,' or a primary level of Christological articulation. The people who theologise are mainly ordinary people; many of them are illiterate and poor and the majority are recent converts who hardly have basic Bible literacy. Their main sources of Christological knowledge are stories from the Gospels, especially the Synoptic Gospels, they hear in church, and their personal experience of Christ through miraculous events.[6] The Christology they articulate emerges when Gospel stories intersect with their contextual experiences. Hence, they focus primarily on the struggles they face and endeavour to find solutions through the work of Christ. In other words, this Christology focuses more on the existential aspects of the work of Christ, such as healing, exorcism and provision, than on the person of Christ. The study showed that many of the respondents were not able to move beyond these functional categories to a deep-rooted understanding of the person of Christ. Even their more advanced categories such as Jesus as the Saviour, Lord and God are the outcome of the former categories.[7] Hence, it is more or less a functional Christology, one which is closely connected with the present aspects of the work of Christ; in other words, soteriological dimensions of Christology are prominent. Again, the eschatological aspect of the work of Christ is underestimated. Although, some of the pastors claimed that they preach about the return of Christ,[8] this aspect did not feature prominently among respondents who are more concerned with the present aspects of the work of Christ. However, in South India, Pentecostals do acknowledge eschatological aspect of Christ's work

[3] See Chapter 6.

[4] Mercy, Interview by author, Kolenchery, Kerala, 28 June 2009.

[5] Ibid.

[6] For example, some of the references heard in the sermons during the participant observation were: Mat. 9:2-8; Mk. 5:21-34; Mk.7:24-30; Lk. 7:36-50; 8:26-39; Jn.5:1-18.

[7] This was the process in which the ontological identity of Jesus developed in NT; see France, 'The Uniqueness of Christ,' 23-24.

[8] Kuttappan, Focus Group Interview, Hebron Church, Rajasthan, 9 August 2009.

as they were introduced to the 'fourfold gospel'. Certainly, people understand and acknowledge Jesus as Saviour and God; nevertheless, these ontological categories are drawn out from existential categories. That is, the ontological dimension of Christology is poorly emphasised or seems to be unknown to the Pentecostals. However, it is an interesting point to note that this characteristic is a universal feature of popular Pentecostal Christology in general.[9]

Another potential problem closely related to the above point is the absence of the Trinitarian context for Christology. Although, ordinary members recognize Jesus to be the son of God, or God, they lack the idea of the ontological relationship between members of the Trinity. They know that God exists as the Father, Son and Holy Spirit but either they do not know the discussion regarding the necessity of the divine equality of Christ (*homoousios*) with the Father or Holy Spirit, or are not concerned about it.[10] Their immediate circumstances have a bearing on this. For them, there is a God; God became a human being to save sinful humanity and Jesus is the Son of God.[11] In the name of Jesus miracles are performed and they happen through the power of the Spirit.[12] The intricate relationship between members of the Trinity and the economy of the Trinity are foreign to this Christology. People experience and visualise a Jesus who acts on their behalf, and therefore, their Christology revolves around the work of Christ. A more advanced theological reflection, which we see in the Johannine gospel, where Jesus is portrayed as the Word (*Logos*), is largely absent. His eternal divine status as the 'Son of God' and his divine essence with God the Father are all missing. Therefore, the notion of his relationship to God the Father needs to be added to this functional Christology to make it more balanced by containing both these aspects. Satyavrata rightly cautions us, 'Anything less than a robust Trinitarian spirituality will find itself in danger of being easily assimilated by the powerful monistic philosophical currents of our day.'[13] This issue naturally places a question mark on their understanding of the divinity of Christ.[14]

6.1.3 Limitations in the Humanity of Jesus

Another area of concern is the lack of understanding of the humanity of Jesus. Undoubtedly, Pentecostals verbalise their belief that Jesus is the incarnation of

---

[9] Walter J. Hollenweger, *The Pentecostals* (Minneapolis: Augsburg Publishing House, 1972), 311-312.

[10] Philipos, Interview by author, Hill-view Church, Rajasthan, 20 September 2009; Joel, Interview by author, Maharashtra, Gujarat, 2 September 2009.

[11] Anish, Interview by author, Maharashtra, 7 September 2009.

[12] Meeraji, Interview by author, Maharashtra, 8 September 2009.

[13] Satyavrata, 'Contextual Perspectives on Pentecostalism,' 213.

[14] Colin E. Gunton, *Father, Son and Holy Spirit: Toward a Fully Trinitarian Theology* (London: T&T Clark, 2003), 58-74; Colin E. Gunton, *The Christian Faith: An Introduction to Christian Doctrine* (Oxford: Blackwell Publishers, 2002), 176-179.

God. However, the humanity of Jesus has been unwittingly sidelined. In practice, the divinity of Jesus is emphasised at the cost of the humanity of Jesus. For them, Jesus is all powerful: able to heal, delivers from evil spiritual and social forces, provides and saves them from their predicament;[15] he is greater than all gods or the gods they worshipped; he is able to rescue them from all possible troubles and therefore he is God.[16] In this way, unknowingly they overlook the humanity of Jesus which is an integral aspect of Christology. In fact, many of them are reluctant to acknowledge Jesus as a human being like us.[17] It is obvious that the context plays an important role, as the prominent understanding at this point is that those who perform miracles are divine (*chamatkar ko namaskar*). This one-sided understanding may stop them from imitating Jesus and carrying out Jesus' model of ministry in their surroundings, which would be detrimental to the growth of the movement in the long run.[18]

At the same time, it is evident from their testimonies that they hold a qualified 'Christology from below'. The justification of this observation is that their Christology is similar to, and in a nutshell can be explained in terms of, the Christology of the Synoptic Gospels. They understand Jesus as one who is among them, solving their immediate problems of physical illness, poverty and delivers them from the threat of social and spiritual powers.[19] He is the one who walks with them and comforts them in their critical junctures.[20] The paradoxical fact is that, although they do not acknowledge Jesus as a human being like us, they wholeheartedly experience and confess his works as a human being as told in the Gospel stories.[21] What we can notice is that this Christology shifts between the divinity and humanity of Jesus. This can be termed a dialectical understanding of the person of Christ: confessing and proclaiming Jesus as divine but experiencing his works as being human. The humanity of Jesus is shrouded in the divinity of Jesus. At this point we find a creative tension between the humanity and the divinity of Jesus. Hence, it is a Christology from above but internally blended with a Christology from below. Consequently, a clear distinction between the divinity and humanity of Jesus cannot be drawn in this Christology. What we have outlined are limitations which may be harmful to the Indian Pentecostal movement in the long run and should be addressed. Therefore, in the next

---

[15] Anand, Interview by author, South Gujarat, 30 September 2009.

[16] Prakash, Interview by author, Maharashtra, 2 September 2009.

[17] Mani, Focus Group Interview, Hebron Church, Rajasthan, 2 August 2009.

[18] John P. Meir, *A Marginal Jew: Rethinking the Historical Jesus* (New York: Doubleday, 1991), 196-201; Marcus J. Borg, *Jesus a New Vision: Spirit, Culture, and the Life of Discipleship* (New York: HarperSanFrancisco, 1987), 1-2.

[19] Joshi, Interview by author, Gujarat, 29 August 2009.

[20] Testimony, Participant Observation, Hill-top Church, 2 July 2009.

[21] Emma, Interview by author, Udaipur, 15 September 2009.

chapter we will recommend some biblical and theological insights to deal with these problems.

6.2 The Nature of Ordinary Indian Pentecostal Christology

We shall now look into the nature of ordinary Pentecostal Christology. As we have seen, theirs is basically a functional Christology emerging from the saving work of Christ. In other words, this Christology is informed and formed by the reflection of the *saving experiences* people undergo in their lives. Therefore, it is closely related to Soteriology. Simultaneously, this Christology moves from functional categories (healer, exorcist, provider, protector) to ontological categories (Lord, God), although the latter group is derived from the former with the theme Jesus as *Saviour* acting as a bridge between these two categories. In actuality, the functional and ontological categories overlap with each other making it difficult for any study to set clear boundaries.

It is obvious from the discussion that this Christology has special characteristics of its own which need discussing to appreciate its worth and usefulness. First of all, it is an *experiential Christology*, which has emerged from the people's intense existential struggles. Most of the Pentecostals come from the lower strata of the society and are constantly confronted by social forces detrimental to their existence. Many of them were either oppressed by evil spiritual forces or physical troubles which result in the draining of their hard-earned resources, inflicting on them a crushing blow leading to poverty. In the midst of such a situation, their new experience of Christ enables them to wade through the struggles; it also lifts them up. Thus, the fundamentals of this Christology are constituted by their emancipating experiences of the work of Christ.[22]

Closely connected with the above characteristics is its intimate relationship to the personal lives of the ordinary people and, therefore it can be termed an *intimate Christology.* Their initial knowledge of Christ is not rooted in formal theological discourse or voluminous information but achieved through an encounter with Christ in their healing, exorcisms or any other immediate needs. Such encounters result in spiritual experience and a new vibrant knowledge and intimacy with Christ. Moreover, all this helps to further build the Christological structure up to form a lofty understanding of Christ. Some of them were Christians before. However, as they testified, they had no personal experience of the person of Christ. Once they joined the movement, intimacy with Christ and knowledge of him increased and this intimacy is actualised through the experience of the Spirit and testified in their immediate surroundings.

[22] Satyavrata, 'Contextual Perspectives on Pentecostalism,' 211; William MacDonald, 'Pentecostal Theology: A Classical View Point,' in *Perspectives on the New Pentecostalism*, edited by Russell P. Spittler (Michigan: Baker Book House, 1976), 61-62.

Besides, as mentioned, the Christological themes which we have explored do not result from theoretical articulation; instead, they are the outcome of intense personal and communitarian reflections on the person and work of Christ. The people verbalise and communicate these themes through testimonies, stories, songs, exposition of biblical narratives and informal conversations in the community to which they are culturally relevant. Therefore, it is a *narrative Christology*. Cook identifies the value of narrative Christology, 'a narrative-centred Christology would seek to maintain the validity and the necessity of particular, concrete experience within a given socio-historical and cultural context precisely in order to sustain the truly catholic and universal character of the mystery that is Jesus.'[23] This communication contributes to deliver a contagious faith to other members of their community and this in turn is transmitted to the wider society. Even though most of them are either illiterate or semi-literate, they convey their Christological perception orally. This oral transmission of life-experiences and Christological themes perfectly fits in the social conditioning of the Indian villages and enables common masses to be attracted to the Pentecostal movement. This sort of transmission of the person and work of Christ was the essential nature of the communication of the first-century church.[24] Interestingly, this is a very basic and common feature of Pentecostal theology more generally, as Hollenweger has rightly commented.[25] Thus, ordinary Indian Pentecostal Christology is an *oral Christology.*[26]

Furthermore, this Christology is formed and articulated in the community on the basis of the struggles of its members, and the solutions they themselves draw with the help of Christological narratives form the basic elements. No professional theologians are involved here. Its ingredients come from individuals in the community; for one, Jesus is the healer, for another, Jesus is the provider, and so on. These themes are put together within a worship context and form a coherent whole and are later verbalised and proclaimed by the ordinary members and directed towards the suffering masses. Accordingly, it is essentially a *communitarian Christology*.

---

[23] Michael L. Cook, *Christology as Narrative Quest* (Minnesota: Liturgical Press, 1997), 31, 29-66.

[24] Casey W. Davis, 'Oral Biblical Criticism: Raw Data in Philippians,' in *Linguistics and New Testament: Critical Junctures*, edited by Stanley E. Porter & D.A. Carson (Sheffield: Sheffield Academic Press, 1999), 96-124; Jan Vansina, *Oral Tradition: A Study in Historical Methodology*, translated by H.M. Wright (New Jersey: Transaction Publishers, 2006), 19-30.

[25] Walter J. Hollenweger, 'Pentecostal Research: Problems and Promises,' in *A Guide to the Study of the Pentecostal Movement*, vol.1, edited by Charles Edwin Jones (London: Scarecrow, 1983), vii-ix; Walter J. Hollenweger, 'Pentecostals and the Charismatic Movement,' in *The Study of Spirituality*, edited by Cheslyn Jones et. al. (London: SPCK, 1986).

[26] Satyavrata, 'Contextual Perspectives on Pentecostalism,' 210.

Closely related to the oral nature of Christology is its 'kerygmatic' nature.[27] Since the Christology is essentially experiential and oral, it is largely communicated in informal settings such as testimonies, conversation and songs. The content of this 'kerygma' is the transforming and liberating power of Christ for the common masses. It is the story of the power of Jesus bringing changes to the lives of ordinary people. It touches the lives of the suffering people as the proclamation is made by the people they know, who were once like them, and who underwent similar predicaments but have now been liberated and transformed. Therefore, the listeners are convinced of what is proclaimed and in many cases it is readily accepted.[28] Moreover, much as in the case of the early Church, this Christology is proclaimed in the power of the Spirit and is seen as being proved by the immediate signs of healing and exorcism.[29] It is not only proclaimed in the physical realm but its effect is also extended even into the 'invisible realm'. Hence, it is a *kerygmatic Christology.*

In addition, it is worth noting that this is a *Pneumatologically-driven Christology*. In other words, it is informed and propelled by the power of the Spirit and proclaimed and enacted through the people who acknowledge the work of the Spirit as they themselves claim.[30] The ordinary members are empowered to venture into the unknown and the Spirit gives power to proclaim the message; the community becomes a channel of liberation in the society, even though the members live in the same conditions themselves.[31] They form an alternative community in the midst of a hostile and oppressive culture with harmful religious practices.

At the same time, it is a *culturally-tuned Christology* as well because it is thoroughly based in the cultural context of the people and the common masses do not feel alienated in their cultural setting while they cherish this Christology. It accommodates the positive aspects of the culture to form and proclaim the message of Christ; their lifestyle and faith expressions are the true reflection of their context. However, it does not advocate the *status quo*, which is often oppressive and harmful for the people. Instead, it transcends and transforms the

---

[27] Kerygma is the systematic statement of the theology of the primitive church as revealed in its preaching. The kerygma was the proclamation of Jesus' deeds, death and resurrection; see R.H. Mounce, 'Kerygma,' *The International Standard Bible Encyclopedia,* vol. 3 (Michigan: Eerdmans, 1986), 9-10.

[28] Joel, Interview, Maharashtra, 2 September 2009.

[29] J. I. H. McDonald, *Kerygma and Didache: The Articulation and Structure of the Earliest Christian Message* (Cambridge: Cambridge University Press, 1980); also see C.H. Dodd, *The Apostolic Preaching and its Developments: Three Lectures* (London: Hodder & Stoughton, 1944).

[30] Mani, Focus Group Interview, Hebron Church, 2 August 2009; Joel, Interview, Maharashtra, 2 September 2009.

[31] See Samuel Solivan, *The Spirit, Pathos and Liberation: Toward an Hispanic Pentecostal Theology* (Sheffield: Sheffield Academic, 1998).

harmful cultural elements of the society.[32] The community is made of people from different castes, people groups and ethnic orientations in which the distinctions of caste, gender and wealth have been blurred.[33] Even women who are not able to speak in the village community are empowered to testify their stories so as to liberate their neighbours.[34]

It is a *transformative and liberative Christology* too. Both the Pentecostal believers and the outsiders alike testify that the outlook and attitude of the people radically changed and was transformed for the better,[35] a transformation which occurred in the social, economic, psychological and spiritual realms of ordinary members. Their newfound faith enables them to stand against the oppressive structure of society. However, it is not to be misunderstood as popular revolution or revolt; instead, silent but definite changes have been taking place in the lives of the people. Moreover, this liberative potential is not limited to the community itself but flows out into the larger society and rescues many. In other words, this Christology empowers people to rescue their own kith and kin who are in the doldrums. Thus, what David Martin asserts is right; in India, Pentecostalism competes with Social Gospel Christianity and Liberationism.[36]

Further, this Christology enables them to face serious challenges such as economic hardships, discrimination and persecution. For the sake of the testimony of Christ people are ready to suffer. Actually many have been falsely accused and persecuted for their faith and jailed while their suffering continues. However, their profound experience of Christ and changes which have taken place in their lives enable them to withstand such perilous situations. Thus, it is an *empowering Christology*.

Another noteworthy credential of this Christology is its missionary nature. The Christological themes which have emerged are directed towards missionary endeavours. The transforming experience of the members of the community along with Gospel stories of healing, exorcism, provision and protection are proclaimed in the larger society. The Gospel stories undergirded by the miraculous interventions in the lives of the hearers validate the impact of this Christology. Every member, knowingly or unknowingly, proclaims these themes through their life-styles, the positive changes in their conditions or in testimonies they give in informal settings. Tony Richie explains this sort of testimony as a typical

---

32 Joel, Interview, Maharashtra, 2 September 2009.

33 Gabriel, 'Reflections on Indian Pentecostalism,' 68.

34 Rosy, Interview by author, Hill-top Church, Rajasthan, 9 August 2009; Bergunder, 'Women and Leadership'.

35 Reji, Focus Group Interview, Hebron Church, 9 August 2009; Nathulal, Maharashtra, 7 September 2009; Miller & Yamamori, *Global Pentecostalism*, 33.

36 David Martin, 'Issues Affecting the Study of Pentecostalism in Asia,' in *Asian and Pentecostal*, 32.

Pentecostal mode of inter-religious dialogue.[37] Many a time the communication of the message happens unknowingly when people watch the marked changes in the conditions of a person and are thus attracted to the message. Of course, the members make it a point to share these themes with others. Therefore, it is essentially a *missionary Christology*.

Another very significant and crucial nature of this Christology is its close proximity and resemblance with the Christology of the Synoptic Gospels and in every sense can be called as *Gospel Christology*. A cursory glance at this point will reveal that the Christological themes which have emerged in the study are the basic building-blocks of Gospel Christology. The Gospel tradition is rich in stories which prove the themes of Jesus as healer, exorcist, provider, and saviour. These narratives in the Gospels take place in a similar setting as that of ordinary Indian Pentecostals, although both are separated by a two thousand year gap. Ill-health, poverty, oppression and evil-spirit infestations form the background of this Christology just as in the Gospels. Even a casual reading of the Gospels and a glimpse into the condition of the people in Indian villages would convince anybody of the glaring similarities of these settings. Moreover, the confessions of people who have experienced healing, exorcism or rescue from perilous situations are the same as those in the gospels. The recipients of these miracles have a lofty understanding of Christ and proclaim him in their context, just as we read in the Gospels.[38]

Another important characteristic of this Christology is its focus on the authority and power of Christ to heal and to deliver from the destructive social, cultural and spiritual forces. Jesus is the greatest of all and is incomparable. Every power whether it is spiritual or temporal, religious or cultural, political or social comes under the authority of Jesus. This idea portrays Christ as the cosmic conqueror of the principalities and powers just as he was portrayed in Colossians (Col. 2:13-15). In the New Testament texts, these powers were recognized as the hostile cosmic powers of the universe that gripped with fear the hearts of many in the Roman world of the day. The popular religion of the first century Mediterranean world conceived of a cosmos haunted by spirits in the heavens, on the Earth and beneath the Earth through association with magic, mysteries or astrology. To remedy this situation, Paul addressed it by announcing that the powers of darkness had been defeated by Christ on the Cross.[39] A similar understanding is prevalent in the context of our study as we have seen: that the

[37] Tony Richie, 'Speaking by the Spirit: A Wesleyan-Pentecostal Theology of Testimony as a Model for Interreligious Encounter and Dialogue in the USA with Global Implications' (PhD Thesis, University of Middlesex, 2010); also see Cartledge, *Testimony in the Spirit*, 146-148.

[38] Mk. 5:7; 7:36; Matt. 14:33 and Lk. 8:39.

[39] D. G. Reid, 'Powers and Principalities,' *DPL*, edited by Gerald F. Hawthorne, Ralph P. Martin, Daniel G. Reid (Illinois: IVP, 1998), CD Rom.

people understand Christ to be victorious over all powers. Therefore we can term it to be a *power Christology*.

It should also be noted that Indian Pentecostal Christology is in tune with the more widespread Pentecostal Christology in which Christ is portrayed as saviour, healer and so on. However, it is not a copy of earlier Pentecostal tradition. Most of the people are unaware that such a Pentecostal Christology exists. It is through their contextual experiences that they have developed these notions of Christ. Nevertheless, it should be noted at this point that, except for a few pastors and some south Indian Pentecostals, not many have advocated the idea of Jesus as 'the soon coming king' as in the 'fourfold Gospel'. This is perhaps understandable, as most of them are reeling under existential struggle. Now we shall turn to analysis to study the affinity of this Christology with the larger Pentecostal tradition and the New Testament.

6.3 Development

Any given system of theology, whether it is biblical or practical, systematic or contextual, needs to include certain basic elements if it is to be called a 'Christian theology'. These elements include scripture, experience, tradition, culture, context, and so on. These basic elements are considered to be the formative factors of any given theology. Christology of a given context also ought to accommodate at least some of these elements if it is to be genuinely an 'ordinary' Christology.

In the case of ordinary Pentecostal Christology we have already explored the context, culture and experience of the people which acted as underlying principles, shaped and coloured it. It is true to these factors. In this section, first we shall try to evaluate ordinary Indian Pentecostal Christology in the light of larger Pentecostal theological traditions to see whether the former has any consonance and continuity with the latter. Secondly, we shall see whether this Christology has a biblical base, especially with respect to the Jesus tradition in order to gauge its suitability as an authentic 'Christology'.

6.3.1 Pentecostal Tradition

We should not overlook the fact that theology is always contextual and takes the shape and colour of the context and other local factors in which it evolves. Moreover, Pentecostalism cannot be explained as a monolithic single structure worldwide but has to be understood as different entities with various hues and colours, springing up from cultural diversities. Even though it is difficult to identify a universal unifying thread, Pentecostal movements the world over have certain characteristic features in common such as emphasis on the work of the Spirit, the idea of Jesus as healer and so on. Moreover, as we have seen, the basic commitment to the fourfold (or fivefold) Gospel also may be considered as a distinguishing feature of the movement.[40]

6.3.1.1 Jesus as Healer and Exorcist

The fourfold Gospel or full Gospel is the fourfold devotion to Jesus Christ as the Saviour, Spirit Baptiser, Healer and Coming King.[41] According to Dayton, the Pentecostal movement developed this doctrine from the background of the Holiness movement and various evangelical revival strands of the nineteenth century.[42] Later, Pentecostal leaders adopted this doctrine and used it effectively in Pentecostal evangelistic campaigns.[43]

However, the unique Pentecostal contribution to this doctrine was the addition of a Pentecostal flavour and a new theological direction. Macchia rightly captures the essence: 'What was unique was how these themes formed a "gestalt" of devotion in the Spirit to Jesus that reconfigured evangelical piety and gave Pentecostalism its Christological centre as well as its theological cogency and direction.'[44] The provision of bodily healing through the atonement and by the gift of the Spirit became one of the main theological emphases of the Pentecostal movement. Dayton considers 'the Divine Healing Movement' of the nineteenth century as one of the 'theological roots of Pentecostalism.'[45] Horton, in his *The Gifts of the Spirit,* says that divine healing is the only way of healing open to

---

[40] Quoted in Donald Dayton, *The Theological Roots of Pentecostalism* (Peabody: Hendrickson Publishers, 1987), 21; see Stanley Horton, *Into All Truth: A Survey of the Course and Content of Divine Revelation* (Springfield, Mo.: Gospel Publishing House, 1955), 13.

[41] This is also often called fivefold Gospel adding Jesus as sanctifier. Dayton, *The Theological Roots,* 19. The 'statement of truth' of the Pentecostal Fellowship of North America (PFNA) calls it full Gospel and draws attention to 'healing for the body' as well as 'holiness' and baptism in the Spirit.

[42] For detailed descriptions see Dayton, *The Theological Roots,* 15-28; Donald Dayton, 'The Rise of the Evangelical Healing Movement in Nineteenth Century America,' *Pneuma* 4/1 (1982): 1-18; Also see Melvin E. Dieter, 'Wesleyan Holiness Aspects of Pentecostal Origins,' in *Aspects of Pentecostal-Charismatic Origins,* edited by Vinson Synan (New Jersey: Logos International, 1975), 67-69. For instance, A. B. Simpson founder of the Christian and Missionary Alliance spoke of Christ as the saviour, sanctifier, healer and coming king. See A.B. Simpson, *The Fourfold Gospel: Jesus as Saviour, Sanctifier, Healer and Coming King* (Orlando, FL: Bridge-Logos, 2007); C. Nienkirchen, 'Simpson, Albert Benjamin,' *NIDPCM,* 1069-70.

[43] Raymond L. Cox, *The Four-Square Gospel* (Los Angeles: Foursquare Publications, 1969), 9. For example, Aimee Semple McPherson, founder of the International Church of the Foursquare Gospel summarises it in characteristic Pentecostal style: Jesus saves us according to John 3:16. He baptises us with the Holy Spirit according to Acts 2:4. He heals our bodies according to James 5:14-15. And Jesus is coming again to receive us unto himself according to 1 Thess. 4:16-17.

[44] Macchia, 'Theology, Pentecostal,' 1123-1124.

[45] For detailed descriptions see Dayton, *The Theological Roots,* 115-141; Kimberly Ervin Alexander, *Pentecostal Healing: Models in Theology and Practice* (Dorset, UK: Deo Publishing, 2006), 8-63.

believers and authorised by the Scriptures.[46] Early Pentecostals were convinced of this and practised the divine healing in their daily life including exorcism.[47]

This Pentecostal emphasis on divine healing and exorcism was true in India and within the larger Asian context. Many of the early Pentecostals in Kerala had supernatural gifts of healing and exorcism,[48] which helped the establishment of the Pentecostal movement at the beginning of the last century.[49] According to K.E. Abraham, founder of the Indian Pentecostal Church (IPC), many of the early Pentecostals joined the movement due to the healing and other miraculous events undertaken in his ministry.[50] Although, earlier Pentecostals did not consider healing and exorcism to be major Pentecostal doctrines,[51] they understood them as instrumental in bringing glory to the Lord and used them extensively in missionary activities.[52] What we can understand from their stories is that divine healing acted as an assurance of God's presence in their personal lives.[53] Occurrence of healing was considered as a medium for evangelism and 'a vivid message from God to the people.'[54] For example, Bergunder, after conducting research on divine healing and exorcism among the Indian Pentecostals, comments that the Pentecostal pastors' practices resembled those of *mantravadis* (black magicians) and this has brought deliverance and attracted many to the Pentecostal movement.[55]

Similarly, in a wider Asian context, healing and exorcism acted as springboards to Pentecostal growth and consolidation. For example, it is claimed that the immediate cause for the rapid growth of the Yoido Full Gospel Church of Yonggi Cho is its emphasis on healing and exorcism to alleviate the sufferings

---

[46] Anderson, *An Introduction, 232.*

[47] For example, Charles Parham wrote in 1902: 'Christ did not leave his believing children without signs...Neither did he send forth his servants to preach vague speculative theories of a world to come, but with mighty power for the relief of suffering humanity: feeding the hungry, clothing the naked; healing the sick; casting out the devils..'. Quoted in Dayton, *The Theological Roots*, 24-25.

[48] See Mathew, *Kerala Penthecosthu Charithram* and Abraham, *Yesukristhuvinte Eliya Dassan.*

[49] Robert F. Cook, *Half a Century of Divine Leading and 37 Years of Apostolic Achievements in South India* (Cleveland, TN: Church of God Foreign Missions Department, 1955), 25-26, 40-41; Mathew, *Kerala Penthecosthu Charithram,* 49-69.

[50] Abraham, *Yesukristhuvinte Eliya Dassan*, 104-105, 108-110.

[51] However, the Ceylon Pentecostal Mission (CPM) had a strict rule against using any medicine and considered divine healing to be an indispensible doctrine of Pentecostalism.

[52] Abraham, *Yesukristhuvinte Eliya Dassan*, 109-110.

[53] P. M. Philip, *Kristhuvil Ente Yathra* (*My Pilgrimage with Christ*) (Kottayam, India: Royal Calling Books, 1999), 17-22; Cook, *Half a Century of Divine Leading,* 33-35, 56.

[54] Cook, *Half a Century of Divine Leading,* 81.

[55] Michael Bergunder, 'Miracle Healing and Exorcism: The South Indian Pentecostal Movement in the Context of Popular Hinduism,' *International Review of Mission* XC/356,357 (January/April, 2001): 101-112.

of the common people (*Minjung*) in their cultural and religious contexts.[56] Park says, 'It [healing] is the most important aspect of the ministry of Yonggi Cho and has contributed to the phenomenal growth of the Church.'[57] This has contributed to the well being of ordinary people, as Ma comments, 'As a result, an "upward mobility" was created, not only in the spiritual and emotional realm but more tangibly in economic and social areas.'[58] This is true in most of the countries of Asia where most of the people suffer social, economic and cultural evils which result in illness and evil spirit infestations.[59]

Early Pentecostal magazines such as *The Apostolic Faith, The Bridegroom's Messenger, The Latter Rain Evangel, Confidence* and others abound with testimonies and theological justification of divine healing and exorcism.[60] In the first issue of *Apostolic Faith* William Seymour reported:

> Canes, crutches, medicine bottles and glasses are being thrown aside as God heals. That is the safe way. No need to keep an old crutch or medicine bottle of any kind around after God heals you.[61]

These periodicals also contained many testimonies about how people were healed of asthma, tuberculosis, evil spirits, blindness and many other serious diseases.[62] Seymour considered health and healing to be intricately linked to salvation and actually, the result of sanctification of the body.[63] Even some of the early Pentecostals rejected the use of medicines and considered them to be evidence of weak faith.[64] Likewise, as McClung asserts, a survey of the literature, history and oral stories of Pentecostalism reveals the centrality of the practice

---

[56] Dongsoo Kim, 'The Healing of Han in Korean Pentecostalism,' *JPT* 15 (1999): 123-139.

[57] Myung Soo Park, 'Korean Pentecostal Spirituality as Manifested in the Testimonies of Members of Yoido Full Gospel Church,' *AJPS* 7/1 (2004): 48.

[58] Wonsuk Ma, 'Asian Pentecostalism: A Religion whose only Limit is the Sky,' *Journal of Beliefs & Values* 25/2 (August 2004): 198.

[59] Trinidad E. Seleky, 'A History of the Pentecostal Movement in Indonesia,' *AJPS* 4/1 (2001): 137; Gani Wiyono, 'Timor Revival: A Historical Study of the Great Twentieth-century Revival in Indonesia,' *AJPS* 4/2 (2001): 227-278; Chin Khua Khai, 'Pentecostalism in Myanmar: An Overview,' *AJPS* 5/1 (2002): 54-55.

[60] See Alexander, *Pentecostal Healing*, 67-70.

[61] *Apostolic Faith* (September, 1906), 1.

[62] See *The Latter Rain Evangel* (August, 1913): 2-11.

[63] Alexander, *Pentecostal Healing,* 78; Similarly, Alexander Boddy advocated that it was through the Cross that sickness is defeated because 'by his stripes we are healed'. Mark J. Cartledge, 'The Early Pentecostal Theology of *Confidence* Magazine (1908-1926): A Version of the Five-Fold Gospel?,' *JEPTA* 28/2 (2008): 126.

[64] Douglas Jacobsen, *Thinking in the Spirit: Theologies of Early Pentecostal Movement* (Indianapolis: Indiana University Press, 2003), 131 and also see Anderson, *An Introduction to*, 232.

of exorcism in the expansion of the movement. However, major Pentecostal denominations did not develop it into a formal doctrine.[65]

Divine healing, the vital theme of Pentecostalism has been recently elucidated by Pentecostal theologians to capture its significance and develop a theology of healing in Pentecostal theology. Thomas elucidates the relationship between the devil and disease, sickness and sin, healing and forgiveness in the New Testament.[66] Cartledge establishes the faith and understanding of ordinary Pentecostal believers in the ministry of healing.[67] Land explains divine healings as 'sign of the eschatological breaking in of the Kingdom of God and last-days restoration for the proclamation of the Gospel of the Kingdom on Earth'.[68] For Pentecostals, healing is a means whereby the Gospel is proclaimed in both the physical and spiritual dimension of life's reality. Thus, healing restores an individual's sense of wholeness.[69] According to F. Martin, this understanding is congruent with the biblical understanding of anthropology.[70] Bridges Johns explains the Pentecostal understanding of divine healing:

> In the ministry of healing there is the expression of the belief that salvation and healing are for the whole person. The laying on of hands and anointing with oil are means whereby Pentecostals give expression to this belief. As recorded in the Gospels, Jesus comes as the great Physician, healing both sin-sick souls and physical sickness. His touch is one which brings *shalom*, restoring wholeness.[71]

Today Pentecostal theology envisions divine healing as an overall liberative activity of God in the life of a disadvantaged person.[72] 'The divine touch upon the human body reveals the good news that even the most weak and despised are worthy of becoming the tabernacle of God's glory. Thus, the outcasts become vessels of honour through which God makes known the mysteries of

---

[65] L. G. McClung Jr., 'Exorcism,' *NIDPCM,* 624; Dayton, *The Theological Roots*, 24; Similarly Keith Warrington elucidates Jesus as Healer in early British Pentecostalism; see Keith Warrington, 'The Role of Jesus as Presented in the Healing Praxis and Teaching of British Pentecostalism: A Re-Examination,' *Pneuma* 25/1 (Spring 2003): 66-92.

[66] John Christopher Thomas, *The Devil, Disease and Deliverance: Origins of Illness in New Testament Thought* (Sheffield: Sheffield Academic Press, 1998); John Christopher Thomas, 'Devil, Disease and Deliverance: James 5:14-16,' *JPT* 2 (1993): 25-50.

[67] Cartledge, *Testimony in the Spirit*, 105-129.

[68] Stephen J. Land, *Pentecostal Spirituality: A Passion for the Kingdom* (Sheffield: Sheffield Academic Press, 1993), 95.

[69] Cheryl Bridges Johns, 'Healing and Deliverance: A Pentecostal Perspective,' *Concilium* 3 (1996): 45-50.

[70] F. Martin, 'Gift of Healing,' *NIDPCM,* 694-698.

[71] Bridges Johns, 'Healing and Deliverance,' 49.

[72] Shaibu Abraham, 'Healing as Liberation: A Pentecostal Perspective,' *Filadelfia Jyoti* (2008): 26-27.

his Kingdom.'[73] Further, Pentecostals understand divine healing as 'a means of achieving deeper solidarity with the oppressed and the suffering creation as well as with the Spirit of redemption at work in healing.'[74] However, Macchia cautions us that one should think critically about sickness in terms of social injustice and poverty.[75] He contends that there are problems with much of the popular teachings of Pentecostal evangelists on healing because of their implicit isolation of sickness from the broader plight of human injustice and suffering. Moreover, the issue of isolation of healing from the work of the Spirit of God in all of creation to bring redemption and liberation is also a serious matter.[76]

Similarly, Pentecostal theologians have tried to explain the Pentecostal perspective on exorcism in a wider context. For Pentecostals, the act of exorcism is the establishment of God's supremacy over the evil powers and signals the in-breaking of the reign of God over the evil structures of this world. However, theology in general has taken a negative attitude towards this issue because twentieth century cosmology relates only to the physical universe and to the physical dimension of reality. Enlightenment thinking and western scientific worldview visualise reality as mechanistic and deterministic, and dichotomise the physical and spiritual, the body and spirit. [77]

However, Pentecostals see reality as a whole, without differentiating into western dualistic categories; as holistic and trans-rational. Bridges Johns describes the Pentecostal view,

> For Pentecostals, truth is not limited to reason...Pentecostals believe that evil spirits may inhabit human beings and use them for evil things.... Much like the ancient church, Pentecostals are engaged in a holy war against the kingdom of darkness...It is fought through the weapons of prayer and often involves fasting…Exorcisms are open confrontations in which the evil ones are cast out and persons rescued for the kingdom of Christ.[78]

Thus, Pentecostals understand the full Gospel as bringing good news for all of life's problems, which is particularly relevant in the societies of the developing world, where disease is rife and access to adequate health care is very rare. Salvation, for Pentecostals, is an all-embracing term, meaning a sense of well-

---

[73] Bridges Johns, 'Healing and Deliverance,' 49.

[74] Frank D. Macchia, 'The Struggle for Global Witness: Shifting Paradigms in Pentecostal Theology,' in *The Globalization of Pentecostalism*, 22.

[75] Macchia, 'The Struggle for Global Witness,' 21.

[76] Macchia says that as a consequence, the popular teaching on healing also tends to be isolated from the final eschatological redemption of the body and renewal of that will occur when the kingdom of God comes in fullness; Macchia, 'The Struggle for Global Witness,' 21.

[77] Abraham, 'Healing as Liberation,' 26.

[78] Bridges Johns, 'Healing and Deliverance,' 48.

being evidenced in freedom from sickness, poverty and misfortune, as well as in deliverance from sin and evil.[79]

6.3.1.2 Jesus as Provider and Protector

Similarly, other themes such as Jesus as provider and protector are not uncommon in Pentecostal tradition. Rather, the lives of early Pentecostal pioneers the world over are the best illustrations for the justification of these Christological notions. Miraculous stories of provision and protection form the bedrock of their faith and assurance; they had the powerful presence of Jesus among them and expressed it through their testimonies.

We need to understand the emergence of these Christological concepts in the deprived circumstances and the opposition and persecution the early Pentecostals suffered. Most of them were from poor backgrounds; however, their faith in the provision of God enabled them to overcome the precarious situation they were in. Early Indian Pentecostals testified to miraculous provision and protection in their lives and in missionary activities. Biographies of early Pentecostal leaders like Ramankutty Paul, K.E. Abraham, P.M. Samuel and K.C. Cherian are full of stories of how God provided miraculously for their material needs.[80] For instance, P.M. Philip, a Pentecostal pioneer of the Indian Pentecostal movement from Kerala, narrates some of his stories of miraculous provision and protection. He received financial provision from a stranger and was protected from a terrible accident.[81]

Similarly, Pentecostal missionaries, as well as ordinary believers the world over also faced perilous opposition from various quarters such as other denominations, other religionists and from governments.[82] In India, the early Pentecostals not only suffered opposition from denominational churches, but many of them were persecuted for their faith and even killed by fundamentalist religious elements.[83]

---

[79] Anderson, *An Introduction to*, 228.

[80] Pulikottil, 'Emergence of Indian Pentecostalism,' 54.

[81] Once Philip was coming from a North Indian missionary trip; reaching Kerala he had to travel by boat to his home. He got the ticket and waited for the boat to leave but it was delayed. Tired of a long journey, he went in a tea shop to have a cup of tea. Meantime, the boat left the place. Now he had only enough money to get to Kottayam a few miles away from his actual destination. He reached Kottayam and began to walk the rest of the distance. Then a voice heard from behind said, 'from where are you coming?' A gentle man came to him, introduced himself and said that he had attended his meeting earlier. He took him to a nearby hotel and provided food and also gave him enough money to reach his destination. As soon as he reached home, the news spread that the boat he had missed had capsized and many people had drowned. Philip, *Kristhuvil Ente Yathra*, 158-164.

[82] See Abraham, *Yesukristhuvinte Eliya Dassan*, 138, 174, 417; Thonnakkal, *Marubhoomiyile Appostalan*, 73-78, 111-113.

[83] Abraham, *Yesukristhuvinte Eliya Dassan;* Chacko, *An Autobiography;* Thomas, *God's Trailblazer;* Mathew, *Kerala Penthecosthu Charithram;* Thonnakkal, *Marubhoomiyile Appostalan*; Kaithamangalam, *Marubhoomiyil Thalarathu;* Simmons, *Vision Mission and a Movement;* K.V. Paul Pillai, *India's Search for Unknown Christ*, 3rd ed. (New Delhi: Indian Inland Mission, 1984).

Kurien Thomas, who was one of the earliest missionaries to North India, also narrates many of his experiences of miraculous provision and protection.[84] Once, he was miraculously protected from an attack,[85] and on another occasion, saved from a train accident.[86]

Similarly, *The Latter Rain Evangel* describes stories of provision and protection to a certain missionary Max Wood Moorhead for the mission work in India. Narrating the incidents he encouraged the young people to go for foreign missions.[87] John Lake, who became a missionary in South Africa (1908), needed $2,000 for expenses for his journey but had nothing. In answer to his prayer an unknown donor from California, sent to a friend four $500 drafts.[88]

The Pentecost Magazine of 1909 reports an incident of miraculous protection of some sisters who were involved in a terrible accident, due to storm burst and rain. According to Ida, one of the persons involved in the incident, '... praise our mighty Keeper, He had fulfilled Ps.34:20 to us: "He keepeth all his bones, not one of them is broken."'[89] Another group of missionaries who worked in West China were attacked by raiders and looted of all their personal belongings. The raiders kidnapped women missionaries but these women were miraculously protected from them, even though they had to undergo perilous situations.[90] What is definite is that these miraculous stories not only served to deepen the faith of the early adherents, but also enabled them to carry out the early mission with great enthusiasm.

---

[84] Thomas, *God's Trailblazer*, 21, 27, 40-41, 51-56; In a missionary trip to the city of Banswara, Rajasthan, he was conducting meetings in the house of a medical doctor. During the meeting, the doctor's son came running with a sword to attack him. However, according to Thomas, some unseen force stopped the young man from striking him.

[85] Thomas, *God's Trailblazer*, 41.

[86] Thomas, *God's Trailblazer*, 51; in another occasion, he was coming from north Bihar; he heard an inner voice compelling him to get out of the train. Recognizing it as the word of the Lord, he refused to travel on it. After a few hours, he got the news that the train derailed and several passengers had been injured.

[87] Max Wood Moorhead, 'The Lord Working for the Unopened Land,' *The Latter Rain Evangel* 6/3 (December 1913): 8-11

[88] T. E. Plumb, 'The Healer: Dr. John Graham Lake,' http://www.enterhisrest.org/charismata/lake_ biography.pdf; (taken from Ward M. Tannenburg, *Let Light Shine Out: The Story of the Assemblies of God in the Pacific Northwest*).

[89] Ida Florence Sackett, '"There Shall Be No Evil Befall Thee,"' *The Pentecost* 1/8 (July 1909): 8; also see C. W. Reinhardt, 'Providential Protection from Storms,' *The Latter Rain Evangel* (February 1913): 21-22.

[90] Ivan S. Kauffman, 'Miraculous Deliverances from Raiders and Robbers,' *The Latter Rain Evangel* (April 1915): 20-24.

6.3.1.3 Jesus as the Saviour, Lord and God

The themes of Jesus as Saviour, Lord and supreme over all other gods are important for Pentecostal movement. Although, Pentecostalism emphasises Spirit baptism and the gifts of the Spirit, all these important doctrines are thoroughly dependent on the bedrock of Christology which exalts Christ as the Saviour, Lord and only God. These Christological notions Pentecostals experience intimately through the work of the Spirit in their personal and community lives. Consequently, they are eager to proclaim Jesus as Saviour and Lord and have no qualms in presenting Jesus as unique. Twentieth-century theological relativism and the onslaught of higher criticism did not deter them from the task of proclamation. It is interesting to observe that when western Protestantism and theology were reeling under the burden of liberalism, Pentecostalism was steadily growing and proclaiming Jesus to be the Saviour. This is all the more true in the Third World situation where multi-religious settings stand against this confession and proclamation. The emergence of the concept of religious pluralism, or the idea of many ways for salvation, did not deter Pentecostals from professing Jesus to be the *only* Saviour.

Early Pentecostals in India were very particular in proclaiming Jesus as the Saviour and Lord and this proclamation was followed by signs and wonders, mainly in terms of divine healing. In Kerala, the Pentecostal proclamation was in the form of the fourfold Gospel and the listeners who were already Christians responded immediately. These proclamations focused on bringing people into a personal relationship with Christ the Lord.[91] Early Pentecostal magazines like *Zion Kahalam* and others underline the early Pentecostals' astute faith in the sovereignty and supremacy of Jesus.

As already discussed, the Christological affirmation in the fourfold Gospel was wholeheartedly assimilated by the early Pentecostals and applied to their lives and mission.[92] The early Pentecostal journals and literature are full of these claims. *The Pentecostal Evangel* boldly asserts, 'He had been made or ordained a Saviour... Christ was manifested to undo, to nullify, to destroy the works of the devil.'[93] They were convinced about the efficacy of the blood of Christ in salvation, 'No blood, no mercy. No blood, no protection.'[94]

The early Pentecostals were accused of the theological error of forsaking the all-sufficiency of Christ and following a Gnostic spirituality, due to their emphasis on Spirit baptism.[95] However, it is clear that the early Pentecostals emphasised

---

[91] Abraham, *Yesukristhuvinte Eliya Dassan*, 96.

[92] Simpson, *The Four-Fold Gospel*, 31; They believed and practiced what Simpson says, 'Christ is called the "mighty to save," because no matter how weak or how wicked the sinner may be, He is able to save him to the uttermost' and 'Salvation comes by confessing Christ as the Saviour'.

[93] No Author, 'Our Jesus,' *The Pentecostal Evangel* 492 (14 April 1923): 1.

[94] No Author, 'When I See the Blood I will Passover You,' *The Pentecostal Evangel* 493 (21 April 1923): 1; No Author, 'The Power of the Blood,' *The Pentecostal Evangel* 495 (5 May 1923): 1.

[95] Macchia, 'The Struggle for Global Witness,' 13.

the supremacy of Christ more than Spirit baptism. For instance, Seymour was categorical about the vitality of Christology and exhorted the people by saying, 'Now, do not go from this meeting and talk about tongues, but try to get people saved'. McClung asserts, 'Seymour, and subsequent Pentecostal leaders since him, had a strong Christology which centred more on the Giver than the gift.'[96] According to Macchia, Pentecostals have never meant to sever Spirit empowerment from the supremacy of Christ in salvation. He contends, 'After all, Pentecostals have always emphasised that Christ is the baptiser in the Spirit.'[97]

Early Pentecostals strongly emphasised the divinity of Jesus and affirmed Jesus as 'the only true God'. *The Pentecostal Evangel* comments: 'The General Council, with the Christian Alliance and all other real Evangelical Christians, believe strongly in the Deity of Jesus Christ.'[98] Whenever there were any attacks against the deity of Christ from liberals, there was a reaction from the Pentecostals. Reacting against liberal attitudes,[99] one article says, 'But I desire to exalt my Jesus as a divine Christ...He was in the form of God, He was equal with God. He is God.'[100] Moreover, they considered Jesus as the only way to salvation and proclaimed this conviction.[101] The name of Jesus is above every name and holds the power to overcome anything in the world,[102] because he has risen from the dead and dwells in us through the power of the Spirit.[103]

---

[96] Stanley H. Frodsham, quoted in L. Grant McClung jr., 'Truth on Fire: Pentecostals and an Urgent Missiology,' *Society for Pentecostal Studies Annual Meeting Papers (1985)* (Cleveland: Society for Pentecostal Studies, 2006): 5, C.D. Rom.

[97] Macchia, 'The Struggle for Global Witness,' 15.

[98] No Author, 'The Only True God,' *The Pentecostal Evangel* 324-325 (24 January 1920): 6-7.

[99] For example, *The Pentecostal Evangel* quotes a liberal view against Jesus and reacts against it strongly: 'They patronizingly speak of Him as a great man and a great teacher, and so forth. I have a clipping concerning a certain professor in a Baptist college in Missouri. This professor states, "I do not subscribe to the deity of Jesus, nor to His vicarious death and intercessory work. I do not worship Christ or pray in His name, I do not believe that He is divine. I cannot accept the statements in the Bible concerning his pre-existence, and I do not believe that Christ is infallible or that He is a safe one to follow." I suppose he prefers to follow his own gigantic mind. This statement from a man, who has been training the preachers of the coming generation, shows how things are going in the religious world'. See, No Author, 'What Think ye of Christ,' *The Pentecostal Evangel* 496 (12 May 1923): 6.

[100] W.T. Gaston, 'What Think ye of Christ,' *The Pentecostal Evangel* 496 (12 May 1923): 6.

[101] No Author, 'The Only Way,' *The Pentecostal Evangel* 499 (2 June 1923): 1; 'There is one way only into this place of, safety, this house of defence, this strong habitation, this fortress of the redeemed: "I am the Way, the Truth, and the Life, no man cometh unto the Father but by Me," see No Author, 'He That Climbeth Up Some Other Way, the Same is a Thief and a Robber,' *The Pentecostal Evangel* 402-403 (23 July 1921): 3.

[102] Smith Wigglesworth, 'The Power of the Name,' *The Pentecostal Evangel* 480-481(20 January 1923): 2.

[103] Smith Wigglesworth, 'Our Risen Christ,' *The Pentecostal Evangel* 490 (31 March 1923): 2.

Although, early Pentecostals were particular about the supremacy of Christ, Pentecostal theologians have not adequately developed a theology that introduces Jesus as the Saviour and Lord in a religious pluralistic context. The reason seems to be that Pentecostals are so deeply involved in the defence of Spirit baptism and glossolalia that Christology has been taken for granted. Moreover, Pentecostals just borrow these ideas from the Evangelical Theology. However, from our study it is very clear that the theological conception of Pentecostals is significantly different from Evangelical Theology and Christology, because of the context and the Spirit-experience. The discussion above shows that the Christology held by the ordinary Pentecostals is compatible with the larger Pentecostal tradition.

6.3.2 New Testament Testimony

Pentecostals have always claimed themselves to be thoroughly biblical and have even been accused of interpreting the Scriptures literally.[104] They are particular in comparing and evaluating their doctrines, experiences and practices in the light of biblical testimony.[105] For Pentecostals, theology means clarifying the message of the Scripture in the service of the fellowship and evangelistic mission of the church.[106] Therefore, the characteristics of various Christological themes that emerged in the study need to be reflected upon and evaluated in the light of the New Testament testimony to the person and work of Christ, in order to fully understand its suitability and reliability within the Indian context. Here, we shall use contemporary New Testament scholarship, especially Gospel studies, Historical Jesus studies and social scientific study of the New Testament which will give us a historical picture of Jesus and the activities he developed in his society, to see how these themes have been portrayed. We shall also look into Pauline scholarship to understand whether the ordinary Indian Pentecostal Christological affirmation of divine titles such as Saviour, Lord and God are in tune with New Testament tradition.

6.3.2.1 Jesus as Healer and Exorcist

As we have noted, the themes of Jesus as healer and exorcist form the core of the Christological understanding of ordinary Pentecostals and also are used as effective tools in missionary activities. This is true in the New Testament testimony, especially in the Gospels.

[104] Kenneth J. Archer, 'Pentecostal Hermeneutics: Retrospect and Prospect,' *JPT* 8 (1996): 65-66; Hollenweger, *The Pentecostals,* 291-307; French L. Arrington, 'The Use of the Bible by Pentecostals,' *Pneuma* 16/1 (Spring 1994): 101.

[105] Anderson, *An introduction to Pentecostalism,* 225-228; Land, *Pentecostal Spirituality,* 19; Arrington, 'The Use of the Bible by Pentecostals,' 105-106.

[106] Macchia clarifies this fact: 'The experiences they expressed and interpreted orally and dramatically were formed in the context of the "strange new world of the Bible." Frank D. Macchia, 'Theology, Pentecostal,' *NIDPCM,* 1120-1121.

'Nothing is more certain about Jesus than that he was viewed by his contemporaries as an exorcist and a healer,' asserts John Meier.[107] Nearly one-fifth of the entire Gospels is devoted to Jesus' healing and the discussions occasioned by it.[108] Kelsey rightly observes, 'The interest Jesus showed in the physical and mental health of human beings was greater than that of any other leader or religious system from Confucius through Hinduism and Buddhism to Islam.'[109]

Jesus devoted a substantial portion of his ministry to performing miracles of healing for a wide variety of people. Mark devotes around thirty one percent of his Gospel to the miracles and healings of Jesus.[110] He focuses on the power of Jesus and on his dramatic confrontations with the forces of Satan (5:1-43).[111] Matthew has his own version of Jesus as healer (15:30-31), *where* he describes those afflicted with several ailments were healed by Jesus and concludes that the crowd 'glorified the God of Israel.'[112]

In Luke's Gospel, both disease and demon possession are attributed to Satan, and the demons regularly recognize Jesus as the Son of God (4:41; 8:28) who is victorious over them. In fact, many writers, such as Achtemeier, believe that of the four Evangelists, it is Luke who himself a physician, makes most clear the possibility of miracles serving as a basis of faith.[113] Jesus' healings in the Gospel of John are pre-eminently signs designed to bring people to faith in Jesus as Son of God (4:54).[114] 'The signs inevitably lead to explanatory discourses which invest them with symbolic and Christological significance,' comments Blomberg.[115] In Acts, there are explicit links between the healing activities of the apostles and that

---

[107] John P. Meier, 'Jesus,' *The New Jerome Biblical Commentary*, rev. ed. (London: Geoffrey Chapman, 1989), 1321.

[108] The Gospels narrate no less than 34 specific miracles performed by Jesus out of which twenty-two are healings. In addition there are fifteen texts that refer to Jesus' miraculous activity in summary fashion; see Morton T. Kelsey, *Psychology, Medicine and Christian Healing* (San Francisco: Harper & Row, Publishers, 1988), 42. For a detailed classification and description of the healing and exorcism stories in the gospels; see John Wilkinson, *The Bible and Healing: A Medical and Theological Commentary* (Michigan: Eerdmans, 1998), 64-69; B. L. Blackburn, 'Miracles and Miracle Stories,' *DJG*, edited by Joel G. Green, Scot McKnight, I. Howard Marshall (Illinois: IVP, 1992), CD Rom.

[109] Kelsey, *Psychology, Medicine*, 41-42.

[110] Blomberg, 'Healing'; also see Andrew Daunton-Fear, *Healing in the Early Church: The Church's Ministry of Healing and Exorcism from the First to the Fifth Century* (Milton Keynes: Paternoster, 2009), 33; Wilkinson, *The Bible and Healing*, 64-69.

[111] Blomberg, 'Healing'; Daunton-Fear, *Healing in the Early Church*, 32-33.

[112] Howard Clark Kee, 'Medicine and Healing,' *ABD*, edited by David Noel Freedman (New York: Doubleday, 1997), CD Rom.

[113] P. J. Achtemeier, 'The Lukan Perspective on the Miracles of Jesus: A Preliminary Sketch,' in *Perspectives in Luke-Acts*, edited by C. H. Talbert (Danville, IL: AABPR, 1978), 153–67.

[114] Harold Remus, *Jesus as Healer* (Cambridge: Cambridge University Press, 1997), 72-75.

[115] Blomberg, 'Healing'; Joel B. Green, 'Healing,' *NDBT*, edited by T. Desmond Alexander & Brian S. Rosner (Downers Grove, Illinois: IVP, 2000), CD Rom.

of Jesus: Acts 9:34 specifies that the healing of the paralytic Aeneas by Peter was by the direct action of Jesus Christ.[116] It is also clear that Jesus sent his disciples out to carry on with the healings and exorcisms.[117]

Similarly, all three Synoptic Gospels agree that the casting out of demons was a significant aspect of Jesus' ministry. According to Twelftree, exorcism stories are the bedrock of reliable data about the historical Jesus and the most compelling evidence of Jesus being an exorcist.[118] The Beelzebul passages[119] clearly depict the power of Jesus over demons as the evidence that God's kingdom had broken into the present world order ruled by Satan.[120] Jesus' authority over the power of Satan was conveyed to his disciples as well.[121] Reese comments: 'In fact, the only activity that runs consistently from the opening summary of Jesus' ministry through the accounts of his miracles and into the commission given to his disciples is the casting out of demons.'[122]

For many scholars, the healing acts of Jesus are problematic, largely 'because there is no room for them among the pattern of conduct and perception available in contemporary U.S. and European social systems'.[123] The Enlightenment mind-set of western scholarship and the contemporary social system in which scholars have been enculturated have given rise to various interpretations of the healing and exorcism of Jesus. Pilch observes, 'The advent of modern science in about the seventeenth century disrupted the bio-psycho-spiritual unity of human consciousness that had existed until then.'[124]

Blackburn contends that there is almost universal agreement among NT scholars that Jesus performed what is regarded as miraculous healings and

---

[116] Kee, 'Medicine and Healing'. In Peter's description of the career of Jesus, he remarks that God's anointing of him with power and thus God's presence with him had been manifested in his good deeds and specifically in his 'healing all that were oppressed by the devil' (Acts 10:38).

[117] Mk. 6:7-13; Matt. 10:5-10; Lk. 9:1-6.

[118] Graham H. Twelftree, *Jesus the Exorcist* (Peabody, Mass: Hendrickson Publishers, 1993); Graham H. Twelftree, *Jesus the Miracle Worker: a Historical & Theological study* (Illinois: IVP, 1999); Graham H. Twelftree, 'Demon, Devil, Satan,' *DJG*; Graham H. Twelftree, 'Miracles of Jesus Marginal or Mainstream?,' *Journal of the Study of the Historical Jesus* 1/1 (2003): 104-124.

[119] The Beelzebul passages deal with the charge that Jesus cast out demons by Beelzebul; see, Matt 12:25–29; Mark 3:23–27; Luke 11:17–22; Mk 3:22 [par. Mt 9:34 and 12:24; Lk 11:15].

[120] David George Reese, 'Demons (New Testament),' *ABD*; Twelftree, 'Demon, Devil, Satan'.

[121] Kee, 'Medicine and Healing'; For example, Matt 10:8; Mark 3:13–19; 6:7–13; Luke 9:1–2; Graham H. Twelftree, *In the Name of Jesus: Exorcism among Early Christians* (Michigan: Baker Academic, 2007).

[122] Reese, 'Demons (New Testament)'.

[123] Stuart L. Love, 'Jesus Heals the Hemorrhaging Woman,' in *The Social Setting of Jesus and the Gospels*, edited by Wolfgang Stegemann, Bruce J. Malina & Gerd Theissen (Minneapolis: Fortress Press, 2002), 85.

[124] John J. Pilch, 'Paul's Ecstatic Trance Experience near Damascus in Acts of the Apostles,' *HTS Teologiese Studies / Theological Studies* 58/2 (2002): 693.

exorcisms. The miracles of healing pass the dissimilarity test and satisfy the criterion of multiple attestations.[125] Gerd Theissen persuasively demonstrates that the accounts of the exorcisms and the healings in the Gospels are to be considered as independent genres with their own motifs.[126]

Some of the Jesus research scholars explain away healing miracles either as mere magic or psychological recovery.[127] However, social-scientific models might better explain healing in the non-western society. According to Love, a model characterised by spirit involvement and aggression may help to better understand illness as a misfortune caused by cosmic forces.[128] Moreover, illness was considered to be impurity.[129] Similarly, the belief that the evil eye may cause illness was prevalent.[130] Every society which depends primarily on animal husbandry for its economic livelihood regards spirit aggression as the predominant cause of illness.[131] Magical practices flourish in pre-industrial settings among all social groups, but especially among lower class urbanites and villagers.[132] 'Restorative magic has prevailed in feudal orders, from the most ancient ones in the Near East to those in the Greek and Roman periods, in Central and Eastern Asia, in Medieval Europe and pre-Columbian America, down to those that survive today,' contends Sjoberg.[133] Since the evil spirits upset the order of life, causing illness and other social or physical disasters, magical practices ward off evil and

---

[125] Blomberg, 'Healing'; Blackburn, 'Miracles and Miracle Stories'; Kelsey, *Psychology, Medicine*, 45. According to Blackburn, however, some like Burton Mack contend that Jesus was not a miracle worker. But Blackburn affirms that sober historical analysis will continue to affirm the high probability that Jesus performed healings and exorcisms. See Burton Mack, *A Myth of Innocence: Mark and Christian Origins* (Philadelphia: Fortress, 1988).

[126] Gerd Theissen, *The Miracle Stories of the Early Christian Tradition*, edited by J. Riches, translated by J. Bowden (Minneapolis: Fortress Press, 1983), 85-94.

[127] For instance, Jesus restored the sight of a blind man of Bethsaida by spitting on the man's eyes and laying on his hands (Mark 8:22–26). In John 9:6, Jesus is described as making mud from spittle and placing it on the eyes of the man born blind, which mud, when washed away, results in his gaining sight. However, as Mark's version of the incident makes clear, the crucial factor is faith in the power transmitted through Jesus (Mark 7:36). Remus, *Jesus as Healer*; Steven L. Davis, *Jesus the Healer* (London: SCM, 1995); John Dominic Crossan, *The Historical Jesus: The Life of a Mediteranean Jewish Peasant* (San Francisco: HarperSanFrancisco, 1992). For a brief survey of scholarship, see Amanda Porterfield, *Healing in the History of Christianity* (New York: Oxford University Press, 2005), 21-36.

[128] Love, 'Jesus Heals the Hemorrhaging Woman,' 86.

[129] Mary Douglas, *Purity and Danger* (London: Routledge and Kegan Paul, 1966); Also see Bruce J. Malina, *The New Testament World: Insight from Cultural Anthropology* (Kentucky: Westminister John Knox Press, 2001), 161-196; for a brief description of concept of purity and impurity, see Stephen Westerholm, 'Clean and Unclean,' *DJG*.

[130] Malina, *The New Testament World,* 120-125.

[131] Love, 'Jesus Heals the Hemorrhaging Woman,' 87.

[132] Gideon Sjoberg, *The Preindustrial City: Past and Present* (New York: Free Press, 1960), 275.

[133] Sjoberg, *The Preindustrial City*, 277-278.

correct imbalances in the spiritual order.[134] Our context comes very close to such a description.

In such societies, both patients and healers are embedded in a cultural system and it is the whole system that heals. Therefore, Jesus as a healer should not be viewed in isolation, but in association with the cultural system.[135] Pilch has identified the *folk sector* as a healing agent, in which villagers with recognised power to treat illness, and Jesus comes in to this category.[136] Elaborating on the healing of the haemorrhaging woman, Love contends that the healing of the woman would enable her to return to her household or become one of the women at the Cross. Returning to her household would open the family to Jesus as their healer, for the household itself would be made whole. Family renewal would mean provision and protection for the woman and increased productivity for the family – essential for the subsistence of agrarian households. The woman's good fortune would spread to her family and other members of her community.[137] Thus, as Horsely asserts, Jesus' healings were not merely isolated acts of individual mercy but part of a larger program of social healing.[138] This is exactly what happens in the Indian context even today, as we have seen.

In the case of exorcism, Western scientific and rational discourse has a tendency to reduce the 'strangeness' of primitive cultures and the dominant role of supernatural elements in daily life.[139] Recently, many biblical interpreters have started to apply current psychological theories as models of explanation for this, such as multiple-personality disorder, which considers possession to be a case of hysteria, mania or epilepsy.[140] These models usually consider possession from a psychoanalytical perspective as the 'projection' of repressed inner emotions or conflict onto another person. However, the possessions in Gospel stories portray a sort of literal 'introjection': the entering and inhabiting of a spirit from outside a person into the inner being of that individual.[141] 'Thus the alien quality of the process, the intravening spirit,' comments Strecker, 'is cut out and replaced by the possessed person's own self.'[142] Similarly, some sociologically oriented approaches

[134] Love, 'Jesus Heals the Hemorrhaging Woman,' 88.

[135] Love, 'Jesus Heals the Hemorrhaging Woman,' 86.

[136] John J. Pilch, 'Sickness and Healing in Luke-Acts,' in *The Social World of Luke-Acts: Models for Interpretation*, edited by J.H. Neyrey (Peabody, Mass: Hendrickson, 1991), 181-209; Love, 'Jesus Heals the Hemorrhaging Woman,' 89.

[137] Love, 'Jesus Heals the Hemorrhaging Woman,' 98.

[138] Richard A. Horsely, *Jesus and Empire: The Kingdom of God and the New World Disorder* (Minneapolis: Fortress Press, 2003), 108-109.

[139] Christian Strecker, 'Jesus and the Demoniacs,' in *The Social Setting of Jesus and the Gospels*, 119.

[140] See Davis, *Jesus the Healer*, 78-89. Strecker, 'Jesus and the Demoniacs,' 119-120.

[141] Strecker, 'Jesus and the Demoniacs,' 120.

[142] Ibid.

run the risk of reducing possession to a strategy of the underprivileged, or of the oppressed, to strengthen their self-esteem, or to protest their condition.[143] In this perspective cases of possession in Jesus' time could have been attributed largely to the prevailing Roman colonial oppression in Palestine.[144]

Taking all these critical remarks into consideration, Strecker interprets possession as *performance*. The possessed person shows odd behaviour such as screaming, uncontrollable raging and teeth-grinding;[145] during the performance, the borders between identity and non-identity, inside and outside, reality and illusion are obscured.[146] Strecker defines the exorcisms of Jesus as transformative performances or *transformances*. Here, the exorcistic actions of Jesus are regarded as performance ritual actions that bring real transformations within possessed persons and their environments.[147] Although, this theory seems to better explain the exorcisms of Jesus, satisfying the scientific and western rational categories, at least in the context where our research was carried out, such an explanation is redundant. For the people, spirit-possessions are very real and they seldom doubt the western dichotomies as westerners do: 'I and not I; identity and alterity; reality and illusion; body and spirit, rationality and irrationality.'[148]

From the above discussion, it follows that it is obvious that the Christological themes of Jesus as healer and exorcist are in tune with the Christology of the Jesus tradition in the Gospels. What Hollenweger asserts cannot be an exaggeration, that Third World oral Pentecostal theology is 'nearer to biblical forms of theology than to the western form of theologising.'[149]

6.3.2.2 Jesus as Provider and Protector

Just as with the healing and exorcism, the themes of Jesus as the provider and protector play important roles in the Christological conception of the ordinary Pentecostal believers. Both these themes are an essential part of the Jesus tradition and form the building blocks of the Christological edifice of Gospel stories. Provision stories are called gift miracles which include the miraculous multiplication of loaves (Mk. 6:30-44); the miraculous fishing trip (Lk. 5:1ff);

[143] Such approaches are used by John Dominic Crossan, Paul W. Hollenbach and many others.

[144] John Dominic Crossan, *Jesus: A Revolutionary Biography* (San Francisco: HarperSan Francisco, 1994), 88-89; Horsely, *Jesus and Empire*, 107-108.

[145] Mk. 1:23-24; 5:2-7; 9:18-22.

[146] Strecker, 'Jesus and the Demoniacs,' 122-123.

[147] Strecker, 'Jesus and the Demoniacs,' 124; Thus, for Strecker, 'approaching possession with performance theory is the best way to shed light on the phenomena, respecting the indigenous experience while preserving its strangeness and opacity to a scientifically justifiable degree'.

[148] Strecker, 'Jesus and the Demoniacs,' 122.

[149] Walter J. Hollenweger, 'Crucial Issues for Pentecostals,' in *Pentecostals after a Century: Global Perspectives on a Movement in Transition,* edited by Allan H. Anderson & Walter J. Hollenweger (Sheffield: Sheffield Academic Press, 1999), 176-191, 178.

the miracle with the wine at Cana (Jn. 2:1ff), and so on. Here the issue is always that Jesus provides material goods in a miraculous way.[150]

According to Theissen and Merz, one of the dominant characteristic features of gift miracle is that it takes place spontaneously; no one asks for it.[151] Underlying them lies a tradition that, Jesus satisfied the hunger of a needy multitude with a small quantity of food that miraculously sufficed them. Marshall comments, 'In this act the early church saw the supernatural power of Jesus to provide for human needs and a picture of his spiritual help.'[152]

In the Gospel of Luke, one could describe Jesus' entire ministry as providing food to the hungry. Jesus' provision of food is a direct continuation of the metaphor of the God who feeds.[153] Nolland asserts that the feeding account is intended by Luke to make a special contribution to the disciples' insight into the 'providing' identity of Jesus.[154] There is also an element of promise in these stories because Jesus seems to be demonstrating that God can be trusted to provide.[155] Mark also presents Jesus as the Shepherd who provides for all of their needs so that they lack nothing.[156]

Several scholars identify the correspondence between the feeding stories and God's provision of manna in the wilderness.[157] Claassens comments, 'Like God, Jesus provides food to the people in a desolate place, evoking provision of manna in the wilderness. And like God's provision of food, there is more than enough for everyone, even leftovers, symbolising the abundance of God's provision of food.'[158] They also show messianic provision and foreshadow the blessings of the

---

[150] Gerd Theissen & Annette Merz, *The Historical Jesus: A Comprehensive Guide*, translated by John Bowden (London: SCM Press, 1998), 294.

[151] Theissen & Merz, *The Historical Jesus*, 294.

[152] I. Howard Marshall, *The Gospel of Luke: A Commentary on the Greek Text, NIGTC* (Exeter: Paternoster Press, 1978), 358.

[153] L. Juliana M. Claassens, *The God who Provides: Biblical Images of Divine Nourishment* (Nashville: Abingdon Press, 2004), 101. For instance, the Magnificant (Lk.1:46-55) depicts God as filling the hungry with good things (v.53). Jesus' ministry becomes a concrete expression of this promise. The beatitudes in Luke 6:21 tell of Jesus blessing the hungry, promising that they will be satisfied; see Joel B. Green, *The Gospel of Luke, NICNT* (Grand Rapids, Michigan: Eerdmans, 1997), 365.

[154] John Nolland, *Luke 1:1-9:20, WBC,* Vol. 35a (Dallas, Texas: Word Books, Publisher, 1998), CD Rom.

[155] L. Shannon Jung, *Food for Life: The Spirituality and Ethics of Eating* (Minneapolis: Fortress Press, 2004), 26.

[156] William L. Lane, *The Gospel of Mark: NICNT* (Michigan: Eerdmans, 1974), 233.

[157] Green, *The Gospel of Luke*, 363; Joseph A. Fitzmyer, *The Gospel According to Luke 1-IX, Anchor Bible* 28 (New York: Doubleday, 1981), 766; I. Howard Marshall, *The Gospel of Luke: A Commentary on the Greek Text, NIGTC* (Exeter: Paternoster Press, 1978), 357.

[158] Claassens, *The God who Provides,* 101.

eschaton.[159] Moreover, the food that Jesus provides is free, echoing the words of Isa. 55:1-2.[160] The Gospel of John places special emphasis on the food that Jesus offers (2:1-11; 6:1-15; 21:1-14). They are all proof of God's provision and signs of the kingdom of God.[161] These miracles suggest the unlimited gifts Jesus makes available; the miracle of abundance in the face of scarcity, of extravagance, of transformation and of new possibilities.[162]

As we have seen in the case of healing and exorcism, there is much scepticism on the historicity of such accounts.[163] According to Hagner, there is no need to deny the historicity of the miracle simply because we have never witnessed a miraculous multiplication of food.[164] Hugh Montefiore, for instance, elaborates on various miraculous provision of food in church history and tries to elucidate the feeding miracles as paranormal phenomena which can be trusted.[165] While commenting on feeding accounts, Marshall also comments, 'If the precise details cannot be proved historically, it is equally impossible to deny on historical grounds that what the Gospels narrate took place in some sort of way.'[166]

The stories of miraculous provision undergird the person of Christ, his divine origin and supremacy. For Marshall, the feeding provides the basis for the confession of Jesus as the Messiah.[167] While commenting on feeding miracles in John's Gospel, Thyen asserts that the underlying theme is Christology.[168] Similarly, Léon-Dufourmy contends that it asserts the mystery of the person of Jesus.[169] At the end of the narrative, the disciples confess Jesus as the Holy One of God.[170] This is similar to the understanding of ordinary Indian Pentecostal Christology.

---

[159] Donald A. Hagner, *Matthew 14-28*, *WBC*, Vol. 33b (Dallas, Texas: Word Books, Publisher, 1998), CD Rom.

[160] Claassens, *The God who Provides*, 101; The providing aspect of the work of Christ is also symbolically portrayed in the Eucharistic meal constituted by Jesus.

[161] Claassens, *The God who Provides*, 102.

[162] Gail R. O'Day, *The Gospel of John*, *NIB*, Vol. IX (Nashville: Abingdon Press, 1995), 539-540; Claassens, *The God who Provides*, 102. In another incident, to pay the temple tax for Jesus and Peter, we see a divine provision of money from a fish (Matt. 17:24). In fact it is not simply mysterious foreknowledge of Jesus but a miracle of divine provision. This miracle is, however, unique in the NT, in that Jesus performs it for his and Peter's own convenience; Hagner, *Matthew 14-28.*

[163] Nolland, *Luke 1:1-9:20.* Nolland cautions us, 'While it is true, however, that we need to make generous allowance for the symbolism involved in the telling of the story, we should not be content to think that the theology and the symbolism have created the account'.

[164] Hagner, *Matthew 14-28.*

[165] Hugh Montefiore, *The Miracles of Jesus* (London: SPCK, 2005), 77-86.

[166] Marshall, *The Gospel of Luke*, 358.

[167] Ibid.

[168] George R. Beasley-Murray, *John*, *WBC*, Vol. 36 (Dallas, Texas: Word Books, Publisher, 1998), CD Rom.

[169] Beasley-Murray, *John.*

[170] Ibid.

Similarly, the Jesus tradition contains deliverance miracles, in which disciples were rescued from different circumstances.[171] They are concerned with the overcoming of hostile forces, defeating the power of nature or the state.[172] According to Theissen and Merz, rescue miracles include the description of the emergency and an epiphany which brings rescue from outside, by the intervention of a divine figure or one who is already present.[173] The calming of the sea proves Jesus to be the protector from forces beyond the control of the disciples.[174] In relation to walking on water, O'Day comments, 'Jesus reveals himself to his disciples in order to allay their fears, to ensure safe passage, to remind them that God has been, is, and will be their rescue.'[175] After the rescue, the question of the disciples, 'Who then is this?', serves to underline the impression of the uniqueness of Jesus. The story was also taken by the early church to symbolize the suffering and tribulation it underwent and the safety and security Jesus offered to them.[176]

However, scholarly scepticism claims that there was no miracle, only a coincidence of timing and that the wind and the waves subsided when Jesus commanded the storm to cease. Nevertheless, Culpepper rightly argues that such an explanation does violence to the story and strips it of its wonder and power.[177] Consequently, the Christological themes of Jesus as the provider and protector have been sufficiently evidenced in the Christological tradition of the Gospel accounts. In the Indian context ordinary believers also experience Jesus as the provider and protector in their everyday lives.

6.3.2.3 Jesus as the Saviour, Lord and God

The Christological titles such as 'Saviour' and 'Lord' refer to the present work and the exalted status of Christ.[178] The first Christians recognised his redemptive role to be universal, unique, complete and definitive[179] and the ancient Christian

---

[171] Such as the stilling the storm (Mk. 4:35-41), the miraculous walking on the water (Mk. 6:45ff) and in the book of Acts the freeing of prisoners (Acts.12:1ff; 16:1ff).

[172] Theissen, *Miracle Stories of Early*, 99.

[173] Theissen & Merz, *The Historical Jesus*, 295.

[174] Perkins, *The Gospel of Mark*, 581; R. Alan Culpepper, *The Gospel of Luke, NIB*, Vol. IX (Nashville: Abingdon Press, 1995), 184-185.

[175] O' Day, *The Gospel of John*, 597

[176] R. T. France, *The Gospel of Mark: A Commentary on Greek Testament, NIGTC* (Michigan: Eerdmans, 2002), 271.

[177] R. Alan Culpepper, *The Gospel of Luke, NIB*, Vol. IX (Nashville: Abingdon Press, 1995), 184.

[178] Oscar Cullmann, *Christology of the New Testament*, 2nd ed. (London: SCM, 1963), 193.

[179] Gerald O' Collins, *Christology: A Biblical, Historical, and Systematic Study of Jesus Christ* (New York: Oxford University Press, 1995), 296.

formulas and confessions undergird this faith.[180] Early Christian theology is in reality almost exclusively Christology.[181]

In the Gospels the idea of Jesus as saviour was closely connected with his mission where salvation is achieved as a present experience resulting from a personal encounter with Jesus.[182] In the healing episode of the paralysed man (Mk. 2:1-12), Jesus' statement that 'the Son of man has authority to forgive sins on Earth' (v.10) has profound Christological significance.[183] This is what is happening among the poor in the Indian context. Their healing experience leads them to acknowledge Jesus as saviour and receive remission of sin in the name of Jesus.

In Pauline literature, according to Luter, saviour means 'one providing salvation,' and often includes the related meanings of 'deliverer' or 'protector;' it is linked to the physical dimension.[184] Christ was the victor and also a liberator from the hostile powers of the sub-lunar cosmos: that vast hierarchy of spiritual authorities and rulers that controlled events in the world of change. Paul himself speaks of conversion as a liberation from the tyranny of these intermediary powers of the cosmos: 'we were in bondage to the ruling spirits of the cosmos' but now saved through Christ (Gal. 4:3-5).[185] Many of the Pentecostals have experienced such liberation and understand Jesus as 'saviour'. Further, according to Witherington, the personal encounter of Paul with the risen Christ would have influenced the Pauline concept of Jesus as saviour.[186] In Galatians 1:11-23 Paul states that he has received his Gospel directly from God by revelation.[187] This

---

[180] Rowan Williams comments, 'Even allowing for the most sceptical reading of the Gospels and Acts, we can say that within about twenty-five years from the likeliest date of Jesus' crucifixion, he was being invoked by Christians as a source of divine favour and almost certainly addressed in public prayer at Christian assemblies'. Rowan Williams, 'A History of Faith in Jesus,' in *The Cambridge Companion to Jesus,* edited by Markus Bockmuehl (Cambridge: Cambridge University Press, 2001), 220; Cullmann, *Christology of the New Testament,* 208; Ben Witherington III, 'Lord,' *DJG.*

[181] Cullmann, *Christology of the New Testament,* 2-3.

[182] I. Howard Marshall, 'Salvation,' *DJG.*

[183] The scribes' indignation ('Who has the power to forgive sins but one, God?' v.7), is caused by Jesus' statement 'Your sins are forgiven'. Such a passive formula is used in the OT for God's forgiveness (Ps. 32:1) and is implied as a claim to make performative statements in God's name. See P. Ellingworth, 'Forgiveness of Sins,' *DJG*; In Lk. 7:36-50 also see a similar incident which underlines the fact that early Jesus tradition has attributed divine title of saviour to Jesus.

[184] A.B. Luter, 'Saviour,' *DPL,* edited by Gerald F. Hawthorne, Ralph P. Martin, & Daniel G. Reid (Illinois: IVP, 1998), CD Rom.

[185] Karen Jo Torjesen, '"You are the Christ": Five Portraits of Jesus from the Early Church,' in *Jesus at 2000,* edited by Marcus J. Borg (Colorado: Westview Press, 1997), 79.

[186] Ben Witherington III, 'Christology,' *DPL.*

[187] J. M. Everts, 'Conversion and Call of Paul,' *DPL*; Witherington III, 'Christology'.

form of personal encounter and the physical dimension of salvation is similar to the experience of Indian Pentecostals.

The title Lord was used by Jesus himself to identify his person and his identity (Mark 12:35-37 cf. Ps.110:7). Witherington cautions us not to dismiss it as the invention of the early church.[188] In the primitive confessional materials Paul's use of *maranatha,* which most probably means '*our Lord, come*' (1Cor. 16:22), strongly suggests 'the reality and presence of glorified Jesus as Lord.'[189] Similarly, in the Christological hymn in Phil. 2:6-11, Jesus has been highly exalted as the *Lord* of all and given the name which is above all names.[190] It is the confession of the lordship which constitutes the climatic worship of all creation.[191] In another 'creedal' passage (1Cor. 8:5-6), Paul acknowledges the existence of many 'gods' and 'lords' but considers Jesus to be the supreme among all. Commenting on the verse, Fee affirms that, for Paul, over against the many lords of paganism there is only one Lord, Jesus Christ, who is the agent of creation and redemption.[192] This confession is all the more relevant to the Pentecostal believers as they encounter many gods and lords, but affirm Jesus as the Lord and God. We find further evidence that the experience of the risen Lord led to the climactic confession of Thomas, 'My Lord and my God' (Jn. 20:28), in which he appears to equate Lordship and Godhood.[193]

The theology of Jesus' lordship becomes explicit after the resurrection and the early Christian reception of the Spirit.[194] Their profound knowledge and experience of Jesus' presence in the worship context, through the Spirit and his intimate presence in their struggles enabled them to address him as 'Lord'. Moreover, when they addressed Jesus as the 'Lord,' the understanding was that he had been exalted over all the earthly authorities.[195] This is what is happening with the Pentecostals, as in the early church. The first Christians were somehow able to accommodate such reverence for Christ within their exclusivist monotheism

---

[188] He says, 'This text should not be abruptly dismissed as reflecting the later theology of the early church, especially inasmuch as there is extensive evidence that Jesus saw himself in messianic terms and at least indirectly made messianic claims'. Witherington III, 'Lord'; Also see Gordon D. Fee, *Pauline Christology: An Exegetical-Theological Study* (Peabody: Hendrickson Publishers, 2007), 393-401.

[189] Williams, 'A History of Faith in Jesus,' 220.

[190] Cullmann, *Christology of the New Testament,* 216-218.

[191] James D.G. Dunn, *The Theology of Paul the Apostle* (Edinburgh: T & T Clark, 1998), 246.

[192] Fee, *Pauline Christology*, 90-91. 'For although there may be so-called gods in heaven or on earth – as indeed there are many 'gods' and many 'lords' yet for us there is one God, the Father… and one Lord, Jesus Christ, through whom are all things and through whom we exist' (1Cor. 8:5-6).

[193] John Macquarrie, *Jesus Christ in Modern Thought* (London: SCM Press, 1990), 45.

[194] Dunn, *The Theology of Paul the Apostle*, 245; Witherington III, 'Lord'; Cullmann, *Christology of the New Testament,* 208.

[195] Cullmann, *Christology of the New Testament,* 208.

inherited from their Jewish background, producing thereby a distinctive 'binitarian' adjustment in this tradition.[196]

The above discussion also points to the fact that the titles such as Saviour and Lord, which had been attributed to God in Old Testament were conferred upon Jesus by the early Christians with all their divine connotations, and they worshipped him without negating the supremacy and divinity of God. Jesus was not worshipped as a second God, or a second-order God; instead Jesus was understood to be of the same essence of God, and of the same saving authority in the cosmos.[197] Edwards portrays it:

> The early church and the New Testament authors inevitably found themselves speaking of Jesus with the same words, symbols, images, statements, and texts by which their Jewish forebears spoke of God... The saving activity of Jesus Christ is the expression of the Saving One who, through the prophet Isaiah, declared, 'I, I am the LORD, and besides me there is no saviour' (43:11).[198]

The same understanding and devotion can evidently be seen in the ordinary Pentecostal believers' attitudes, words, life-styles as well as in the way they address Jesus as the Saviour and Lord in their worship contexts. As a result, they are not wary of acknowledging Jesus as supreme and unique over all other gods they know and do not hesitate in proclaiming him God.

To summarise, Indian Pentecostal Christology unwittingly lacks a strong ontological identity of Jesus and the humanity of Jesus which are vital for any Christology. We have also noted some of the characteristics of this Christology, which make it a valid Christology for ordinary people in India. It is obvious that Pentecostal Christology is compatible with the larger Pentecostal tradition, as well as with New Testament testimonies to the person and work of Christ. Therefore, this Christology can rightly be termed to be a 'Pentecostal and biblical Christology'.

---

[196] Larry W. Hurtado, *Lord Jesus Christ: Devotion to Jesus in Earliest Christianity* (Michigan: Eerdmans, 2003), 134-153; Richard J. Bauckham, *God Crucified: Monotheism and Christology in the New Testament* (Carlisle: Paternoster Press, 1998), 25-42.

[197] James R. Edwards, *Is Jesus the only Saviour?* (Michigan: Eerdmans, 2005), 111.

[198] Edwards, *Is Jesus the only Saviour?*, 113.

Chapter 7

Indian Pentecostal Christology: Constructive Proposal

In chapter six we highlighted the affinity of ordinary Indian Pentecostal Christology with the larger Pentecostal tradition and recent Pentecostal scholarship. Here we shall endeavour to rescript the ordinary Indian Pentecostal Christology, by engaging with contemporary Pentecostal and Charismatic scholarship as dialogue partners. This rescripting exercise with Pentecostal theology will help to place the ordinary Christology into the wider academic context. In the light of rescripting, we shall also offer a specific constructive proposal for ordinary Christology, which is in effect the thesis of this research project.

We shall group the themes of ordinary Christology into two categories: functional and ontological. Jesus as healer, exorcist, provider and protector are themes related to the existential struggles of the community and the way they perceive Jesus in relation to answers to those struggles, and can therefore be termed functional Christology. The last two themes, Jesus as Lord and God speak about the ontological identity of Jesus where he is understood to be above all. The theme 'Saviour' acts as a bridge between the functional and ontological categories and portrays his presence among the ordinary people and his supremacy and unique status as God. These Christological identities form the narrative structure of the community and define its identity, way of life and spirituality. They also act as a point of contact with non-Pentecostals and people of other religious traditions. We shall now turn to functional and ontological Christological articulations of Pentecostal theology to place ordinary Christology on a firm footing.

It can be rightly argued that Pentecostalism is more Jesus-centred than Spirit-centred.[1] This is because Pentecostal proclamation revolves around the 'Full Gospel' (fourfold or fivefold Gospel) in which Jesus is proclaimed as saviour, (sanctifier), healer, Spirit-baptiser and the soon coming king.[2] A glance into the elements of the 'Full Gospel' suggests that they are closely related to soteriological aspects and, hence, point toward a functional Christology. These elements have been intimately appropriated and proclaimed in everyday experiences of ordinary Pentecostals.

The unique theology of Pentecostalism is neither tongue-speaking nor sanctification but the 'Full Gospel' which provides a historical and theological pattern to analyse the movement.[3] According Thomas the theological heart of Wesleyan Pentecostalism is the 'Full Gospel' and as a result, Pentecostal theology should be structured around these central tenets. A theology based on the 'Full Gospel' can reveal the ways in which Pentecostalism, as a movement, is both similar to and dissimilar from other movements within Christendom.[4] Similarly, Kärkkäinen argues that a valid Pentecostal theology is to focus on Jesus Christ as the centre of the 'Full Gospel' and is a methodological gateway to a balanced theology. Christology and Pneumatology are interwoven in that, whatever Christ is, he is in the Spirit: Jesus Christ as the Saviour, healer and so on. And conversely, whatever the Spirit effects in the believer's life, be it salvation, healing or Spirit-baptism, it is the work of the Lord, Jesus Christ.[5] Thus, it could be suggested that Pentecostal Christology is basically a functional Christology of the 'Full Gospel' with a pneumatological emphasis.

7.1 Functional Pentecostal Christology

One of the unique features of Pentecostalism is its insistence in applying the work of Christ in every aspect of believers' lives. What is read in the Bible has to be experienced in life in their contextual circumstances, in the power of the Spirit. This leads Pentecostals to appropriate Jesus' actions in the Gospels literally. Jesus has healed many, so healing is available even today. Jesus has provided for the

---

[1] Keith Warrington, *Pentecostal Theology: A Theology of Encounter* (London: T&T Clark, 2008), 34.

[2] It is to be noted that different people use the terms 'fourfold' or 'fivefold' interchangeably but denote the same idea. See A. B. Simpson, *The Fourfold Gospel: Jesus as Saviour, Sanctifier, Healer and Coming King* (Orlando, FL: Bridge-Logos, 2007); Dayton, *The Theological Roots,* 15-28.

[3] Dayton has shown that Pentecostalism borrowed a fourfold-devotion to Jesus Christ as Saviour, Spirit Baptizer, Healer, and Coming King from the Holiness movement and other evangelical strands. Dayton, *The Theological Roots,* 15-28; Dayton, 'The Rise of the Evangelical Healing Movement,' 1-18.

[4] John Christopher Thomas, 'Pentecostal Theology in the Twenty-First Century: 1998 Presidential Address,' *Pneuma* 20 (1998): 3-19, 17.

[5] Veli-Matti Kärkkäinen, 'David's Sling: The Promise and Problem of Pentecostal Theology Today: A Response to D. Lyle Dabney,' *Pneuma* 23 (2001): 147-152, 152.

poor, so his ability to provide for believers is still anticipated and experienced. Archer explains:

> When Pentecostals read Scripture, they do so from within their cultural-contextual worldview. They read Scripture as the marginalised people of the latter rain. At the centre of the dramatic narrative is Jesus, the divine-human Messiah. Jesus is a mighty miracle worker empowered by the Holy Spirit.[6]

Pentecostals understand that Christ acts here and now through the work of the Spirit. Christology in Pentecostalism is, therefore, rightly termed pneumatological Christology, and this dimension of Christology has been rightly emphasised by Pentecostalism from the beginning. Land, speaking about Pentecostal spirituality affirms that, 'Pentecostal spirituality is Christocentric precisely because it is pneumatic; its fivefold Gospel is focused on Christ because of its starting point in the Holy Spirit...In Pentecostal spirituality, Jesus Christ is the centre and the Holy Spirit is the circumference.'[7] Thus, the 'Full Gospel' functions as the central narrative conviction of the Pentecostal community.[8]

Pentecostals embrace the Full Gospel, which places Jesus and the Spirit at the centre of God's dramatic redemptive story. The proclamation of the Full Gospel is the declaration of the redemptive activity of God in Christ Jesus and the Holy Spirit to the community. These confessional-doxological statements flow out of the redemptive encounter with the living Word, Jesus Christ, who is present in their community through the powerful presence of the Holy Spirit.[9] In line with this Pentecostal orientation, Archer argues that to uphold the identity of Pentecostal theology, it is essential to articulate it 'Pneumatologically and organise it around the fivefold Gospel.' Furthermore, a Pentecostal theology can avoid the Christo-monistic tendency of Reformation theology of the Word by affirming and addressing the missional role of the Spirit, in conjunction with the missional role of Jesus. Thus, he affirms that 'Spirit Christology would more correctly reflect the Pentecostal story and scriptural testimony.'[10] Alfaro, from a Latin American Hispanic context, also emphasizes that Spirit Christology is a more suitable paradigm for constructing a Pentecostal Christology, provided it

[6] Kenneth J. Archer, *The Gospel Revisited: Towards a Pentecostal Theology of Worship and Witness* (Oregon: Pickwick Publications, 2011), 42.

[7] Land, *Pentecostal Spirituality*, 23.

[8] Kenneth J. Archer, 'A Pentecostal Way of Doing Theology: Method and Manner,' *IJST* 9/3 (July 2007): 312.

[9] Archer, 'A Pentecostal Way of Doing Theology,' 312.

[10] Archer, 'A Pentecostal Way of Doing Theology,' 301-314.

is grounded in the experience, faith, and worship of its community and oriented toward liberative praxis.[11]

Additionally, from the beginnings of the movement, Pentecostals read the Gospels within the framework of a Spirit-Christology, where Christ was seen to be carrying out his ministry in the power of the Spirit; this is a popular understanding among Pentecostals. Although, ordinary Pentecostals as a rule tend to over-emphasise the divinity of Jesus at the cost of his humanity; in relation to the earthly ministry of Jesus, especially regarding miracles, they firmly affirm him as truly human. The general perception is that

> As God, Jesus was able to...heal the sick...but he has chosen not to 'use' his divinity, and he also made it clear that – in his humanity – he was utterly powerless. The miraculous did not occur because Jesus was God, but because he was filled with the Spirit without measure and always moved in perfect harmony with the Father.[12]

Similarly, Williams in his *Renewal Theology* also points towards the Pentecostal-Charismatic position.

> We now emphasize that the ministry of Jesus, in terms of His preaching the Good News, healing, deliverance, and many miraculous deeds, flowed out of His anointing by the Holy Spirit. It would be a mistake, therefore, to assume that Jesus did such mighty works because He was the Son of God. Rather, it was His Spirit-anointed humanity and the power resting on that humanity that lay behind His ministry in word and deed.[13]

This Spirit-empowerment is understood to be a model of ministry for Christians and Pentecostals firmly believe that the same power is granted to them through Spirit-baptism and enables them to act like Jesus (Jn.14:12).

Therefore, the functional Christology of Pentecostal scholarship is firmly anchored in Pneumatology and we shall explore it from the vantage point of the Spirit-anointing of Jesus. To this end, we shall take Pentecostal scholars Menzies and Shelton as dialogue partners; they expound Pentecostal Christology from the Lucan Pneumatological perspective.

Menzies argues that Luke has purposefully redacted his sources to show that Jesus was a Spirit-anointed person who accomplished all the miraculous

---

[11] Sammy G. Alfaro, 'Foundations for a Hispanic Pentecostal Christology: A Constructive and Liberative Approach' (PhD Thesis, Dallas: Fuller Theological Seminary, 2008).

[12] C. Dye, *Healing Anointing: Hope for a Hurting World* (London: Hodder and Stoughton, 1997), 28, quoted in Warrington, *Pentecostal Theology*, 52.

[13] Rodman J. Williams, *Renewal Theology,* Vol.1 (Michigan: Zondervan, 1988), 339.

feats through the power of the Spirit.[14] It is generally argued that descent of the Spirit at Jordan brought Jesus into a new and deeper existential awareness of God as Father, and it also gave him a sense of becoming Son and Messiah. For Dunn, the Spirit initiates Jesus into the new age and covenant at the River Jordan.[15] However, Menzies suggests that the descent of the Spirit and the divine declaration underline the fact that Jesus was equipped for his messianic task and this signals the beginning of his Spirit-led ministry. He asserts, '..Jesus' pneumatic anointing, rather than being the source of his unique filial relationship to God or his initiation into the new age, is the means by which Jesus equipped for his messianic task.'[16] In the temptation narrative, Luke specifically adds, 'Jesus, *full of Holy Spirit*, returned from the Jordan' (Lk. 4:1), to stress his redactional emphasis. It signifies that Jesus, as one who has been filled with the Spirit at Jordan, has constant access to the Spirit of God.[17] The same phrase was used in the case of Stephen (Acts 6:5; 7:55) and Barnabas (Acts 11:24). Thus, for Menzies, Luke's description of Jesus as 'full of Holy Spirit' indicates that Jesus was empowered to carry out his divinely appointed task rather than pointing to the uniqueness of Jesus' experience of the Spirit. Luke also adds that Jesus returned to Galilee 'filled with the *power* of Spirit,' which is neither found in Mark nor Matthew. This insertion, according to Menzies, points forward to the preaching of Jesus in Nazareth (4:15, 18-19) and to the exorcism in Capernaum.[18]

In the sermon of Jesus at Nazareth (Lk.4: 18-19), Luke altered the wording of the quotation from Isa. 61:1-2. He omitted 'bind up the broken-hearted' and inserted 'let the oppressed go free,' due to his distinctive prophetic Pneumatology and also to emphasise the liberating power of Jesus' Spirit-inspired preaching and activities, which effect salvation. Here Luke views Jesus' entire ministry as well as his Spirit-anointing in prophetic terms.[19] Thus, for Menzies, all of Jesus' earthly ministry, including the miracles, were carried out by the power of the Spirit. Along with the above argument, according to Menzies, this understanding has implications for the believers. The pneumatic anointing of Jesus at the Jordan and that of the disciples at Pentecost suggests that, for Luke, Pentecost was for the disciples what the Jordan was for Jesus. The logical corollary is that, at Pentecost, the Spirit came upon the disciples in order to turn them into effective witnesses.[20]

---

[14] Robert P. Menzies, *Empowered for Witness: The Spirit in Luke-Acts* (London: T&T Clark, 2004), 133-134.

[15] Menzies, *Empowered for Witness*, 135-137; James D. G. Dunn, *Baptism in the Holy Spirit: A Re-examination of the New Testament Teaching on the Gift of the Spirit in Relation to Pentecostalism Today* (London: SCM, 1970), 28.

[16] Menzies, *Empowered for Witness*, 137-138.

[17] Ibid., 139.

[18] Ibid., 139-143.

[19] Ibid., 155.

[20] Ibid., 174.

Shelton also brings out his functional Christology from Luke-Acts in a similar vein. He argues that, for Luke, Jesus being the recipient of the Holy Spirit is 'mighty in words and deeds.'[21] According to Shelton, Luke does not show as much interest as Paul in the Spirit's role in conversion and who believers in Christ are; rather, power for mission captures most of Luke's attention.[22] By comparing and contrasting the references regarding the Spirit in the Synoptic Gospels, Shelton argues that Luke's distinct interest was to prove that the endowment of the Spirit enables the recipient to witness authoritatively. Even in the case of Jesus this is true; anointing was given to him to proclaim the good-news, to release the captives, to confront and defeat the devil, to heal and to do wonders (Lk. 4:14, 18ff).[23]

Luke, like other evangelists, sees the descent of the dove during the baptism of Jesus as a messianic sign and he also reiterates the sonship concept from the genealogy, emphasising that Jesus is the Son of God (Lk. 3:38). Also in the temptation account Satan's query, 'If you are the Son of God..' attests the traditional significance of the descent of the Spirit found in all four Gospels. However, in addition to these references, Luke frequently and overtly declares that after the descent of the dove, Jesus was 'full of Holy Spirit' and empowered to do mighty works. More importantly, of all the Gospel writers only Luke notes this.[24] Shelton argues that this was a baptism of the Spirit for Jesus one which was similar to that of the believers, although there was one quantitative difference, that Jesus poured out the same Spirit upon the believers.[25]

In the temptation account, Luke describes Jesus as 'full of Holy Spirit,' which is meant to show that this would result in inspired speech (Acts. 6:3,5,8,10; 7:55; 11:23-24). Luke implies that Jesus was filled with the Spirit to conquer temptation. According to Shelton, Luke intended to tell his readers that Jesus overcame the suggestions of the devil, not by performing a miracle (4:3), but by the words handed down to him by the Spirit.[26] What is vital in Luke's unique presentation of the temptation is that it makes a strong statement on Jesus' human nature. Jesus is described in the same terms as other human beings, however,

---

[21] He asserts, 'In Luke-Acts the recipient of the Holy Spirit are, like Moses, "mighty in... words and deeds" (Acts.7:22), even as Jesus himself was "mighty in deed and word" (Lk.24:19)'. See James B. Shelton, *Mighty in Word and Deed: The Role of the Holy Spirit in Luke-Acts* (Oregon: Wipf and Stock Publishers, 2000), 6.

[22] Shelton, *Mighty in Word and Deed*, 6.

[23] Ibid., 6-13.

[24] See Lk. 4:1, 18; 10:21; 24:19; Acts 1:2; 2:22; 10:38; Shelton, *Mighty in Word and Deed*, 48-49.

[25] Shelton, *Mighty in Word and Deed*, 49-50; also see Dunn, *Baptism in the Holy Spirit*, 24.

[26] However, this does not mean that the words of Jesus are mere magical formulas that enable him automatically to render the temptation ineffective or that the Spirit's power is a neutral magical power put to any use. Jesus overcame the temptation because of his continuous relationship with the Father. Shelton, *Mighty in Word and Deed*, 59.

empowered by the Spirit. Luke's use of 'full of the Holy Spirit' and 'led by the Spirit' makes it doubly clear that Jesus' temptations were real and that he was truly human. He relied not on his own power and resources but on God's. Otherwise, the temptations would have been a pre-arranged drama, a mere sham. This is why Luke uses the same terms to express Jesus' relationship with the Spirit and that of believers. The temptations of Jesus are real, as real as anyone else's dilemmas. He overcomes evil as God expects all people to triumph—through the power of the Holy Spirit. The inspired words that enable Jesus to overcome all of this originate from his experience with God's Spirit of power.[27]

In the inauguration of Jesus' public ministry, only Luke mentions that, Jesus returned to Galilee in the 'power of the Spirit' (4:14) and that he read from Isaiah's scroll in the Nazareth synagogue 'the Spirit of the Lord is upon me' (4:18-19).[28] In the book of Acts, Luke emphasised the Spirit in Jesus' ministry, when he recounts early apostolic preachings. Peter, for example, associates Jesus with spiritual power (2:22; 4:27; 10:38), while John the Baptist is associated with repentance (10:37; 19:4).[29] Luke also specifically connects the miracle ministries of Jesus and the early church with the Spirit who is the source of miracle-working power and authority.[30] Thus, because of his Spirit-anointing, Jesus became 'mighty in deed and word' (Lk. 24:19; Acts.10:38).

The natural corollary both Menzies and Shelton draw from their theses is that believers are Spirit-baptised to be mighty prophets. Under the power of the Spirit, believers were 'mighty in deed and word,' just as Jesus was.[31] Stronstad also argues that, by virtue of having been filled with the Spirit of prophecy, the believers become the eschatological community of prophets.[32] Therefore, it is vital 'to recapture Luke's vision of God's people as the prophethood of all believers.'[33]

7.2 Rescripting Ordinary Christology

Let us turn to rescripting the ordinary Christology in the light of the above discussion. It is clear from the idea expressed above that Pentecostal Christology understands Jesus' earthly activities in terms of Spirit-anointing as well as in

---

[27] The same Spirit who empowered Jesus will enable his followers to speak against opposition, just as he predicted: 'And when they bring you before the synagogues and the rulers and authorities, do not be anxious how or what you are to answer or what you are to say; for the Holy Spirit will teach you in that very hour what you ought to say' (Luke 12:11-12), Shelton, *Mighty in Word and Deed,* 60.

[28] Shelton, *Mighty in Word and Deed,* 63.

[29] Ibid., 67.

[30] Ibid., 74-82.

[31] Ibid., 157.

[32] Roger Stronstad, 'Affirming Diversity: God's People as a Community of Prophets,' *Pneuma* 17/2 (Fall 1995): 145-157, 145 (Presidential address of Society for Pentecostal Studies, 1994).

[33] Stronstad, 'Affirming Diversity,' 157.

human terms. Here the 'Full Gospel' comes alive. Using Ted Peters' analogy of systematic theology to be a 'wheel' and the 'hub' of the wheel as the Gospel of Jesus Christ, Archer argues that Pentecostal theology structured around the 'Full Gospel' and centred upon Jesus Christ, gives the movement its unique theological identity. 'The Theological centre is the person of Jesus Christ, and protruding out of the centre are the five spokes which serve to explain the significance of the story of Jesus Christ for the community and the world. These spokes are the central narrative convictions of the Pentecostal story.'[34] Thus, for Archer, the 'Full Gospel' is crucial in order to understand the origins and enduring accents of emerging Pentecostal theologies. Further, the Christ that occupies the centre of Pentecostal theology is not an abstract or ideological principle, but the living Christ who still accomplishes the will of the Father through the power of the Spirit today.[35] The discussion of Lucan Christology by Menzies and Shelton also provides us with the following data: that Jesus performed all his miracles by the power of the Spirit.

Similarly, it has been sufficiently demonstrated that the ordinary Christological articulation of the Indian Pentecostals is integrally connected to their testimonies and proclamation of Jesus as healer, exorcist, saviour, God and so on. They understand Jesus in functional categories and introduce Jesus to others in these terms. Indian Pentecostals also firmly believe that these signs and wonders take place through the power of the Spirit. Therefore, the functional Christology of ordinary Indian Pentecostals is similar to the conceptions of the 'Full Gospel'.

However, theological expressions of Pentecostal movements the world over have different emphases and outlooks. Accordingly, ordinary Pentecostal Christology shows certain differences from the 'Full Gospel', just as we have seen, one of the elements, 'Christ as the Coming King' is largely missing (due to the contextual struggles).[36] Using the same analogy Archer used, for ordinary Indian Pentecostals, the 'hub' is the person of Jesus Christ and his Gospel. However, the number of spokes is bigger. There are seven spokes in the wheel; Jesus is proclaimed as the healer, exorcist, provider, protector, Saviour, Lord and God. The rim of the wheel is the work of the Spirit. It is also clear that this functional Christology has radically transformed their conditions, making them strong enough to face the perilous situations they undergo and to rescue many from similar predicaments.

Jesus as healer and exorcist is at the very core of the Christological experience and conviction of the Pentecostals at the primary level and this also helps to disseminate the Gospel's message to the wider community. These themes not only heal ordinary people physically but renew and recreate their wounded psyche and broken world to give them a new life by healing the collective mind of the community and giving a new direction. This conviction is closely related to the

[34] Archer, *The Gospel Revisited*, 15.

[35] Macchia, 'Theology, Pentecostal,' *NIDPCM*, 1124.

[36] However, in South India, especially in Kerala, this understanding is prevalent.

revival fervour still prevalent in the community and understood to be the work of the Spirit.

Archer underlines this revival fervour in wider Pentecostal theology. According to him, the latter rain motif played a prominent role in the fashioning of the narrative tradition of the early Pentecostal community, by providing the basic structure for the Pentecostal story.[37] In fact there would be no Pentecostal story without this revival motif. It enabled the Pentecostals to hold together the message of the Full Gospel because it provided a coherent explanation for the restoration of the supernatural gifts. It also provided the primary organisational structure for the Pentecostal story,[38] which is true of ordinary Pentecostals who very often appeal to the manifestation of miracles to validate their message. What Archer says is true of Indian Pentecostal Christology, '"Signs and wonders" became an important "proof" for validating the Pentecostal story, and with this came the development of a "signs theology."'[39]

According to Archer, early Pentecostals read the whole Bible through the Book of Acts which was taken to be the beginning and end point in the development of biblical doctrines.[40] However, for Indian Pentecostals, especially those who come from contexts such as sickness, spirit worldview, poverty and religious and cultural oppression, similar Gospel stories, especially from the Synoptic Gospels, act as the fulcrum of their interpretation. The stories of healing, exorcism, provision and protection pass through the 'ordinary hermeneutical grid' of Pentecostal believers and shape Christological themes which change their lives. For them, these stories are not mere doctrine rather they are life, because in truth, they recreate their shattered lives. Ordinary Pentecostals internalise miracle stories in personal and community life and proclaim Jesus to be the Saviour in their society. This portrayal of Jesus acts as the restorative momentum to the members of traditional churches and to the people of other religious traditions. It is to be noted that the background of the Pentecostal movement in the early years of the last century, and the cultural and religious context of Indian Pentecostalism are entirely different. Indian Pentecostals live and work among people of other religious faiths, therefore, the Christological understanding needs to be extended to the understanding and to the appreciation of other religious traditions.

Besides, these primary themes liberate the marginalised and oppressed from their wretched situation and empower them to rise above such denigrating elements in society. Here Jesus is understood to be deliverer. Even more, because they still live in their hostile circumstances, they are ready to come all out, for the sake of Christ. Archer agrees with this, 'The Pentecostals were marginalised people who heeded the call to empty themselves of "self-love" and "self-will" and

[37] Archer, *The Gospel Revisited,* 27.

[38] Ibid., 27-30.

[39] Ibid., 30.

[40] Ibid., 35-36.

immerse themselves in the latter rain outpouring, which was the restoration of the Gospel of Christ for the preparation and participation of the end-time harvest.'[41] This element is vital for ordinary Christology and therefore, we shall re-examine it later.

7.3 Ontological Pentecostal Christology

Our concern at this point is to look into the Pentecostal mode of ontological Christology developed in recent Pentecostal scholarship. Several Pentecostal scholars endorse Spirit Christology in this regard. Hunter supports Spirit Christology, 'so long as Christology and Pneumatology are seen in a Trinitarian structure.'[42] Habets holds that a Trinitarian Spirit Christology satisfies the requirements for a biblical Christology when it is seen, not as a replacement for, but as a complement to the existing Logos Christology.[43] His main emphasis is that Spirit Christology needs to be developed from a Trinitarian framework to avoid denying the ontological identity of Christ with God.[44] Therefore, here we shall take Ralph Del Colle, the Roman Catholic Charismatic theologian, as our dialogue partner, since he speaks in Pentecostal terms and advocates a classical Trinitarian position in Spirit Christology.[45]

According to Del Colle, the experiential reality in Spirit baptism among Pentecostals and Charismatics becomes the basis for their spirituality. Pentecostal spirituality is essentially concerned with a communion in which God, the self, the neighbour and all of creation are known in prayer and praise of God, witnessing the risen Christ through the power of the Spirit.[46] Taking this idea forward, Del Colle argues that the 'knowledge of God,' or 'religious affection' appropriate for the Christian, is one that brings transformative conversion and praxis, the presence of God mediated by the risen Lord in the Holy Spirit.[47] What is unique to Pentecostal experience is that this transformation is marked by an experimental effusion of the Spirit as gift and empowerment. Thus, Pentecostalism intrinsically holds that the presence of God is Christologically and Pneumatologically inscribed

[41] Archer, *The Gospel Revisited,* 31.

[42] Harold D. Hunter, 'The Resurgence of Spirit Christology,' *European Pentecostal Theological Association Bulletin 11* (1992), http://www.fullnet.net/np/archives/writings/epta.html (accessed 1 September 2010); Harold D. Hunter, 'Spirit-Christology: Dilemma and Promise,' *Heythrop Journal* 24 (1983): 127-140, 266-277.

[43] *Myk Habets,* 'Spirit Christology: Seeing in Stereo,' *JPT* 11/2 (2003): 216-228.

[44] *Steven M. Studebaker,* 'Integrating Pneumatology and Christology: A Trinitarian Modification of Clark H. Pinnock's Spirit Christology,' *Pneuma* 28/1 (Spring 2006): 8, 5-20.

[45] Ralph Del Colle, *Christ and the Spirit: Spirit Christology in Trinitarian Perspective* (Oxford University Press, 1994).

[46] Ralph Del Colle, 'Spirit Christology: Dogmatic Foundations for Pentecostal-Charismatic Spirituality,' *JPT* 3 (1993): 94.

[47] Ralph Del Colle, 'Schleiermacher and Spirit Christology: Unexplored Horizons of the Christian Faith,' *IJST* 1/3 (1999): 288-289.

into our regenerated human faculties. That is, there is no relationship with Christ, without the awareness of the Spirit and vice versa.[48]

Consequently, Del Colle proposes a Spirit Christology from a Trinitarian perspective. The true Gospel portrayal of Jesus emerges only when the Christological event is understood to be a thoroughly Trinitarian event.[49] That is, God the Father effects salvation through the Son and in the Spirit; Jesus is both 'Son' and 'Spirit-bearer'. Therefore, the theological elaboration of this idea in the direction of Christian doctrine leads to the construction of Spirit Christology which attempts to represent this reality in the realm of our understanding faithfully.[50] He explains the relevance of Spirit Christology:

> To contemplate the person of Jesus Christ in the light of the Pentecostal-charismatic experience is to explicate the confession of 'truly human' and 'truly divine' within the ambit of a Spirit anointed and transfigured human being that is God's communicative and salvific relation to humanity. He is the mediator of life, mission and our deepest human identity, what we can describe in the language of election as our calling to exist in graced filial relation to God, the source of all reality.[51]

Thus, Spirit experience can truly contribute to an ontological understanding of Christ because it emphasises both his divinity and his humanity.

According to Del Colle, Trinitarian Spirit Christology proposes that the work of God in Jesus Christ proceeds of the Spirit and is enacted in the Spirit such that the Spirit becomes a gift to humanity in divinizing and missionising power.[52] Moreover, taking the idea of David Coffey, he argues that the Spirit creates, sanctifies and unites the assumed humanity of Jesus to the divine Son, so that the same Spirit as the Spirit of the Son may be poured out as a gift, enacting a regenerated, empowered and transfigured humanity so that in the eschaton God may be all in all (1Cor.15:28).[53] It is significant to note that Pentecostal-Charismatic spirituality contributes to a theological recognition of Trinitarian Spirit Christology because 'it apprehends in Spirit baptism/renewal of the living

---

[48] Del Colle, 'Spirit Christology,' 93.

[49] Del Colle, *Christ and the Spirit*, 4; That is, 'the relationship between Jesus and God and the role of Christ in redemption cannot be fully understood unless there is an explicitly pneumatological dimension'.

[50] Ralph Del Colle, 'Trinity and Temporality: A Pentecostal/Charismatic Perspective,' *JPT* 8 (1996): 101.

[51] Del Colle, 'Spirit Christology,' 94.

[52] Ibid., 106.

[53] Del Colle, *Christ and the Spirit*, 124. Some of the Charismatic and Pentecostal theologians use the Spirit Christology of David Coffey for their Spirit Christologies (Del Colle, Steven M. Studebaker). We shall look into the Spirit Christology of David Coffey in a later section of the Chapter, to propose a Trinitarian Spirit Christology for ordinary Indian Pentecostal Christology.

agency and presence of Christ and the Holy Spirit, as co-inhering but distinct, in the full inheritance of Christian initiation.'[54] The believer knows Christ to be Baptizer in the Spirit and the Spirit is the *Paraclete* who glorifies Christ in the manifestation of *charismata* and the formation of virtue. Here Trinitarian distinctions are not a matter of speculation but of lived experience and Christian witnessing. Moreover, the 'Full Gospel' is central to the Pentecostal-Charismatic experience that understands Christ as Saviour and Baptizer in the Spirit. In this experience there is an existential awareness of the effusion of the Holy Spirit as gift of the risen *kyrios*.[55] The key issue for a systematic Trinitarian Spirit Christology is whether or not the Son and the Spirit can be distinguished in the Christian experience of grace. The *Christus praesens* is known through the proclamation that effectively announces salvation. Likewise, prayer and petition for the outpouring of the Holy Spirit, the epicletic dimension associated with the *Spiritus praesens* (Lk.11:13; 24:49), implies a distinction from the *Christus praesens*.[56] Thus, the Pentecostal-Charismatic experience reveals the Trinitarian deep structure of Christian faith and theology.

Del Colle also attempts to address three major issues of contemporary theology, with the help of his Trinitarian Spirit Christology. They are (1) contextual issues of culture and human experience; (2) emancipatory concerns of social praxis and a just society, and (3) religious pluralism and the quest for dialogue.[57] We shall address the last two of these concerns in relation to ordinary Indian Pentecostal Christology later.

7.4 Rescripting Ordinary Christology

Now we shall turn to rescript the ontological elements which are integral parts of ordinary Christology. It was noted above that Indian Pentecostals attribute titles such as Lord and God to Christ, as they experience miraculous intervention in their lives. Jesus who has rescued them from sickness and evil spirits is also the saviour of their entire lives. That is, the saving acts begin with the body and proceed to the inner being and to salvation from sin. Their proclamation of Jesus as Lord and God underlines their basic conviction that Jesus is greater than all the other gods.

However, as we explained in chapter six, although ordinary Pentecostals emphasise and proclaim Jesus as Lord and God, ordinary Christology lacks a Trinitarian understanding and an ontological identity (both divinity and humanity). Their knowledge of Jesus as Lord begins with their salvation experience which is closely related to their bodily healing, deliverance and protection from social and spiritual forces and provisions in their strugglesome lives. They also

[54] Del Colle, 'Spirit Christology,' 106.

[55] Del Colle, 'Spirit Christology,' 106-107; Del Colle, 'Trinity and Temporality,' 111.

[56] Del Colle, 'Spirit Christology,' 107; Del Colle, *Christ and the Spirit*, 174-179.

[57] Del Colle, *Christ and the Spirit*, 195-213.

experience the constant presence and work of Christ in their daily life. These experiences, along with preaching and teaching about the greatness of Jesus Christ in the church enable them to see him as Lord of their lives. Within the worship context of the community, where the work of the Spirit is appreciated and the experience of the baptism of Spirit gives a further boost to this understanding. Then they extend the Lordship of Christ into every realm of their community and into the larger society. For them, Jesus is greater than all and he is the supreme God.

Therefore, for Indian Pentecostals a Spirit Christology addressing both the divinity and humanity of Jesus with equal emphasis is significant. It needs to be rooted in the biblical tradition, especially the Gospel accounts, which are the primary source of theologising of ordinary believers. Moreover, it has to do justice to traditional Trinitarian Christology, Pentecostal identity and to contextual factors which give rise to ordinary Pentecostal Christology. Del Colle's explanation goes along with this line:

> Reference to Jesus Christ is true to the Gospel only when the Christological event is understood to be a thoroughly Trinitarian event, an event in which God effects salvation through the Son and in the Spirit. In terms commensurate with the earliest strata of the canonical Gospels we can state that Jesus is revealed as one who stands in a unique relationship to the God of Israel, that is, his 'Abba relation' and as one who is filled with the Spirit without measure (Jn. 3:34).[58]

The ontological Christology proposed by Del Colle is essentially a Trinitarian framework which emphasises the divinity and the humanity of Jesus equally while upholding the person and work of the Spirit, which gives Pentecostal spirituality its identity. It is interesting to note that he begins his Spirit Christology from Spirit-experience, which is similar to the understanding of ordinary Pentecostals. Ordinary Pentecostals are unable to articulate their experiences into neat categories and turn them into a formal Christology but their rich Christological and pneumatological experiences can be taken to be stepping stones to a more ontologically oriented understanding of Christ, as Del Colle explains. At this point, ordinary Indian Pentecostal Christology can develop an ontological Christology in Trinitarian terms by defining the relationship between the Christ and the Spirit and the Christ and the Father. This understanding is relevant to a Pentecostal Christology, as Studebaker argues that integration of the Pentecostal experience of the Spirit with theological reflection is the key distinguishing factor of Pentecostal theology.[59]

[58] Del Colle, 'Spirit Christology,' 93.

[59] Studebaker, 'Integrating Pneumatology and Christology,' 19-20.

7.5 Constructive Proposal

In the light of rescription, critical evaluation and the context of Indian Pentecostals it is feasible to make certain proposals, considering ordinary Indian Pentecostal Christology's inherent weaknesses and contextual issues it faces. From the study it has become clear that three areas need to be addressed, namely, first, the 'Trinitarian' element of Christology in the light of lack of a concrete understanding of the divinity and humanity of Jesus (ontological); second, the 'dialogical' element in the context of religious pluralism and persecution; third, the 'liberative' elements in the situation of exploitations and marginalisation. The ideas of the Trinitarian model of Spirit Christology presented by David Coffey will be proposed to add a Trinitarian emphasis as scholars like Del Colle and Studebaker have done. In relation to other religious traditions we shall engage with a few Pentecostal scholars who have specialised in this area, while from a liberation perspective we shall present ideas from the study of the historical Jesus.

7.5.1 Trinitarian Spirit Christology

We shall now explore important elements of Trinitarian Spirit Christology which are to be added to Indian Pentecostal Christology. Australian Roman Catholic theologian David Coffey shows that Spirit Christology is a necessary complement to *Logos* Christology.[60] Exploring the idea of 'the Holy Spirit as the mutual love of the Father and the Son,' he expounds Jesus' divine Sonship and the bestowal of the Spirit on Jesus in the Gospels. The mutual love model posits that the Father generated the Son from eternity and that the Holy Spirit proceeds and subsists as the mutual love of the Father for the Son and of the Son for the Father. The Spirit is the love that indissolubly unites the Father and the Son. The identity of the Holy Spirit as mutual love does not depersonalize the Spirit. The Spirit is a unique divine person whose activity is that of uniting the other two divine persons.[61]

Both Matthew and Luke convey the same idea that both the conception of Jesus and divine Sonship were bestowed upon Jesus through the work of the Spirit.[62] Coffey also compares the idea of the Suffering Servant of Isaiah with Jesus; both of them were endowed with the Spirit for specific vocations. But, the Son had a unique love relationship with the Father, which enabled Jesus to address God as '*abba*'. The Spirit was Jesus' love for the Father and the Father's love for Jesus. In Christ, this love brings the deepest nature of Spirit and hence, the Christ-event became the revelation of the Trinity itself.[63] So for Coffey, the activity of

---

[60] Del Colle discusses the Spirit Christology of David Coffey, Del Colle, *Christ and Spirit,* 91-140.

[61] Studebaker, 'Integrating Pneumatology and Christology,' 11-12.

[62] David Coffey, 'The Holy Spirit as the Mutual Love of the Father and the Son,' *TS* 51/2 (1990): 203.

[63] Coffey, 'The Holy Spirit as the Mutual Love,' 204-205; Christina Manohar, *Spirit Christology: An Indian Christian Perspective* (Delhi: ISPCK, 2009), 96.

Christ is 'neither simply divine nor simply human, but something unique, divine-human, theandric.[64]

Coffey observes that, in Johannine Christology, the Spirit does not play an active role in the work of Christ as in the Synoptic Gospels. Theology in general has followed the Johannine trajectory. However, for a balanced Christology, the incarnational Christology of John, which assumes Christ's human nature by the *Logos,* needs to be complemented by the Synoptic Christology, which speaks about the role of the Spirit in incarnation.[65] John identifies the incarnation as the product of an act of the Father's love and the Synoptic Gospels as an act of the Holy Spirit. Thus, the conclusion is that 'the Holy Spirit is the love of God expressed *ad extra* who unites the divine Son with humanity in Jesus Christ.'[66]

Moreover, Coffey is keen to establish the ontological character of Christ; both the divinity and humanity; '..the radical bestowal of the Holy Spirit is the cause of the total human reality of Jesus, which is the same as his divine Sonship.'[67] That is, the Spirit is central to both who Christ is and what he did. Ontologically, Jesus Christ is the union of the divine Son with humanity because the Spirit creates, sanctifies, and unites the humanity to the divine Son. Functionally, Christ can perform his redemptive mission precisely because of the activity of God's Spirit in realizing the hypostatic union.[68]

In relation to the ontological unity of Christ with the Father Coffey asserts, 'The Spirit was given to him as *God's* Spirit; it set up a relationship, a bond, with *God,* which was realised in the course of his life and especially in his death, though naturally this realisation was in the course of his dealings with others.'[69] Jesus' appropriation of the Spirit means that it became a principle of action, as is the case with the Father himself, and was the pointer of his divinity. Jesus received the Spirit from the Father *but made it his own.* Moreover, Jesus bestows the Spirit to his fellow human beings which shows that Jesus, like the Father, is divine (Acts. 2:33).[70]

---

[64] David Coffey, 'The Theandric Nature of Christ,' *TS* 60/3 (1999): 413-415; Coffey explains, 'Christ was neither simply human nor simply nonhuman...While it is true (and important) to stress that the Word assumed a human nature like ours, it is also true that it is rendered unique, theandric, in the act of assumption. For hypostatic union is not a natural potency of human nature. It is a supernatural potency, one that would allow a human nature, God so willing, to be borne by grace beyond its natural limits to an absolute fulfilment. On the part of Christ's human nature it is this transcendence of natural limits along with its unsurpassable outcome in hypostatic union that justifies my use of the word "theandric" in its regard'.

[65] Coffey, 'The Theandric Nature of Christ,' 428.

[66] Studebaker, 'Integrating Pneumatology and Christology,' 16.

[67] Coffey, 'The Holy Spirit as the Mutual Love,' 218.

[68] Studebaker, 'Integrating Pneumatology and Christology,' 18-19.

[69] Coffey, 'The Holy Spirit as the Mutual Love,' 217.

[70] Ibid., 217-219.

However, there is a marked difference between the Spirit experience of Jesus and that of ordinary believers which also underlines his ontological status with God; 'Ordinary Christians, to whom the Spirit is also given, also relate to God in the power of the Spirit, and in death give themselves to Him in the Spirit, but though they "receive" and "possess" the Spirit, they can never appropriate it, as Jesus does.'[71]

Coffey also sees *communicatio idiomatum* as the ontological communication from the divine to the human nature of Christ. This is the Father's communication of his being through the Spirit in and at the inception of his life.[72] This makes Christ the unique, only begotten Son of God and places him in a unique ontological relationship with the Father by the Spirit. This is the Jesus whom we see in the Gospels. He is entirely human and in his human nature Jesus relates to the Father. By the special action of the Holy Spirit, Jesus in a human way, just as the divine Son in the Trinity depends on the Father, is taken into the Trinity. Moreover, this enabled the communication of human experience and suffering to the Trinity; 'All of Jesus' human experiences, including his sufferings, are imported into the life of Trinity...'[73] However, this does not compromise divine transcendence, since there is a dialectic of identity and non-identity between the existence of the Son in his divine and in his human nature.[74]

This expounding of the divinity and humanity of Jesus, in terms of Spirit activity, is significant because it balances the one-sided approach of ordinary Christological articulations described above. As explained here, it is thoroughly Trinitarian and underscores the ontological status of Christ. It makes room for the humanity of Jesus and gives credence to his relationship to and reliance on the Spirit for his activities in his context. Here Del Colle's Spirit Christology which emphasises the ontological status of Jesus should be added to give ordinary Christology a Pentecostal/Charismatic flavour. Indian Christology has also endeavoured to present a Christology which delineates the divinity as well as the ontological identity of Jesus. As already seen, Upadhyaya's use of the *sat-cit-*

---

[71] Coffey, 'The Holy Spirit as the Mutual Love,' 217-218.

[72] Coffey, 'The Theandric Nature of Christ,' 424-425. This means that the properties of the Divine Word are ascribed to the man Jesus, and that the properties of the man Jesus are predicated of the Word. This doctrine had a long history in patristic Christology. In Reformation times the Lutheran doctrine of the Eucharist demanded the transference of the attribute of ubiquity from the divine to the human nature of Christ. The principle of the *communicatio idiomatum* was therefore invoked and interpreted as a real participation in attributes. The Reformed tradition which (unlike Luther) held that the finite could not contain the infinite was regarded to be valid as a turn of speech but not for describing a real transfer or sharing of qualities. See H.E.W. Turner, 'Communicatio Idiomatum,' *A New Dictionary of Christian Theology*, edited by Alan Richardson & John Bowden (London: SCM, 1983), 113; also see Jürgen Moltmann, *The Crucified God: The Cross of Christ as the Foundation and Criticism of Christian Theology* (London: SCM, 1974), 231-235.

[73] Coffey, 'The Theandric Nature of Christ,' 425.

[74] Ibid.

ananda concept which explains the Trinity is valuable in establishing Christ's ontological relationship with God as well as in structuring a Trinitarian Christology within the Indian religious context.[75] However, we need to be cautious not to impose these overtly religious and philosophical categories on ordinary Indian Pentecostals. Similarly, Rayan in his Spirit-Christology, emphasises the humanity of Jesus. These ideas are appropriate for an ontological Christological construct of Pentecostal Christology in the Indian context and ought to be included in ordinary Christology.

7.5.2 Dialogical Spirit Christology

Encountering people of other religions and sharing Christ is a way of life for Indian Pentecostals; thus, they are affected by the issue of religious pluralism with all of its practical aspects. Moreover, most of them have come from other religions. Therefore, as Anderson comments, there is an urgent need to ponder the relationship between the Christian Gospel and the ancient pre-Christian religions that continue to give meaning to people's understanding of their lives. Demonizing these religions will not help the cause of evangelism and the healthy growth of the church today.[76] Although, Pentecostals are generally hesitant to discuss the issue of religious pluralism and related questions, recently Pentecostal scholars are beginning to appreciate the need for dialogue with other religions and have developed a theology of religions. Richie contends that it is not appropriate to relegate all religious experience beyond the border of the institutional church to the demonic realm. According to Richie, although there is no salvation outside Christ, that does not mean that there is no possibility of salvation outside the church.[77]

Now more pastors and evangelists encounter people of other faiths. Taking this reality into consideration, Kärkkäinen argues that it is vital to include theology of religions in the Christian educational curriculum. He also elaborates on the implications of the doctrine of Trinity when approaching religious pluralism.[78] According to Richie, a valid, vibrant Pentecostal theology of religions that does not compromise biblical, historic Christianity or act condescendingly or

[75] Upadhyaya explicates Christ as 'infinite in being' (*nirguna*), yet he is also 'with relations' (*saguna*) and so personal and knowable; see chapter 5.

[76] Allan Anderson, 'Towards a Pentecostal Missiology for the Majority World,' *AJPS* 8/1 (2005): 38.

[77] Tony Richie, '"The Unity of Spirit": Are Pentecostals Inherently Ecumenists and Inclusivists?,' *JEPTA* 26/1 (2006): 31-33.

[78] Veli-Matti Kärkkäinen, *An Introduction to the Theology of Religions: Biblical, Historical, & Contemporary Perspectives* (Illinois: IVP, 2003), 20; Veli-Matti Kärkkäinen, *Trinity and Religious Pluralism: The Doctrine of the Trinity in Christian Theology of Religions* (Hants: Ashgate, 2004); Samuel Solivan, 'Interreligious Dialogue: An Hispanic American Pentecostal Perspective,' in *Grounds for Understanding: Ecumenical Responses to Religious Pluralism*, edited by S. Mark Heim (Michigan: Eerdmans, 1998), 37-45.

contemptuously toward other world religions, is both possible and desirable for Pentecostals and for our friends in the interfaith venture.[79]

Amos Yong argues that the stress of Charismatic-Pentecostal Pneumatology on the universality of experience of God through the Spirit may contribute to a contemporary Christian theology of religions.[80] He sees the presence of the Spirit active in creation and in all cultures, which includes religions because the Spirit has been poured out on all flesh.[81] The emphasis of pneumatic elements enables Pentecostals to be open to other religious traditions. According to him, a Pentecostal-Charismatic theology of religions should free human beings for participation in interreligious dialogue. The goal of such dialogue is not merely to agree on similarities, rather even the 'activity of apologetics needs to be included in acknowledging such conversations to be in the service of the righteousness, peace and truth that characterise the Kingdom of God.'[82] He articulates 'pneumatological imagination,' as an experience of and orientation to the Holy Spirit through which one may determine the presence of the Holy Spirit. He also stresses that it is vital to discern the absence of the divine or presence of the demonic in other religious traditions.[83]

Yong proposes a theological framework for interfaith encounter. First, God is universally present by his Spirit; therefore, he sustains religions for his divine purposes. Second, the Spirit ushers in the Kingdom of God and hence, the signs of the Kingdom are made manifest through the Spirit's presence. Third, when there are signs of resistance to and activity against the Kingdom of God, the Spirit can be said to be absent from religions.[84] Nonetheless, he emphasises that the possibility of the presence of the Spirit in other religions should not de-emphasise the centrality of Christ to salvation, nor should it undermine the importance of evangelism.[85]

---

[79] Tony Richie, 'Neither Naïve nor Narrow: A Balanced Pentecostal Approach to Christian Theology of Religions,' *Presented to the Annual Meeting of the American Academy of Religion,* (Philadelphia, PA: November 19-22, 2005): 2, http://www.ncccusa.org/pdfs/naive.pdf (accessed 2 November 2010); also see Richie, 'Speaking by the Spirit: A Wesleyan-Pentecostal Theology of Testimony'.

[80] Amos Yong, *Discerning the Spirit(s): A Pentecostal-Charismatic Theology of Religions, JPT Supplement Series* (Sheffield: Sheffield Academic Press, 2000), 29-30.

[81] Amos Yong, *The Spirit Poured Out on All Flesh: Pentecostalism and the Possibility of Global Theology* (Michigan: Baker Academic, 2005).

[82] Yong, *Discerning the Spirit(s),* 313.

[83] Amos Yong, '"Not Knowing Where the Wind Blows ...": On Envisioning a Pentecostal-Charismatic Theology of Religions,' *JPT* 14 (1999): 81-83.

[84] Cartledge, *Testimony in the Spirit,* 144; Also see Yong, Yong, *The Spirit Poured Out on All Flesh,* 250–253.

[85] Amos Yong, *Beyond the Impasse: Toward a Pneumatological Theology of Religion* (Michigan: Eerdmans, 2003), 52-53.

Similarly, Richie, draws on the narrative of Acts 2 and the day of Pentecost, offers a Pentecostal perspective of dialogue.[86] The outpouring of the Spirit enabled a diversity of tongues; the many tongues retain their particularity even as they point to the unity of the one Spirit. These tongues represent, at least potentially, many religions, which in turn point to the redemption of religions (eschatologically), as well as of languages and cultures. The tongues or testimonies of the religious other must first be heard in their own terms, before a theology of religion can be constructed. This will involve a critical analysis of religious beliefs and practices, using a 'hermeneutic of charity.'[87]

With this background, Richie proposes a model of Pentecostal engagement based on the notion of testimony; telling others of what God has done in one's life in order to encourage them. It can be transformative for the testifier and hearer alike. It contains significant autobiographical elements and doxological content. Use of testimony as a way of interreligious dialogue benefits Pentecostals, since it is integral to Pentecostal spirituality and helps Pentecostals to retain their original energy and vitality.[88]

Hollenweger, however, develops a theology of 'dialogical evangelism' that is less rigid and more respectful regarding mutual sharing between religious others that decry too a sharp demarcation between Christian mission and interfaith dialogue. This is based on the encounter of Peter and Cornelius (Acts 10), and is used as a biblical model for contemporary Pentecostals. Significantly, both participants learn from each other as the Holy Spirit is poured out afresh.[89]

It seems that pneumatological elements in Christological articulation make it possible to interact with other religious traditions. Added to that, for ordinary Indian Pentecostals the centrality of Christ is a point of contact with other religionists, as we have seen. This point of contact is actualised through their testimonies and activities of signs and wonders which happen through the agency of the Spirit. Moreover, ordinary Pentecostal Christology can take cues from Indian Christology which emphasises dialogue for religious harmony, especially for the liberation of oppressed people. In an Indian and an Asian scenario, many voices advocate interreligious dialogue and they can be useful for ordinary Pentecostal Christology. However, a cautious approach is needed so that the supremacy of

---

[86] Richie, 'Speaking by the Spirit,' 89-90; Cartledge, *Testimony in the Spirit*, 147-148.

[87] Richie, 'Speaking by the Spirit,' 113-115; also see Richie, 'Continuing the Conversation on King: My Really Final Response to Tony Moon?,' *JPT* 19/1 (2010): 170-179; Richie, 'Getting Back to the Heart of the Matter: The Way Forward and a Final Response to Tony Moon,' *JPT* 18/1 (2009): 141-149; Richie, 'God's Fairness to People of All Faiths: A Respectful Proposal to Pentecostals for Discussion Regarding World Religions,' *Pneuma* 28/1 (Spring 2006): 105-119.

[88] Richie, 'Speaking by the Spirit,' 165-166.

[89] Walter J. Hollenweger, 'Critical Issues for Pentecostals,' in *Pentecostals after a Century: Global Perspectives on a Movement in Transition,* edited by Allan H. Anderson & Walter J. Hollenweger (Sheffield: Sheffield Academic Press, 1999), 176-191; Walter J. Hollenweger, 'Evangelism: A Non-Colonial Model,' *JPT* 7 (1995): 116-121.

Christ is not undermined. M.M. Thomas advocates dialogue between Christians and non-Christians (both religious and secular) to involve in the political struggle for the transformation of the Asian society. Similarly, Appasamy's idea of Jesus as *avatara* as well as the cultural Christology of Amaladoss can be included in the Pentecostal model of dialogue which always undergirds evangelical endeavours. Here Sadhu Sundar Singh's approach to Christology has still greater value in the cultural and religious contexts of Indian villages, as he emphasises the mystical and practical elements of Christology. Developing suitable cultural and religious models of mission and evangelism, like Sundar Singh's, emphasising the work of the Spirit and the mystical aspects which would touch the heart of the Indian masses, the majority of which are ordinary people, should be the priority of Pentecostal missiologists and theologians.[90]

Richie rightly endorses a typical Pentecostal position: 'Inclusivism by no means necessitates even a nascent compromise of Christian integrity or of Pentecostal theology and spirituality; rather, it enables Pentecostals to witness with respect to everyone of the limitless love of God in his Son by the power of the Spirit.'[91] Since ordinary Pentecostals constantly interact with people of other faiths and also come under the attack of extremist elements, this notion needs to be included in an Indian Pentecostal Christology.

7.5.3 Liberative Spirit Christology

For a liberative Spirit Christology, we shall propose the picture of Jesus who, by the anointing of the Spirit, acted as an agent of liberation in his own context. Before we chart our course, it is to be noted that Pentecostals naturally shy away from overt social involvement due to their understanding of holiness. However, it is important to emphasise that the holiness Pentecostal spirituality advocates is not an inward-looking and world-shunning piety; rather it is outgoing and world-affirming.[92] Dempster argues that the baptism in the Spirit and the gifts of the Spirit restored the Spirit's empowering in witness. Hence, Pentecostals witness as prophets by virtue of works which are empowered by the Spirit and by words which are inspired by the Spirit.[93] Taking Luke's portraits of the people of God of the new age, Stronstad argues that by virtue of having been filled with the Spirit of prophecy, the believers became the eschatological community of

[90] Using Indian spiritual categories such as storytelling, using parables and a mission without tight ecclesiastical binding can be helpful. See P. Surya Prakash, 'Contribution of Sadhu Sundhar Singh to the Indigenous Christian movement in India,' in *Christianity is Indian,* 113-127.

[91] Richie, '"The Unity of Spirit,"' 34.

[92] Shaibu Abraham, *Pentecostal Theology of Liberation: Holy Spirit and Holiness in the Society* (New Delhi: Christian World Imprints, 2014).

[93] Murray W. Dempster, 'Pentecostal Social Concern and the Biblical Mandate for Social Justice,' *Pneuma* 9/2 (Fall 1987): 147.

prophets.[94] Therefore, Pentecostal believers stand in the heritage of the Spirit-anointed, Spirit-filled, Spirit-led and Spirit-empowered prophet Jesus who is the prophet *per se*[95] and who carried out a prophetic ministry of renouncing the evils of his society. The holiness Jesus envisioned was not of exclusion but of embracing and compassionate participation.[96] Interestingly, early Pentecostals understood Spirit baptism to be power for mission that not only included evangelism but also addressed social issues such as slavery, women's rights, child labour, slum conditions and illiteracy.[97] It was a subversive and revolutionary movement, not based upon either philosophic ideology or critical reflection. It was a movement that experienced God's divine liberation through the Holy Spirit.[98] Therefore, it is feasible to propose a liberative Christology for Indian Pentecostals.

As we have already seen, issues such as the caste-system, poverty, oppression, communalism and the resultant social unrest and even armed struggles, make life miserable for ordinary people. Therefore, in our construction of a liberative Spirit Christology it is vital to present a picture of Jesus acting against similar issues in the power of the Spirit in his society. Recent scholarship in Gospel studies, especially the social scientific study of the New Testament and the Historical Jesus research have shed ample light upon the life and ministry of Jesus and these can help us to draw a picture of Jesus and of how he acted within his society.[99] Here we shall concentrate on the historical sketch of first century Palestine and the portrayal of the historical Jesus by Marcus Borg, as they come closer to the Indian situation.

Borg explains Jesus' social and religious context in terms of ritual purity (holiness) and resultant injustices and oppression, and introduces Jesus as someone who acted against those evils in the power of the Spirit and identified with the

[94] Stronstad, 'Affirming Diversity,' 145.

[95] Ibid., 148.

[96] Marcus J. Borg, *Meeting Jesus Again for the First Time: The Historical Jesus and the Heart of Contemporary Faith* (New York: HarperSanFrancisco, 1994); Marcus J. Borg, *Conflict, Holiness and Politics in the Teaching of Jesus* (New York: The Edwin Mellen Press, 1984).

[97] Bridges Johns, *Pentecostal Formation*, 65-66.

[98] Ibid., 69.

[99] For a detailed account see Ben Witherington III, *The Jesus Quest: The Third Search for the Jew of Nazareth* (Illinois: IVP, 1995); James H. Charlesworth, *Jesus within Judaism: New Light from Exiting Archaeological Discoveries* (New York: Doubleday, 1988); James H. Charlesworth & Petr Pokorny (eds.), *Jesus Research: An International Perspective* (Michigan: Eerdmans, 2009); Theissen & Merz, *The Historical Jesus*; Wolfgang Stegemann, Bruce J. Malina & Gerd Theissen (eds.), *The Social Setting of Jesus and the Gospels* (Minneapolis: Fortress Press, 2002); Ekkehard W. Stegemann & Wolfgang Stegemann. *The Jesus Movement: A Social History of its First Century* (Edinburg: T&T Clark, 1999); Jerome H. Neyrey (ed.), *The Social World of Luke-Acts* (Peabody, MA: Hendrickson, 1991).

'untouchables' and the poor.[100] It is interesting to note that Borg identifies Jesus' activities in his context as a result of his Spirit-empowerment which is similar to Pentecostal functional Christology and the Trinitarian mode of Spirit Christology we have outlined above.

This portrayal of Jesus is highly significant within the Indian context as a large section of the population still reel under the evil effect of the caste system and its resultant discrimination. Soares-Prabhu, speaking from the Indian context, describes Jesus as the Spirit-filled evangeliser and Spirit-empowered exorcist.[101] Therefore, ordinary Pentecostals may feel at home with a picture of Jesus which gives them a model to follow a life of discipleship.[102] It is appropriate to add this portrayal of Jesus as a building block of Pentecostal Christology.

7.5.3.1 Jesus in His Context

According to Borg, Jesus' relationship to the Spirit had great implications for his ministry. One of the most important characteristics of Jesus' ministry was his deep involvement with the socio-political and economic life of his own people.[103] Unlike other renewal movements which 'separated' themselves from people and depicted God and religion in exclusive terms, Jesus advocated an 'open' stream which would accommodate even 'sinners,' 'outcasts' and gentiles and introduced a God who was merciful and gracious to all.[104] He was not only born in a particular culture with its political, religious and economic complexities but was also fully involved in it and to some extent even shaped by it.[105]

The society of his time was divided into various groups determined by three basic elements: power, privilege and prestige.[106] The overwhelming majority of the populace belonged to 'lower-stratum groups' who inhabited largely in rural

---

[100] Marcus J. Borg, *Jesus a New Vision: Spirit, Culture, and the Life of Discipleship* (New York: HarperSanFrancisco, 1987); Marcus J. Borg, *Jesus in Contemporary Scholarship* (Pennsylvania: Trinity Press International, 1994); Borg, *Meeting Jesus Again*; Borg, *Conflict, Holiness and Politics.*

[101] George M. Soares-Prabhu, *The Dharma of Jesus*, edited by Francis Xavier O'sa (Maryknoll: Orbis Books, 2003): 19-22.

[102] Jon Sobrino, *Jesus the Liberator: A Historical-Theological Reading of Jesus of Nazareth* (Kent: Burns & Oates, 1994), 47-55; John P. Meir, *A Marginal Jew: Rethinking the Historical Jesus* (New York: Doubleday, 1991), 196-201; Borg, *Jesus a New Vision*, 1-2.

[103] Theissen & Merz, *The Historical Jesus*, 125-150; T. Raymond Hobbs, 'The Political Jesus: Discipleship and Disengagement,' in *The Social Setting of Jesus and the Gospels*, 251-281.

[104] Theissen and Merz, *The Historical Jesus*, 146.

[105] See John Howard Yoder, *The Politics of Jesus* (Michigan: Eerdmans, 1994); Gerd Theissen, *The Gospels in Context: Social and Political History in the Synoptic Tradition*, translated by Linda M. Maloney (Edinburgh: T&T Clark, 1992).

[106] Stegemann & Stegemann, *The Jesus Movement*, 60ff.

areas and which included peasants, artisans, labourers and slaves.[107] They were characterised by their absolute poverty. *Ptochoi*, the Greek word used for the poor in the New Testament denotes the people who were hungry and thirsty, had only rags for clothes and lacked lodging or hope.[108] This description is similar to the description of the poor in the Indian context.

Roman rule had direct economic consequences which had a huge impact on the Jewish social world. It added a tax burden upon the ordinary people, who were already paying temple tax and other forms of tithing required by the law.[109] This resulted in increasing debt for the poor and in the confiscation of land belonging to the marginal farmers, followed by arrest, torture and slavery of the family.[110] Further, Roman rule perpetuated injustice and was chronically oppressive and brutal. Such a situation of sharp social differences created unrest, conflict and even rebellion by slaves and very poor peasants from rural areas.[111]

In such a context, he had a message, the message of the Kingdom of God which would change the existing social structure into an entity of God's reign;[112] this was not achieved through force, but through service and peace-making.[113] In the Kingdom, the poor were considered to be the blessed and the meek as powerful (Matt. 5:3ff; Lk.6:20ff). It led to freedom, fellowship and justice.[114] Borg rightly comments, 'Like Amos, Micah, and Jeremiah, Jesus challenged the domination system of his day, a hierarchical and oppressive social order with sharp social boundaries ruled over by a small class of urban elites. He not only challenged that system; he also had an alternative social vision.'[115] Thus, Jesus was *political* but not in a conventional sense.[116]

---

[107] Bruce J. Malina, *The Social Gospel of Jesus: The Kingdom of God in Mediterranean Perspective* (Minneapolis: Fortress Press, 2001), 19-22; Stegemann & Stegemann give a detailed account of social situation and stratification of ancient Mediterranean societies; see, Stegemann & Stegemann, *The Jesus Movement*, 60-95.

[108] Stegemann & Stegemann, *The Jesus Movement*, 92.

[109] Stegemann & Stegemann, *The Jesus Movement*, 116-125; Borg, *Jesus a New Vision*, 84-86.

[110] Douglas E. Oakman, 'The Countryside in Luke-Acts,' *The Social World of Luke-Acts,* 163-164; Malina, *The Social Gospel of Jesus*, 27; Stegemann & Stegemann, *The Jesus Movement*, 134-136.

[111] Richard A. Horsley, *The Liberation of Christmas: The Infancy Narratives in Social Context* (New York: Crossroad, 1988), 127-143; K.C. Hanson, 'Jesus and Social Bandits,' in *The Social Setting of Jesus and the Gospels*, 285-291.

[112] G. R. Beasley-Murray, *Jesus and the Kingdom of God* (Exeter: Paternoster, 1986); Malina, *The Social Gospel of Jesus.*

[113] Gerd Theissen, 'The Political Dimension of Jesus' Activities,' in *The Social Setting of Jesus and the Gospels*, 225-250.

[114] Soares-Prabhu, *The Dharma of Jesus*, 67.

[115] Marcus J. Borg (ed.), 'From Galilean Jew to the Face of God: The Pre-Easter and Post-Easter Jesus,' *Jesus at 2000,* edited by Marcus J. Borg (Colorado: Westview Press, 1997), 11.

[116] Yoder, *The Politics of Jesus*; Hobbs, 'The Political Jesus'; Borg, *Jesus in Contemporary Scholarship*, 100-107.

Holiness/Purity System

One of the vexing issues of his society was the practice of holiness. According to Borg, the dominant ethos and the paradigm structuring of the Jewish social world in first century Palestine was 'Be holy as God is holy' (Lev. 19:2), holiness understood as purity.[117] The purity laws acted as boundaries between outsiders and insiders.[118] The core value was God's holiness, understood as to order the world, separation from everything unclean taken as ritual purity.[119] It created social boundaries between pure and impure, righteous and sinners, whole and not whole, male and female, Jew and Gentile.[120]

Purity is a social system organised around the polarities of pure and impure, clean and unclean.[121] These polarities apply to persons, places, things, times, and social groups. One's purity status depended to some extent, on birth[122] in such a way that a person born to the priestly family was more holy than a common man.[123] One's degree of holiness also depended on behaviour. Those who observed the purity codes were considered as 'the pure' while the non-observant were termed 'outcasts' or 'sinners' and included occupational groups such as tax-collectors and perhaps shepherds. In a purity system sin becomes a matter of being impure or ritually unclean and rendered one 'untouchable.'[124]

Physical wholeness was also associated with purity and lack of wholeness with impurity. People who were maimed, the chronically ill, lepers, eunuchs were considered to be impure. Purity and impurity were also associated with the contrast between male and female. Men in their natural state were thought to be more pure than women. The natural bodily process of childbirth and menstruation

---

[117] Borg, *Jesus in Contemporary Scholarship*, 26; 'Holiness generated a social world ordered as a purity system, with sharp boundaries not only between places, things, and times, but also between persons and social groups,' says Borg.

[118] Stegemann & Stegemann, *The Jesus Movement*, 142; Wolfgang Stegemann, 'The Contextual Ethics of Jesus,' in *The Social Setting of Jesus and the Gospels*, 52.

[119] Jerome H. Neyrey, 'The Symbolic Universe of Luke-Acts: 'They Turn the World Upside Down,' in *The Social World of Luke-Acts,* 276; Archaeological evidences also confirm the purity system, see Craig A. Evans, 'Context, Family and Formation,' in *The Cambridge Companion to Jesus*, edited by Markus Bockmuehl (Cambridge: The Cambridge University Press, 2001), 12.

[120] For a detailed discussion see Borg, *Conflict, Holiness and Politics*, 56-72; Borg, *Meeting Jesus Again*, 52.

[121] Mary Douglas defines a purity system as an orderly cultural system; see, Mary Douglas, *Purity and Danger: An Analysis of Pollution and Taboo* (London: Routledge and Kegan Paul, 1966).

[122] Neyrey, 'The Symbolic Universe of Luke-Acts,' 285; Westerholm, 'Clean and Unclean,' 131.

[123] For instance, at the top of the purity ladder stood the high priest and he was the holiest of all; followed by priests, Levites, Jewish men, women, converts, and gentiles and so on. Neyrey, 'The Symbolic Universe of Luke-Acts,' 279.

[124] Borg, *Meeting Jesus Again*, 51.

were considered to be a source of impurity and, hence, women had only second-class status in the society.[125]

Purity was also observed in relation to place. At the centre of the purity system was the temple which was taken to be the geographic and cultic centre of Israel's purity map. The temple's 'Holy of Holies' was the point of greatest holiness and from it concentric circles of decreasing degrees of holiness radiated outward ending at the borders of 'the holy land.'[126] The land of Israel was considered holier than other lands. Holiness was observed in relation to things, time and social groups and objects related to the temple were considered to be holier. Certain food items were considered impure; the Sabbath day was holier than other days; Israelites were God's chosen people and, therefore, a holy nation. Since Gentiles were not God's people, they were considered unholy.[127]

The purity system had political and economic implications too. According to Borg, the ruling elites used these laws to further their own agenda. The income of the temple and the temple elites depended upon the observance of purity laws to some extent while tithing was closely linked to purity; un-tithed produce was thus impure and would not be purchased by the observant. This might have resulted in a sort of economic boycott and further exploitation.[128] There are many such similarities between the caste system and the Jewish purity system. Such a predicament is what Dalits, Tribals and lower castes face in India even today.[129]

Jesus, however, directly and repeatedly challenged the dominant socio-political and economic paradigm of his society and advocated an alternative vision. In the teachings and activities of Jesus we see a comprehensive alternative social and spiritual vision, which foresaw a 'Kingdom' community, a community not shaped by the ethos of purity, but by compassion and relationship.

Compassion as Holiness

According to Sobrino, the ministry of Jesus, especially his miracles, were a demonstration of his compassion.[130] His charismatic power attracted crowds, largely the poor and despised such as women, tax collectors and leprosy affected

---

[125] William Countryman, *Dirt, Greed, and Sex* (Philadelphia: Fortress, 1988), 28-30.

[126] The order was Holy of Holies, Holy Place, court of the priests, court of men, court of women, and court of gentiles and so on. Neyrey, 'The Symbolic Universe of Luke-Acts,' 278-279.

[127] Neyrey, 'The Symbolic Universe of Luke-Acts,' 280-282.

[128] Borg, *Jesus in Contemporary Scholarship*, 110.

[129] Anderson H.M. Jeremiah, 'Exploring New Facets of Dalit Christology: Critical Interaction with J.D. Crossan's Portrayal of the Historical Jesus,' in *Dalit Theology in Twenty-First Century: Discord Voices, Discerning Pathways*, edited by Sathianathan Clarke, Deena Bandhu Manchala & Philip Vinod Peacock (New Delhi: Oxford University Press, 2010), 160.

[130] 'The miracles not only demonstrate Jesus' power as healer...but mainly his reaction to the sorrows of the poor and weak'. Sobrino, *Jesus the Liberator*, 90; D. J. Williams, 'Mercy,' *DJG*.

people.[131] Similarly, Borg identifies Jesus' activities with Spirit and compassion. For Jesus, compassion was the central quality of God and the central moral quality of a life centred in God. Hence, Jesus deliberately replaced 'Be holy as God is holy' by 'Be compassionate as God is compassionate (Lk.6:36).'[132]

Table Fellowship

One of the most radical acts of Jesus against the purity system was his table fellowship or 'open commensality,' sharing the meals with the poor, the tax-collectors and the outcasts to rebuild a community on radically different principles, 'based on an egalitarian sharing of spiritual and material power at the most grass-roots level.'[133] Pharisees and teachers of the law would not eat with somebody who was impure, since that would make them unholy.[134] The rules related to meals were deeply embedded in the purity system;[135] refusing to share a meal was a form of social exclusion.

The open table fellowship of Jesus was thus perceived as a challenge to the ideology of the purity class.[136] It had socio-political and religious connotations which included the ritually impure in the fellowship of a messianic community and placed them at a par with those who were higher in the social ladder of the purity system.[137] Moreover, in a patriarchal society, Jesus' message was deliberately addressed even to prostitutes; Jesus accepted the touch and kiss of a prostitute and assured her of forgiveness (Lk. 36-50).[138] These credentials of Jesus need to be accommodated into Indian Pentecostal Christology, where many are still considered to be untouchables.

---

[131] Theissen & Merz, *The Historical Jesus*, 217.

[132] Borg, *Meeting Jesus Again*, 46-48; He adds that compassion has particularly rich connotations because of its etymology: its roots in both Hebrew and Aramaic means womb. To be compassionate is to be 'like womb' with its evocations of nourishing, life-giving, and encompassing. It is the opposite of purity in many ways, perhaps most notably in its inclusiveness. See Borg, *Jesus in Contemporary*, 153-154.

[133] J.D. Crossan, *The Historical Jesus: The Life of a Mediterranean Jewish Peasant* (San Francisco: HarperSanFrancisco, 1991), 344; S. Scott Bartchy, 'The Historical Jesus and Honour Reversal at the Table,' *The Social Setting of Jesus and the Gospels*, 175-183.

[134] Jesus was accused of 'eating with tax-collectors and sinners' and was with being 'a glutton and a drunkard, a friend of tax-collectors and sinners'. S. Scott Bartchy, 'Table Fellowship,' *DJG*; Dennis E. Smith, 'Table Fellowship,' *ABD*.

[135] Jerome H. Neyrey, 'Ceremonies in Luke-Acts: The Case of Meals and Table Fellowship,' in *The Social World of Luke-Acts*, 378.

[136] Borg, *Meeting Jesus Again*, 55-56.

[137] Craig Blomberg, *Contagious Holiness: Jesus' Meals with Sinners* (Leicester: Apollos, 2005), 97-163; Borg, *Meeting Jesus Again*, 55-56; Bartchy, 'Table Fellowship'.

[138] Theissen & Merz, *The Historical Jesus*, 219-222.

Temple Cleansing

At its climax, the cleansing of the temple characterises Jesus' opposition toward the interpretation of the religious authorities as regards holiness. This action can be interpreted in religious, messianic, prophetic and political terms. Mark presents the action in the temple as a deliberate act (Mk. 11:11).[139] It was an indictment of what was taking place in the temple; it became a centre of an economically exploitative system dominated by ruling elites. His ire was not against the poor merchants. This was obvious by Jesus' combining and quoting of two OT passages: 'Is it not written: "My house will be called a house of prayer for all nations?" (Isa. 56:7), but you have made it "a den of robbers" (Jer. 7:11).' The line from Isaiah comes from one of the most inclusive visions of the temple community in the Bible. The temple was to include eunuchs, foreigners and outcasts. The second phrase is from Jeremiah's famous temple sermon, in which he indicted the Jerusalem elites of his day. It was they who acted unjustly, oppressing aliens, orphans and widows and shedding the blood of the innocent in the temple. As in the days of Jeremiah, the religious elites had turned the temple into a den of robbers and violent people. Thus, the action was directed against the perpetuators of the purity system who were profiteering from the temple system.[140] In this episode, Dalit theologian Nirmal sees 'a pre-figuration of the vindication of the Dalit struggle for their prayer and worship rights.'[141]

Thus, Jesus on the one hand erected a formidable challenge against the purity system; on the other hand, he reinterpreted holiness in terms of compassion, loving relationships and inclusiveness. This inclusive vision of Jesus' activity was reflected in the early church; it acted as an alternative community with remarkable social radicalism by the power of the Spirit. In a world with sharp social boundaries, it included women, untouchables, the poor, the maimed and the marginalised. The story of baptism of the Ethiopian eunuch and the conversion and inclusion of Cornelius in the church depict the inclusiveness of the movement. Borg comments: 'As a boundary shattering movement, it was a social reality with an alternative vision of human life in community. This, too, is connected to the Spirit: *there is something boundary-shattering about the activity and experience of the Spirit.*'[142] Life in the Spirit does not draw one away from culture and society. It is not an individualistic vision

---

[139] W.R. Herzog II, 'Temple Cleansing'.

[140] Borg, *Jesus in Contemporary Scholarship*, 115-116; W.R. Herzog II, 'Temple Cleansing;' The response from the authorities confirms this: 'The chief priests and the teachers of the law heard this and began looking for a way to kill him... (Mk.11:18)'.

[141] Balasundaram, *Contemporary Asian,* 169-170.

[142] Borg, *Jesus in Contemporary Scholarship*, 153-154 (italics added for emphasis).

but it creates a new community, or an alternative culture. It was so with Jesus and his followers.[143]

Therefore, ordinary Pentecostals need a ministry of the Spirit and compassion and a Christology that accommodates these ideals. Such approaches are actually followed in Indian Christologies to address issues such as poverty, the caste-system, and economic exploitation as we have seen. The Christology of M.M. Thomas, Dalit Christology and the Indian version of liberation theology present Christ as the liberator of the poor. The Spirit Christology of Rayan emphasises the humanity of Jesus to accelerate the liberative efforts. Wilfred suggests a *kenotic* Christology in the context of communal frenzy and marginalisation of the poor. There are many other voices, both theological and secular, which contribute to the emancipation of the downtrodden in the Indian context. An Ordinary Pentecostal Christology should accommodate their credentials to make it more akin to the Gospel accounts of Jesus and to enhance liberative potential. What is important is to have a 'pneumatological imagination,' as Yong proposed, to discern them.[144] Archer suggestively comments,

> ...orthopathos puts us in touch with the compassionate redemptive liberation of Jesus Christ and the Holy Spirit. This redemptive liberation is anchored in the very passion of God manifested paradigmatically in the ministry of Jesus and the ongoing work of the Christian community empowered and impassioned by the Spirit. We must do theology from a conjunctive methodology that takes seriously orthopathos as the integrative centre for our Pentecostal theology without setting aside either praxis or dogma.[145]

To summarise our discussion, it is clear that the Christological themes of ordinary Pentecostals have a major impact upon the lives of the people. However, lack of a systematic articulation of a Christology triggers Christological misconceptions and also prevents them from involving themselves overtly in their contexts. This study urges the thesis that a constructive Christology among Indian Pentecostals should articulate a Spirit Christology with Trinitarian, dialogical and liberative emphasis, one that would bring the necessary correction and impetus to their Christology, thus making it a suitable Christology for an Indian context.

---

[143] Borg, *Jesus a New Vision*, 194. He says, '...the heart of biblical tradition is "charismatic," its origin lies in the experience of the Spirit-endowed people who became radically open to the other world and whose gifts were extraordinary'; Borg, *Jesus a New Vision*, 32.

[144] Yong, '"Not Knowing Where the Wind Blows ..."'; Yong, *Beyond the Impasse.*

[145] Archer, 'A Pentecostal Way of Doing Theology,' 310-311.

Chapter 8

Conclusion

In the previous chapters we have explored ordinary Pentecostal Christology and its various aspects. In this final chapter, we shall summarise what we have discussed so far. We shall also highlight this Christology's significant contributions to the Indian, Asian and global contexts. Finally, we shall identify major areas for further research, so that various other significant aspects of Indian Pentecostal theology, particularly Pentecostal Christology may be unravelled for wider Pentecostal scholarship.

Chapter one highlighted the growth and present state of Pentecostalism in India. The movement is making a positive impact among the poor, Dalits, Tribal groups and ordinary people. However, the movement has not articulated its variegated theological heritage for its consolidation and further growth. Therefore, it is argued that a Christology developed from the people's side would help the movement to steer its course into the future and enable it to face various obstacles. In order to achieve this, a qualitative research is proposed.

Chapter two argued the importance and necessity of contextual and practical expressions of theology and Christology in particular. Since Indian Pentecostalism largely exists among ordinary people, it is proposed that a practical approach is essential to draw out various aspects of Christological articulations. For this purpose, an empirical research is proposed. The rest of the chapter discussed various research methods used for data collection. We employed various methods such as formal interviews and informal interviews (ethnography), focus groups, participant observation, informal conversations with Pentecostal members and pastors and documentary analysis.

In chapter three we discussed various issues in the Indian context which affect the general populace and Pentecostals in particular and contribute to the Christological articulation of Pentecostals. It explained that, although India is experiencing major growth and development in the social and economic realms, only a few enjoy the fruits. The ordinary people suffer the effects of various anomalies which have existed for a long time and also now the negative effects of economic liberalisation and an unbridled consumer market. The most pressing issues affecting common people are poverty and lack of health-care facilities. Dalits and Tribal people face the evil effect of the caste system and resultant untouchability and economic exploitation. Moreover, their cultural and spiritual situation have been identified and analysed to see how do they affect their lives. For Pentecostals, along with all these issues, the issues of frenzied hostility and persecution create a piquant situation, affect their psyche and social life badly and threaten their safe existence.

Chapter four deals with Christologies prevalent in the Indian Christian theological milieu which could be possible dialogue partners for Indian Pentecostal Christology. These Christologies emerged in response to four broader concerns within the Indian context, namely secular, religious, cultural and socio-political concerns. We selected a few from each category and explored their ideas. It is argued that certain elements such as taking culture positively, emphasising the liberative aspect of Christology and appreciating dialogue, among others, need to be taken into account and accommodated by a Pentecostal Christology. However, Christological proposals of some of them are not useful for Pentecostal Christology, since they do not appreciate the divinity and supremacy of Christ. Pentecostal Christology needs to be discerning when appropriating ideals from some of them.

Chapter five deals with the ordinary Indian Pentecostal Christology that emerged from the intimate experiences of ordinary believers who were undergoing various struggles. We identified their immediate context and explained that the Christological articulation they cherish stems from their profound contextual and spiritual experiences. We identified seven major Christological themes, namely, (1) in the context of illness and lack of health-care Jesus is their healer; (2) in the wake of troubles and oppression from evil spiritual forces, the person of Christ comes as the exorcist; (3) in the midst of extreme poverty, they experience Jesus as the provider; (4) in their struggle and persecution, Jesus comes to their rescue and is seen as the protector. These experiential categories enable them to identify Jesus as (5) the Saviour while their continued dependency on Jesus and his continuous presence among them embolden them to confess him to be (6) the Lord. The worship, the work of the Spirit in their lives and teachings from the Bible in churches enable them to make this confession. This new understanding ultimately leads them to proclaim (7) Jesus as God. It is amply clear that these Christological notions have brought radical changes in their personal, family and social lives.

In the first part of Chapter six we evaluated the Christology of Indian Pentecostals critically. It has an appropriate mix of both a Christology from below and a Christology from above. However, it lacks an ontological conception of the person of Christ. Moreover, it lacks an understanding of the full humanity of Jesus. These deficiencies can be problematic in the long run. Secondly, we identified several characteristic features of ordinary Christology which are salient features of this Christology. Thirdly, we have also endeavoured to identify its consonance and continuity, in relation to the larger Pentecostal tradition and the New Testament testimony of the person of Christ in order to present it to the larger Pentecostal and Christian audience. It explained that this Christology is compatible with both Pentecostal tradition and the New Testament testimony of the person of Christ.

In Chapter seven we rescripted the ordinary Christology in conversation with Pentecostal scholarship to present it constructively to the wider scholarship. In response to the evaluation, rescripting and contextual factors, we also proposed Trinitarian, dialogical and liberative elements which might be added to the ordinary Christology to enrich it and give it added value and meaning. It is believed that these proposals would help Indian Pentecostals to involve themselves actively in their society and enable them to liberate many from the struggles.

This research and its findings have wider significance in Indian, Asian and global contexts in relation to theology, especially Christology. It can also a make rich contribution to Asian and global Pentecostal theology.

Firstly, it emerged that a Christology needs to touch the lives and struggles of ordinary people in order to make it relevant to their context and to achieve this, the ingredients of this Christology must derive from ordinary people. This thesis sends out the message that Christology has to be articulated taking its input from the personal and communal spiritual dimensions of the people.

Secondly, a Christology in an Indian/Asian context should appreciate and appropriate 'signs and wonders,' such as healing and exorcism to alleviate immediate struggles of ordinary people. Along with these elements, the pneumatological dimension should also be included, to actualise liberative efforts in the context of marginalisation and oppression. This Christology may encourage other endeavours in taking these elements seriously.

Thirdly, it is obvious from the research that the missionary dimension of Christology is an indispensible element in disseminating the message of Christ to the people who are in need. The liberative potential of this proposed Indian Pentecostal Christology can be communicated effectively by ordinary people through their experience and testimony. This research will facilitate the appropriation by other Christologies of the evangelistic and missionary dimension in Christological articulation. It may also help to take ordinary people's testimonies as a valid source for theology. Moreover, emphasising the missionary element and the people's testimonies would enable other Christologies to uphold the supremacy and uniqueness of Christ, in the context of religious pluralism.

This Christology stands as the first attempt to articulate the Christology of Indian Pentecostalism within a hundred years of this movement's existence; moreover, it is also an initial approach to bring out a Christology from the people's side. This research is also unique in its attempt to articulate the history of the North Indian Pentecostal movement. This research also opens a new vista in the theological thinking of the Pentecostal community in India due to the fact that it enables them to appreciate various facets of their theological heritage and history, and to articulate them for the consolidation of the movement and mission while helping to establish the movement's identity in a hostile environment. This also could contribute to the cause of theological education providing methodology, context and content for Christology. This project can also act as a catalyst to similar endeavours in the Asian and global contexts. This may also encourage Pentecostal theologians worldwide to appreciate and explore the rich and colourful spiritual, theological and historical heritage of Indian Pentecostalism and its contribution to the global Pentecostal heritage, which are largely ignored.

This study has been an exploration into the Christological notions of ordinary Indian Pentecostals. In the course of the research various theological issues which have a great impact upon people and the larger society have emerged. These issues suggest a few potential areas for further research into Pentecostal theology especially Christology.

One of the important insights that emerged during this research is that Christological notions have changed every area of the life of the people: personal, family, spiritual, economic and social. Given their dismal situation, it is difficult to make such a vast change. Therefore, an in-depth study is needed to understand how these changes have been taking place: how Christological notions affect their inherited worldview and change it for better; how a believer who still lives in such a situation is able to rescue others. These questions need to be dealt with from both sociological and theological angles, to fully recognize the intricate forces and processes behind them.

It has also emerged during this research that Christological formation and the experience of the Spirit are inseparably conjoined for Indian Pentecostals. The gifts of the Spirit, such as healing and exorcism, are carried out in the name of Jesus. A detailed and deeper research is needed to explore their relationship and the point of intersection. It is also significant to see how the gifts of Spirit such as healing and miracles enrich the Christological understanding of a person and of a community.

Another significant element to be investigated is the relationship between Christology and Soteriology. In the context of a primitive worldview and of oppression by evil spiritual forces, it is interesting to see how people understand the work of Christ. What is the relevance of the suffering of Christ? How do people understand the Cross of Christ? Here their idea of sin also needs to be unearthed to appreciate nuances of Christology people hold.

It is also important to identify the relationship between Christology and ecclesiology. Christological notions form in the crucible of the experience of the community in which the composition of the community plays a crucial role. The worship context and teachings in the church shape Christological ideas. Moreover, the community acts as a liberation agent in the context of oppressive cultural and religious settings. Therefore, it is significant to find the relationship between these aspects, which requires a detailed analysis to augment the liberative momentum of the community.

It is also vital to look at the means and methods to communicate Christological themes to pastors and theological students to appreciate and develop further dimensions of Christological elements of the community. This effort may help the larger Pentecostal community as well as Pentecostal scholarship.

Thus, this research brought into light the Christology of ordinary Pentecostals formed in their particular context. It revealed that their context, history, revival fervour, personal and communal experiences have heavily impacted their Christological articulations, while their Christological concepts have radically changed their existence and enabled them to rescue their compatriots from similar situations. This articulation may help to further the liberative mission endeavours, consolidation of the Pentecostal movement, theological self-assertion of Indian Pentecostals, as well as the Asian and global theological enterprises of Pentecostalism and the larger Christian churches.

Bibliography

Abraham, P. G. *Caste and Christianity: A Pentecostal Perspective.* Kumbhaza, India: Crown Books, 2003.

Abraham, Shaibu. *Pentecostal Theology of Liberation: Holy Spirit and Holiness in the Society.* New Delhi: Christian World Imprints, 2014.

________ *The History of the Pentecostal Movement in North India: Unfolding its Social and Theological Contexts.* New Delhi: Christian World Imprints, 2017.

Acharya, Akash & M. Kent Ranson. 'Health Care Financing for the Poor: Community-based Health Insurance Schemes in Gujarat.' *EPW* (17 Sept. 2005): 4141-4150. http://epw.in.ezproxye.bham.ac.uk/epw/uploads/articles/1133.pdf (accessed 25 Nov. 2009).

Achtemeier, P. J. 'The Lukan Perspective on the Miracles of Jesus: A Preliminary Sketch.' In *Perspectives in Luke-Acts.* Edited by C. H. Talbert. Danville, IL: AABPR, 1978.

Aiyar, Shankkar. 'Richest Politicians.' *India Today* (23 Feb. 2009). http://indiatoday.intoday.in/site/story?sId=28888&secid=30 (accessed 10 Nov. 2009).

________ 'Inclusive Inequality.' *India Today* (24 Sept. 2007). http://indiatoday.intoday.in/site/story/Inclusive+inequality/1/1235.html (accessed 12 Nov. 2009).

Alangaram, A. *Christ of the Asian People: Towards an Asian Contextual Theology.* Bangalore: Asia Trading Corporation, 2001.

Aleaz, K. P. *The Relevance of Relation in Sankara's Advaita Vedanta.* Delhi: Kant Publications, 1996.

Alexander, Kimberly Ervin. *Pentecostal Healing: Models in Theology and Practice.* Dorset, UK: Deo Publishing, 2006.

Alfaro, Sammy G. Foundations for a Hispanic Pentecostal Christology: A Constructive and Liberative Approach. PhD Thesis, Dallas: Fuller Theological Seminary, 2008.

Amaladoss, Michael. *The Asian Jesus*. New Delhi: IDCR/ISPCK, 2005.

Ambedkar, B. R. 'Philosophy of Hinduism.' *Dr Babasaheb Ambedkar: Writings and Speeches,* Vol. 3. Bombay: Department of Education, Government of Maharashtra, 1987, (first published 1936).

Anderson, Allan. *An Introduction to Pentecostalism.* Cambridge: Cambridge University Press, 2004.

________ & Edmond Tang (eds.). *Asian and Pentecostal: The Charismatic Face of Christianity in Asia.* Carlisle: Regnum Books International, 2005.

________ 'Revising Pentecostal History in Global Perspective.' In *Asian and Pentecostal: The Charismatic Face of Christianity in Asia.* Edited by Allan Anderson & Edmond Tang. Carlisle: Regnum Books International, 2005.

________ 'Towards a Pentecostal Missiology for the Majority World.' *AJPS* 8/1 (2005): 29-47.

________ *Spreading Fires*: *The Missionary Nature of Early Pentecostalism.* London: SCM, 2007.

Anderson, Robert M. *Vision of the Disinherited: The Making of American Pentecostalism.* New York: Oxford University Press, 1979.

Andrews, C. F. *Sadhu Sundar Singh: A Personal Memoir.* London: Hodder and Stoughton, 1937.

Andrews, Sonia & Sailesh Mohan. 'User Charges in Health Care: Some Issues.' *EPW* (14 Sept. 2002): 373-375.

Appasamy, A. J. *Sundar Singh: A Biography.* Madras: Christian Literature Service, 1966.

Archer, Kenneth J. 'Pentecostal Hermeneutics: Retrospect and Prospect.' *JPT* 8 (1996): 63-81.

________ 'A Pentecostal Way of Doing Theology: Method and Manner.' *IJST* 9/3 (July 2007): 301-314.

________ *The Gospel Revisited: Towards a Pentecostal Theology of Worship and Witness.* Oregon: Pickwick Publications, 2011.

Arles, Siga. 'Indigenous Pentecostal Church Growth at KGF (Kolar Gold Field), Karnataka.' In *Christianity is Indian: The Emergence of an Indigenous Community,* rev. ed. Edited by Roger E. Hedlund. Delhi: ISPCK, 2004.

Arrington, French L. 'The Use of the Bible by Pentecostals.' *Pneuma* 16/1 (Spring 1994): 101-108.

Assemblies of God, Division of Foreign Missions. 'Brussels Statement on Evangelization and Social Concern.' *Transformation* 16/2 (1999): 41-43.

Astley, Jeff. 'In Defense of "Ordinary Theology."' *British Journal of Theological Education* 13/1 (Aug. 2002): 21-35.

________ *Ordinary Theology: Looking, Listening and Learning in Theology.* Hants: Ashgate, 2002.

________ & Ann Christie. *Taking Ordinary Theology Seriously, The Grove Pastoral Series.* Cambridge: Grove Books Limited, 2007.

________ & Christie, Ann. 'Ordinary Soteriology: A Qualitative Study.' In *Empirical Theology in Texts and Tables: Qualitative, Quantitative and Comparative Perspectives.* Edited by Leslie J. Francis, Mandy Robbins & Jeff Astley. Leiden: Brill, 2009.

Athappilly, Sebastian. *Theology in India: Essays on Christ, Church and Eucharist.* Bangalore: Dharmaram Publication, 2005.

Athreya, Venkatesh. 'Far from Healthy.' *Frontline* 27/01 (2-15 Jan 2010). http://www.frontlineonnet.com/stories/20100115270108400.htm (accessed 4 Jan. 2010).

Augustine, P.A. *The Bhils of Rajasthan.* New Delhi: Indian Social Institute, 1986.

Ayrookhuziel, Abraham M. 'Distinctive Characteristics of Folk Traditions.' In *Religions of the Marginalised: Towards a Phenomenology and Methodology of Study.* Edited by Gnana Robinson. Delhi: ISPCK, 1998.

Balasundaram, F. J. *Contemporary Asian Christian Theology.* Delhi: ISPCK, 1995.

Balasuriya, Tissa. 'Christologies in Dialogue in EATWOT: An Asian Historical Perspective.' *Voices from Third World* XVIII/2 (Dec. 1995): 46-70.

Ballard, Paul & John Pritchard. *Practical Theology in Action: Christian Thinking in the Service of the Church and Society.* London: SPCK, 1996.

Bandyopadhyay, Jayanta. 'Endless Thirst.' *India Today* (6 Oct. 2008). http://indiatoday.intoday.in/site/story?sId=16141&secid=3 (accessed 17 Nov. 2009).

Banerjee, Abhijit, Angus Deaton & Esther Duflo. 'Health Care Delivery in Rural Rajasthan.' *EPW* (28 Feb. 2004): 944-949. http://epw.in.ezproxye.bham.ac.uk/epw/uploads/ articles/7389.pdf (accessed 25 Nov. 2009).

Bardhan, Pranab. 'Poverty and Inequality in China and India: Elusive Link with Globalisation.' *EPW* (22 Sept. 2007): 3849-3852. http://epw.in.ezproxye.bham.ac.uk/epw/uploads/articles/11058.pdf (accessed 25 Nov. 2009).

Barrett, David B. & Todd M. Johnson. 'Annual Statistical Table on Global Mission.' *IBMR,* 23 (January, 1999): 24-25.

________ George T. Kurian & Todd M. Johnson (eds.). *World Christian Encyclopedia,* 2nd ed. New York: Oxford University Press, 2001.

Bartchy, S. Scott. 'Table Fellowship.' *Dictionary of Jesus and the Gospels.* Edited by Joel G. Green, Scot McKnight & I. Howard Marshall. Illinois: IVP, 1992 (CD Rom).

________ 'The Historical Jesus and Honour Reversal at the Table.' In *The Social Setting of Jesus and the Gospels*. Edited by Wolfgang Stegemann, Bruce J. Malina & Gerd Theissen. Minneapolis: Fortress Press, 2002.

Basu, Kaushick. http://www.ndtv.com/news/videos/video_player.php?id=1190535 (accessed 6 Jan. 2010).

Basu, Samit. 'Brave New Demography: Youth Power.' *India Today* (14 Dec. 2009). http://indiatoday.intoday.in/site/story?sId=73519&secid=30 (accessed 16 Dec. 2009).

Bauckham, Richard J. *God Crucified: Monotheism and Christology in the New Testament.* Carlisle: Paternoster Press, 1998.

________ *Jesus and the Eyewitnesses: The Gospels as Eyewitness Testimony.* Michigan: Eerdmans, 2006.

________ *The Gospels as Eyewitness Testimony.* Cambridge: Grove Books, 2008.

Bauman, Chad M. *Christian Identity and Dalit Religion in Hindu India, 1868-1947.* Michigan: Eerdmans, 2008.

Bavadam, Lyla. 'Growing Unease.' *Frontline* 26/24 (21 Nov. – 4 Dec. 2009). http://www.frontlineonnet.com/fl2624/stories/20091204262400900.htm (accessed 16 Dec. 2009).

Beasley-Murray, George. R. *Jesus and the kingdom of God.* Exeter: Paternoster, 1986.

________ *John, WBC*, vol. 36. Dallas, Texas: Word Books, Publisher, 1998.

Bedi, Mohender Singh. *Drinking Behaviour and Development in Tribal Areas.* Udaipur, India: Himanshu Publications, 1998.

Bergmann, Sigurd. *God in Context: A Survey of Contextual Theology.* Hants: Ashgate, 2003.

Bergunder, Michael. 'Miracle Healing and Exorcism: The South Indian Pentecostal Movement in the Context of Popular Hinduism.' *International Review of Mission* XC/356, 357 (Jan./April 2001): 101-112.

________ 'Women and Leadership in the South Indian Pentecostal Movement.' *Dharma Deepika* 6/2 (July-December 2002): 35-40.

________ 'Ministry of Compassion: D.G.S. Dhinakaran, Christian Healer-Prophet from Tamilnadu.' In *Christianity is Indian: The Emergence of an Indigenous Community*, rev. ed. Edited by Roger E. Hedlund. Delhi: ISPCK, 2004.

________ 'Constructing Indian Pentecostalism: On Issues of Methodology and Presentation.' In *Asian and Pentecostal: The Charismatic Face of Christianity in Asia.* Edited by Allan Anderson & Edmond Tang. Carlisle: Regnum Books International, 2005.

________ *The South Indian Pentecostal Movement in the Twentieth Century.* Cambridge: Eerdmans, 2008.

Bevans, Stephen B. *Models of Contextual Theology,* rev. ed. Maryknoll: Orbis Books, 2002.

Bhat, Ramesh & Nishant Jain. 'Analysis of Public and Private Healthcare Expenditures.' *EPW* (7 Jan. 2006): 58-68.

Bhatnagar, Rashmi Dube, et. al. *Female Infanticide in India: A Feminist History.* New York: State University of New York Press, 2005.

Bhupta, Malini. 'The Job Bonanza.' *India Today* (7 May 2007). http://www.indiatoday.com/itoday/20070507/cover1.html (accessed 9 Nov. 2009).

Blackburn, B. L. 'Miracles and Miracle Stories.' *Dictionary of Jesus and the Gospels.* Edited by Joel G. Green, Scot McKnight & I. Howard Marshall. Illinois: IVP, 1992 (CD Rom).

Blomberg, C. L. 'Healing.' *Dictionary of Jesus and the Gospels.* Edited by Joel G. Green, Scot McKnight & I. Howard Marshall. Illinois: IVP, 1992 (CD Rom).

________ 'Where Do We Start Studying Jesus.' In *Jesus Under Fire: Modern Scholarship Reinvents the Historical Jesus.* Edited by Michael J. Wilkins & J. P. Moreland. Carlisle: Paternoster, 1996.

________ *Contagious Holiness: Jesus' Meals with Sinners.* Leicester: Apollos, 2005.

Bobb, Dilip. 'Year of Revival.' *India Today* (11 Jan. 2010). http://indiatoday.intoday.in/site/Story/77320/Cover%20Story/Year+of+revival.html (acessed 14 Jan. 2010).

Bonney, Richard. *Harvest of Hatred: The Concerned Citizen's Tribunal Report of Gujarat 2002.* Delhi: Media House, 2004.

Borg, Marcus J. *Conflict, Holiness and Politics in the Teaching of Jesus.* New York: The Edwin Mellen Press, 1984.

________ *Jesus a New Vision: Spirit, Culture, and the Life of Discipleship.* New York: HarperSanFrancisco, 1987.

________ *Jesus in Contemporary Scholarship.* Pennsylvania: Trinity Press International, 1994.

________ *Meeting Jesus Again for the First Time: The Historical Jesus and the Heart of Contemporary Faith.* New York: HarperSanFrancisco, 1994.

________ 'From Galilean Jew to the Face of God: The Pre-Easter and Post-Easter Jesus.' In *Jesus at 2000.* Edited by Marcus J. Borg. Colorado: Westview Press, 1997.

Bornkamm, Gunther. *Jesus of Nazareth.* New York: Harper & Row, 1960.

Bose, Ashish. 'India's Disturbing Health Card.' *EPW* (15 Dec. 2007): 10-13. http://epw.in.ezproxye.bham.ac.uk/epw/uploads/articles/11314.pdf (accessed 25 Nov. 2009).

Bose, Kaly. 'Conversions not due to Coercion, but due to Caste-Inferiority.' *Indian Currents* (25-31 Jan 1999): 19-21.

Boyd, Robin. *An Introduction to Indian Christian Theology*, rev. ed. Madras: The Christian Literature Service, 1975.

Brass, Paul R. *The Production of Hindu-Muslim Violence in Contemporary India.* Washington DC: University of Washington Press, 2003.

________ 'Development of an Institutionalised Riot System in Meerut City, 1961 to 1982.' *EPW* (30 Oct. 2004): 4839-4848. http://epw.in.ezproxyd.bham.ac.uk/epw/uploads/articles/8354.pdf (accessed 10 Dec. 2009).

Brown, Colin. 'Historical Jesus, Quest of.' *Dictionary of Jesus and the Gospels.* Edited by Joel G. Green, Scot McKnight & I. Howard Marshall. Illinois: IVP, 1992 (CD Rom).

Brown, Raymond E. *Jesus God and Man: Modern Biblical Reflections.* London: Geoffrey Chapman, 1968.

________ *An Introduction to New Testament Christology.* London: Geoffrey Chapman, 1994.

Browning, Don S. *A Fundamental Practical Theology.* Minneapolis: Fortress Press, 1991.

Bryman, Alan. *Social Research Methods,* 2nd ed. Oxford: Oxford University Press, 2004.

Bueno, Ronald N. 'Listening to the Margins: Re-historicising Pentecostal Experiences and Identities.' In *The Globalization of Pentecostalism.* Edited by M. W. Dempster, B. D. Klaus & D. Petersen. Carlisle: Regnum, 1999.

Burgess, Stanley M. 'Pentecostalism in India: An Overview.' *AJPS* 4/1 (2001): 85-98.

________ & Gary B. McGee, 'Signs and Wonders.' *The New International Dictionary of Pentecostal and Charismatic Movement.* Edited by Stanley M. Burgess. Michigan: Zondervan, 2002, 1063-1068.

Cartledge, Mark J. 'Empirical Theology: Inter-or Intra-disciplinary?' *Journal of Beliefs & Values* 20/1 (1999): 98-104.

________ *Practical Theology: Charismatic and Empirical Perspectives.* Waynesboro, GA: Paternoster Press, 2003.

________ 'The Early Pentecostal Theology of *Confidence* Magazine (1908-1926): A Version of the Five-Fold Gospel?' *The Journal of the European Pentecostal Theological Association* 28/2 (2008): 117-130.

________ *Testimony in the Spirit.* Farnham: Ashgate, 2010.

Census India. http://www.censusindia.gov.in/Census_Data_2001/India_at_glance/glance.aspx (accessed 15 Dec 2009).

Cerillo jr., Agustus. 'Interpretive Approaches to the History of American Pentecostal Origins.' *Pneuma* 19/1 (Spring, 1997): 30-32.

Chacko, M. K. *An Autobiography.* Delhi: Pastor M. K. Chacko, 1976.

Chacko, M. V. *Daivasasthram* (*Systematic Theology*), 2nd ed. Secunderabad: OM Authentic Books, 2002.

Chakrabarty, Dipesh. 'The Power of Superstition in Public Life in India.' *EPW* (17 May 2008): 16-19.

Chakraborty, Debashis, D. Shyam Babu & Manashi Chakravorty. 'Atrocities on Dalits: What the District Level Data Say on Society-State Complicity.' *EPW* (17 June 2006): 2478-2481. http://epw.in.ezproxyd. bham.ac.uk/epw/uploads/articles/2221.pdf (accessed 16 Dec. 2009).

Chakraborty, Somen. 'Blood Bath in Bihar: Caste Unabated.' *Indian Currents* (15-21 Feb. 1999): 16-20.

Chandra, Ramesh (ed.). *Liberation and Dalit Articulation of Dalits.* Delhi: Isha Books, 2004.

Chatterji, Angana. 'Hindutva's Violent History.' *Tehelka* 5/36 (13 Sept. 2008). http://www.tehelka.com/story_main40.asp?filename=Ne130908HindutvasViolentHistory.asp (accessed 10 Dec. 2009).

Chengappa, Raj & Ramesh Vinayak. 'Grain Drain.' *India Today* (11 June 2007). http://www.indiatoday.com/itoday/20070611/cover1.html (accessed 17 Nov. 2009).

________ 'India's Best Colleges.' *India Today* (2 June 2008). http://India today.intoday.in/site/story?sId=8688&secid=30 (accessed 16 Dec. 2009).

________ 'Higher Education: How to Clean the Mess.' *India Today* (13 July 2009). http://indiatoday.intoday.in/site/Story/49794/Higher+Educa tion:+How+to+clean+the+mess.html?page=0 (accessed 18 Nov. 2009).

________ 'How Stem Cells can Save your Life.' *India Today* (25 Jan. 2010). http://indiatoday.intoday.in/site/Story/79189/Cover%20Story/How+stem+cells+can+save+your+life.html (accessed 29 Jan. 2010).

Cherian, Abraham T. 'A Study of the Religion of the Bhils of Jhadol Taluk in Udaipur, Rajasthan and Their Response to Christian Faith in the Post-Independent Period.' Unpublished MTh Thesis, Asian Institute of Theology, Bangalore, India, 2001.

________ 'Contribution of Churches and Missions to the Bhils of Rajasthan.' Unpublished PhD Thesis, Asian Institute of Theology, Bangalore, India, 2005.

Cherian, M.T. *Hindutva Agenda and Minority Rights: A Christian Response.* Bangalore: Centre for Contemporary Christianity, 2007.

Christie, Ann. 'Who Do You Say I Am?: Answers from the Pews.' *The Journal of Adult Theological Education* 4/2 (2007): 181-194.

Church of North India. http://www.cnisynod.org/beginning.aspx (accessed 8 Jan. 2010).

Claassens, L. Juliana M. *The God who Provides: Biblical Images of Divine Nourishment.* Nashville: Abingdon Press, 2004.

Clark, Mathew. 'Questioning Every Consensus: A Plea for a Return to the Radical Roots of Pentecostalism.' *AJPS* 5/1 (2002): 73-86.

Clarke, Sathianathan. *Dalits and Christianity: Subaltern Religion and Liberation Theology in India.* New Delhi: Oxford University Press, 1999.

Coffey, David. 'The Holy Spirit as the Mutual Love of the Father and the Son.' *TS* 51/2 (1990): 193-229.

________ 'The Theandric Nature of Christ.' *TS* 60/3 (1999): 405-431.

Collins, Gerald O'. *Christology: A Biblical, Historical, and Systematic Study of Jesus Christ.* New York: Oxford University Press, 1995.

Constitution of India. http://india.gov.in/govt/documents/english/coi_part_full.pdf (accessed 10 Jan. 2010).

Cook, Robert F. *Half a Century of Divine Leading and 37 Years of Apostolic Achievements in South India*. Cleveland, TN: Church of God Foreign Missions Department, 1955.

Cook, Michael L. *Christology as Narrative Quest.* Minnesota: Liturgical Press, 1997.

Copley, Antony. *Religions in Conflict: Ideology, Cultural Contact and Conversion in Late Colonial India*. Delhi, India: Oxford University Press, 1997.

Corbin, Juliet & Anselm Strauss. *Basics of Qualitative Research: Grounded Theory Procedures and Techniques*. Newbury Park, CA: Sage Publications, 1990.

Coulter, Dale. '"Delivered By the Power of God": Toward a Pentecostal Understanding of Salvation.' *IJST* 10/4 (October 2008): 447-467.

Cox, Harvey. *Fire from Heaven: The Rise of Pentecostal Spirituality and the Reshaping of Religion in the Twenty-first Century.* London: Cassell, 1996.

Cox, Raymond L. *The Four-Square Gospel.* Los Angeles: Foursquare Publications, 1969.

Creswell, John W. *Research Design: Qualitative, Quantitative, and Mixed Methods Approach.* London: Sage Publications, 2003.

Cross, F.L. and E.A. Livingston (eds.). 'Pentecostalism.' *The Oxford Dictionary of the Christian Church,* 3rd ed. Oxford: Oxford University Press, 1997, 1253-1254.

Crossan, John Dominic. *The Historical Jesus: The Life of a Mediterranean Jewish Peasant.* San Francisco: HarperSanFrancisco, 1991.

_________ *Jesus: A Revolutionary Biography.* San Francisco: HarperSan Francisco, 1994.

Cullmann, Oscar. *Christology of the New Testament,* 2nd ed. London: SCM, 1963.

Culpepper, R. Alan. *The Gospel of Luke, The New Interpreters Bible,* Vol. IX. Nashville: Abingdon Press, 1995.

D'mello, Bernard. 'What is Maoism?' *EPW* 44/47 (21 Nov. 2009): 39-48. http://epw.in/epw/uploads/articles/14167.pdf (accessed on 5 Jan. 2010)

Dasan, Ebenezer D. 'Conversion and Persecution in South Gujarat.' In *Conversion in a Pluralistic Context: Perspectives and Context.* Edited by Krickwin C. Marak & Plamthodathil S. Jacob. Delhi: ISPCK, 2000.

Daunton-Fear, Andrew. *Healing in the Early Church: The Church's Ministry of Healing and Exorcism from the First to the Fifth Century.* Milton Keynes: Paternoster, 2009.

David, M. D. *Missions: Cross-Cultural Encounter and Change in Western India.* Delhi: ISPCK, 2001.

Davis, Casey W. 'Oral Biblical Criticism: Raw Data in Philippians.' In *Linguistics and New Testament: Critical Junctures.* Edited by Stanley E. Porter & D.A. Carson. Sheffield: Sheffield Academic Press, 1999.

Davis, Steven L. *Jesus the Healer.* London: SCM, 1995.

Dayton, Donald. 'The Rise of the Evangelical Healing Movement in Nineteenth Century America.' *Pneuma* 4/1 (1982): 1-18.

_________ *The Theological Roots of Pentecostalism.* Peabody: Hendrick-son Publishers, 1987.

De Mesa, Jose M. & Lode L. Wostyn. *Doing Christology: The Re-Appropriation of a Tradition.* Quezon City, Philippines: Claretian Publications, 1989.

Debroy, Bibek. 'A Case for India Whining.' *India Today* (24 Sept. 2007). http://indiatoday.intoday.in/site/story?sId=1230&secid=30 (accessed 14 Nov. 2009).

Del Colle, Ralph. 'Spirituality in Light of Spirit-Christology.' In *Drinking From Our Own Wells: Defining a Pentecostal-Charismatic Spirituality.* Edited by Cheryl Bridges Johns. Springfield: Society for Pentecostal Studies, 1992.

_________ 'Spirit-Christology: Dogmatic Foundations for Pentecostal-Charismatic Spirituality.' *JPT* 3 (1993): 91-112.

________ *Christ and Spirit: Spirit-Christologies in Trinitarian Perspective.* Oxford: Oxford University Press, 1994.

________ 'Trinity and Temporality: A Pentecostal/Charismatic Perspective.' *JPT* 8 (1996): 99-113.

________ 'The Triune God.' In *The Cambridge Companion to Christian Doctrine.* Edited by Colin E. Gunton. Cambridge: Cambridge University Press, 1997.

________ 'Schleiermacher and Spirit-Christology: Unexplored Horizons of the Christian Faith.' *IJST* 1/3 (1999): 286-307.

Dempster, Murray W. 'Pentecostal Social Concern and the Biblical Mandate for Social Justice.' *Pneuma* 9/2 (Fall 1987): 129-153.

Deshpande, Ashwini & Katherine Newman. 'Where the Path Leads: The Role of Caste in Post-University Employment Expectations.' *EPW* (13 Oct. 2007): 4133-4140. http://epw.in.ezproxyd.bham.ac.uk/epw/uploads/ articles/11134.pdf (accessed 15 Dec. 2009).

Deshpande, Satish. 'Exclusive Inequalities: Merit, Caste and Discrimination in Indian Higher Education Today.' *EPW* (17 June 2006): 2438-2444. http://epw.in.ezproxyd.bham.ac.uk/epw/uploads/articles/2212.pdf (accessed 15 Dec. 2009).

Devasahayam V (ed.). *Frontiers of Dalit Theology.* Delhi: ISPCK, 1997.

Dieter, Melvin E. 'Wesleyan-Holiness Aspects of Pentecostal Origins.' In *Aspects of Pentecostal-Charismatic Origins.* Edited by Vinson Synan. New Jersey: Logos International, 1975.

Dirks, Nicholas. *Castes of Mind: Colonialism and the Making of Modern India.* New Jersey: Princeton University Press, 2001.

Dodd, C.H. *The Apostolic Preaching and its Developments: Three Lectures.* London: Hodder & Stoughton, 1944.

Douglas, Mary. *Purity and Danger: An Analysis of Pollution and Taboo.* London: Routledge and Kegan Paul, 1966.

Duewel, Wesley. *Revival Fire.* Michigan: Zondervan Publishing House, 1995.

Dunn, James D. G. *Baptism in the Holy Spirit: A Re-examination of the New Testament Teaching on the Gift of the Spirit in Relation to Pentecostalism Today.* London: SCM, 1970.

________ *Jesus and the Spirit.* London: SCM Press, 1975.

________ *Christology in the Making: An Inquiry into the Origins of the Incarnation.* London: SCM, 1980.

________ *The Theology of Paul the Apostle.* Edinburgh: T & T Clark, 1998.

Dye, C. *Healing Anointing: Hope for a Hurting World.* London: Hodder and Stoughton, 1997.

Dyer, Helen S. (comp.). *Revival in India 1905-1906.* Akola, Maharashtra: Alliance Publications, 1987.

Economic Research Foundation, New Delhi. 'Government Health Expenditure in India: A Benchmark Study.' *Macroscan* (August 2006). http://www. macroscan. com/anl/oct06/anl301006Health_Expenditure.htm (accessed 4 Jan. 2010).

Editor. 'From the Mission Field.' *Cross & Crown* 26/2 (Dec. 95-Jan. 96): 21.

________ 'Tortured for Christ.' *Cross & Crown* (July-August 1997): 11-13.

________ 'Arrested on False Charges.' *Cross & Crown* 37/3 (Jan.-Feb. 2008): 21.

Editorial. 'Communal Violence in Orissa.' *EPW* (5 Jan. 2008): 6.

________ 'Restraining Child Marriage.' *EPW* XLIV/15 (11 April 2009): 7.

________ 'Caste Out, Yet Again.' *EPW* XLIV/20 (16 May 2009): 5-6. http://epw. in.ezproxyd.bham.ac.uk/epw/uploads/articles/13508.pdf (accessed 15 Dec. 2009).

Edwards, James R. *Is Jesus the only Saviour?* Michigan: Eerdmans, 2005.

Ellingworth, P. 'Forgiveness of Sins.' *Dictionary of Jesus and the Gospels.* Edited by Joel G. Green, Scot McKnight & I. Howard Marshall. Illinois: IVP, 1992 (CD Rom).

Engineer, Asghar Ali & Amarjit S. Narang (eds.). *Minorities and Police in India.* New Delhi: Manohar Publishers, 2006.

________ 'Communal Riots, 2004.' *EPW* (5 Feb. 2005): 517-520. http://epw. in.ezproxye.bham.ac.uk/epw/uploads/articles/142.pdf (accessed 2 Dec. 2009).

Evans, Craig A. *Life of Jesus Research: An Annotated Bibliography.* Leiden: Brill, 1989.

________ 'What Did Jesus Do?' In *Jesus Under Fire: Modern Scholarship Reinvents the Historical Jesus.* Edited by Michael J. Wilkins & J.P. Moreland. Carlisle: Paternoster, 1996.

________ 'Context, Family and Formation.' In *The Cambridge Companion to Jesus.* Edited by Markus Bockmuehl. Cambridge: The Cambridge University Press, 2001.

Everts, J. M. 'Conversion and Call of Paul.' *DPL.* Edited by Gerald F. Hawthorne, Ralph P. Martin & Daniel G. Reid. Illinois: IVP, 1998 (CD Rom).

Fallon, P. 'A Critical Evaluation of the Hindu Interpretation of Christ.' *Indian Journal of Theology* 18/1 (Jan.-Mar. 1969): 81-87.

Farley, Edward. *Theologia: The Fragmentation and Unity of Theological Education.* Philadelphia: Fortress Press, 1983.

Fee, Gordon D. 'Philippians 2:5-11: Hymn or Exalted Pauline Prose?' *Bulletin of Biblical Research* 2 (1992): 29-46.

________ *Pauline Christology: An Exegetical-Theological Study.* Peabody: Hendrickson Publishers, 2007.

Finch, Helen & Jane Lewis, 'Focus Group.' In *Qualitative Research Practice: A Guide for Social Science Students and Researchers.* Edited by Jane Ritchie & Jane Lewis. London: Sage Publications, 2003.

Firth, C.B. *An Introduction to Indian Church History.* Delhi: ISPCK, 1976.

Fitzmyer, Joseph A. *The Gospel According to Luke 1-IX, Anchor Bible* 28. New York: Doubleday, 1981.

Flemming, Dean. *Contextualization in the New Testament: Pattern for Theology and Mission.* Illinois: IVP, 2005.

Flick, Uwe. *An Introduction to Qualitative Research.* London: Sage Publications, 1998.

Forrester, Duncan B. *Truthful Action: Explorations in Practical Theology.* Edinburgh: Clark, 2000.

France, R. T. 'The Uniqueness of Christ.' *Evangelical Review of Theology* 17/1 (Jan-Mar 1993): 9-28.

________ *The Gospel of Mark: A Commentary on Greek Testament, NIGTC.* Michigan: Eerdmans, 2002.

Francis, T. Dayanandan (ed.). *The Christian Bhakti of A. J. Appasamy: A Collection of His Writings.* Madras: CLS, 1992.

Frykenberg, Robert. E. 'Christianity in South India Since 1500: Historical Studies of Trans-cultural Interactions within Hindu-Muslim Environments.' *Dharma Deepika* (Dec. 1997): 3-7

Fuchs, Ottmar. 'Relationship between Practical Theology and Empirical Research.' *Journal of Empirical Theology* 14/2 (2001): 5-19.

Full Gospel Assembly of God Church (FGAG). http://salvationband.wordpress.com/2009/01/30/revpaul-thangiah-%E2%80%93-fgag/ (accessed 22 Dec. 2009).

Gabriel, Reuben Louis. 'Reflections on Indian Pentecostalism: Trends and Issues.' *Dharma Deepika* 2 (July-Dec. 2002): 67-76.

Galanter, Marc. *Competing Equalities: Law and the Backward Classes in India.* New Delhi: Oxford, 1984.

Garitte, Gérard & J. N. Farquhar. *The Apostle Thomas in India According to the Acts of Thomas.* Kottayam, Kerala, 1972.

Gaston, W.T. 'What Think ye of Christ.' *The Pentecostal Evangel* 496 (May 12, 1923): 6.

George, A. C. 'Pentecostal Beginnings in Travancore, South India.' *AJPS* 4/2 (2001): 215-37.

________ *Trailblazers for God: A History of the Assemblies of God of India.* Bangalore: SABC Publications, 2004.

Ghanakan, C. G. 'Charismata and Compassion: Dhinakaran, Charismatic Healing and Pastoral Pentecostalism in South-India – A Practical Assessment.' Unpublished PhD Thesis, University of Birmingham, Birmingham, England, 2006.

Ghosh, Jayati. 'Securing Food for the People.' *Macroscan* (18 Aug. 2009). http://www.macroscan.org/cur/aug09/cur180809Food.htm (accessed 16 Nov. 2009).

Golwalker, M.S. *We or Our Nationhood Defined.* Nagpur, India: Bharath Publications, 1939.

Gonsalves, Francis. '"Destroy Christians, Kill them, Jai Sriram!": The Traumatic Experience on a Black Christmas Day.' *Indian Currents* (4-10 Jan. 1999): 20-22.

________ 'Debating Conversions.' *Indian Currents* (8-14 Feb. 1999): 35-36.

Gopalakrishnan, K. 'Ideals of Secularism on Test in India.' *Indian Currents* (15-21 Feb. 1999): 22-23.

Green, Joel B. *The Gospel of Luke, NICNT.* Grand Rapids, Michigan: Eerdmans, 1997.

________ 'Healing.' *NDBT.* Edited by T. Desmond Alexander & Brian S. Rosner. Downers Grove, Illinois: IVP, 2000 (CD Rom).

Green, Michael. *I Believe in the Holy Spirit.* London: Hodder & Stoughton, 1975.

Groome, Thomas H. *Christian Religious Education: Sharing our Story and Vision.* San Francisco: Harper & Row, 1980.

Gupta, Tilak D. 'Maoism in India: Ideology, Programme and Armed Struggle.' *EPW* (22 July 2006): 3172-3176. http://epw.in/epw/uploads/articles/791.pdf (accessed 5 Jan. 2010).

Gunton, Colin E. *The Christian Faith: An Introduction to Christian Doctrine.* Oxford: Blackwell Publishers, 2002.

Gutierrez, Gustavo. *A Theology of Liberation: History, Politics, and Salvation,* rev. ed. London: SCM, 2001.

Habets, Myk. 'Spirit Christology: Seeing in Stereo.' *JPT* 11/2 (2003): 216-228.

Hagner, Donald A. *Matthew 14-28, Word Biblical Commentary,* vol. 33b. Dallas, Texas: Word Books, 1998.

Haight, Roger. 'The Case for Spirit-Christology.' *TS* 53 (1992): 257-287.

Hamerton-Kelly, R.G. *Pre-existence, Wisdom, and the Son of Man.* Cambridge: Cambridge University Press, 1973.

Hammersley, Martyn. *Reading Ethnographic Research,* 2nd ed. London: Longman, 1988.

Hanson, K.C. 'Jesus and Social Bandits.' In *The Social Setting of Jesus and the Gospels.* Edited by Wolfgang Stegemann, Bruce J. Malina & Gerd Theissen. Minneapolis: Fortress Press, 2002.

Hardiman, David. 'Healing, Medical Power and the Poor: Contests in Tribal India.' *EPW* (21 April 2007): 1404-08.

________ & Gauri Raje. 'Practices of Healing in Tribal Gujarat.' *EPW* (1 March 2008): 43-50.

Harris, Murray J. *Jesus as God.* Grand Rapids: Baker, 1992.

Hastings, Adrian. 'Incarnation.' *The Oxford Companion to Christian Thought.* Edited by Adrian Hastings Alistair Mason, Hugh S. Pyper. Oxford: Oxford University Press, 2000.

Hedlund, Roger E. *Quest for Identity: India's Churches of Indigenous Origin, The 'Little Tradition' in Indian Christianity.* Delhi: ISPCK, 2000.

________ *Christianity is Indian: The Emergence of an Indigenous Community,* rev. ed. Delhi: ISPCK, 2004.

________ 'Critique of Pentecostal Mission by a Friendly Evangelical.' *AJPS* 8/1 (2005): 67-94.

________ 'Indigenous Pentecostalism in India.' In *Asian and Pentecostal: The Charismatic Face of Christianity in Asia.* Edited by Allan Anderson & Edmond Tang. Carlisle: Regnum Books International, 2005.

Heiler, Friedrich. *The Gospel of Sadhu Sundar Singh.* London: George Allen & Unwin Ltd., 1927.

Heitink, Gerben. *Practical Theology: History, Theory, Action Domain.* Michigan: Eerdmans, 1999.

Heredia, Rudolf C. 'No Entry, No Exit: Savarna Aversion towards Dalit Conversion.' *EPW* (9 Oct. 2004): 4543-55.

________ *Changing Gods: Rethinking Conversion in India.* New Delhi: Penguin Books, 2007.

Herzog II, W.R. 'Temple Cleansing.' *Dictionary of Jesus and the Gospels.* Edited by Joel G. Green, Scot McKnight & I. Howard Marshall. Illinois: IVP, 1992 (CD Rom).

Hiebert, Paul G. 'Spiritual Warfare and World View.' In *Missiology for the 21st Century: South Asian Perspective.* Edited by Roger E. Hedlund & Paul Joshua Bhakiaraj. Delhi: ISPCK, 2004.

Hillman, Streeter Burnett & A.J. Appasamy. *The Sadhu: A Study in Mysticism and Practical Religion.* London: Macmillan and Company, 1922.

Hiscock, Geoff. *India's Store Wars: Retail Revolution and the Battle for the Next 500 million Shoppers.* Singapore: John Wiley & Sons (Asia) Pte. Ltd, 2008.

Hobbs, T. Raymond. 'The Political Jesus: Discipleship and Disengagement.' In *The Social Setting of Jesus and the Gospels.* Edited by Wolfgang Stegemann, Bruce J. Malina & Gerd Theissen. Minneapolis: Fortress Press, 2002.

Hollenweger, Walter J. *The Pentecostals.* Minneapolis: Augsburg Publishing House, 1972.

________ 'Pentecostal Research: Problems and Promises.' In *A Guide to the Study of the Pentecostal Movement*, vol.1. Edited by Charles Edwin Jones. London: Scarecrow, 1983.

________ 'Pentecostals and the Charismatic Movement.' In *The Study of Spirituality.* Edited by Cheslyn Jones, et al. London: SPCK, 1986.

________ 'Evangelism: A Non-Colonial Model.' *JPT* 7 (1995): 107-128.

________ *Pentecostalism: Origins and Developments Worldwide.* Peabody: Hendrickson Publishers, 1997.

________ 'Critical Issues for Pentecostals.' In *Pentecostals after a Century: Global Perspectives on a Movement in Transition.* Edited by Allan Anderson & Walter J. Hollenweger. Sheffield: Sheffield Academic Press, 1999.

Hong, Young-Gi. 'Church and Mission: A Pentecostal Perspective.' *International Review of Mission* XC/358 (July 2001): 289-308.

Horsley, Richard A. *Jesus and Empire: The Kingdom of God and the New World Disorder.* Minneapolis: Fortress Press, 2003.

________ *The Liberation of Christmas: The Infancy Narratives in Social Context.* New York: Crossroad, 1988.

Horton, Stanley. *Into All Truth: A Survey of the Course and Content of Divine Revelation.* Springfield, Mo.: Gospel Publishing House, 1955.

Hrangkhuma, F. 'Church in India.' In *Church in Asia Today: Challenges and Opportunities.* Edited by Saphir Athyal. Singapore: Asian Lausanne Committee for World Evangelism, 1996.

________ 'Factors that Contributed to the Arrest of Mass Movements Towards Christianity in India.' In *Christianity in India: Search for Liberation and Identity.* Edited by F. Hrangkhuma. Delhi: ISPCK, 2000.

________ (ed.). *Christianity in India: Search for Liberation and Identity.* Delhi: ISPCK, 2000.

Hunter, Harold D. 'Spirit-Christology: Dilemma and Promise.' *Heythrop Journal* 24 (1983): 127-140, 266-277.

________ 'The Resurgence of Spirit Christology.' *European Pentecostal Theological Association Bulletin 11* (1992). http://www.fullnet.net/np/archives/writings/epta.html (accessed 1 Sept. 2010).

Hurtado, Larry W. 'Lord.' *Dictionary of Paul and His Letters.* Edited by Gerald F. Hawthorne, Ralph P. Martin & Daniel G. Reid. Illinois: IVP, 1998 (CD Rom).

________ *Lord Jesus Christ: Devotion to Jesus in Earliest Christianity.* Michigan: Eerdmans, 2003.

________ 'The Binitarian Pattern of Earliest Christian Devotion and Early Doctrinal Development.' In *The Place of Christ in Liturgical Prayer: Trinity, Christology, and Liturgical Theology.* Edited by Bryan D. Spinks. Minnesota: Liturgical Press, 2008.

Ilaiah, Kancha. *Why I am not a Hindu: A Sudra Critique of Hindutva Philosophy, Culture and Political Economy,* 2nd ed. Calcutta: Samya, 2005.

Inbody, Tyron L. *The Many Faces of Christology.* Nashville: Abingdon Press, 2002.

Irvin, Dale T. 'Pentecostal Historiography and Global Christianity: Rethinking the Question of Origins.' *Pneuma* 27/1 (Spring 2005): 35-50.

Jacobs, Alan. *Looking Before and After: Testimony and the Christian Life.* Michigan: Eerdmans, 2008.

Jacobsen, Douglas. *Thinking in the Spirit: Theologies of Early Pentecostal Movement.* Indianapolis: Indiana University Press, 2003.

Jenkins, Philip. *The Next Christendom: The Coming of Global Christianity.* Oxford: Oxford University Press, 2002.

________ *The New Faces of Christianity: Believing the Bible in the Global South.* Oxford: Oxford University Press, 2006.

Jenkins, S.D.L. The Human Son of God and the Holy Spirit: Toward a Pentecostal Incarnational Spirit-Christology. PhD dissertation, Marquette University, 2004.

Jenks, David. *Six Great Missionaries of the Sixteenth and Seventeenth Centuries.* London: A. R. Mowbray, 1930.

Jeremiah, Anderson H.M. 'Exploring New Facets of Dalit Christology: Critical Interaction with J.D. Crossan's Portrayal of the Historical Jesus.' In *Dalit Theology in Twenty-First Century: Discord Voices, Discerning Pathways.* Edited by Sathianathan Clarke, Deena Bandhu Manchala & Philip Vinod Peacock. New Delhi: Oxford University Press, 2010.

Jeyakumar, D. Arthur. *History of Christianity in India: Selected Themes.* Delhi: ISPCK, 2004.

________ 'Group Conversion Movements to Christianity in the Indian Sub-Continent.' *Indian Church History Review* XXXIX/2 (Dec 2005): 63-73.

Jeyaraj, Daniel. 'Editorial – Pentecostalism.' *Dharma Deepika* 6/2 (July-Dec. 2002): 2-3.

Jha Praveen & Mario Negre. 'Indian Economy in the Era of Contemporary Globalisation: Some Core Elements of the Balance Sheet.' *Macroscan* (17 May 2007). http://www.macroscan.org/anl/may07/anl170507Indian%20 Economy.htm (accessed 10 Nov. 2009).

Jodhka, Surinder S. & Katherine Newman. 'In the Name of Globalisation: Meritocracy, Productivity and the Hidden Language of Caste.' *EPW* (13 Oct. 2007): 4125-4132.

John, P.R. 'Towards Indian Christology.' In *Seeking New Horizons*. Edited by Leonard Fernando. Delhi: ISPCK, 2002.

Johns, Cheryl Bridges. *Pentecostal Formation: A Pedagogy among the Oppressed.* Sheffield: Sheffield Academic Press, 1993.

________ 'Healing and Deliverance: A Pentecostal Perspective.' *Concilium* 3 (1996): 45-50.

Johns, Jackie David & Cheryl Bridges Johns. 'Yielding to the Spirit: A Pentecostal Approach to Group Bible Study.' *JPT* 1/1 (1992): 109-134.

________ Yielding to the Spirit: The Dynamic of a Pentecostal Model of Praxis.' In *The Globalization of Pentecostalism.* Edited by M.W. Dempster, B.D. Klaus & D. Petersen. Carlisle: Regnum, 1999.

Johnson, Todd M., David B. Barrett & Peter F. Crossing. 'Christianity 2010: A View from the New Atlas of Global Christianity.' *IBMR* 34/1 (Jan. 2010). http://www.internationalbulletin.org/system/files/2010-01-029-johnson.pdf (accessed 9 Jan. 2010).

Jones, Arun W. 'Faces of Pentecostalism in North India Today.' *Society* 46/6 (Nov. 2009): 504–509.

Jones, W.W. 'Mass Movement as Missionary Dream and Reality.' *Indian Church History Review* XXVIII/2 (1994): 135-151.

Jose, Tisy. 'Conversion: A Convenient Mask.' *Indian Currents* (18-24 January, 1999): 10-13.

Joshi, Prabhakar. *Ethnography of the Primitive Tribes in Rajasthan*. Jaipur, India: Printwell, 1995.

Joy, K.T. *The Mar Thoma Church: A Study of its Growth and Contribution.* Kottayam, Kerala: Good Shepherd Press, 1986.

Judge, Paramjit S. & Gurpreet Bal. *Mapping Dalits*. Jaipur, India: Rawat Publication, 2009.

Jung, L. Shannon. *Food for Life: The Spirituality and Ethics of Eating.* Minneapolis: Fortress Press, 2004.

Kaithamangalam, Thomson Thomas. *Marubhoomiyil Thalarathu* (Not Tired in the Desert: A Biography of Thomas Mathew). Udaipur, India: Cross and Crown Publications, 1996.

Kanungo, Pralay. 'Co-opting Dalits into the Hindutva Fold.' *EPW* (19 May 2007): 1852-54. http://epw.in.ezproxyd.bham.ac.uk/epw/uploads/articles/10631.pdf (accessed 16 Dec. 2009).

Kappen, Sebastian. *Jesus and Cultural Revolution: An Asian Perspective.* Bombay: A Build Publication, 1983.

________ 'Towards an Indian Theology of Liberation.' In *Leave the Temple.* Edited by Felix Wilfred. Trichirapally, India: Carmel, 1992.

Kärkkäinen, Veli-Matti. 'David's Sling: The Promise and Problem of Pentecostal Theology Today: A Response to D. Lyle Dabney.' *Pneuma* 23 (2001): 147-152.

________ *Pneumatology: The Holy Spirit in Ecumenical, International, and Contextual Perspective.* Michigan: Baker Academic, 2002.

________ 'Spirituality as a Resource for Social Justice: Reflections from the Catholic-Pentecostal Dialogue.' *AJPS* 6/1 (2003): 83-96.

________ *An Introduction to the Theology of Religions: Biblical, Historical, & Contemporary Perspectives.* Illinois: IVP, 2003.

________ *Christology: A Global Introduction.* Michigan: Baker Academic, 2003.

________ *Trinity and Religious Pluralism: The Doctrine of the Trinity in Christian Theology of Religions.* Hants: Ashgate, 2004.

Karthikeyan, V. 'Religion in Politics.' *Indian Currents* (15-21 Feb. 1999): 13.

Katapali, Daniel. 'Indigenous Missions and the Savara Tribal Church of Srikakulam.' In *Christianity is Indian: The Emergence of an Indigenous Community,* rev. ed. Edited by Roger E. Hedlund. Delhi: ISPCK, 2004.

Kauffman, Ivan S. 'Miraculous Deliverances from Raiders and Robbers.' *The Latter Rain Evangel* (April, 1915): 20-24.

Kee, Howard Clark. 'Medicine and Healing.' *The Anchor Bible Dictionary.* Edited by David Noel Freedman. New York: Doubleday, 1997 (CD Rom).

Kelsey, Morton T. *Psychology, Medicine and Christian Healing.* San Francisco: Harper & Row, Publishers, 1988.

Khai, Chin Khua. 'Pentecostalism in Myanmar: An Overview.' *AJPS* 5/1 (2002): 51-71.

Khattar, Jagdish. 'The Paths to Prosperity: Low Cost Transport.' *India Today* (14 Dec. 2009). http://indiatoday.intoday.in/site/Story/73518/Cover%20 Story/The+paths+to+prosperity.html (accessed 20 Dec. 2009).

Kim, Dongsoo. 'The Healing of Han in Korean Pentecostalism.' *JPT* 15 (1999): 123-139.

Kim, Elijah Jong Fil. 'Filipino Pentecostalism in a Global Context.' *AJPS* 8/2 (2005): 235-254.

Kim, Kirsteen. Mission Pneumatology with Special Reference to the Indian Theologies of the Holy Spirit of Stanley Samartha, Vandana, and Samuel Rayan. PhD Thesis, University of Birmingham, 2001.

________ *Mission in Spirit: The Holy Spirit in Indian Christian Theologies.* Delhi: ISPCK, 2003.

Kim, Sebastian C. H. *In Search of Identity: Debates on Religious Conversion in India.* New Delhi: Oxford, 2003.

Kim, Seyoon. *The Origin of Paul's Gospel.* Oregon: Wipf & Stock, 2007.

Knight, Gordon. 'The Necessity of God Incarnate.' *International Journal for Philosophy of Religion* 43 (1998): 1–16.

Kochukunju, Muthapackal. "Malankara Kanda Maha Unarv" (Malayalam) (The Great Revival that Saw Malankara). *Maranatha Voice* (10 Oct. 2006): 8-9 & 14.

Krishna Reddy, G.V. 'Lessons in Nation Building.' *India Today* (24 Aug. 2009). http://indiatoday.intoday.site/Story/56580/Cover%20Story/Lessons+in+nation+building.html (accessed 25 Nov. 2009).

Kumar, Bachchan. *The Bhils: An Ethno-Historic Analysis.* Delhi: Sharada Publishing House, 1997.

Küster, Volker. *The Many Faces of Jesus Christ.* London: SCM, 2001.

Kydd, R.A.N. 'Healing in the Christian Church.' *The New International Dictionary of Pentecostal and Charismatic Movements.* Edited by Stanley M. Burgess. Michigan: Zondervan, 2002, 698-711.

Lackey, Jennifer. *Learning from Words: Testimony as a Source of Knowledge.* Oxford: Oxford University Press, 2010.

Lakra, Benjamin. 'Conversion and Tribals of India.' *Indian Currents* (8-14 Feb. 1999): 39-41.

Lal, Deepak. *The Hindu Equilibrium: Cultural Stability and Economic Stagnation – India c 1500BC-AD1980, vol. I.* Oxford: Clarendon Press, 1989.

Lalpekhlua, L. H. *Contextual Christology: A Tribal Perspective.* Delhi: ISPCK, 2007.

Lampe, G.W.H. *The Seal of the Spirit*, 2nd ed. London: SPCK, 1967.

Land, Stephen J. *Pentecostal Spirituality: A Passion for the Kingdom.* Sheffield: Sheffield Academic Press, 1993.

Lane, A.N.S. 'Anselm.' *New Dictionary of Theology.* Edited by Sinclair B. Ferguson & David F. Wright. Illinois: IVP, 2000 (CD-Rom).

Lane, William L. *The Gospel of Mark: New International Commentary on the New Testament.* Michigan: Eerdmans, 1974.

Lee, Young-Hoon. 'Korean Pentecost: The Great Revival of 1907.' *AJPS* 4/1 (2001): 73-83.

Legard, Robin, Jill Keegan & Kit Ward. 'In-depth Interviews.' In *Qualitative Research Practice: A Guide for Social Science Students and Researchers*. Edited by Jane Ritchie & Jane Lewis. London: Sage Publications, 2003.

Letham, R. 'Trinity, Triune God.' *Global Dictionary of Theology.* Edited by William A. Dyrness & Veli-Matti Karkkainen. Nottingham: IVP, 2008.

Levison, J. & P. Pope-Levison. 'Christology.' *Global Dictionary of Theology.* Edited by William A. Dyrness & Veli-Matti Kärkkäinen. Nottingham: IVP, 2008.

Lim, D.S. 'Evangelism in the Early Church.' In *New Testament and Its Developments.* Edited by R.P. Martin & Peter H. Davis. Leicester: IVP, 1997.

Lipner, Julius & Gispert-Sauch, George (eds.). *The Writings of Brahmabandhab Upadhyaya,* vol. 1. Bangalore: The United Theological College, 1991.

Lobo, Joseph. *Encountering Jesus Christ in India.* Bangalore: Asian Trading Corporation, 2005.

Lobo, Lancy. *Globalisation, Hindu Nationalism and Christians in India.* Jaipur: Rawat, 2002.

________ 'Adivasis, Hindutva and Post-Godhra Riots in Gujarat.' *EPW* (30 Nov. 2002): 4844-4849. http://epw.in.ezproxye.bham.ac.uk/epw/uploads/articles/9761.pdf (accessed 2 Dec. 2009).

Longchar, A. Wati. *An Emerging Asian Theology: Tribal Theology Issue, Method and Perspective.* Jorhat, India: Tribal Study Centre, 2000.

Lott, Eric. *Vedantic Approaches to God.* London: The MacMillan Press, 1980.

Love, Stuart L. 'Jesus Heals the Hemorrhaging Woman.' In *The Social Setting of Jesus and the Gospels.* Edited by Wolfgang Stegemann, Bruce J. Malina & Gerd Theissen. Minneapolis: Fortress Press, 2002.

Lovett, Leonard. 'Liberation: A Dual-Edged Sword.' *Pneuma* 9/2 (Fall, 1987): 155-171.

Lukose, Wessly. 'A Contextual Missiology of the Spirit: A Study of Pentecostalism in Rajasthan, India.' Unpublished PhD Thesis, University of Birmingham, England, 2009.

Luter, A. B. 'Saviour.' *Dictionary of Paul and His Letters.* Edited by Gerald F. Hawthorne, Ralph P. Martin & Daniel G. Reid. Illinois: IVP, 1998 (CD Rom).

Ma, Wonsuk. 'Asian (Classical) Pentecostalism: Theology in Context.' *Dharma Deepika* 6/2 (July-Dec 2002): 13-33.

________ 'Asian Pentecostalism: A Religion whose only Limit is the Sky.' *Journal of Beliefs & Values* 25/2 (August 2004): 191-204.

________ 'Full Circle Mission: A Possibility of Pentecostal Missiology,' *AJPS* 8/1 (2005): 5-27.

Macchia, Frank D. 'The Struggle for Global Witness: Shifting Paradigms in Pentecostal Theology.' In *The Globalization of Pentecostalism*. Edited by M.W. Dempster, B.D. Klaus & D. Petersen. Carlisle: Regnum, 1999.

________ 'Theology, Pentecostal.' *NIDPCM*. Edited by Stanley M. Burgess. Michigan: Zondervan, 2002, 1120-1141.

MacDonald, William. 'Pentecostal Theology: A Classical View Point.' In *Perspectives on the New Pentecostalism*. Edited by Russell P. Spittler. Michigan: Baker Book House, 1976.

Mack, Burton. *A Myth of Innocence: Mark and Christian Origins*. Philadelphia: Fortress, 1988.

Macquarrie, John. *Jesus Christ in Modern Thought*. London: SCM Press, 1990.

Madheswaran, S. & Paul Attewell. 'Caste Discrimination in the Indian Urban Labour Market: Evidence from the National Sample Survey.' *EPW* (13 Oct. 2007): 4146-53. http://epw.in.ezproxyd.bham.ac.uk/epw/uploads/articles/11136.pdf (accessed 12 Dec. 2009).

Malina, Bruce J. *The New Testament World: Insight from Cultural Anthropology*. Kentucky: Westminster John Knox Press, 2001.

________ The *Social Gospel of Jesus: The Kingdom of God in Mediterranean Perspective*. Minneapolis: Fortress Press, 2001.

Manna, G.C. 'On Calibrating the Poverty Line for Poverty Estimation in India.' *EPW* (28 July 2007): 3108-3115.

Manohar, Christina. *Spirit Christology: An Indian Christian Perspective*. Delhi: ISPCK, 2009.

Marsh, Clive. *Christ in Focus: Radical Christocentrism in Christian Theology*. London: SCM, 2005.

Marshall, I. Howard. *The Gospel of Luke: A Commentary on the Greek Text, NIGTC*. Exeter: Paternoster Press, 1978.

________ 'Salvation.' *DJG*. Edited by Joel G. Green, Scot McKnight, I. Howard Marshall. Illinois: IVP, 1992 (CD Rom).

Martin, David. *Tongues of Fire: The Explosion of Protestantism in Latin America*. Cambridge, MA: Basil Blackwell, 1990.

________ 'Issues Affecting the Study of Pentecostalism in Asia.' In *Asian and Pentecostal: The Charismatic Face of Christianity in Asia*. Edited by Allan Anderson & Edmond Tang. Carlisle: Regnum Books International, 2005.

Martin, F. 'Gift of Healing.' *NIDPCM*. Edited by Stanley M. Burgess. Michigan: Zondervan, 2001, 694-698.

Martin, Paul C. 'The Ceylon Pentecostal Mission.' In *Christianity is Indian: The Emergence of an Indigenous Community* rev. ed. Edited by Roger E. Hedlund. Delhi: ISPCK, 2004.

Massey, James. 'Christians in North India: Historical Perspective with Special Reference to Christians in Panjab.' *Religion and Society* XXXIV/3 (Sept. 1987): 88-106.

________ *Down Trodden: The Struggle of India's Dalits for Identity, Solidarity and Liberation.* Geneva: WCC Publications, 1997.

________ 'Christianity Among the Dalits in North India with Special Reference to Punjab.' In *Christianity in India: Search for Liberation and Identity.* Edited by F. Hrangkhuma. Delhi: ISPCK, 2000.

Mathew, C. V. *Saffron Mission: A Historical Analysis of Modern Hindu Missionary Ideologies and Practices.* New Delhi: ISPCK, 1999.

Mathew, Saju. *Kerala Penthecosthu Charithram,* 2nd ed. Bilaspur, India: Margam Books, 2006.

McClung, L.G. Jr. 'Exorcism.' *NIDPCM.* Edited by Stanley M. Burgess. Michigan: Zondervan, 2001, 624-628.

________ 'Evangelism.' *NIDPCM.* Edited by Stanley M. Burgess. Michigan: Zondervan, 2002, 617-620.

________ 'Truth on Fire: Pentecostals and an Urgent Missiology.' *Society for Pentecostal Studies Annual Meeting Papers (1985).* Cleveland: Society for Pentecostal Studies, 2006 (CD Rom).

McCready, Douglas. *He Came Down From Heaven: The Preexistence of Christ and the Christian Faith.* Illinois: IVP, 2005.

McDonald, J. I. H. *Kerygma and Didache: The Articulation and Structure of the Earliest Christian Message.* Cambridge: Cambridge University Press, 1980.

McGavran, Donald. *Understanding Church Growth.* Grand Rapids: Eerdmans, 1970.

McGee, Gary B. 'Pentecostal Phenomena and Revivals in India: Implications for Indigenous Church Leadership.' *International Bulletin of Missionary Research* 20/3 (July 1996): 112-117.

________ '"Latter Rain" Falling in the East: Early-Twentieth-Century Pentecostalism in India and the Debate over Speaking in Tongues.' *Church History* 68/3 (1999): 648-665.

________ & S. M. Burgess. 'India.' *NIDPCM.* Michigan: Zondervan, 2002, 118-126.

________ 'Missions, Overseas (North American Pentecostal),' *NIDPCM.* Michigan: Zondervan, 2002, 885-901.

________ 'Pentecostal and Pentecostal-like Movements (1860-1910).' *NIDPCM*. Michigan: Zondervan, 2002, 118-119.

________ 'The Calcutta Revival of 1907 and the Reformulation of Charles Parham's Bible Evidence Doctrine.' *AJPS* 6/1 (2003): 123-143.

McKnight, Scot. 'Who is Jesus?: An Introduction to Jesus Studies.' In *Jesus Under Fire: Modern Scholarship Reinvents the Historical Jesus.* edited by Michael J. Wilkins & J. P. Moreland. Carlisle: Paternoster, 1996.

Meier, John P. 'Jesus.' *The New Jerome Biblical Commentary*, rev. ed. London: Geoffrey Chapman, 1989.

________ *A Marginal Jew: Rethinking the Historical Jesus.* New York: Doubleday, 1991.

Menon, Amarnath K. 'Tackling the Red Terror.' *India Today* (26 Oct. 2009). http://indiatoday.intoday.in/site/Story/66450/Cover%20Story/Tackling+the+Red+Terror.html.

Menzies, William W. & Robert P. Menzies, *Spirit and Power: Foundations of Pentecostal Experience.* Michigan: Zondervan, 2000.

Menzies, Robert P. *Empowered for Witness.* Sheffield: Sheffield Academic Press, 2001.

Migliore, Daniel L. *Faith Seeking Understanding: An Introduction to Christian Theology.* Michigan: Eerdmans, 1991.

Miller, Basil. *Praying Hyde: A Man of Prayer.* Michigan: Zondervan Publishing House, 1943.

Miller, Albert G. 'Pentecostalism as a Social Movement: Beyond the Theory of Deprivation.' *JPT* 9 (1996): 97-114.

Miller, Donald E. & Tetsunao Yamamori. *Global Pentecostalism: The New Face of Christian Social Engagement.* Berkeley: University of California Press, 2007.

Mishra, M.K. *Indian Social Problems.* Jaipur, India: Mark Publishers, 2009.

Mittal, Sunil Bharati. 'Market Unbound.' *India Today* XXXIV/34 (August 18-24, 2009): 60.

Modi, S.K. *Socio-Economic Development of Dalits in India.* New Delhi: Navyug Publishers, 2009.

Moffett, Samuel Hugh. *A History of Christianity in Asia: Beginnings to 1500,* vol.1, 2nd rev. ed. New York: Orbis Books, 1998.

________ *A History of Christianity in Asia: 1500-1900,* Vol. II. New York: Orbis Books, 2005.

Mohanty, P. K. *Encyclopaedia of Scheduled Tribes in India,* 5 vols. Delhi: Isha Books, 2006.

Moltmann, Jürgen. *The Crucified God: The Cross of Christ as the Foundation and Criticism of Christian Theology.* London: SCM Press, 1974.

________ *The Way of Jesus Christ: Christology in Messianic Dimensions.* London: SCM Press, 1990.

________ *The Spirit of Life: A Universal Affirmation.* Minneapolis: Fortress, 1992.

Montefiore, Hugh. *The Miracles of Jesus.* London: SPCK, 2005.

Mooij, Jos & S. Mahendra Dev. 'Social Sector Priorities: An Analysis of Budgets and Expenditures in India in the 1990s.' *Development Policy Review* 22/1(Jan. 2004): 97-120.

Moorhead, Max Wood. 'The Lord Working for the Unopened Land.' *The Latter Rain Evangel* 6/3 (Dec. 1913): 8-11.

Morris, Thomas V. *The Logic of God Incarnate.* Ithaca: Cornell University Press, 1986.

Moule, C.F.D. *The Origin of Christology.* Cambridge: Cambridge University Press, 1977.

Mounce, R. H. 'Kerygma.' *The International Standard Bible Encyclopedia,* vol. 3. Michigan: Eerdmans, 1986, 9-10.

Mouw, Richard J. *Consulting the Faithful: What Christian Intellectuals can Learn from Popular Religion.* Michigan: Eerdmans, 1994.

Mujumdar, N. A. 'Rural Development: New Perceptions.' *EPW* (28 Sept 2002): 3983-3987. http://epw.in.ezproxyd.bham.ac.uk/epw/uploads/articles/4601.pdf (accessed 16 Nov 2009).

Mukherjee, Anit N. & Krishanu Karmakar. 'Untreated Morbidity and Demand for Healthcare in India: An Analysis of National Sample Survey Data.' *EPW* (15 Nov 2008): 71-77. http://epw.in.ezproxye.bham.ac.uk/epw/uploads/articles/12871.pdf (accessed 25 Nov. 2009).

Mukhopadhayay, Abhiroop & Indira Rajaraman. 'Rural Unemployment 1999-2005: Who Gained, Who Lost?' *EPW* (28 July 2007): 3116-3120.

Mundadan, A. Mathias. *History of Christianity in India, vol I: From the Beginning up to the Middle of the Sixteenth Century (up to 1542).* Bangalore: Church History Association of India, 1989.

________ The Path of Indian Theology. Bangalore: Dharmaram Publications, 1998.

________ 'The Changing Task of Christian History.' In *Enlarging the Story: Perspectives on Writing World Christian History.* Edited by Wilbert R. Shenk. Maryknoll, NY: Orbis Books, 2002.

Nagaraj, K. 'Farmer Suicides in India: Magnitudes, Trends and Spatial Patterns.' *Macroscan* (March 2008), http://www.macroscan.org/anl/mar08/pdf/Farmers_Suicides.pdf (accessed 18 Nov. 2009).

Nagaraja Rao, P. *Introduction to Vedanta,* 3rd ed. Bombay: Bharatiya Vidya Bhavan, 1966.

Narayana Murthy, N. R. *A Better India, A Better World.* New Delhi: Penguin Books India Pvt. Ltd, 2009.

Narayana, K. V. 'Changing Health Care System.' *EPW* (22-29 March 2003): 1230-1241.

Nayak, Abhijit. 'Orissa Atrocities not Fit to Print.' *Dharma Deepika* 13/2 (July-Dec. 2009): 3-10.

Negi, B.S. *Child Marriage in India.* New Delhi: Mittal Publication, 1993.

Neill, Stephen. *Out of Bondage: Christ and the Indian Villager.* London: Church of England Zenana Missionary Society, 1930.

Neufeldt, Ronald. *Hindu-Christian Dialogue: Perspectives and Encounter.* Edited by Harold Coward. Maryknoll: Orbis Books, 1989.

New Life Assembly of God, Chennai. http://www.nlag.org.in/about_us.htm (accessed 22 Dec. 2009).

Newbigin, Lesslie. *The Gospel in a Pluralist Society.* Michigan: Eerdmans, 1989.

Newman, Paul W. *A Spirit-Christology: Recovering the Biblical Paradigm of Christian Faith.* New York: University Press of America, 1987.

Neyrey, Jerome H. 'Ceremonies in Luke-Acts: The Case of Meals and Table Fellowship.' In *The Social World of Luke-Acts.* Edited by Jerome H. Neyrey. Peabody, MA: Hendrickson, 1991.

________ 'The Symbolic Universe of Luke-Acts: 'They Turn the World Upside Down.' In *The Social World of Luke-Acts.* Edited by Jerome H. Neyrey. Peabody, MA: Hendrickson, 1991.

Nicholls, Bruce J. *Contextualization: A Theology of Gospel and Culture.* Exeter: Paternoster, 1979.

________ 'Our Witness to the Uniqueness and Finality of the Lord Jesus Christ in a Pluralistic World – Editorial.' *Evangelical Review of Theology* 17/1 (Jan-Mar 1993): 3-8.

________ 'Contextualization.' *New Dictionary of Theology.* Edited by Sinclair B. Ferguson & David F. Wright. Illinois: IVP, 2000 (CD Rom).

Nienkirchen, C. 'Simpson, Albert Benjamin.' *The New International Dictionary of Pentecostal and Charismatic Movements.* Edited by Stanley M. Burgess. Michigan: Zondervan, 2001, 1069-70.

Nirmal, A. P. 'Towards a Christian Dalit Theology.' In *A Reader in Dalit Theology.* Edited by A.P. Nirmal. Madras: Gurukul, n.d.

________ 'Dalit Theology.' In *Transcending Boundaries.* Edited by Aravind P. Nirmal. Bombay: Vikas Adhyan Kendra, 1995.

No Author. 'Evangelization, Proselytism and Common Witness: The Report from the Fourth Phase of the International Dialogue 1990-1997 between the Roman Catholic Church and Some Classical Pentecostal Churches and Leaders,' *AJPS* 2/1 (January 1999): 105-151.

________ 'Expansion for Profit: Health Care.' *EPW* (24 Aug. 2002): 3476. http://epw.in.ezproxye.bham.ac.uk/epw/uploads/articles/9714.pdf (accessed 25 Nov. 2009).

________ 'He That Climbeth Up Some Other Way, the Same is a Thief and a Robber.' *The Pentecostal Evangel* 402-403 (23 July 1921): 3.

________ 'Our Jesus.' *The Pentecostal Evangel* 492 (April 14, 1923): 1.

________ 'Pentecostal Conversion in the Popular Perception of the Sacred: Some Methodological Elements for its Analysis.' *Voices from the Third World* XIV/2 (December 1991): 51-75.

________ 'Sangh's Reconversion Mela Fizzles Out.' *Indian Currents* (22-28 Feb. 1999): 13.

________ 'The Only True God.' *The Pentecostal Evangel* 324-325 (January 24, 1920): 6-7.

________ 'The Only Way.' *The Pentecostal Evangel* 499 (June 2, 1923): 1;

________ 'The Power of the Blood.' *The Pentecostal Evangel* 495 (May 5, 1923): 1.

________ 'What Think ye of Christ.' *The Pentecostal Evangel* 496 (May 12, 1923): 6.

________ 'What's hot.' *India Today* (9 Nov. 2009). http://indiatoday.intoday. in/site/Story/68638/Lifestyle/What (accessed 16 Dec. 2009).

________ 'When I See the Blood I will Pass over You.' *The Pentecostal Evangel* 493 (21 April 1923): 1.

Nolland, John. *Luke 1:1-9:*20: *WBC* 35a. Dallas, Texas: Word Books, 1998.

Nongsiej, T. 'Revival Movement in Khasi-Jaintia Hills.' In *Churches of Indigenous Origin in Northeast India* Edited by O. L. Snaitang. Delhi: ISPCK, 2000.

O'Brien, Peter T. *Colossians, Philemon, WBC* 44. Dallas, Texas: Word Books, 1982.

________ *The Epistle to the Philippians.* Michigan: Eerdmans, 1991.

O'Day, Gail R. *The Gospel of John, The New Interpreters Bible,* vol. IX. Nashville: Abingdon Press, 1995.

Oakman, Douglas E. 'The Countryside in Luke-Acts.' In *The Social World of Luke-Acts.* Edited by Jerome H. Neyrey. Peabody, MA: Hendrickson, 1991.

Omvedt, Gail. 'Caste System and Hinduism.' *EPW* (13 March 2004): 1179-80. http://epw.in.ezproxyd.bham.ac.uk/epw/uploads/articles/8133.pdf (accessed 10 Dec. 2009).

Orr, J. Edwin. *Evangelical Awakenings in Southern Asia.* Minneapolis: Bethany Fellowship, 1975.

________ The Outpouring of the Spirit in Revival and Awakening and its Issue in Church Growth (British Church Growth Association, 2000). http://www.churchmodel.org.uk/Orr%20HS%20BOOKLET%20A4.pdf (accessed 12 Jan. 2010).

Pandey, Vineeta. 'The Road to Development in Rural India is Literally a Road.' *DNA* (10 Dec. 2009). http://www.dnaindia.com/india/report_the-road-to-development-in-rural-india-is-literally-a-road_1322070 (accessed 18 Dec. 2009).

Panikkar, K. N. 'Foreword.' *Hindutva and Dalits: Perspectives for Understanding Communal Praxis.* Kolkata: Samya, 2005.

________ 'Ways of Hindutva.' *Frontline* 26/07 (Mar. 28-Apr. 10, 2009). http://www.frontlineonnet.com/fl2607/stories/20090410260702600.htm

Panikkar, Raimundo. *The Unknown Christ of Hinduism: Towards an Ecumenical Christophany.* London: Darton, Longman & Todd, 1981.

Panini, M. N. 'Caste, Race and Human Rights.' *EPW* (1 Sept. 2001): 3344-46.

Paradkar, Balwant A. M. 'Hindu Interpretation of Christ from Vivekananda to Radhakrishnan.' *Indian Journal of Theology* 18/1 (Jan-Mar 1969): 65-80.

Parappally, Jacob. *Emerging Trends in Indian Christology.* Bangalore: IIS Publications, 1995.

Park, Myung Soo. 'Korean Pentecostal Spirituality as Manifested in the Testimonies of Members of Yoido Full Gospel Church.' *AJPS* 7/1 (2004): 35-56.

Parmar, S.L. 'The Church in North India.' *Ecumenical Review* XX/1 (Jan. 1968): 72-83.

Paswan, Sanjay. *Encyclopaedia of Dalits in India,* vols. 1-14. Delhi: Kalpaz Publications, 2004.

Pati, Biswamoy. 'Identity, Hegemony, Resistance: Conversions in Orissa, 1800-2000.' *EPW* (3 Nov. 2001): 4202-4212.

Patnaik, Utsa. 'Neoliberalism and Rural Poverty in India.' *EPW* (28 July 2007): 3132-3150.

________ 'A World of Distress.' *Frontline* 26/07 (Mar. 28-Apr. 10, 2009). http://www.frontlineonnet.com/fl2607/stories/20090410260701100.htm (accessed 11 Nov 2009).

Pattison, Stephen. *The Challenge of Practical Theology.* London: Jessica Kingsley Publishers, 2007.

Paul Pillai, K. V. *India's Search for Unknown Christ* 3rd ed. New Delhi: Indian Inland Mission, 1984.

Paul, Sam. 'Christian Council Disappointed with Treatment of Dalit Issues at Un Anti-Racism Conference.' *All India Christian Council* (30 April 2009). http://indianchristians.in/news/content/view/2986/42/ (accessed 15 Dec. 2009).

Pelikan, Jaroslav. *The Christian Tradition: A History of Development of Doctrine, The Emergence of Catholic Tradition (100-600).* Chicago: University of Chicago Press, 1971.

Perayil, Varghese. *The Oath of Coonan Cross.* Adoor, Kerala: Kerala Study Centre, 2007.

Perkins, Pheme. *The Gospel of Mark, The New Interpreters Bible,* vol. VIII. Nashville: Abingdon Press, 1995.

Perrin, Norman. *Rediscovering the Teaching of Jesus.* New York: Harper & Row, 1967.

Petersen, Douglas. *Not by Might nor by Power – A Pentecostal Theology of Social Concern in Latin America.* Oxford: Regnum, 1996.

Petersen, Douglas. 'Missions in the Twenty-First Century: Toward a Methodology of Pentecostal Compassion.' *Transformation* 16/2 (1999): 54–59.

Philip, Finny. 'The Thomas Mathews Revolution.' *Cross and Crown* 36/1 (Nov. 2005 - March 2006): 18-23.

Philip, Glory M. 'Celestial Celebration of Saints: Navapur `07.' *Cross & Crown* 37/2 (Nov-Dec 2007): 11-16.

Philip, P. M. *Kristhuvil Ente Yathra* (*My Pilgrimage with Christ*). Kottayam, India: Royal Calling Books, 1999.

Philip, T. M. *The Encounter Between Theology and Ideology.* Chennai: CLS, 1986.

Philipose, A. *The Apostolic Origin and Early History of the Syrian Church of Malabar.* London: The Christian Literature Society, 1904.

Pickett, J. Waskom. *Christian Mass Movements in India.* New York: Abingdon, 1933.

Pilch, John J. 'Sickness and Healing in Luke-Acts.' In *The Social World of Luke-Acts: Models for Interpretation.* Edited by J.H. Neyrey. Peabody, Mass: Hendrickson, 1991.

________ 'Paul's Ecstatic Trance Experience near Damascus in Acts of the Apostles.' *HTS Teologiese Studies/Theological Studies* 58/2 (2002): 690-70. http://www.hts.org.za/index.php/HTS/article/view/560 (accessed 2 September 2010).

Pinnock, Clark H. *Flame of Love: A Theology of the Holy Spirit.* Illinois: IVP, 1996.

Pinto, Ambrose. 'Dalits: Victims of an Oppressive Caste System.' *Indian Currents* (9-15 August, 1999): 29-34.

Plumb, T. E. 'The Healer: Dr. John Graham Lake.' http://www.enterhisrest. org/charismata/lake_biography.pdf (accessed 10 March 2010).

Porterfield, Amanda. *Healing in the History of Christianity.* New York: Oxford University Press, 2005.

Prabhakar, M. E. (ed.). *Towards a Dalit Theology*. Delhi: ISPCK, 1989.

________ 'The Search for a Dalit Theology.' In *Towards a Dalit Theology.* Edited by M. E. Prabhakar. Delhi: ISPCK, 1989.

Prafulladas. 'Project Orissa.' *Frontline* 25/19 (13-26 Sept 2008). http://www.frontlineonnet.com/fl2519/stories/20080926251900400.htm (accessed Dec. 10, 2009)

Prakash, P. Surya. 'Contribution of Sadhu Sundhar Singh to the Indigenous Christian Movement in India.' In *Christianity is Indian: The Emergence of an Indigenous Community,* rev. ed. Edited by Roger E. Hedlund. Delhi: ISPCK, 2004.

Prasada Rao, I., B. Kangadurai, P. K. Jain, & Neelam Jain. 'Information System for Rural Road Network Planning - A Case Study.' *GIS Development* (8 Oct. 2009). http://www.gisdevelopment.net/application/Utility/transport/mi03218.htm (accessed 18 Nov. 2009).

Puligandla, Ramakrishna. *Fundamentals of Indian Philosophy*. New Delhi: D.K. Printworld, 1997.

Pulikottil, Paulson. 'As East and West Met in God's Own Country: Encounter of Western Pentecostalism with Native Pentecostalism in Kerala.' http://www.pctii.org/cyberj/cyberj10/paulson.html (accessed 10 Jan. 2010).

________ 'Emergence of Indian Pentecostalism.' *Dharma Deepika* 6/2 (July-Dec. 2002): 47-58.

________ 'Ramankutty Paul: A Dalit Contribution to Pentecostalism.' In *Asian and Pentecostal: The Charismatic Face of Christianity in Asia.* Edited by Allan Anderson and Edmond Tang. Carlisle: Regnum Books International, 2005.

Puniyani, Ram. 'Communalism and Minorities.' *Religion and Society* 49/1 (March 2004), 1-9.

________ *Contours of Hindu Rashtra: Hindutva, Sangh Parivaar and Contemporary Politics.* Delhi: Kalpaz Publications, 2006.

Purie, Aroon. 'From the Editor-in-Chief.' *India Today* (19 Oct. 2009), http://indiatoday.intoday.in/site/story?sId=65455&secid=39 (accessed December 16, 2009).

Qaiser, Rizwan. 'Communalism and the Conceptualisation of "Hindu Rashtra."' *Social Action* 44 (Jan-Mar 1994): 81-96.

Raj, M. C. *Dalitology.* Tumkur, India: Ambedkar Resource Centre, 2001.

Raj, Albones. 'Mass Religious Conversion as Protest Movement: A Framework.' *Religion and Society* XXVIII/4 (1981): 58-66.

Raju, M. P. 'Thou art Untouchable, Thou shalt Remain so.' *Indian Currents* (9-15 Aug. 1999): 24-28.

Ram, Fakir. *Dalit Awakening Moving Upward.* Delhi: Swastik Publications, 2010.

Ramachandran, R. & T. K. Rajalakshmi. 'Unhealthy Trend.' *Frontline* 26/07 (28 March - 10 April 2009). http://www.frontlineonnet.com/fl2607/stories/20090410260702100.htm (accessed 14 Nov. 2009).

Ramakrishnan, Venkitesh & Ajoy Ashirwad Mahaprashasta. 'Victims always.' *Frontline* 26/24 (21 Nov.-Dec. 04, 2009). http://www.Frontline onnet.com/fl2624/stories/20091204262400400.htm (accessed 15 Dec. 2009).

Rambachan, Anantanand. 'A Hindu Look at Jesus.' *Vidhyajyoti Journal of Theological Reflection* 58/12 (Dec. 1994): 771-776.

Rao, S. Srinivasa. 'Dalits in Education and Workforce.' *EPW* (20 July 2002): 2998-3000. http://epw.in.ezproxyd.bham.ac.uk/epw/uploads/articles/4367.pdf (accessed 15 Dec. 2009).

Rayan, Samuel. *Breath of Fire – The Holy Spirit: Heart of the Christian Gospel.* London: Geoffrey Chapman, n.d.

________ 'The Justice of God.' In *Living Theology in Asia.* Edited by John C. England. London: SCM, 1981.

Reese, David George. 'Demons (New Testament).' *The Anchor Bible Dictionary.* Edited by David Noel Freedman. New York: Doubleday, 1997 (CD Rom).

Reid, D. G. 'Powers and Principalities.' *Dictionary of Paul and His Letters.* Edited by Gerald F. Hawthorne, Ralph P. Martin & Daniel G. Reid. Illinois: IVP, 1998 (CD Rom).

Reinhardt, C. W. 'Providential Protection from Storms.' *The Latter Rain Evangel* (Feb. 1913): 21-22.

Remus, Harold. *Jesus as Healer.* Cambridge: Cambridge University Press, 1997.

Richie, Tony 'Neither Naïve Nor Narrow: A Balanced Pentecostal Approach to Christian Theology of Religions.' *Presented to the Annual Meeting of the*

American Academy of Religion. Philadelphia, PA (19-22, November 2005). http://www.ncccusa.org/pdfs/naive.pdf (accessed 2 November 2010).

________ '"The Unity of Spirit": Are Pentecostals Inherently Ecumenists and Inclusivists?' *JEPTA* 26/1 (2006): 21-35.

________ 'God's Fairness to People of All Faiths: A Respectful Proposal to Pentecostals for Discussion Regarding World Religions.' *Pneuma* 28/1 (Spring 2006): 105-119.

________ 'Getting Back to the Heart of the Matter: The Way Forward and a Final Response to Tony Moon.' *JPT* 18/1 (2009): 141-149.

________ 'Continuing the Conversation on King: My Really Final Response to Tony Moon?' *JPT* 19/1 (2010): 170-179.

Risley, H. H. & E. A. Gait. *Census of India 1921, Religion*. Calcutta: Superintendent Government Printing, India, 1923. http://www.archive.org/stream/cu31924014522746#page/n179/mode/2up (accessed 11 July 2010).

Ritchie, Jane, Jane Lewis & Gilian Elam. 'Designing and Selecting Samples.' In *Qualitative Research Practice: A Guide for Social Science Students and Researchers*. Edited by Jane Ritchie & Jane Lewis. London: Sage Publications, 2003.

Ro, Bong Rin. 'Evangelical Response to Religious Pluralism.' *Evangelical Review of Theology* 17/1 (Jan.-Mar. 1993): 70-81.

Robson, Colin. *Real World Research: A Resource for Social Scientists and Practitioner-Researchers*. Oxford: Blackwell, 2002.

Rosato, Philip J. 'Spirit-Christology: Ambiguity and Promise.' *TS* 38 (1977): 423-449.

Rosling, Hans. 'Asia's Rise - How and When.' *TED India* 2009. Filmed Nov. 2009, Posted Nov. 2009. http://www.ted.com/talks/hans_rosling_asia _s_rise_ how_and_when. html (accessed 4 Jan. 2010).

Rossman, G. B. & S. F. Rallis. *Learning in the Field: An Introduction to Qualitative Research*. Thousand Oaks, CA: Sage Publications, 1988.

Sackett, Ida Florence. '"There Shall Be No Evil Befall Thee."' *The Pentecost* 1/8 (July 1909): 8.

Samuel Kutty, T. S. *The Place and Contribution of Dalits in Select Pentecostal Churches in Central Kerala from 1922-1972*. Delhi: ISPCK, 2000.

Samuel, J. 'A Study on the Influence of Rajasthan Pentecostal Church in the Socio-Economic Upliftment of the Bhil Tribes in Udaipur District.' Unpublished MTh Thesis, Asian Institute of Theology, Bangalore, India, 2006.

Samuel, V. C. *The Council of Chalcedon Re-examined*. Madras: The Christian Literature Society, 1977.

Sanjana. 'There is a Limit to Religious Freedom': Interview with *Karnataka Home Minister* Dr V.S. Acharya. *Tehelka 5/38 (27 Sept. 2008).* http://www.tehelka.com/story_main40.asp?Filename=Ne270908in coldblood.asp (accessed 23 Dec. 2009).

_________ 'An Unholy Crusade.' *Tehelka* 5/39 (4 Oct 2008). http://www. tehelka.com/story_main40.asp?filename=Ne041008coverstory.asp (accessed 22 Dec. 2009).

Sankar, Deepa & Vinish Kathuria. 'Health System Performance in Rural India: Efficiency Estimates Across States.' *EPW* (27 March 2004): 1427-1433.

Sarkar, Sumit. 'Conversion and Politics of Hindu Right.' *EPW* (26 June 1999): 1691-1700.

Satyavrata, Ivan M. 'Contextual Perspectives on Pentecostalism as a Global Culture: A South Asian View.' In *The Globalization of Pentecostalism*. Edited by M.W. Dempster, B.D. Klaus & D. Petersen. Carlisle: Regnum, 1999.

Saumya. 'Communalism: Narratives in Chhattisgarh.' *EPW* 43/2 (12 Jan. 2008): 38-44. http://epw.in.ezproxye.bham.ac.uk/epw/uploads/articles/11428.pdf (accessed 2 Dec., 2009).

Saxena, L. L. *The Bhils of Rajasthan – Their Habitat, Economy and Society*. Jodhpur, India: Books Treasure, 2000.

Sayeed, Vikhar Ahmed. 'Now, Karnataka.' *Frontline* 25/20 (27 Sept.-10 Oct. 2008). http://www.frontlineonnet.com/fl2520/stories/2008101025200 2500.htm (accessed 23 Dec. 2009).

Schmälzle, Udo. 'Empirical Research in Practical Theology as a Strategy of Intervention.' *Journal of Empirical Theology* 16/1 (2003): 5-19.

Schreiter, Robert J. *Constructing Local Theologies.* New York: Orbis Books, 1985.

Seleky, Trinidad E. 'A History of the Pentecostal Movement in Indonesia,' *AJPS* 4/1 (2001): 131–148.

Seleky, Trinidad E. 'The Organization of the Philippine Assemblies of God and the Role of Early Missionaries.' *AJPS* 8/2 (2005): 271-287.

Sen, Amartya. 'Social Exclusion: Concept, Application, and Scrutiny.' *Working Paper, Social Development Paper No 1.* Manila: Asian Development Bank, June, 2000, 1-54. http://scholar.google.co.uk.ezproxyd.bham.ac.uk/scholar?hl=en&rlz=1R2RNTN_enGB348&q=author:%22Sen%22+intitle:%22Social+exclusion:+Concept,+application,+and+scrutiny%22+&um=1&ie=UTF-8&oi=scholarr (accessed 10 Dec. 2009).

Sengupta, Roshni. 'Communal Violence in India: Perspectives on Causative Factors.' *EPW* (14 May 2005): 2046-2050.

Shah, A. M. 'The Tribes – So-Called – of Gujarat: In the Perspective of Time.' *EPW* 38/2 (11 Jan. 2003): 95-97.

Shah, Ghanshyam. 'Conversion, Reconversion and the State: Recent Events in the Dangs.' *EPW* (6 Feb. 1999): 312-318; http://epw.in/epw/uploads/articles/8620.pdf (accessed 2 May 2010).

Shaji, K. A. 'Holy Ghost on Malabar Coast.' *Tehelka* 4/42 (27 Oct 2007). http://www.tehelka.com/story_main34.asp?filename=Ne271007holyghost.asp (accessed 22 Dec. 2009).

Sharma, Aravind. *The Philosophy of Religion and Advaita Vedanta.* Delhi: Sri Satguru Publications, 1997.

Shaull, Richard & Waldo Cesar. *Pentecostalism and the Future of the Christian Churches.* Michigan: Eerdmans, 2000.

Shelton, James B. *Mighty in Word and Deed.* Oregon: Wipf and Stock Publishers, 2000.

Shenk, Wilbert R. (ed.). *Enlarging the Story: Perspectives on Writing World Christian History.* Maryknoll: Orbis, 2002.

Sheth, D. L. 'Political Communalisation of Religions and the Crisis of Secularism.' *EPW* XLIV/39 (26 Sept 2009): 71-79. http://epw.in.ezproxye.bham.ac.uk/epw/uploads/articles/13967.pdf (accessed 2 Dec. 2009).

Sheth, Jagdish N. 'Great Ideas, Great Minds.' *India Today* (6 Oct. 2008). http://indiatoday.intoday.in/site/story?sId=16109&secid=30 (accessed 16 Dec. 2009).

Simha, Vijay. 'In the name of God.' *Tehelka 5/36 (13 Sept. 2008).* http://www.tehelka.com/story_main40.asp?filename=Ne130908CoverStory.asp (accessed 23 Dec. 2009).

Simmons, Roger. *Vision Mission and a Movement: The Story of Dr. Thomas Mathews and the Native Missionary Movement.* Richardson, TX: Native Missionary Movement, 2008.

Simpson, A. B. *The Fourfold Gospel: Jesus as Saviour, Sanctifier, Healer and Coming King.* Orlando, FL: Bridge-Logos, 2007.

Singaram, Charles. 'The Question of Method in Dalit Theology.' Unpublished PhD Thesis, University of Birmingham, Birmingham, 2004.

Singh, Abhay. 'Palamu Reconversions a Mystery.' *Indian Currents* (22-28 February, 1999): 14.

Singh, K. S. *The Scheduled Tribes.* Delhi: Oxford University Press, 1994.

Singh, Sadhu Sundar. 'The Living Christ.' In *Readings in Indian Christian Theology.* Edited by R.S. Sugirtharaja & Cecil Hargreaves. London: SPCK, 1993.

Sjoberg, Gideon. *The Preindustrial City: Past and Present.* New York: Free Press, 1960.

Smart, Ninian & Steven Konstantine. *Christian Systematic Theology in a World Context.* London: Marshal Pickering, 1991.

Smith, Dennis E. 'Table Fellowship.' *The Anchor Bible Dictionary.* Edited by David Noel Freedman. New York: Doubleday, 1997 (CD Rom).

Snaitang, O. L. 'The Indigenous Pentecostal Movement in Northeast India.' *Dharma Deepika* 6/2 (July-Dec 2002): 5-11.

Snehi, Yogesh. 'Female Infanticide and Gender in Punjab.' *EPW* (11 Oct. 2003): 4302-4305.

Snell, Jeffrey T. 'Beyond the Individual and into the World: A Call to Participation in the Larger Purpose of the Spirit on the Basis of Pentecostal Theology.' *Pneuma* 14/1 (Spring, 1992): 43-57.

Soares-Prabhu, George M. *Fascism of Sangh Parivar.* New Delhi: Media House, 2000.

________ *The Dharma of Jesus.* Edited by Francis Xavier O'sa. Maryknoll: Orbis Books, 2003.

Sobrino, Jon *Christology at the Crossroads: A Latin American Approach.* Maryknoll: Orbis Books, 1978.

________ *Jesus the Liberator: A Historical-Theological Reading of Jesus of Nazareth.* Kent: Burns & Oates, 1994.

Sodani, P. R. 'Determinants of Demand for Healthcare in Surveyed Tribal Households of Selected Three Districts of Rajasthan.' *Demography India* 28/2 (1997): 257-271.

Solivan, Samuel. 'Interreligious Dialogue: An Hispanic American Pentecostal Perspective.' In *Grounds for Understanding: Ecumenical Responses to Religious Pluralism.* Edited by S. Mark Heim. Michigan: Eerdmans, 1998.

________ *The Spirit, Pathos and Liberation: Toward an Hispanic Pentecostal Theology.* Sheffield: Sheffield Academic, 1998.

Son, Bong-Ho. 'Uniqueness of Christ and Social Justice.' *Evangelical Review of Theology* 17/1 (Jan-Mar 1993): 93-109.

South Asia Human Rights Documentation Centre. 'Anti-Conversion Laws: Challenges to Secularism and Fundamental Rights,' *EPW* (January 12, 2008): 63-73.

Special Correspondent. 'Hate Campaign against Christians may not be Spontaneous, Really.' *Indian Currents* (15-21 Feb. 1999): 30-31.

Sridhar, V. 'Numbers Game.' *Frontline* 16/25 (27 Nov. 1999).

________ 'Retail Invasion.' *Frontline* 24/13 (30 June-13 July, 2007). http://www.frontlineonnet.com/fl2413/stories/20070713005300400.htm (accessed 18 Dec. 2009).

Srinivasan, K. & S. K. Mohanty. 'Deprivation of Basic Amenities by Caste and Religion.' *EPW* (14 Feb 2004): 728-735. http://epw.in.ezproxyd. bham.ac.uk/epw/uploads/articles/9484.pdf (accessed 15 Dec. 2009).

Stegemann, Ekkehard W. & Wolfgang Stegemann. *The Jesus Movement: A Social History of its First Century.* Edinburg: T&T Clark, 1999.

Stegemann, Wolfgang. 'The Contextual Ethics of Jesus.' In *The Social Setting of Jesus and the Gospels.* Edited by Wolfgang Stegemann, Bruce J. Malina & Gerd Theissen. Minneapolis: Fortress Press, 2002.

Strachan, G. *The Pentecostal Theology of Edward Irving.* Peabody, MA: Hendrickson, 1988.

Strecker, Christian. 'Jesus and the Demoniacs.' In *The Social Setting of Jesus and the Gospels.* Edited by Wolfgang Stegemann, Bruce J. Malina & Gerd Theissen. Minneapolis: Fortress Press, 2002.

Streeter, Burnett Hillman & A. J. Appasamy. *The Sadhu: A Study in Mysticism and Practical Religion.* London: Macmillan and Company, 1922.

Stringer, Ernest T. *Action Research,* 2nd ed. London: Sage, 1999.

Stronstad, Roger. *The Charismatic Theology of St. Luke.* Massachusets: Hendricksen Publishers, 1984.

________ 'Affirming Diversity: God's People as a Community of Prophets.' *Pneuma:* 17/2 (Fall 1995): 145-157.

________ *The Prophethood of All Believers – A Study in Luke's Charismatic Theology.* Sheffield: Sheffield Academic Press, 1999.

Studebaker, Steven M. 'Integrating Pneumatology and Christology: A Trinitarian Modification of Clark H. Pinnock's Spirit Christology.' *Pneuma* 28/1 (Spring 2006): 5-20.

Sugirtharajah, R. S. (ed.). 'Prologue and Perspective.' *Asian Faces of Jesus – Faith and Culture Series.* Maryknoll: Orbis Books, 1993.

Suico, Joseph. 'Pentecostalism: Towards a Movement of Social Transformation in the Philippines.' *Journal of Asian Mission* 1/1 (1999): 7-19.

________ 'Pentecostalism and Social Change,' *AJPS* 8/2 (2005): 195-213.

Sumithra, Sunand. *Revolution as Revelation: A Study of M. M. Thomas's Theology.* New Delhi: Theological Research and Communications Institute, 1984.

________ *Christian Theologies from an Indian Perspective.* Bangalore: Theological Book Trust, 1995.

Sundar, Nandini. 'Bastar, Maoism and Salwa Judum.' *EPW* (22 July 2006): 3187-3192. http://epw.in/epw/uploads/articles/795.pdf. (accessed 5 Jan. 2010).

Sundaram, K. 'Employment and Poverty in India 2000-2005.' *EPW* (28 July 2007): 3121-3131.

Swinton, John & Harriet Mowat. *Practical Theology and Qualitative Research.* London: SCM, 2006.

Synan, Vinson. 'A Healer in the House? A Historical Perspective on Healing in the Pentecostal/Charismatic Tradition.' *AJPS* 3/2 (2000): 189-201.

Thampu, Valson. 'National Debate on Conversions.' *Indian Currents* (18-24 Jan. 1999): 16-17.

Thangaraj, M. Thomas. *The Crucified Guru: An Experiment in Cross-Cultural Christology*. Nashville: Abingdon Press, 1994.

Theissen, Gerd. *Miracle Stories of Early Christian Tradition.* Edited by John Riches. Edinburgh: T&T Clark, 1983.

________ *The Gospels in Context: Social and Political History in the Synoptic Tradition*, translated by Linda M. Maloney. Edinburgh: T&T Clark, 1992.

________ and Annette Merz. *The Historical Jesus: A Comprehensive Guide*, translated by John Bowden. London: SCM Press, 1998.

________ 'The Political Dimension of Jesus' Activities.' In *The Social Setting of Jesus and the Gospels.* Edited by Wolfgang Stegemann, Bruce J. Malina & Gerd Theissen. Minneapolis: Fortress Press, 2002.

Thekkedath, Joseph. *History of Christianity in India Vol. II, From the Middle of the Sixteenth Century to the Seventeenth Century.* Bangalore: Theological Publications in India, 1982.

Thomas, John Christopher. 'The Devil, Disease and Deliverance: James 5.14-16.' *JPT* 2 (1993): 25-50.

________ 'Pentecostal Theology in the Twenty-First Century: 1998 Presidential Address.' *Pneuma* 20 (1998): 3-19.

________ *The Devil, Disease and Deliverance: Origins of Illness in New Testament Thought.* Sheffield: Sheffield Academic Press, 1998.

Thomas, Kurien. *God's Trailblazer in India and Around the World.* Itarsi, India: Kurien Thomas, 1986.

Thomas, M. M. *The Christian Response to the Asian Revolution.* London: SCM, 1966.

________ *The Acknowledged Christ of Indian Renaissance.* Madras: CLS, 1970.

________ *Salvation and Humanisation.* Bangalore: Christian Institute for the Study of Religion and Society, 1971.

________ *The Secular Ideologies of India and the Secular Meaning of Christ.* Madras: CLS, 1976.

________ *The Realisation of the Cross.* Madras: CLS, 1972.

________ 'My Pilgrimage in Mission.' In *Frontiers in Asian Christian Theology: Emerging Trends.* Edited by R.S. Sugirtharajah. Maryknoll: Orbis Books, 1994.

Thomas, P. *Christians and Christianity in India and Pakistan.* London: George Allen & Unwin, 1954.

Thomas, V. P. 'Indian Christian Approaches to the Knowledge of Christ.' *Indian Journal of Theology* 18/1 (Jan-Mar 1969): 88-99.

Thomas, V. V. 'Pentecostalism Among the Dalits in Kerala from 1909 to the Present: A Subaltern Reading.' *UBS Journal* 3/2 (September 2005): 89-94.

Thompson, Paul. *The Voice of the Past: Oral History,* 2nd ed. New York: Oxford University Press, 1988.

Thonnakkal, Thomas. *Marubhoomiyile Appostalan (The Apostle of the Desert: A Biography of Thomas Mathews).* Udaipur, India: Cross and Crown, 2004.

Thorat, Sukhdeo & Joel Lee. 'Caste Discrimination and Food Security Programmes.' *EPW* (24 Sept 2005): 4198-4201. http://epw.in.ezproxyd.bham.ac.uk/epw/uploads/articles/1149.pdf (accessed 16 Dec. 2009).

________ & Katherine S. Newman. 'Caste and Economic Discrimination: Causes, Consequences and Remedies.' *EPW* (13 Oct 2007): 4121-4124. http://epw.in.ezproxyd.bham.ac.uk/epw/uploads/ articles/11132.pdf (accessed 12 Dec. 2009).

________ & Nidhi Sadana. 'Caste and Ownership of Private Enterprises.' *EPW* 44/23 (6 June 2009): 13-16.

Tillich, Paul. *Courage to Be.* New Haven: Yale University Press, 1952.

Tripathi, V.K. 'Conversion and Purification Issues are Mischievous.' *Indian Currents* (22-28 Feb. 1999): 15-16.

Turner, H.E.W. 'Communicatio Idiomatum.' *A New Dictionary of Christian Theology.* Edited by Alan Richardson & John Bowden. London: SCM, 1983, 113.

Twelftree, Graham H. 'Demon, Devil, Satan.' *Dictionary of Jesus and the Gospels.* Edited by Joel G. Green, Scot McKnight & I. Howard Marshall. Illinois: IVP, 1992 (CD Rom).

________ *Jesus the Exorcist.* Peabody, Mass: Hendrickson Publishers, 1993.

________ Jesus the Miracle Worker: a Historical & Theological study. Illinois: IVP, 1999.

________ 'Miracles of Jesus Marginal or Mainstream?' *Journal of the Study of the Historical Jesus* 1/1 (2003): 104-124.

________ *In the Name of Jesus: Exorcism among Early Christians.* Michigan: Baker Academic, 2007.

Upadhyaya, Brahmabandhab. 'The Hymn of the Incarnation.' *The Twentieth Century* 1/1 (1901): 7-8.

van der Ven, Johannes A. *Practical Theology: An Empirical Approach.* Kampen: Kok Pharos, 1993.

________ 'An Empirical or a Normative Approach to Practical Theological Research?' *Journal of Empirical Theology* 15/2 (2002): 5-33.

Vansina, Jan. *Oral Tradition: A Study in Historical Methodology*. Translated by H.M. Wright. New Jersey: Transaction Publishers, 2006.

Varghese, T.P. (ed.). *Penthecosthu Daivasasthram (Pentecostal Theology)*, rev. ed. Thiruvalla, Kerala: Readers Publications, 2002.

Varghese, V. Titus & P.P. Philip, *Glimpses of the History of the Christian Churches in India.* Madras: The Christian Literature Society, 1983.

Vargis, P.G. *Christuvinuvendi Himalaya Sanukkalil.* Pathankot, India: Indian Evangelical Team.

Varshney, Ashutosh. *Ethnic Conflict and Civic Life: Hindus and Muslims in India.* New Haven: Yale University Press, 2002.

Vishwanath, L. S. 'Female Foeticide and Infanticide.' *EPW* (1 Sept 2001): 3411-3412.

________ 'Female Infanticide: The Colonial Experience.' *EPW* (29 May 2004): 2313-2318.

Visvanathan, Shiv. 'The Race for Caste: Prolegomena to the Durban Conference.' *EPW* (7 July 2001): 2512-2516. http://epw.in.ezproxyd.bham.ac.uk/epw/uploads/articles/5628.pdf (accessed 17 Dec. 2009)

________ 'Durban and Dalit Discourse.' *EPW* (18 Aug. 2001): 3123-3127, http://epw.in.ezproxyd.bham.ac.uk/epw/uploads/articles/5776.pdf (accessed Dec. 17, 2009).

Wagner, C. Peter. *Look Out! The Pentecostals are Coming.* Illinois: Creation House, 1973.

Wagstaff, Adam. 'Poverty and Health Sector Inequalities.' *Bulletin of the World Health Organisation* 80/2 (2002). http://www.scielosp.org/scielo.php?pid=S0042-96862002000200004&script=sciarttext&tlng=en (accessed 3 Jan. 2010).

Warrington, Keith. 'The Role of Jesus as Presented in the Healing Praxis and Teaching of British Pentecostalism: A Re-Examination.' *Pneuma* 25/1 (Spring 2003): 66-92.

________ *Pentecostal Theology: A Theology of Encounter.* London: T&T Clark, 2008.

Watson, Hubert Manohar. *Towards a Relevant Christology in India Today: An Appraisal of the Christologies of John Hick, Jürgen Moltmann and Jon Sobrino.* Frankfurt am Main: Peter lang, 2002.

Webster, John C. B. *The Christian Community and Change in Nineteenth Century North India.* Delhi: Macmillan, 1976.

Wessels, Anton. *Images of Jesus.* London: SCM, 1990.

Westerholm, Stephen. 'Clean and Unclean.' *Dictionary of Jesus and the Gospels.* Edited by Joel G. Green, Scot McKnight & I. Howard Marshall. Illinois: IVP, 1992 (CD Rom).

Wigglesworth, Smith. 'The Power of the Name.' *The Pentecostal Evangel* 480-481(20 Jan 1923): 2.

________ 'Our Risen Christ.' *The Pentecostal Evangel* 490 (31 March 1923): 2.

Wilfred, Felix. *On the Bank of Ganges: Doing Contextual Christology,* rev. ed. Delhi: ISPCK, 2005.

Wilfred, H. 'In Fond Memory of P.S. Samuel.' *Hallelujah* 11/12 (15 June 2006): 6-7.

Wilkinson, John. *The Bible and Healing: A Medical and Theological Commentary.* Michigan: Eerdmans, 1998.

Wilkinson, Steven I. *Votes and Violence: Electoral Competition and Communal Riots in India.* New Delhi: Cambridge University Press, 2005.

________ 'Communal Riots in India.' *EPW* (29 Oct. 2005): 4768-4770. http://epw.in.ezproxyd.bham.ac.uk/epw/uploads/articles/1313.pdf (accessed 10 Dec. 2009).

Williams, Rodman J. *Renewal Theology, Vol.1.* Michigan: Zondervan, 1988.

Williams, Rowan. 'A History of Faith in Jesus.' In *The Cambridge Companion to Jesus.* Edited by Markus Bockmuehl. Cambridge: Cambridge University Press, 2001.

Wilson, Everett A. 'They Crossed the Red Sea, Didn't They?: Critical History and Pentecostal Beginning.' In *The Globalization of Pentecostalism*, edited by M.W. Dempster, B.D. Klaus & D. Petersen. Carlisle: Regnum, 1999.

Witherington, Ben III. 'Lord.' *Dictionary of Jesus and the Gospels.* Edited by Joel G. Green, Scot McKnight & I. Howard Marshall. Illinois: IVP, 1992 (CD Rom).

________ *Jesus the Sage.* Minneapolis: Fortress Press, 1994.

________ *The Jesus Quest: The Third Search for the Jew of Nazareth.* Illinois: IVP, 1995.

________ 'Christology.' *Dictionary of Paul and His Letters.* Edited by Gerald F. Hawthorne, Ralph P. Martin & Daniel G. Reid. Illinois: IVP, 1998 (CD Rom).

Wiyono, Gani. 'Timor Revival: A Historical Study of the Great Twentieth-century Revival in Indonesia.' *AJPS* 4/2 (2001): 227-278.

World Bank. 'India: Raising the Sites-Better Health Systems for India's Poor - Findings, Analysis, and Options.' *Health, Nutrition, and Population Series.* Washington DC, 2002.

World Health Organisation. 'Macroeconomics and Health: Investing in Health for Economic Development.' *Report of the Commission on Macroeconomics and Health.* Geneva: WHO, 2001.

Yeshu Darbar. http://www.aaidu.org/yeshuDarbar.htm (accessed 23 Dec. 2009).

Yoder, John Howard. *The Politics of Jesus.* Michigan: Eerdmans, 1994.

Yong, Amos. '"Not Knowing Where the Wind Blows ...": On Envisioning a Pentecostal-Charismatic Theology of Religions.' *JPT* 14 (1999): 81-112.

________ *Discerning the Spirit(s): A Pentecostal-Charismatic Theology of Religions, Journal of Pentecostal Theology Supplement Series.* Sheffield: Sheffield Academic Press, 2000.

________ *the Impasse: Toward a Pneumatological Theology of Religion.* Michigan: Eerdmans, 2003.

________ *The Spirit Poured Out on All Flesh: Pentecostalism and the Possibility of Global Theology.* Michigan: Baker Academic, 2005.

Index

T

U

V

W